A Concise Dictionary of New Testament Greek

This Dictionary provides students, pastors, and other readers of the Bible with a convenient and useful source of word meanings and English glosses for the entire vocabulary of the Greek New Testament. In addition to reflecting the full range of semantic uses and nuances with appropriate examples, according to the most recent lexical research, the Concise Dictionary includes the following features: identifying the part of speech, listing cognate key words, noting principal parts for each verb as used in the New Testament (giving the frequency of use in the New Testament), and citing the New Testament reference for each word used only once. The Dictionary also identifies enclitics, postpositives, and non-Greek words, and contains numerous cross references for irregular forms. It should prove to be an essential accompaniment to any course of NT Greek or serious study of the Bible in its original form.

WARREN C. TRENCHARD is Professor of New Testament and Early Christian Literature at La Sierra University, Riverside, California. He is author of the highly successful *The Student's Complete Vocabulary Guide to the Greek New Testament* and its second edition entitled *Complete Vocabulary Guide to the Greek New Testament* (Zondervan, 1993, 1998).

A CONCISE
DICTIONARY OF
NEW TESTAMENT
GREEK

WARREN C. TRENCHARD

CAMBRIDGE
UNIVERSITY PRESS

CAMBRIDGE UNIVERSITY PRESS
Cambridge, New York, Melbourne, Madrid, Cape Town, Singapore, São Paulo,
Delhi, Mexico City

Cambridge University Press
The Edinburgh Building, Cambridge CB2 8RU, UK

Published in the United States of America by Cambridge University Press, New York

www.cambridge.org
Information on this title: www.cambridge.org/9780521521111

5 \14

First published 2003
9th printing 2013

Printed and bound in the United Kingdom by the MPG Books Group

The SymbolGreek II font used to print this work is available from Linguist's Software, Inc.,
PO Box 580, Edmonds, WA 98020–0580, USA; tel. (425) 775-1130
www.linguistsoftware.com.

A catalogue record for this publication is available from the British Library

ISBN 978-0-521-81815-5 Hardback
ISBN 978-0-521-52111-6 Paperback

To Mark, David, and Kevin —
sons to whom I entrust the future

CONTENTS

PREFACE

This dictionary represents the maturation of a project that I began in 1990 with research and preparation for a comprehensive vocabulary guide to the Greek New Testament. Based on a computer database that I developed over two years, the first product was *The Student's Complete Vocabulary Guide to the Greek New Testament* (Zondervan, 1992). In 1998, it was released in revised form with a shortened title, as indicated below. However, for many years, I felt the need to greatly expand the database, especially in the area of word meanings, and issue the results in a small dictionary of the Greek New Testament. The result is *A Concise Dictionary of New Testament Greek*.

There are several fine small dictionaries available for students, pastors, and others who read the Greek New Testament, most notably the one by Barclay Newman listed below. This dictionary inevitably contains much of the same information. However, it is also unique in providing cognate key words, frequency data, and references for all words that occur only once in the New Testament. The *Concise Dictionary* also identifies enclitics, postpositives, and non-Greek words.

Among the many works that I have consulted in preparing this dictionary, I want particularly to acknowledge the following:

Abbott-Smith, G. *A Manual Greek Lexicon of the New Testament*. 3d ed. New York: Charles Scribner's Sons, 1937.

Aland, Barbara, Kurt Aland, Johannes Karavidopolous, Carlo M. Martini, and Bruce M. Metzger. *The Greek New Testament*. 4th rev. ed. Stuttgart: Deutsche Bibelgesellschaft, 1998.

Blass, F., and A. Debrunner. *A Greek Grammar of the New Testament and Other Early Christian Literature*. Translated and revised by Robert W. Funk. Chicago: The University of Chicago Press, 1961.

Concordance to the Novum Testamentum Graece of Nestle–Aland, 26th Edition, and to the Greek New Testament, 3rd Edition. 3d ed. Edited by the Institute for New Testament Textual Research and the Computer Center of Münster University. Berlin: Walter de Gruyter, 1987.

Danker, Frederick William. *A Greek–English Lexicon of the New Testament and Other Early Christian Literature*. Based on Walter Bauer, *Grieschisch–deutsches Wörterbuch zu den Schriften des Neuen Testaments und der früchristlichen Literatur*. 6th ed. Edited by Kurt Aland and Barbara Aland with Viktor Reichmann, and on previous English editions by W.F. Arndt, F.W. Gingrich, and F.W. Danker. Chicago: The University of Chicago Press, 2000.

GRAMCORD Morphological Search Engine 2.4bm.

Greenlee, J. Harold. *A New Testament Greek Morpheme Lexicon*. Grand Rapids, MI: Zondervan Publishing House, 1983.

Kohlenberger III, John R., Edward W. Goodrick, and James A. Swanson. *The Exhaustive Concordance to the Greek New Testament*. Grand Rapids, MI: Zondervan Publishing House, 1995.

Liddell, Henry George, and Robert Scott. *A Greek–English Lexicon*. New ed. by Henry Stuart Jones. Oxford: Clarendon Press, 1940.

Louw, Johannes P., and Eugene A. Nida, eds. *Greek–English Lexicon of the New Testament Based on Semantic Domains*. 2 vols. 2d ed. New York: United Bible Societies, 1989.

Moule, C.F.D. *An Idiom-Book of New Testament Greek*. 2d ed. Cambridge: Cambridge University Press, 1959.

Moulton, James Hope. *A Grammar of New Testament Greek*. 4 vols. Vol. 2 edited by Wilbert Francis Howard. Vols. 3 and 4 edited by Nigel Turner. Edinburgh: T&T Clark, 1906–1976.

Moulton, James Hope, and George Milligan. *The Vocabulary of the Greek Testament Illustrated from the Papyri and Other Non-Literary Sources*. London: Hodder and Stoughton, 1930.

Newman, Jr., Barclay M. *A Concise Greek–English Dictionary of the New Testament*. Stuttgart: Deutsche Bibelgesellschaft, 1993.

Robertson, A.T. *A Grammar of the Greek New Testament in Light of Historical Research*. Nashville, TN: Broadman Press, 1934.

Trenchard, Warren C. *Complete Vocabulary Guide to the Greek New Testament*. Rev. ed. Grand Rapids, MI: Zondervan Publishing House, 1998.

I am pleased to express my deep gratitude to several persons who helped with this project. My former student, Liisa Hawes, and my son, Mark Trenchard, worked on the initial database. My assistants, Joyce Arevalo and David Oceguera, entered material into the current database. My friend, Tom Zapara, provided funds for computer equipment. My dean, John Jones, gave support and encouragement. My editor at Cambridge, Kevin Taylor, believed in this project from the beginning and greatly facilitated its realization. My family, especially my wife Marilyn, patiently put up with my fixation on this for longer than reasonable.

INTRODUCTION

A Concise Dictionary of New Testament Greek is intended to provide students, pastors, and others with a convenient and useful source of word meanings and English glosses and with other information concerning the vocabulary of the Greek New Testament. It assumes that users have a working knowledge of New Testament Greek grammar and syntax and a basic understanding of Greek word formation.

The entries in this dictionary contain information in the following order and formatting: headword in boldface type, part of speech, cognate key word(s) in parentheses, type of proper word, indication of a non-Greek word or one of non-Greek origin, principal parts of verbs, meanings and glosses in italic type, frequency of NT use in parentheses, and NT references for words that occur only once. Of course, no entry will have all of these. What follows will explain each of these components.

Headword

Usually, the entries list headwords for each entry according to BDAG, including the voice form of verbs. The listing of the very common πορεύομαι instead of πορεύω is a notable exception. When an entry lists a verb in the active voice that occurs in the NT only in the middle and/or passive, this fact is noted in the meaning. Likewise, entries indicate that certain words listed as adjectives occur in the NT only as substantives. The alternate forms of words are included only if such forms appear in the NT.

The spelling, accentuation, and capitalization of headwords typically follow what appears in UBS[4]. This includes the representation of certain Aramaic and Hebrew words used in direct quotations without accents or breathing marks, for example αββα and ηλι. In some cases, entries separately list words (e.g. ἐάνπερ) that appear in BDAG under the entries for other words (ἐάν). This reflects the usage in UBS[4].

Many headwords represent irregular or other forms of words found elsewhere in the dictionary and are cross-referenced to them. Some headwords occur in the NT only as variant readings in UBS[4], N[27], or an earlier edition of either. A few listings provide information about the results of compounding certain prepositions to words beginning with particular letters, for example συνπ-.

Part of speech

Entries give the part of speech of each headword. The exceptions include certain non-Greek words (e.g. ελωι) and cross references. The designations of parts of speech usually follow BDAG.

Cognate key word(s)

This part of the entry lists up to three key words that share a cognate relationship with the headword, if there is a cognate word in the NT. The determination of cognate word groups and their related key words largely follows those identified by J. Harold Greenlee in *A New Testament Greek Morpheme Lexicon*. A few entries list key words that are prepositional compounds (e.g. ἐπιποθέω), if all the related words in the NT represent the same compound. Of course, such words are not actually cognate key words and are provided merely as a convenience for users.

If only one root of a multi-root word is represented in the NT, entries list only one key word. An asterisk (*) indicates that the headword is itself the key word to which other words are related. A hyphen in front of a key word (e.g. -βαίνω) means that the key word appears in the NT only in compounds.

Because they are so numerous and their presence so obvious, entries do not list prepositions as key words for prepositional compounds, except for words that derive solely from prepositions. Furthermore, entries do not give key words for headwords that occur in the NT only as variant readings or for proper words. The one exception to the latter is Ζεύς, because it is the basis of the common words διοπετής and εὐδία. The form εὐ- is a prefix and thus not listed as a key word.

Type of proper word

Proper words are capitalized as headwords and are identified in one of three ways. Names of persons (pers.) include the names of human persons, deities, and titles associated with each. Included in this category are the names of the twelve sons of Jacob, even though they are occasionally used to identify places.

Names of places (pla.) refer to the names of countries, regions, cities, towns, geographical features and phenomena, and buildings. They also include nouns related to languages and the inhabitants of particular places, as well as the corresponding proper adjectives and adverbs.

Other proper words (oth.) include the names of religious, philosophical, political, and social groups and the words used to describe their members. A few miscellaneous proper words (e.g. Ἀσιάρχης and Χερούβ) also fall into this category.

Non-Greek word

Entries identify the non-Greek words among the vocabulary of the NT, as well as the Greek words that derived directly from another language. These include words from Aramaic, Coptic, Hebrew, Latin, and Persian. A few are listed simply as Semitic. Greek words that derived from original loanwords (e.g. the derivatives of βύσσινος) or that entered Greek very early (e.g. συκάμινος) are usually not identified.

Principal parts

For verbs, entries list the principal parts that are found in the NT. If none are listed, this means that the verb occurs only in the present principal part (present and/or imperfect tenses). Principal parts are not included for verbs that appear in the NT only as variant readings. Some principal parts contain more than one form.

Because the forms ἐρῶ, εἶπον, εἴρηκα, εἴρημαι, and ἐρρέθην and their compounds are always used in the NT for λέγω and its compounds outside the present and imperfect, I have listed them among the principal parts of λέγω and the related verbs. Likewise, I have given εἶδον as the predominant aorist principal part of ὁράω.

Meanings and glosses

The heart of each entry is the listing of the headword's meaning or the English glosses that represent its range of uses in the NT. For these meanings and glosses and the main semantic nuances into which they are divided, I draw extensively on BDAG, with input from the other sources listed in the Preface and my own observations.

Entries divide these meanings and glosses into their main semantic nuances, separated by semicolons with the glosses and examples within a particular nuance separated by commas. For example, **κρίμα, ατος, τό** n. (κρίνω) *dispute, lawsuit; decision, degree; judging, judgment, authority to judge; judicial verdict, condemnation, punishment, sentence.*

Also separated in this way are the distinct meanings associated with particular forms or functions, for example passive voice or substantive form. These are identified in parentheses at the end of the section to which they pertain. For example, **λοιπός, ή, όν** adj. (λείπω) *left, remaining; other, rest (of); from now on, in the future, henceforth, beyond that, in addition, finally, furthermore, therefore* (neut. as adv.).

Where a classification or description relates to more than one main nuance, this is identified at the beginning of the first of these main nuances, and pertains to all the main nuances that follow until one comes to another such description or to the end of the entry. For example, **ἔξω** adv. (ἐκ) *outside; outer, outside, foreign* (as adj.); *out; outsider* (w. art.); adv. prep. w. gen. *outside; out, out of*.

Only words and phrases in italic typeface represent meanings and English glosses. Italicized expressions within parentheses associated with one of these meanings or glosses are intended to be a possible element of the meaning or gloss, for example *settle (down)*. If the parenthetical expression is in regular typeface, it is intended to be explanatory, for example *to cast against* (of votes). Likewise, the word "or" is used frequently to convey an alternative element of the meaning or gloss and is not intended to be part of the meaning, for example *to pour out* or *down over*.

Often the word is not used in the NT in the particular form represented by the headword (e.g. active voice for verbs or attributive or predicate use for adjectives). Usually, entries list the meaning of the headword form followed after a semicolon by the meaning of the form used in the NT. For example, **μαραίνω** v. (*) aor. pass. ἐμαράνθην. *to destroy; die out, fade, disappear, wither* (pass. in NT).

Many of these nuances include unusual or idiomatic examples from the text of the NT. For example, **πλησμονή, ῆς, ἡ** n. (πίμπλημι) *satiety, satisfaction, gratification,* πρὸς πλησμονὴν τῆς σαρκός *self-indulgence*.

When giving parsing information in cross references, entries use the following assumptions for various types of words, unless otherwise stated. For verbs: indicative, active, first person, singular. For imperatives: second person, singular. For participles: active, singular, masculine, nominative. For nouns: masculine, nominative, singular. Also, unless otherwise stated aorist = 1 aorist, perfect = 1 perfect, future = 1 future. Thus, for example "aor." means "1 aor. ind. act. 1 sg."; "2 aor. pass. ptc." means "2 aor. pass. ptc. sg. masc. nom."

Frequency

The frequency information reflects the number of times a word is used in the NT. The main sources for the data, which are not intended to be definitive, are the *Concordance to the Novum Testamentum Graece, The Exhaustive Concordance to the Greek New Testament*, and GRAMCORD. Only words that appear in the text of UBS[4], including those printed within square brackets, are used in the count. Crasis forms have their own frequency numbers. However, the individual parts of these contracted words are also counted in computing the frequency of the individual words. I have not provided frequency numbers for words that occur only as variant readings in the NT. Instead, the abbreviation "v.l." appears within the parentheses.

Reference

The last component of the entry is the reference provided for all words that occur only once in the NT. This information is not given for words that occur in the NT only as variant readings.

ABBREVIATIONS

New Testament books

Mt	Matthew	1 Ti	1 Timothy
Mk	Mark	2 Ti	2 Timothy
Lk	Luke	Tit	Titus
Jn	John	Phlm	Philemon
Ac	Acts	Heb	Hebrews
Rom	Romans	Jas	James
1 Cor	1 Corinthians	1 Pt	1 Peter
2 Cor	2 Corinthians	2 Pt	2 Peter
Gal	Galatians	1 Jn	1 John
Eph	Ephesians	2 Jn	2 John
Phil	Philippians	3 Jn	3 John
Col	Colossians	Jd	Jude
1 Th	1 Thessalonians	Rev	Revelation
2 Th	2 Thessalonians		

Other abbreviations

1	first person	comp.	comparative
2	second person	conj.	conjunction
3	third person	contr.	contraction, contracted
abs.	absolute	Cop.	Coptic
abstr.	abstract	correl.	correlative
acc.	accusative	cult.	cultic
act.	active	dat.	dative
adj.	adjective	demonstr.	demonstrative
adv.	adverb, adverbial	distr.	distributive
alt.	alternate	emph.	emphasis
aor.	aorist	encl.	enclitic
Ara.	Aramaic	esp.	especially
art.	article	ex.	example
attrib.	attributive	excl.	exclamation
aux.	auxiliary	ext.	extended
BDAG	*A Greek–English Lexicon of the New Testament and Other Early Christian Literature*, 4th ed.	fem.	feminine
		fig.	figurative
		form.	formula
		fut.	future

gen.	genitive	pla.	name of a place
Heb.	Hebrew	plpf.	pluperfect
impers.	impersonal	pos.	positive
impf.	imperfect	poss.	possible, possibly
impv.	imperative	posses.	possessive
indef.	indefinite	postpos.	postpositive
inf.	infinitive	pred.	predicate
infer.	inferential	predom.	predominantly
instr.	instrumental	pref.	preferred
interj.	interjection	prep.	preposition
interrog.	interrogative	pres.	present
intr.	intransitive	prob.	probably
Lat.	Latin	pron.	pronoun
lit.	literal	prop.	properly
masc.	masculine	ptc.	participle
met.	metaphorical	recip.	reciprocal
mid.	middle	ref.	reference
mng(s).	meaning(s)	reflex.	reflexive
mor.	moral	rel.	relative
n.	noun	s.	see
N^{27}	Nestle–Aland, *Novum Testamentum Graece*, 27th ed.	Sem.	Semitic
		sg.	singular
		somet.	sometimes
neg.	negative	subj.	subjunctive
neut.	neuter	subst.	substantive
nom.	nominative	superl.	superlative
NT	New Testament	temp.	temporal
oft.	often	trans.	transitive
opp.	opposite	UBS^4	United Bible Societies, *The Greek New Testament*, 4th ed.
opt.	optative		
oth.	other proper name		
part.	particle	untransl.	untranslatable
pass.	passive	usu.	usually
Per.	Persian	v.	verb
pers.	name of a person, personal	v.l.	variant reading(s) only
personif.	personified	voc.	vocative
pf.	perfect	w.	with
pl.	plural		

Ἀαρών, ὁ n. pers. *Aaron.* (5)

Ἀβαδδών, ὁ n. pers. *Abaddon.* (1) Rev 9:11

ἀβαρής, ές adj. (βάρος) *light weight, not burdensome* (fig. in NT). (1) 2 Cor 11:9

αββα Ara. *father, abba.* (3)

Ἄβελ, ὁ n. pers. *Abel.* (4)

Ἀβιά, ὁ n. pers. *Abijah.* (3)

Ἀβιαθάρ, ὁ n. pers. *Abiathar.* (1) Mk 2:26

Ἀβιληνή, ῆς, ἡ n. pla. *Abilene.* (1) Lk 3:1

Ἀβιούδ, ὁ n. pers. *Abiud.* (2)

Ἀβραάμ, ὁ n. pers. *Abraham.* (73)

ἄβυσσος, ου, ἡ n. (βυθός) *depth, abyss; underworld.* (9)

Ἄγαβος, ου, ὁ n. pers. *Agabus.* (2)

ἀγαγεῖν s. ἄγω (2 aor. inf.).

ἀγαθοεργέω v. (ἀγαθός, ἔργον) *to do good, confer benefits.* (1) 1 Ti 6:18

ἀγαθοποιέω v. (ἀγαθός, ποιέω) aor. ἠγαθαποίησα. *to do good, be helpful; do what is right.* (9)

ἀγαθοποιΐα, ας, ἡ n. (ἀγαθός, ποιέω) *doing good, doing right.* (1) 1 Pt 4:19

ἀγαθοποιός, όν adj. (ἀγαθός, ποιέω) *doing good, upright; one who does good* (subst. in NT). (1) 1 Pt 2:14

ἀγαθός, ή, όν adj. (*) *useful, beneficial; good, beneficent; kind, generous; good things, possessions, what is good, good deeds* (subst.). (102)

ἀγαθουργέω v. contr. of ἀγαθοεργέω *to do good, confer benefits.* (1) Ac 14:17

ἀγαθωσύνη, ης, ἡ n. (ἀγαθός) *goodness, uprightness; generosity.* (4)

ἀγαλλίασις, εως, ἡ n. (ἀγαλλιάω) *exultation, extreme joy.* (5)

ἀγαλλιάω v. (*) aor. ἠγαλλίασα; aor.
pass. ἠγαλλιάθην. *to exult, be glad, overjoyed.* (11)

ἄγαμος, ον adj. (γάμος) *unmarried; unmarried man* or *woman* (subst. in NT). (4)

ἀγανακτέω v. (*) aor. ἠγανάκτησα. *to be aroused, indignant, angry.* (7)

ἀγανάκτησις, εως, ἡ n. (ἀγανακτέω) *indignation.* (1) 2 Cor 7:11

ἀγαπάω v. (*) fut. ἀγαπήσω; aor. ἠγάπησα; pf. ἠγάπηκα; pf. pass. ἠγάπημαι; aor. pass. ἠγαπήθην. *to love, cherish, have affection for; take pleasure in, enjoy, long for, show love; prove one's love.* (143)

ἀγάπη, ης, ἡ n. (ἀγαπάω) *love, esteem, affection, regard; love-feast, fellowship meal.* (116)

ἀγαπητός, ή, όν adj. (ἀγαπάω) *only beloved, only; beloved, dear, prized, valued.* (61)

Ἀγάρ, ἡ n. pers. *Hagar.* (2)

ἀγγαρεύω v. Per. fut. ἀγγαρεύσω; aor. ἠγγάρευσα. *to press into service, requisition, force, compel.* (3)

ἀγγεῖον, ου, τό n. (ἄγγος) *vessel, flask, container.* (1) Mt 25:4

ἀγγελία, ας, ἡ n. (ἄγγελος) *message; instruction, command.* (2)

ἀγγέλλω v. (ἄγγελος) *to announce, tell.* (1) Jn 20:18

ἄγγελος, ου, ὁ n. (*) *messenger, envoy; angel.* (175)

ἄγγος, ους, τό n. (*) *vessel, container.* (1) Mt 13:48

ἄγε interj. pres. impv. of ἄγω *come!* (2)

ἀγέλη, ης, ἡ n. (ἄγω) *herd (of pigs).* (7)

ἀγενεαλόγητος, ον adj. (λέγω, γίνομαι) *without genealogy.* (1) Heb 7:3

ἀγενής, ές adj. (γίνομαι) *base, low, insignificant.* (1) 1 Cor 1:28

ἀγιάζω v. (ἅγιος) aor. ἡγίασα; pf. pass. ἡγίασμαι; aor. pass. ἡγιάσθην. *to consecrate, dedicate, make holy; sanctify; reverence; purify.* (28)

ἁγιασμός, οῦ, ὁ n. (ἅγιος) *holiness, consecration, sanctification.* (10)

ἅγιος, α, ον adj. (*) *holy, sacred, dedicated to God; pure, perfect, worthy of God; holy thing, holy one(s), saints, sanctuary* (subst.). (233)

ἁγιότης, ητος, ἡ n. (ἅγιος) *holiness, holy character.* (1) Heb 12:10

ἁγιωσύνη, ης, ἡ n. (ἅγιος) *holiness.* (3)

ἀγκάλη, ης, ἡ n. (*) *arm.* (1) Lk 2:28

ἄγκιστρον, ου, τό n. (ἄγκυρα) *fishhook.* (1) Mt 17:27

ἄγκυρα, ας, ἡ n. (*) *anchor.* (4)

ἄγναφος, ον adj. (γναφεύς) *unbleached, unshrunken, unsized, new.* (2)

ἁγνεία, ας, ἡ n. (ἅγιος) *purity, chastity.* (2)

ἁγνίζω v. (ἅγιος) aor. ἥγνισα; pf. ἥγνικα; pf. pass. ἥγνισμαι; aor. pass. ἡγνίσθην. *to purify, cleanse.* (7)

ἁγνισμός, οῦ, ὁ n. (ἅγιος) *purification.* (1) Ac 21:26

ἀγνοέω v. (γινώσκω) aor. ἡγνόησα. *to not know, be ignorant; not recognize, ignore; not understand; sin unintentionally.* (22)

ἀγνόημα, ατος, τό n. (γινώσκω) *sin committed in ignorance.* (1) Heb 9:7

ἄγνοια, ας, ἡ n. (γινώσκω) *ignorance; sin* (poss.). (4)

ἁγνός, ή, όν adj. (ἅγιος) *pure, holy, innocent, chaste.* (8)

ἁγνότης, ητος, ἡ n. (ἅγιος) *purity, sincerity.* (2)

ἁγνῶς adv. (ἅγιος) *purely, sincerely.* (1) Phil 1:17

ἀγνωσία, ας, ἡ n. (γινώσκω) *ignorance, lack of spiritual discernment, ignorant talk.* (2)

ἄγνωστος, ον adj. (γινώσκω) *unknown.* (1) Ac 17:23

ἀγορά, ᾶς, ἡ n. (ἀγοράζω) *market place.* (11)

ἀγοράζω v. (*) aor. ἡγόρασα; pf. pass. ἡγόρασμαι; aor. pass. ἡγοράσθην. *to buy, purchase; acquire as property.* (30)

ἀγοραῖος, ον adj. (ἀγοράζω) *pertaining to a market; market people, rabble, court sessions* (pl. subst. in NT). (2)

ἄγρα, ας, ἡ n. (*) *catching, catch.* (2)

ἀγράμματος, ον adj. (γράφω) *uneducated, illiterate.* (1) Ac 4:13

ἀγραυλέω v. (ἀγρός) *to live outdoors.* (1) Lk 2:8

ἀγρεύω v. (ἄγρα) aor. ἤγρευσα. *to catch; catch unawares* (fig. in NT). (1) Mk 12:13

ἀγριέλαιος, ου, ἡ n. (ἀγρός, ἐλαία) *wild olive tree.* (2)

ἄγριος, α, ον adj. (ἀγρός) *wild; uncontrolled, stormy.* (3)

Ἀγρίππας, α, ὁ n. pers. *Agrippa.* (11)

ἀγρός, οῦ, ὁ n. (*) *countryside, land; farm, estate* (pl.); *arable land, field.* (36)

ἀγρυπνέω v. (ἄγρα, ὕπνος) *to be alert; look after, care for.* (4)

ἀγρυπνία, ας, ἡ n. (ἄγρα, ὕπνος) *sleeplessness.* (2)

ἄγω v. (*) fut. ἄξω; aor. ἤγαγον; aor. pass. ἤχθην. *to lead, bring; bring along; lead away, arrest; guide, encourage; celebrate, observe; go.* (67)

ἀγωγή, ῆς, ἡ n. (ἄγω) *way of life, conduct.* (1) 2 Ti 3:10

ἀγών, ῶνος, ὁ n. (*) *contest, race; struggle, fight* (fig. in NT). (6)

ἀγωνία, ας, ἡ n. (ἀγών) *distress, anguish, anxiety.* (1) Lk 22:44

ἀγωνίζομαι v. (ἀγών) pf. pass. ἡγώνισμαι. *to engage in a contest; fight, struggle, strain.* (8)

Ἀδάμ, ὁ n. pers. *Adam.* (9)

ἀδάπανος, ον adj. (δαπάνη) *free of charge.* (1) 1 Cor 9:18

Ἀδδί, ὁ n. pers. *Addi.* (1) Lk 3:28

ἀδελφή, ῆς, ἡ n. (ἀδελφός) *sister, fellow believer.* (26)

ἀδελφός, οῦ, ὁ n. (*) *brother* (somet.
pl. = *brothers and sisters); fellow believer, associate, compatriot, neighbor.*
(343)
ἀδελφότης, ητος, ἡ n. (ἀδελφός) *broth-
erhood, a fellowship.* (2)
ἄδηλος, ον adj. (δῆλος) *not clear, unseen, latent; indistinct.* (2)
ἀδηλότης, ητος, ἡ n. (δῆλος) *uncer-
tainty.* (1) 1 Ti 6:17
ἀδήλως adv. (δῆλος) *uncertainly.* (1) 1
Cor 9:26
ἀδημονέω v. *to be distressed, troubled,
anxious.* (3)
ᾅδης, ου, ὁ n. *Hades, underworld, place
of the dead; Hades* (personif.). (10)
ἀδιάκριτος, ον adj. (κρίνω) *nonjudg-
mental, impartial; unwavering* (poss.).
(1) Jas 3:17
ἀδιάλειπτος, ον adj. (λείπω) *unceasing, constant.* (2)
ἀδιαλείπτως adv. (λείπω) *constantly,
unceasingly.* (4)
ἀδικέω v. (δίκη) fut. ἀδικήσω; aor.
ἠδίκησα; aor. pass. ἠδικήθην. *to do
wrong, be in the wrong, treat unjustly;
injure, damage.* (28)
ἀδίκημα, ατος, τό n. (δίκη) *wrong,
crime, misdeed.* (3)
ἀδικία, ας, ἡ n. (δίκη) *wrongdoing; un-
righteousness, wickedness, injustice.*
(25)
ἄδικος, ον adj. (δίκη) *unjust, crooked,
dishonest, untrustworthy.* (12)
ἀδίκως adv. (δίκη) *unjustly.* (1) 1 Pt
2:19
Ἀδμίν, ὁ n. pers. *Admin.* (1) Lk 3:33
ἀδόκιμος, ον adj. (δέχομαι) *not standing the test, unqualified, worthless,
base.* (8)
ἄδολος, ον adj. (δόλος) *without deceit,
unadulterated, pure.* (1) 1 Pt 2:2
Ἀδραμυττηνός, ή, όν adj. pla. *of
Adramyttium.* (1) Ac 27:2
Ἀδρίας, ου, ὁ n. pla. *Adriatic Sea.* (1)
Ac 27:27
ἀδρότης, ητος, ἡ n. *abundance.* (1) 2
Cor 8:20

ἀδυνατέω v. (δύναμαι) fut. ἀδυνατήσω.
to be powerless; it is impossible
(impers. in NT). (2)
ἀδύνατος, ον adj. (δύναμαι) *powerless,
impotent; impossible.* (10)
ἀδυσβάστακτος, ον adj. *not too difficult
to bear.* (v.l.)
ᾄδω v. (ᾠδή) *to sing.* (5)
ἀεί adv. (*) *always; continually, constantly.* (7)
ἀετός, οῦ, ὁ n. *eagle, vulture.* (5)
ἄζυμος, ον adj. (ζέω) *without fermenta-
tion;* subst. *unleavened bread; festival
of unleavened bread.* (9)
Ἀζώρ, ὁ n. pers. *Azor.* (2)
Ἄζωτος, ου, ἡ n. pla. *Azotus.* (1) Ac 8:40
ἀήρ, ἀέρος, ὁ n. *air; sky, space.* (7)
ἀθανασία, ας, ἡ n. (θνήσκω) *immort-
ality.* (3)
ἀθέμιτος, ον adj. *not allowed, forbid-
den; wanton, disgusting.* (2)
ἄθεος, ον adj. (θεός) *without God, god-
less.* (1) Eph 2:12
ἄθεσμος, ον adj. (τίθημι) *lawless, un-
principled; lawless person* (subst. in
NT). (2)
ἀθετέω v. (τίθημι) fut. ἀθετήσω; aor.
ἠθέτησα. *to declare invalid, nullify, ignore; reject, not recognize, disallow.*
(16)
ἀθέτησις, εως, ἡ n. (τίθημι) *annulment,
removal.* (2)
Ἀθῆναι, ῶν, αἱ n. pla. *Athens.* (4)
Ἀθηναῖος, α, ον adj. pla. *Athenian; an
Athenian* (subst.). (2)
ἀθλέω v. (*) aor. ἤθλησα. *to compete (in
a contest).* (2)
ἄθλησις, εως, ἡ n. (ἀθλέω) *contest;
hard struggle* (fig. in NT). (1) Heb
10:32
ἀθροίζω v. (θροέω) pf. pass. ἤθροισμαι.
to collect, gather. (1) Lk 24:33
ἀθυμέω v. (θυμός) *to be discouraged,
lose heart, become dispirited.* (1) Col
3:21
ἀθῷος, ον adj. (τίθημι) *innocent.* (2)
αἴγειος, α, ον adj. *of a goat.* (1) Heb
11:37

αἰγιαλός, οῦ, ὁ n. (ἅλας) *shore, beach.* (6)

Αἰγύπτιος, α, ον adj. pla. *Egyptian; an Egyptian* (subst.). (5)

Αἴγυπτος, ου, ἡ n. pla. *Egypt.* (25)

ἀΐδιος, ον adj. (ἀεί) *eternal.* (2)

αἰδώς, οῦς, ἡ n. (*) *modesty.* (1) 1 Ti 2:9

Αἰθίοψ, οπος, ὁ n. pla. *an Ethiopian; Ethiopian* (adj.). (2)

αἷμα, ατος, τό n. (*) *blood; life-blood, death, murder;* σὰρξ καὶ αἷμα *human nature.* (97)

αἱματεκχυσία, ας, ἡ n. (αἷμα, -χέω) *shedding of blood.* (1) Heb 9:22

αἱμορροέω v. (αἷμα, ῥέω) *to bleed, suffer with hemorrhage.* (1) Mt 9:20

Αἰνέας, ου, ὁ n. pers. *Aeneas.* (2)

αἴνεσις, εως, ἡ n. (αἶνος) *praise.* (1) Heb 13:15

αἰνέω v. (αἶνος) *to praise.* (8)

αἴνιγμα, ατος, τό n. (αἶνος) *riddle, indirect image.* (1) 1 Cor 13:12

αἶνος, ου, ὁ n. (*) *praise.* (2)

Αἰνών, ἡ n. pla. *Aenon.* (1) Jn 3:23

αἵρεσις, εως, ἡ n. (αἱρέω) *sect, party, school, faction, dissension; opinion, dogma.* (9)

αἱρετίζω v. (αἱρέω) aor. ἡρέτισα. *to choose.* (1) Mt 12:18

αἱρετικός, ή, όν adj. (αἱρέω) *factious, causing divisions.* (1) Tit 3:10

αἱρέω v. (*) fut. αἱρήσω; aor. εἷλα, εἷλον. *to choose, prefer* (mid. in NT). (3)

αἴρω v. (*) fut. ἀρῶ; aor. ἦρα; pf. ἦρκα; pf. pass. ἦρμαι; aor. pass. ἤρθην. *to lift up, take up, pick up, raise; take, carry, carry away remove; conquer, kill, destroy, cut off, blot out; withdraw; keep in suspense; depart; arise* (pass.). (101)

αἰσθάνομαι v. (*) aor. ἠσθόμην. *to understand.* (1) Lk 9:45

αἴσθησις, εως, ἡ n. (αἰσθάνομαι) *discernment, insight.* (1) Phil 1:9

αἰσθητήριον, ου, τό n. (αἰσθάνομαι) *sense, faculty.* (1) Heb 5:14

αἰσχροκερδής, ές adj. (αἰσχρός, κέρδος) *fond of dishonest gain, avaricious.* (2)

αἰσχροκερδῶς adv. (αἰσχρός, κέρδος) *in fondness for dishonest gain, greedily.* (1) 1 Pt 5:2

αἰσχρολογία, ας, ἡ n. (αἰσχρός, λέγω) *obscene speech, dirty talk.* (1) Col 3:8

αἰσχρός, ά, όν adj. (*) *shameful, disgraceful, dishonest.* (4)

αἰσχρότης, ητος, ἡ n. (αἰσχρός) *shamefulness, obscenity, indecent behavior.* (1) Eph 5:4

αἰσχύνη, ης, ἡ n. (αἰσχρός) *modesty, shame; disgrace; shameful deed.* (6)

αἰσχύνω v. (αἰσχρός) aor. pass. ᾐσχύνθην. *to be ashamed; be put to shame, disgraced* (mid. and pass. in NT). (5)

αἰτέω v. (*) fut. αἰτήσω; aor. ᾔτησα; pf. ᾔτηκα. *to ask, ask for, demand, request.* (70)

αἴτημα, ατος, τό n. (αἰτέω) *request, demand.* (3)

αἰτία, ας, ἡ n. (*) *cause, reason; relationship; charge, ground for complaint; accusation.* (20)

αἴτιος, α, ον adj. (αἰτία) *responsible; cause, source, reason, ground for complaint* (subst. in NT). (5)

αἰτίωμα, ατος, τό n. (αἰτία) *charge, complaint.* (1) Ac 25:7

αἰφνίδιος, ον adj. (ἄφνω) *sudden.* (2)

αἰχμαλωσία, ας, ἡ n. (ἅλωσις) *captivity; captives, prisoners of war.* (3)

αἰχμαλωτεύω v. (ἅλωσις) aor. ᾐχμαλώτευσα. *to capture, take captive.* (1) Eph 4:8

αἰχμαλωτίζω v. (ἅλωσις) aor. pass. ᾐχμαλωτίσθην. *to capture, make captive; mislead, deceive.* (4)

αἰχμάλωτος, ου, ὁ n. (ἅλωσις) *captive.* (1) Lk 4:18

αἰών, ῶνος, ὁ n. (*) *very long time, past, earliest times, eternity,* εἰς τὸν αἰῶνα *forever, never* (w. neg.); *age; world; Aeon* (personif.). (122)

αἰώνιος, α, ον adj. (αἰών) *long ago; eternal (of God); without end, eternal, everlasting.* (71)

ἀκαθαρσία, ας, ἡ n. (καθαρός) *dirt, refuse; immorality, vileness* (fig.). (10)

ἀκάθαρτος, ον adj. (καθαρός) *impure, unclean* (cult.)*; impure, unclean* (mor.). (32)

ἀκαιρέομαι v. (καιρός) *to have no time, no opportunity.* (1) Phil 4:10

ἀκαίρως adv. (καιρός) *untimely, out of season.* (1) 2 Ti 4:2

ἄκακος, ον adj. (κακός) *innocent, guileless, unsuspecting.* (2)

ἄκανθα, ης, ἡ n. (ἄκρον) *thorn-plant, thorn.* (14)

ἀκάνθινος, η, ον adj. (ἄκρον) *thorny.* (2)

ἄκαρπος, ον adj. (καρπός) *unfruitful, fruitless; useless, unproductive* (fig.). (7)

ἀκατάγνωστος, ον adj. (γινώσκω) *beyond reproach, above criticism.* (1) Tit 2:8

ἀκατακάλυπτος, ον adj. (καλύπτω) *uncovered.* (2)

ἀκατάκριτος, ον adj. (κρίνω) *uncondemned, without a proper trial, without due process.* (2)

ἀκατάλυτος, ον adj. (λύω) *indestructible, endless.* (1) Heb 7:16

ἀκατάπαυστος, ον adj. (παύω) *unceasing, restless.* (1) 2 Pt 2:14

ἀκαταστασία, ας, ἡ n. (ἵστημι) *disturbance, tumult; disorder, unruliness, insurrection.* (5)

ἀκατάστατος, ον adj. (ἵστημι) *unstable, restless.* (2)

Ἀκελδαμάχ n. pla. *Akeldama, Field of Blood.* (1) Ac 1:19

ἀκέραιος, ον adj. (κεράννυμι) *unmixed; pure, innocent* (fig. in NT). (3)

ἀκλινής, ές adj. (κλίνω) *without wavering, firmly.* (1) Heb 10:23

ἀκμάζω v. (ἄκρον) aor. ἤκμασα. *to bloom, be ripe.* (1) Rev 14:18

ἀκμήν adv. (ἄκρον) *even yet, still.* (1) Mt 15:16

ἀκοή, ῆς, ἡ n. (ἀκούω) *hearing; listening; ear; fame, report, rumor, account, message, proclamation.* (24)

ἀκολουθέω v. (*) fut. ἀκολουθήσω; aor. ἠκολούθησα; pf. ἠκολούθηκα. *to come after; accompany; be a disciple, follow* (fig.)*; follow* (lit.). (90)

ἀκούω v. (*) fut. ἀκούσω, ἀκούσομαι; aor. ἤκουσα; pf. ἀκήκοα; aor. pass. ἠκούσθην. *to hear; grant a hearing; learn, learn about; heed, obey; listen to; understand, have heard.* (428)

ἀκρασία, ας, ἡ n. (κράτος) *lack of self-control, self-indulgence.* (2)

ἀκρατής, ές adj. (κράτος) *without self-control, dissolute.* (1) 2 Ti 3:3

ἄκρατος, ον adj. (κεράννυμι) *unmixed, full strength.* (1) Rev 14:10

ἀκρίβεια, ας, ἡ n. (ἀκριβής) *exactness, precision, strictness.* (1) Ac 22:3

ἀκριβής, ές adj. (*) *exact, strict.* (1) Ac 26:5

ἀκριβόω v. (ἀκριβής) aor. ἠκρίβωσα. *to ascertain* or *inquire precisely.* (2)

ἀκριβῶς adv. (ἀκριβής) *accurately, carefully, well.* (9)

ἀκρίς, ίδος, ἡ n. *locust, grasshopper.* (4)

ἀκροατήριον, ου, τό n. (ἀκροατής) *audience hall, auditorium.* (1) Ac 25:23

ἀκροατής, οῦ, ὁ n. (*) *hearer.* (4)

ἀκροβυστία, ας, ἡ n. (ἄκρον) *foreskin; uncircumcision, uncircumcised man, Gentile* (fig.)*; noncircumcised, Gentiles* (abstr.). (20)

ἀκρογωνιαῖος, α, ον adj. (ἄκρον, γωνία) *lying at the extreme corner; cornerstone* (subst. in NT). (2)

ἀκροθίνιον, ου τό n. (ἄκρον) *booty, spoils* (pl. in NT). (1) Heb 7:4

ἄκρον, ου, τό n. (*) *high point, top, tip, end.* (6)

Ἀκύλας, ὁ n. pers. *Aquila.* (6)

ἀκυρόω v. (κύριος) aor. ἠκύρωσα. *to make void.* (3)

ἀκωλύτως adv. (κωλύω) *without hindrance.* (1) Ac 28:31

ἄκων, ουσα, ον adj. (ἑκών) *unwilling; unwillingly* (adv. in NT). (1) 1 Cor 9:17

ἀλάβαστρος, ου, ὁ, ἡ n. *alabaster vase.* (4)

ἀλαζονεία, ας, ἡ n. (ἀλαζών) *pretension, arrogance, pride.* (2)

ἀλαζών, όνος, ὁ n. (*) *boaster, braggart.* (2)

ἀλαλάζω v. *to wail loudly, clang, crash.* (2)

ἀλάλητος, ον adj. (λαλέω) *unexpressed, wordless.* (1) Rom 8:26

ἄλαλος, ον adj. (λαλέω) *mute, unable to speak; mute person* (subst.). (3)

ἅλας, ατος, τό n. (*) *salt.* (8)

ἀλείφω v. (*) aor. ἤλειψα. *to anoint.* (9)

ἀλεκτοροφωνία, ας, ἡ n. (ἀλέκτωρ, φωνή) *crowing of a cock, cockcrow, before dawn, third watch of the night* (12–3 a.m.). (1) Mk 13:35

ἀλέκτωρ, ορος, ὁ n. (*) *cock, rooster.* (12)

Ἀλεξανδρεύς, έως, ὁ n. pla. *an Alexandrian.* (2)

Ἀλεξανδρῖνος, η, ον adj. pla. *Alexandrian.* (2)

Ἀλέξανδρος, ου, ὁ n. pers. *Alexander.* (6)

ἄλευρον, ου, τό n. (ἀλήθω) *wheat flour.* (2)

ἀλήθεια, ας, ἡ n. (λανθάνω) *truthfulness, dependability; truth; reality,* κατὰ ἀλήθειαν *rightly,* ἐν ἀληθείᾳ *indeed, truly,* ἐπ᾽ ἀληθείας *in accordance with the truth, truly.* (109)

ἀληθεύω v. (λανθάνω) *to be truthful, tell the truth.* (2)

ἀληθής, ές adj. (λανθάνω) *truthful, righteous, honest; true; real, genuine.* (26)

ἀληθινός, ή, όν adj. (λανθάνω) *true, trustworthy; reliable; real, genuine, authentic.* (28)

ἀλήθω v. (*) *to grind.* (2)

ἀληθῶς adv. (λανθάνω) *truly, in truth, really, actually.* (18)

ἁλιεύς, έως, ὁ n. (ἅλας) *one who fishes, fisherman.* (5)

ἁλιεύω v. (ἅλας) *to fish.* (1) Jn 21:3

ἁλίζω v. (ἅλας) aor. pass. ἡλίσθην. *to salt.* (2)

ἁλίσγημα, ατος, τό n. *pollution.* (1) Ac 15:20

ἀλλ᾽ = ἀλλά before vowels.

ἀλλά part. (ἄλλος) *but, yet, rather,* ἀλλὰ καί *but also; nevertheless; yet, certainly, but rather; now, then.* (638)

ἀλλάσσω v. (ἄλλος) fut. ἀλλάξω; aor. ἤλλαξα; aor. pass. ἠλλάγην. *to change, alter; exchange.* (6)

ἀλλαχόθεν adv. (ἄλλος) *from or at another place.* (1) Jn 10:1

ἀλλαχοῦ adv. (ἄλλος) *elsewhere, in another direction.* (1) Mk 1:38

ἀλληγορέω v. (ἄλλος, ἀγοράζω) *to speak allegorically.* (1) Gal 4:24

ἀλληλουϊά Heb. *hallelujah, praise Yahweh.* (4)

ἀλλήλων pron. (ἄλλος) *each other, one another, mutually* (gen. of recip. pron.). (100)

ἀλλογενής, ές adj. (ἄλλος, γίνομαι) *foreign; foreigner* (subst. in NT). (1) Lk 17:18

ἅλλομαι v. (*) aor. ἡλάμην. *to leap, spring up; well up, bubble up* (fig.). (3)

ἄλλος, η, ο adj. (*) *other,* ἄλλος ... ἄλλος *one ... another; another, different; more; the other* (subst.). (155)

ἀλλοτριεπίσκοπος, ου, ὁ n. (ἄλλος, σκοπός) *one who meddles in the affairs of others, busybody.* (1) 1 Pt 4:15

ἀλλότριος, α, ον adj. (ἄλλος) *belonging to another, not one's own, strange; hostile;* (subst.) *stranger, alien; enemy.* (14)

ἀλλόφυλος, ον adj. (ἄλλος, φύω) *alien, foreign; a Gentile* (subst. in NT). (1) Ac 10:28

ἄλλως adv. (ἄλλος) *otherwise, in another way.* (1) 1 Ti 5:25

Ἀλμεί, ὁ n. pers. *Almi.* (v.l.)

ἀλοάω v. (*) *to thresh.* (3)

ἄλογος, ον adj. (λέγω) *without reason, unreasoning; contrary to reason, absurd.* (3)

ἀλόη, ης, ἡ n. *aloes* (aromatic juice used for embalming). (1) Jn 19:39

ἅλς, ἁλός, ὁ n. *salt*. (v.l.)
ἁλυκός, ή, όν adj. (ἅλας) *salty*. (1) Jas 3:12
ἄλυπος, ον adj. (λύπη) *free from anxiety*. (1) Phil 2:28
ἅλυσις, εως, ἡ n. *chain; imprisonment*. (11)
ἀλυσιτελής, ές adj. (λύω, τέλος) *unprofitable, of no help*. (1) Heb 13:17
Ἄλφα, τό n. *alpha* (first letter of the Greek alphabet). (3)
Ἀλφαῖος, ου, ὁ n. pers. *Alphaeus*. (5)
ἅλων, ωνος, ἡ n. (ἀλοάω) *threshing floor; threshed grain* (fig. in NT). (2)
ἀλώπηξ, εκος, ἡ n. *fox*. (3)
ἅλωσις, εως, ἡ n. (*) *capture, catching*. (1) 2 Pt 2:12
ἅμα adv. *at the same time; together; together with* (adv. prep. w. dat.); ἅμα πρωΐ *early in the morning*. (10)
ἀμαθής, ές adj. (μανθάνω) *ignorant*. (1) 2 Pt 3:16
ἀμαράντινος, η, ον adj. (μαραίνω) *unfading*. (1) 1 Pt 5:4
ἀμάραντος, ον adj. (μαραίνω) *unfading*. (1) 1 Pt 1:4
ἁμαρτάνω v. (*) fut. ἁμαρτήσω; aor. ἡμάρτησα, ἥμαρτον; pf. ἡμάρτηκα. *to sin, commit a sin*. (43)
ἁμάρτημα, ατος, τό n. (ἁμαρτάνω) *sin, transgression*. (4)
ἁμαρτία, ας, ἡ n. (ἁμαρτάνω) *sin* (an act); *sinfulness; sin* (a power). (173)
ἀμάρτυρος, ον adj. (μάρτυς) *without witness*. (1) Ac 14:17
ἁμαρτωλός, όν adj. (ἁμαρτάνω) *sinful; sinner, irreligious* or *unobservant person* (subst.). (47)
ἄμαχος, ον adj. (μάχη) *peaceable*. (2)
ἀμάω v. aor. ἤμησα. *to mow*. (1) Jas 5:4
ἀμέθυστος, ου, ἡ n. (μεθύω) *amethyst*. (1) Rev 21:20
ἀμελέω v. (μέλει) aor. ἡμέλησα. *to neglect, be unconcerned, disregard*. (4)
ἄμεμπτος, ον adj. (μέμφομαι) *blameless, faultless*. (5)
ἀμέμπτως adv. (μέμφομαι) *blamelessly, blameless*. (2)

ἀμέριμνος, ον adj. (μεριμνάω) *free from care, out of trouble*. (2)
ἀμετάθετος, ον adj. (τίθημι) *unchangeable; unchangeableness* (neut. subst.). (2)
ἀμετακίνητος, ον adj. (κινέω) *immovable, firm*. (1) 1 Cor 15:58
ἀμεταμέλητος, ον adj. (μέλει) *not to be regretted, without regret, irrevocable*. (2)
ἀμετανόητος, ον adj. (νοῦς) *unrepentant*. (1) Rom 2:5
ἄμετρος, ον adj. (μέτρον) *immeasurable*, εἰς τὰ ἄμετρα *beyond limits*. (2)
ἀμήν Heb. *amen, let it be so, truly; the Amen* (Christ). (129)
ἀμήτωρ, ορος adj. (μήτηρ) *without a mother*. (1) Heb 7:3
ἀμίαντος, ον adj. (μιαίνω) *undefiled, pure*. (4)
Ἀμιναδάβ, ὁ n. pers. *Amminadab*. (3)
ἄμμος, ου, ἡ n. *sand*. (5)
ἀμνός, οῦ, ὁ n. *lamb*. (4)
ἀμοιβή, ῆς, ἡ n. *return, recompense, repayment*. (1) 1 Ti 5:4
ἄμπελος, ου, ἡ n. (*) *vine, grapevine*. (9)
ἀμπελουργός, οῦ, ὁ n. (ἄμπελος, ἔργον) *vinedresser, gardener*. (1) Lk 13:7
ἀμπελών, ῶνος, ὁ n. (ἄμπελος) *vineyard, orchard*. (23)
Ἀμπλιᾶτος, ου, ὁ n. pers. *Ampliatus*. (1) Rom 16:8
ἀμύνομαι v. aor. ἡμυνάμην. *to help, assist, defend, retaliate*. (1) Ac 7:24
ἀμφιάζω v. *to clothe*. (v.l.)
ἀμφιβάλλω v. (βάλλω) *to cast* (a fishnet). (1) Mk 1:16
ἀμφίβληστρον, ου, τό n. (βάλλω) *casting-net*. (1) Mt 4:18
ἀμφιέζω v. (ἱμάτιον) *to clothe*. (1) Lk 12:28
ἀμφιέννυμι v. (ἱμάτιον) pf. pass. ἡμφίεσμαι. *to clothe, dress*. (3)
Ἀμφίπολις, εως, ἡ n. pla. *Amphipolis*. (1) Ac 17:1

ἄμφοδον, ου, τό n. (ὁδός) *street*. (1) Mk 11:4

ἀμφότεροι, αι, α adj. *both; all*. (14)

ἀμώμητος, ον adj. (μέμφομαι) *blameless, unblemished*. (1) 2 Pt 3:14

ἄμωμον, ου, τό n. *amomum (an Indian spice plant)*. (1) Rev 18:13

ἄμωμος, ον adj. (μέμφομαι) *unblemished; blameless*. (8)

Ἀμών, ὁ n. pers. *Amon*. (v.l.)

Ἀμώς, ὁ n. pers. *Amos*. (3)

ἄν part. (*) postpos. conditional part., part. of contingency (untransl.); somet. used for ἐάν. (166)

ἄν' = ἀνά before vowels.

ἀνά prep. (*) w. acc. *up, up to* (lit. not in NT); w. μέσον *among, in the midst of, between*; w. μέρος *in turn*; w. numbers *each, apiece*. (13)

ἀναβαθμός, οῦ, ὁ n. (-βαίνω) *step; flight of stairs* (pl.). (2)

ἀναβαίνω v. (-βαίνω) fut. ἀναβήσομαι; aor. ἀνέβην; pf. ἀναβέβηκα. *to go up, ascend, embark, climb up, come up, grow up; enter, arise*. (82)

ἀναβάλλω v. (βάλλω) aor. ἀνέβαλον. *to adjourn, postpone*. (1) Ac 24:22

ἀναβιβάζω v. (-βαίνω) aor. ἀνεβίβασα. *to bring up, pull up*. (1) Mt 13:48

ἀναβλέπω v. (βλέπω) aor. ἀνέβλεψα. *to look up; regain sight, gain sight, receive sight*. (25)

ἀνάβλεψις, εως, ἡ n. (βλέπω) *recovery of sight*. (1) Lk 4:18

ἀναβοάω v. (βοή) aor. ἀνεβόησα. *to cry out, shout*. (1) Mt 27:46

ἀναβολή, ῆς, ἡ n. (βάλλω) *postponement, delay*. (1) Ac 25:17

ἀνάγαιον, ου, τό n. (γῆ) *room upstairs*. (2)

ἀναγγέλλω v. (ἄγγελος) fut. ἀναγγελῶ; aor. ἀνήγγειλα; aor. pass. ἀνηγγέλην. *to report; disclose, announce, proclaim, preach*. (14)

ἀναγεννάω v. (γίνομαι) aor. ἀνεγέννησα; pf. pass. ἀναγεγέννημαι. *to cause to be born again, beget again*. (2)

ἀναγινώσκω v. (γινώσκω) aor. ἀνέγνων; aor. pass. ἀνεγνώσθην. *to read, read aloud*. (32)

ἀναγκάζω v. (ἀνάγκη) aor. ἠνάγκασα; aor. pass. ἠναγκάσθην. *to compel, force; invite, strongly urge, press*. (9)

ἀναγκαῖος, α, ον adj. (ἀνάγκη) *necessary; intimate, close*. (8)

ἀναγκαστῶς adv. (ἀνάγκη) *by compulsion*. (1) 1 Pt 5:2

ἀνάγκη, ης, ἡ n. (*) *necessity, pressure*; w. inf. *it is necessary, one must*; w. ἐξ *under pressure, necessarily*; w. κατὰ *by pressure; distress, calamity; torture*. (17)

ἀναγνωρίζω v. (γινώσκω) aor. pass. ἀνεγνωρίσθην. *to learn to know again, become reacquainted*. (1) Ac 7:13

ἀνάγνωσις, εως, ἡ n. (γινώσκω) *reading, public reading*. (3)

ἀνάγω v. (ἄγω) aor. ἀνήγαγον; aor. pass. ἀνήχθην. *to lead up, bring up; bring before; offer up; put out to sea, set sail* (mid. or pass.). (23)

ἀναδείκνυμι v. (δείκνυμι) aor. ἀνέδειξα. *to show clearly, reveal something hidden; appoint, commission*. (2)

ἀνάδειξις, εως, ἡ n. (δείκνυμι) *commissioning, installation*. (1) Lk 1:80

ἀναδέχομαι v. (δέχομαι) aor. ἀνεδεξάμην. *to accept, receive; welcome*. (2)

ἀναδίδωμι v. (δίδωμι) aor. ἀνέδωκα. *to deliver, hand over*. (1) Ac 23:33

ἀναζάω v. (ζάω) aor. ἀνέζησα. *to be resurrected, be alive again; spring into life, come to life*. (2)

ἀναζητέω v. (ζητέω) aor. ἀνεζήτησα. *to look for, search for*. (3)

ἀναζώννυμι v. (ζώννυμι) aor. ἀνέζωσα. *to bind up, gird up*. (1) 1 Pt 1:13

ἀναζωπυρέω v. (ζάω, πῦρ) *to rekindle*. (1) 2 Ti 1:6

ἀναθάλλω v. (θηλάζω) aor. ἀνέθαλον. *to cause to grow* or *bloom again, revive*. (1) Phil 4:10

ἀνάθεμα, ατος, τό n. (τίθημι) *cursed, accursed; a curse*. (6)

ἀναθεματίζω v. (τίθημι) aor. ἀνεθεμάτισα. *to put under a curse, curse.* (4)

ἀναθεωρέω v. (θεάομαι) *to examine, look carefully at; consider.* (2)

ἀνάθημα, ατος, τό n. (τίθημι) *votive offering.* (1) Lk 21:5

ἀναίδεια, ας, ἡ n. (αἰδώς) *shamelessness, impertinence, impudence.* (1) Lk 11:8

ἀναίρεσις, εως, ἡ n. (αἱρέω) *murder, killing.* (1) Ac 8:1

ἀναιρέω v. (αἱρέω) fut. ἀνελῶ; aor. ἀνεῖλον, ἀνεῖλα; aor. pass. ἀνηρέθην. *to take away, abolish; do away with, destroy, kill, slay, condemn to death; take up, claim* (mid.). (24)

ἀναίτιος, ον adj. (αἰτία) *innocent.* (2)

ἀνακαθίζω v. (καθίζω) aor. ἀνεκάθισα. *to sit up, sit upright.* (2)

ἀνακαινίζω v. (καινός) *to renew, restore.* (1) Heb 6:6

ἀνακαινόω v. (καινός) *to renew.* (2)

ἀνακαίνωσις, εως, ἡ n. (καινός) *renewal.* (2)

ἀνακαλύπτω v. (καλύπτω) pf. pass. ἀνακεκάλυμμαι. *to uncover, unveil.* (2)

ἀνακάμπτω v. (κάμπτω) fut. ἀνακάμψω; aor. ἀνέκαμψα. *to return.* (4)

ἀνάκειμαι v. (κεῖμαι) *to lie, recline; recline at table, dine* (NT). (14)

ἀνακεφαλαιόω v. (κεφαλή) aor. ἀνεκεφαλαίωσα. *to sum up, recapitulate, bring together.* (2)

ἀνακλίνω v. (κλίνω) fut. ἀνακλινῶ; aor. ἀνέκλινα; aor. pass. ἀνεκλίθην. *to lay down, lay, put to bed; seat at table; lie down, recline to eat* (pass.). (6)

ἀνακράζω v. (κράζω) aor. ἀνέκραξα, ἀνέκραγον. *to cry out, shout.* (5)

ἀνακρίνω v. (κρίνω) aor. ἀνέκρινα; aor. pass. ἀνεκρίθην. *to question, examine, inquire about; hear a case, judge; call to account, discern.* (16)

ἀνάκρισις, εως, ἡ n. (κρίνω) *investigation, (preliminary) hearing.* (1) Ac 25:26

ἀνακυλίω v. *to roll away.* (v.l.)

ἀνακύπτω v. (κύπτω) aor. ἀνέκυψα. *to stand erect, straighten oneself; stand tall.* (4)

ἀναλαμβάνω v. (λαμβάνω) aor. ἀνέλαβον; aor. pass. ἀνελήμφθην. *to take up; take; take along, take on board.* (13)

ἀναλημφθείς s. ἀναλαμβάνω (aor. pass. ptc.).

ἀνάλημψις, εως, ἡ n. (λαμβάνω) *ascension; death* (poss.). (1) Lk 9:51

ἀναλίσκω and ἀναλόω v. (ἅλωσις) aor. ἀνήλωσα; aor. pass. ἀνηλώθην. *to destroy, consume.* (2)

ἀναλογία, ας, ἡ n. (λέγω) *proportion,* w. κατά *in agreement with.* (1) Rom 12:6

ἀναλογίζομαι v. (λέγω) aor. ἀνελογισάμην. *to consider carefully.* (1) Heb 12:3

ἄναλος, ον adj. (ἅλας) *without salt, saltless.* (1) Mk 9:50

ἀναλόω = ἀναλίσκω.

ἀνάλυσις, εως, ἡ n. (λύω) *departure, death.* (1) 2 Ti 4:6

ἀναλύω v. (λύω) aor. ἀνέλυσα. *to depart, return, die.* (2)

ἀναμάρτητος, ον adj. (ἁμαρτάνω) *without sin.* (1) Jn 8:7

ἀναμένω v. (μένω) *to wait for, expect.* (1) 1 Th 1:10

ἀναμιμνήσκω v. (μιμνήσκομαι) fut. ἀναμνήσω; aor. pass. ἀνεμνήσθην. *to remind; remember* (pass.). (6)

ἀνάμνησις, εως, ἡ n. (μιμνήσκομαι) *reminder, remembrance.* (4)

ἀνανεόω v. (νέος) *to renew.* (1) Eph 4:23

ἀνανήφω v. (νήφω) aor. ἀνένηψα. *to return to one's senses.* (1) 2 Ti 2:26

Ἀνανίας, ου, ὁ n. pers. *Ananias.* (11)

ἀναντίρρητος, ον adj. (ῥῆμα) *not to be contradicted, undeniable.* (1) Ac 19:36

ἀναντιρρήτως adv. (ῥῆμα) *without objection.* (1) Ac 10:29

ἀνάξιος, ον adj. (ἄξιος) *unworthy, incompetent.* (1) 1 Cor 6:2

ἀναξίως adv. (ἄξιος) *in an unworthy or careless manner, unworthily*. (1) 1 Cor 11:27

ἀνάπαυσις, εως, ἡ n. (παύω) *stopping, ceasing; rest, relief; resting-place.* (5)

ἀναπαύω v. (παύω) fut. ἀναπαύσω; aor. ἀνέπαυσα; pf. pass. ἀναπέπαυμαι; aor. pass. ἀνεπάην. *to cause to rest, give rest, refresh, revive;* mid. *rest; rest upon.* (12)

ἀναπείθω v. (πείθω) *to induce, incite.* (1) Ac 18:13

ἀνάπειρος, ον adj. *crippled.* (2)

ἀναπέμπω v. (πέμπω) fut. ἀναπέμψω; aor. ἀνέπεμψα. *to send (up), send back.* (5)

ἀνάπεσε, ἀναπεσεῖν s. ἀναπίπτω (2 aor. impv., 2 aor. inf.).

ἀναπηδάω v. (-πηδάω) aor. ἀνεπήδησα. *to jump up, stand up.* (1) Mk 10:50

ἀναπίπτω v. (πίπτω) aor. ἀνέπεσον, ἀνέπεσα. *to lie down, recline* (esp. to eat)*; lean, lean back.* (12)

ἀναπληρόω v. (πληρόω) fut. ἀναπληρώσω; aor. ἀνεπλήρωσα. *to make complete; fulfill; fill a gap, replace; occupy, fill.* (6)

ἀναπολόγητος, ον adj. (λέγω) *without excuse, inexcusable.* (2)

ἀναπτύσσω v. (πτύσσω) aor. ἀνέπτυξα. *to unroll.* (1) Lk 4:17

ἀνάπτω v. (ἅπτω) aor. pass. ἀνήφθην. *to kindle, set fire.* (2)

ἀναρίθμητος, ον adj. (ἀριθμός) *innumerable, countless.* (1) Heb 11:12

ἀνασείω v. (σείω) aor. ἀνέσεισα. *to stir up, disturb, upset, incite.* (2)

ἀνασκευάζω v. (σκεῦος) *to tear down; upset, unsettle* (fig. in NT). (1) Ac 15:24

ἀνασπάω v. (σπάω) fut. ἀνασπάσω; aor. pass. ἀνεσπάσθην. *to draw or pull up.* (2)

ἀνάστα s. ἀνίστημι (2 aor. impv.).

ἀνάστασις, εως, ἡ n. (ἵστημι) *rising up, rise; resurrection.* (42)

ἀναστατόω v. (ἵστημι) aor. ἀνεστά-τωσα. *to disturb, trouble, upset, cause a revolt.* (3)

ἀνασταυρόω v. (σταυρόω) *to crucify, crucify again.* (1) Heb 6:6

ἀναστενάζω v. (στενός) aor. ἀνεστέναξα. *to sigh deeply.* (1) Mk 8:12

ἀνάστηθι s. ἀνίστημι (2 aor. impv.).

ἀναστρέφω v. (στρέφω) fut. ἀναστρέψω; aor. ἀνέστρεψα; aor. pass. ἀνεστράφην. *to act, behave, conduct oneself, live* (pass.)*; return, come back.* (9)

ἀναστροφή, ῆς, ἡ n. (στρέφω) *way of life, conduct, behavior.* (13)

ἀνατάσσομαι v. (τάσσω) aor. ἀνεταξάμην. *to arrange in proper order; organize in a series, compose, compile* (fig. in NT). (1) Lk 1:1

ἀνατέθραμμαι s. ἀνατρέφω (pf. pass.).

ἀνατέλλω v. (ἀνατολή) aor. ἀνέτειλα; pf. ἀνατέταλκα. *to cause to spring or rise up; rise, spring up, dawn, come up; be a descendant.* (9)

ἀνατίθημι v. (τίθημι) aor. ἀνέθηκα. *to communicate, refer, declare, lay before* (mid. in NT). (2)

ἀνατολή, ῆς, ἡ n. (*) *rising; east, orient; dawn; east* (pl.). (11)

ἀνατρέπω v. (τροπή) aor. ἀνέτρεψα. *to cause to fall, overturn, destroy; upset, ruin.* (3)

ἀνατρέφω v. (τρέφω) aor. ἀνέθρεψα; pf. pass. ἀνατέθραμμαι; aor. pass. ἀνετράφην. *to bring up, care for; rear, train.* (3)

ἀναφαίνω v. (φαίνω) aor. ἀνέφανα. *to light up, cause to appear, come in sight of; appear* (pass.). (2)

ἀναφέρω v. (φέρω) aor. ἀνήνεγκα, ἀνήνεγκον. *to take* or *lead up, bring up; offer up; take up, bear.* (10)

ἀναφωνέω v. (φωνή) aor. ἀνεφώνησα. *to cry out.* (1) Lk 1:42

ἀναχθείς s. ἀνάγω (aor. pass. ptc.).

ἀνάχυσις, εως, ἡ n. (-χέω) *wide stream, flood.* (1) 1 Pt 4:4

ἀναχωρέω v. (χωρέω) aor. ἀνεχώρησα. *to go away, withdraw, retire, take refuge; return.* (14)

ἀνάψυξις, εως, ἡ n. (ψύχω) *breathing space, relaxation, relief, rest*. (1) Ac 3:20

ἀναψύχω v. (ψύχω) aor. ἀνέψυξα. *to give a breathing space, revive, refresh*. (1) 2 Ti 1:16

ἀνδραποδιστής, οῦ, ὁ n. (ἀνήρ, πούς) *slave-dealer, kidnapper*. (1) 1 Ti 1: 10

Ἀνδρέας, ου, ὁ n. pers. *Andrew*. (13)

ἀνδρίζομαι v. (ἀνήρ) *to conduct oneself in a manly* or *courageous way, act like a man*. (1) 1 Cor 16:13

Ἀνδρόνικος, ου, ὁ n. pers. *Andronicus*. (1) Rom 16:7

ἀνδροφόνος, ου, ὁ n. (ἀνήρ, φονεύω) *murderer*. (1) 1 Ti 1:9

ἀνέβην s. ἀναβαίνω (2 aor.).

ἀνέγκλητος, ον adj. (καλέω) *blameless, irreproachable*. (5)

ἀνέγνων s. ἀναγινώσκω (2 aor.).

ἀνέθην, ἀνείς s. ἀνίημι (aor. pass., 2 aor. ptc.).

ἀνεθρεψάμην s. ἀνατρέφω (aor. mid.).

ἀνεῖλα, ἀνεῖλον s. ἀναιρέω (1 aor., 2 aor.).

ἀνεκδιήγητος, ον adj. (ἄγω) *indescribable* (good sense). (1) 2 Cor 9:15

ἀνεκλάλητος, ον adj. (λαλέω) *inexpressible*. (1) 1 Pt 1:8

ἀνέκλειπτος, ον adj. (λείπω) *unfailing, inexhaustible*. (1) Lk 12:33

ἀνεκτός, όν adj. (ἔχω) *bearable, endurable, tolerable*. (5)

ἀνελεήμων, ον adj. (ἔλεος) *unmerciful*. (1) Rom 1:31

ἀνελεῖν, ἀνέλω s. ἀναιρέω (aor. inf., fut.).

ἀνέλεος, ον adj. (ἔλεος) *merciless*. (1) Jas 2:13

ἀνελήμφθην s. ἀναλαμβάνω (aor. pass.).

ἀνεμίζω v. (ἄνεμος) *to be moved by the wind* (pass. in NT). (1) Jas 1:6

ἄνεμος, ου, ὁ n. (*) *wind*; w. οἱ τέσσαρες *four directions* (pl.). (31)

ἀνένδεκτος, ον adj. (δέχομαι) *impossible*. (1) Lk 17:1

ἀνεξεραύνητος, ον adj. (ἐρωτάω) *un-*searchable, unfathomable*. (1) Rom 11:33

ἀνεξίκακος, ον adj. (ἔχω, κακός) *patient, tolerant*. (1) 2 Ti 2:24

ἀνεξιχνίαστος, ον adj. (ἴχνος) *inscrutable, incomprehensible, fathomless*. (2)

ἀνεπαίσχυντος, ον adj. (αἰσχρός) *unashamed*. (1) 2 Ti 2:15

ἀνεπίλημπτος, ον adj. (λαμβάνω) *irreproachable*. (3)

ἀνέρχομαι v. (ἔρχομαι) aor. ἀνῆλθον. *to go up, come up*. (3)

ἄνεσις, εως, ἡ n. (-ἵημι) *some liberty* or *freedom; relaxing, rest, relaxation, relief*. (5)

ἀνέστην s. ἀνίστημι (2 aor.).

ἀνετάζω v. (-ἐτάζω) *to give a hearing*. (2)

ἄνευ prep. *without, without the knowledge and consent of* (adv. prep. w. gen. in NT). (3)

ἀνεύθετος, ον adj. (τίθημι) *unsuitable, poor, unfavorably situated*. (1) Ac 27:12

ἀνευρίσκω v. (εὑρίσκω) aor. ἀνεῦρα, ἀνεῦρον. *to find (by searching)*. (2)

ἀνέχω v. (ἔχω) fut. ἀνέξω; aor. ἀνέσχον. mid. in NT *to endure, bear with, put up with, listen patiently to; accept a complaint*. (15)

ἀνεψιός, οῦ, ὁ n. *cousin*. (1) Col 4:10

ἀνέῳγα, ἀνέῳξα s. ἀνοίγω (pf., aor.).

ἀνήγαγον s. ἀνάγω (2 aor.).

ἀνήγγειλα, ἀνηγγέλην s. ἀναγγέλλω (aor., 2 aor. pass.).

ἄνηθον, ου, τό n. *dill*. (1) Mt 23:23

ἀνῆκα s. ἀνίημι (aor.).

ἀνήκω v. (ἥκω) *to refer* or *relate to; it is proper* or *fitting* (impers. in NT). (3)

ἀνήμερος, ον adj. *savage, brutal*. (1) 2 Ti 3:3

ἀνήνεγκον s. ἀναφέρω (2 aor.).

ἀνήρ, ἀνδρός, ὁ n. (*) *man (male), husband, grown man; someone, person*. (216)

ἀνῃρέθην s. ἀναιρέω (aor. pass.).

ἀνήφθην s. ἀνάπτω (aor. pass.).

ἀνήχθην s. ἀνάγω (aor. pass.).
ἀνθ᾽ = ἀντί before rough breathing.
ἀνθέξομαι s. ἀντέχω (fut. mid.).
ἀνθίστημι v. (ἵστημι) aor. ἀντέστην; pf. ἀνθέστηκα. *to set oneself against, oppose; resist, stand one's ground, withstand.* (14)
ἀνθομολογέομαι v. (ὅμοιος, λέγω) *to praise, thank.* (1) Lk 2:38
ἄνθος, ους, τό n. *blossom, flower.* (4)
ἀνθρακιά, ᾶς, ἡ n. (ἄνθραξ) *charcoal fire.* (2)
ἄνθραξ, ακος, ὁ n. (*) *charcoal, burning embers.* (1) Rom 12:20
ἀνθρωπάρεσκος, ον adj. (ἄνθρωπος, ἀρέσκω) *trying to please people; one who tries to please people, fawner* (subst. in NT). (2)
ἀνθρώπινος, η, ον adj. (ἄνθρωπος) *human.* (7)
ἀνθρωποκτόνος, ου, ὁ n. (ἄνθρωπος, -κτείνω) *murderer.* (3)
ἄνθρωπος, ου, ὁ n. (*) *human being; people, associates* (pl.)*; human being* (limitation), κατὰ ἄνθρωπον *from a human standpoint; man* (male)*, husband, son, slave; someone, one, person; being; fellow; friend, sir.* (550)
ἀνθύπατος, ου, ὁ n. *proconsul* (Roman governor of a senatorial province). (5)
ἀνίημι v. (-ἵημι) aor. ἀνῆκα; aor. pass. ἀνέθην. *to loosen, unfasten; abandon, desert; give up, cease from.* (4)
ἄνιπτος, ον adj. (νίπτω) *unwashed.* (2)
ἀνίστημι v. (ἵστημι) fut. ἀναστήσω; aor. ἀνέστησα, ἀνέστην. *to raise, erect, raise up; bring to life; procreate; rise, stand up; rise up, come back from the dead; arise, rebel; set out, get ready.* (108)
Ἄννα, ας, ἡ n. pers. *Anna.* (1) Lk 2:36
Ἄννας, α, ὁ n. pers. *Annas.* (4)
ἀνόητος, ον adj. (νίπτω) *unintelligent, foolish, dull-witted.* (6)
ἄνοια, ας, ἡ n. (νίπτω) *folly, foolishness; fury.* (2)
ἀνοίγω v. (*) fut. ἀνοίξω; aor. ἤνοιξα, ἀνέῳξα, ἠνέῳξα; pf. ἀνέῳγα; pf.

pass. ἀνέῳγμαι, ἠνέῳγμαι; aor. pass. ἠνοίχθην, ἀνεῴχθην, ἠνεῴχθην. *to open, be open.* (77)
ἀνοικοδομέω v. (οἶκος, δῶμα) fut. ἀνοικοδομήσω. *to build up again, rebuild.* (2)
ἄνοιξις, εως, ἡ n. (ἀνοίγω) *opening.* (1) Eph 6:19
ἀνοιχθήσομαι s. ἀνοίγω (fut. pass.).
ἀνομία, ας, ἡ n. (νόμος) *lawlessness; lawless deed.* (15)
ἄνομος, ον adj. (νόμος) *outside or without law, Gentile; lawless, wicked, criminal; lawless one* (subst.). (9)
ἀνόμως adv. (νόμος) *without law, lawlessly.* (2)
ἀνορθόω v. (ὀρθός) fut. ἀνορθώσω; aor. ἀνώρθωσα; aor. pass. ἀνωρθώθην. *to rebuild, restore; straighten, strengthen.* (3)
ἀνόσιος, ον adj. (ὅσιος) *unholy, wicked.* (2)
ἀνοχή, ῆς, ἡ n. (ἔχω) *forbearance, clemency, tolerance.* (2)
ἀντ᾽ = ἀντί before smooth breathing.
ἀνταγωνίζομαι v. (ἀγών) *to struggle.* (1) Heb 12:4
ἀντάλλαγμα, ατος, τό n. (ἄλλος) *something given in exchange.* (2)
ἀνταναπληρόω v. (πληρόω) *to fill up, complete, supplement.* (1) Col 1:24
ἀνταποδίδωμι v. (δίδωμι) fut. ἀνταποδώσω; aor. ἀνταπέδωκα; aor. pass. ἀνταπεδόθην. *to repay, pay back, requite* (obligation)*; repay, pay back* (retribution). (7)
ἀνταπόδομα, ατος, τό n. (δίδωμι) *repayment, reward; recompense, retribution.* (2)
ἀνταπόδοσις, εως, ἡ n. (δίδωμι) *repaying, reward.* (1) Col 3:24
ἀνταποκρίνομαι v. (κρίνω) aor. pass. ἀνταπεκρίθην. *to answer in turn, reply, answer back.* (2)
ἀντεῖπον s. ἀντιλέγω (2 aor.).
ἀντέχω v. (ἔχω) fut. ἀνθέξω. mid. in NT *to cling to, hold fast to, be devoted to; help.* (4)

ἀντί prep. (*) w. gen. *instead of, in place of; for, as, after; in behalf of; because of, for the purpose of,* ἀνθ' ὧν *because; therefore.* (22)
ἀντιβάλλω v. (βάλλω) *to exchange,* w. λόγοι *discuss.* (1) Lk 24:17
ἀντιδιατίθημι v. (τίθημι) *to oppose oneself, be opposed* (mid. in NT). (1) 2 Ti 2:25
ἀντίδικος, ου, ὁ n. (δίκη) *accuser, plaintiff; opponent, enemy.* (5)
ἀντίθεσις, εως, ἡ n. (τίθημι) *contradiction.* (1) 1 Ti 6:20
ἀντικαθίστημι v. (ἵστημι) aor. ἀντικατέστην. *to oppose, resist.* (1) Heb 12:4
ἀντικαλέω v. (καλέω) aor. ἀντεκάλεσα. *to invite in return.* (1) Lk 14:12
ἀντίκειμαι v. (κεῖμαι) *to be opposed to, be in opposition to; opponent, enemy, adversary* (subst. ptc.). (8)
ἄντικρυς adv. (ἀντί) adv. prep. w. gen. in NT *opposite.* (1) Ac 20:15
ἀντιλαμβάνω v. (λαμβάνω) aor. ἀντέλαβον. mid. in NT *to come to the aid of, help; take part in, devote oneself to, practice; enjoy, benefit by.* (3)
ἀντιλέγω v. (λέγω) aor. ἀντεῖπον. *to speak against, contradict,* w. μή and inf. *deny; oppose, refuse; say in return.* (11)
ἀντίλημψις, εως, ἡ n. (λαμβάνω) *help, helpful deed.* (1) 1 Cor 12:28
ἀντιλογία, ας, ἡ n. (λέγω) *contradiction, dispute; hostility, rebellion.* (4)
ἀντιλοιδορέω v. (λοίδορος) *to revile in return.* (1) 1 Pt 2:23
ἀντίλυτρον, ου, τό n. (λύω) *ransom.* (1) 1 Ti 2:6
ἀντιμετρέω v. (μέτρον) aor. pass. ἀντεμετρήθην. *to measure in return.* (1) Lk 6:38
ἀντιμισθία, ας, ἡ n. (μισθός) *recompense, exchange, penalty, reward.* (2)
Ἀντιόχεια, ας, ἡ n. pla. *Antioch.* (18)
Ἀντιοχεύς, έως, ὁ n. pla. *an Antiochene, man from Antioch.* (1) Ac 6:5
ἀντιπαρέρχομαι v. (ἔρχομαι) aor. ἀντιπαρῆλθον. *to pass by on the opposite side.* (2)
Ἀντιπᾶς, ᾶ, ὁ n. pers. *Antipas.* (1) Rev 2:13
Ἀντιπατρίς, ίδος, ἡ n. pla. *Antipatris.* (1) Ac 23:31
ἀντιπέρα adv. (πέραν) adv. prep. w. gen. in NT *opposite.* (1) Lk 8:26
ἀντιπίπτω v. (πίπτω) *to resist, oppose.* (1) Ac 7:51
ἀντιστρατεύομαι v. (στρατιά) *to be at war with.* (1) Rom 7:23
ἀντιτάσσω v. (τάσσω) *to oppose, resist* (mid. in NT). (5)
ἀντίτυπος, ον adj. (τύπος) *corresponding to; copy, antitype, representation* (subst.). (2)
ἀντίχριστος, ου, ὁ n. (χρίω) *Antichrist.* (5)
ἀντλέω v. (*) aor. ἤντλησα; pf. ἤντληκα. *to draw* (water). (4)
ἄντλημα, ατος, τό n. (ἀντλέω) *bucket.* (1) Jn 4:11
ἀντοφθαλμέω v. (ὁράω) *to look directly at, face.* (1) Ac 27:15
ἄνυδρος, ον adj. (ὕδωρ) *waterless, dry.* (4)
ἀνυπόκριτος, ον adj. (κρίνω) *genuine, sincere.* (6)
ἀνυπότακτος, ον adj. (τάσσω) *independent, not made subject; undisciplined, disobedient, rebellious.* (4)
ἄνω adv. (ἀνά) *above,* ἕως ἄνω *to the brim; up, upward; above* (as adj.)*; what is above, heaven* (subst.). (9)
ἀνῶ s. ἀνίημι (aor. subj.).
ἄνωθεν adv. (ἀνά) *from above, from heaven; from the beginning, for a long time; again, anew.* (13)
ἀνωτερικός, ή, όν adj. (ἀνά) *upper, inland.* (1) Ac 19:1
ἀνώτερος, α, ον adj. (ἀνά) neut. as adv. in NT *higher; preceding, above, earlier.* (2)
ἀνωφελής, ές adj. (ὠφελέω) *useless; harmful.* (2)
ἀξίνη, ης, ἡ n. (*) *ax.* (2)

ἄξιος, α, ον adj. (*) corresponding, comparable, worthy, in keeping with, deserving, proper; fit, deserving, good enough. (41)

ἀξιόω v. (ἄξιος) aor. ἠξίωσα; pf. pass. ἠξίωμαι; aor. pass. ἠξιώθην. to consider worthy or deserving; deem, hold an opinion, request, ask. (7)

ἀξίως adv. (ἄξιος) worthily, in a manner worthy of, suitably. (6)

ἀόρατος, ον adj. (ὁράω) unseen, invisible. (5)

Ἀουλία, ας, ἡ n. pers. alt. form of Ἰουλία. (v.l.)

ἀπ᾽ = ἀπό before smooth breathing.

ἀπαγγέλλω v. (ἄγγελος) fut. ἀπαγγελῶ; aor. ἀπήγγειλα; aor. pass. ἀπηγγέλην. to report, announce, tell; proclaim, confess, declare, w. ἵνα command. (45)

ἀπάγχω v. aor. ἀπῆγξα. to hang oneself (mid. in NT). (1) Mt 27:5

ἀπάγω v. (ἄγω) aor. ἀπήγαγον; aor. pass. ἀπήχθην. to lead off, take away; bring before, lead away; lead, run; be misled, be carried away (pass.). (15)

ἀπαίδευτος, ον adj. (παῖς) uninstructed, uneducated, uninformed. (1) 2 Ti 2:23

ἀπαίρω v. (αἴρω) aor. pass. ἀπήρθην. to take away (pass. in NT). (3)

ἀπαιτέω v. (αἰτέω) to ask for, demand back; demand, desire. (2)

ἀπαλγέω v. pf. ἀπήλγηκα. to become callous, dead to feeling; be despondent. (1) Eph 4:19

ἀπαλλάσσω v. (ἄλλος) aor. ἀπήλλαξα; pf. pass. ἀπήλλαγμαι. to free, release; pass. leave, depart; come to a settlement. (3)

ἀπαλλοτριόω v. (ἄλλος) pf. pass. ἀπηλλοτρίωμαι. to estrange, alienate; be estranged, be excluded (pass. in NT). (3)

ἀπαλός, ή, όν adj. tender. (2)

ἀπαντάω v. (ἀπό, ἀντί) fut. ἀπαντήσω; aor. ἀπήντησα. to meet, come toward. (2)

ἀπάντησις, εως, ἡ n. (ἀπό, ἀντί) meeting; to meet (w. εἰς in NT). (3)

ἅπαξ adv. (*) once, ἅπαξ καὶ δίς again and again, more than once; once for all. (14)

ἀπαράβατος, ον adj. (-βαίνω) permanent, unchangeable. (1) Heb 7:24

ἀπαρασκεύαστος, ον adj. (σκεῦος) not ready, unprepared, not in readiness. (1) 2 Cor 9:4

ἀπαρθῶ s. ἀπαίρω (aor. pass. subj.).

ἀπαρνέομαι v. (ἀρνέομαι) fut. ἀπαρνήσομαι; aor. ἀπηρνησάμην; aor. pass. ἀπηρνήθην. to deny, not recognize; deny oneself. (11)

ἀπαρτισμός, οῦ, ὁ n. (ἄρτι) completion. (1) Lk 14:28

ἀπαρχή, ῆς, ἡ n. (ἄρχω) first fruits, first portion, first; birth certificate. (9)

ἅπας, ασα, αν adj. (πᾶς) all, whole (w. subst. and art.); all, everybody, everything (w. no subst.). (34)

ἀπασπάζομαι v. (ἀσπάζομαι) aor. ἀπησπασάμην. to take leave of, say farewell to. (1) Ac 21:6

ἀπατάω v. (ἀπάτη) aor. pass. ἠπατήθην. to deceive, mislead, lead astray. (3)

ἀπάτη, ης, ἡ n. (*) deception, deceitfulness, seduction; pleasure, pleasantness, lust. (7)

ἀπάτωρ, ορος adj. (πατήρ) fatherless, without a father. (1) Heb 7:3

ἀπαύγασμα, ατος, τό n. (αὐγή) radiance. (1) Heb 1:3

ἀπαχθῆναι s. ἀπάγω (aor. pass. inf.).

ἀπέβαλον s. ἀποβάλλω (2 aor.).

ἀπέβην s. ἀποβαίνω (2 aor.).

ἀπέδειξα s. ἀποδείκνυμι (aor.).

ἀπέδετο s. ἀποδίδωμι (2 aor. mid. 3 sg.).

ἀπεδίδουν s. ἀποδίδωμι (impf.).

ἀπέθανον s. ἀποθνήσκω (2 aor.).

ἀπεθέμην s. ἀποτίθημι (aor. mid.).

ἀπεῖδον s. ἀφοράω (2 aor.).

ἀπείθεια, ας, ἡ n. (πείθω) disobedience, disbelief. (7)

ἀπειθέω v. (πείθω) aor. ἠπείθησα. to disobey, be disobedient, disbelieve. (14)

ἀπειθής, ἐς adj. (πείθω) *disobedient*. (6)
ἀπειλέω v. (ἀπειλή) aor. ἠπείλησα. *to threaten, warn*. (2)
ἀπειλή, ῆς, ἡ n. (*) *threat, threatening*. (3)
ἄπειμι v. (εἰμί) *to be absent, be away*. (7)
ἄπειμι v. (-εῖμι) *to go, come*. (1) Ac 17:10
ἀπεῖπον s. ἀπολέγω (2 aor.).
ἀπείραστος, ον adj. (πεῖρα) *without temptation, unable to be tempted*. (1) Jas 1:13
ἄπειρος, ον adj. (πεῖρα) *unacquainted with, unaccustomed to*. (1) Heb 5:13
ἀπεκαλύφθην s. ἀποκαλύπτω (aor. pass.).
ἀπεκατεστάθην, ἀπεκατέστην s. ἀποκαθίστημι (aor. pass., aor.).
ἀπεκδέχομαι v. (δέχομαι) *to await eagerly, wait*. (8)
ἀπεκδύομαι v. (δύνω) aor. ἀπεξεδυσάμην. *to take off, strip off; disarm*. (2)
ἀπέκδυσις, εως, ἡ n. (δύνω) *removal, stripping off*. (1) Col 2:11
ἀπεκρίθην s. ἀποκρίνομαι (aor. pass.).
ἀπεκτάνθην, ἀπέκτεινα s. ἀποκτείνω (aor. pass., aor.).
ἀπέλαβον s. ἀπολαμβάνω (2 aor.).
ἀπελαύνω v. (ἐλαύνω) aor. ἀπήλασα. *to drive away*. (1) Ac 18:16
ἀπελεγμός, οῦ, ὁ n. (ἐλέγχω) *refutation, exposure, discredit*. (1) Ac 19:27
ἀπελεύθερος, ου, ὁ n. (ἐλεύθερος) *freedperson*. (1) 1 Cor 7:22
ἀπελεύσομαι, ἀπελήλυθα, ἀπῆλθον s. ἀπέρχομαι (fut. mid., 2 pf., 2 aor.).
ἀπέλιπον s. ἀπολείπω (2 aor.).
Ἀπελλῆς, οῦ, ὁ n. pers. *Apelles*. (1) Rom 16:10
ἀπελπίζω v. (ἐλπίς) *to expect back* or *in return*. (1) Lk 6:35
ἀπέναντι adv. (ἀπό, ἐν, ἀντί) adv. prep. w. gen. in NT *opposite, before, against, contrary to*. (5)
ἀπενεγκεῖν, ἀπενεχθῆναι s. ἀποφέρω (2 aor. inf., aor. pass. inf.).

ἀπέπεσα s. ἀποπίπτω (aor.).
ἀπέπλευσα s. ἀποπλέω (aor.).
ἀπεπνίγην s. ἀποπνίγω (2 aor. pass.).
ἀπέραντος, ον adj. (πέραν) *endless, limitless*. (1) 1 Ti 1:4
ἀπερισπάστως adv. (σπάω) *without distraction*. (1) 1 Cor 7:35
ἀπερίτμητος, ον adj. (τομός) *uncircumcised; obdurate, stubborn* (fig. in NT). (1) Ac 7:51
ἀπέρχομαι v. (ἔρχομαι) fut. ἀπελεύσομαι; aor. ἀπῆλθον; pf. ἀπελήλυθα. *to go away, depart, go, come* or *go to; leave, pass away; go out, spread; go after; go off; follow*. (117)
ἀπεστάλην, ἀπέσταλχα, ἀπέστειλα s. ἀποστέλλω (2 aor. pass., 2 pf., aor.).
ἀπέστην, ἀπέστησα s. ἀφίστημι (2 aor., 1 aor.).
ἀπεστράφην s. ἀποστρέφω (2 aor. pass.).
ἀπέχω v. (ἔχω) *to be paid in full, receive in full; to suffice, be enough; be distant; keep away, abstain, refrain from* (mid.). (19)
ἀπήγαγον s. ἀπάγω (2 aor.).
ἀπῆγξα s. ἀπάγχω (aor.).
ἀπῆεσαν s. ἄπειμι (impf. 3 pl.).
ἀπήλασα s. ἀπελαύνω (aor.).
ἀπῆλθον s. ἀπέρχομαι (2 aor.).
ἀπήλλαγμαι s. ἀπαλλάσσω (pf. pass).
ἀπήρθην s. ἀπαίρω (aor. pass.).
ἀπιστέω v. (πείθω) aor. ἠπίστησα. *to disbelieve, refuse to believe; be unfaithful*. (8)
ἀπιστία, ας, ἡ n. (πείθω) *unbelief; unfaithfulness*. (11)
ἄπιστος, ον adj. (πείθω) *unbelievable, incredible; without faith, unbelieving*. (23)
ἁπλότης, ητος, ἡ n. (*) *simplicity, sincerity, ingenuousness; generosity, liberality*. (8)
ἁπλοῦς, ῆ, οῦν adj. (ἁπλότης) *single, sincere, without guile, healthy*. (2)
ἁπλῶς adv. (ἁπλότης) *sincerely, openly, without reservation*. (1) Jas 1:5
ἀπό prep. (*) w. gen. *from, away from* (separation); *out from, since; down*

from, from (source)*; away from, from, about* (distance)*; because of, with the help of, with, for, of, by, by means of*. (646)

ἀποβαίνω v. (-βαίνω) fut. ἀποβήσομαι; aor. ἀπέβην. *to go away, get out; turn out, lead to.* (4)

ἀποβάλλω v. (βάλλω) aor. ἀπέβαλον. *to take off, shed; lose.* (2)

ἀποβλέπω v. (βλέπω) *to look, pay attention.* (1) Heb 11:26

ἀπόβλητος, ον adj. (βάλλω) *rejected.* (1) 1 Ti 4:4

ἀποβολή, ῆς, ἡ n. (βάλλω) *rejection; loss.* (2)

ἀπογίνομαι v. (γίνομαι) aor. ἀπεγένομην. *to die.* (1) 1 Pt 2:24

ἀπογραφή, ῆς, ἡ n. (γράφω) *census, registration.* (2)

ἀπογράφω v. (γράφω) aor. ἀπέγραψα; pf. pass. ἀπογέγραμμαι. *to register, record.* (4)

ἀποδείκνυμι v. (δείκνυμι) aor. ἀπέδειξα; pf. pass. ἀποδέδειγμαι. *to make, proclaim, appoint; display, attest; prove.* (4)

ἀπόδειξις, εως, ἡ n. (δείκνυμι) *proof.* (1) 1 Cor 2:4

ἀποδεκατόω v. (δέκα) *to tithe, give one tenth; collect a tithe.* (4)

ἀπόδεκτος, ον adj. (δέχομαι) *pleasing, acceptable.* (2)

ἀποδέχομαι v. (δέχομαι) aor. ἀπεδεξάμην. *to welcome, accept, recognize, praise.* (7)

ἀποδημέω v. (δῆμος) aor. ἀπεδήμησα. *to go on a journey; be away, be absent.* (6)

ἀπόδημος, ον adj. (δῆμος) *away on a journey.* (1) Mk 13:34

ἀποδίδωμι v. (δίδωμι) fut. ἀποδώσω; aor. ἀπέδωκα; aor. pass. ἀπεδόθην. *to give up, yield, award; pay, pay out, fulfill, give; give back, return, repay; render, reward; sell, trade* (mid.). (48)

ἀποδιορίζω v. (ὁρίζω) *to divide, separate.* (1) Jd 19

ἀποδοκιμάζω v. (δέχομαι) aor. ἀπεδο-

κίμασα; pf. pass. ἀποδεδοκίμασμαι; aor. pass. ἀπεδοκιμάσθην. *to reject.* (9)

ἀποδοχή, ῆς, ἡ n. (δέχομαι) *acceptance, approval.* (2)

ἀποθανοῦμαι s. ἀποθνῄσκω (fut. mid.).

ἀπόθεσις, εως, ἡ n. (τίθημι) *removal, getting rid of.* (2)

ἀποθήκη, ης, ἡ n. (τίθημι) *storehouse, barn.* (6)

ἀποθησαυρίζω v. (τίθημι) *to store up, lay up.* (1) 1 Ti 6:19

ἀποθλίβω v. (θλίβω) *to press upon, crowd.* (1) Lk 8:45

ἀποθνῄσκω v. (θνῄσκω) fut. ἀποθανοῦμαι; aor. ἀπέθανον. *to die, decay; face death, be mortal.* (111)

ἀποκαθίστημι and **ἀποκαθιστάνω** v. (ἵστημι) fut. ἀποκαταστήσω; aor. ἀπεκατέστην; aor. pass. ἀπεκατεστάθην. *to restore, reestablish, cure, give back, restore.* (8)

ἀποκαλύπτω v. (καλύπτω) fut. ἀποκαλύψω; aor. ἀπεκάλυψα; aor. pass. ἀπεκαλύφθην. *to reveal, disclose, bring to light, make fully known.* (26)

ἀποκάλυψις, εως, ἡ n. (καλύπτω) *revelation, disclosure.* (18)

ἀποκαραδοκία, ας, ἡ n. (κρανίον, δέχομαι) *eager expectation.* (2)

ἀποκαταλλάσσω v. (ἄλλος) aor. ἀποκατήλλαξα. *to reconcile.* (3)

ἀποκατάστασις, εως, ἡ n. (ἵστημι) *restoration.* (1) Ac 3:21

ἀπόκειμαι v. (κεῖμαι) *to be put* or *laid away; reserve; it is certain, one is destined* (impers.). (4)

ἀποκεφαλίζω v. (κεφαλή) aor. ἀπεκεφάλισα. *to behead.* (4)

ἀποκλείω v. (κλείω) aor. ἀπέκλεισα. *to close, shut.* (1) Lk 13:25

ἀποκόπτω v. (κόπτω) fut. ἀποκόψω; aor. ἀπέκοψα. *to cut off, cut away, make a eunuch of, castrate, cut.* (6)

ἀπόκριμα, ατος, τό n. (κρίνω) *official report, decision, verdict.* (1) 2 Cor 1:9

ἀποκρίνομαι v. (κρίνω) aor. ἀπεκρινάμην; aor. pass. ἀπεκρίθην. *to answer, reply; continue, begin, speak up;* w. εἶπον or λέγω *answer and say, say.* (231)

ἀπόκρισις, εως, ἡ n. (κρίνω) *answer.* (4)

ἀποκρύπτω v. (κρύπτω) aor. ἀπέκρυψα; pf. pass. ἀποκέκρυμαι. *to hide, keep secret.* (4)

ἀπόκρυφος, ον adj. (κρύπτω) *hidden, secret.* (3)

ἀποκτείνω and ἀποκτέννω v. (-κτείνω) fut. ἀποκτενῶ; aor. ἀπέκτεινα; aor. pass. ἀπεκτάνθην. *to kill; put to death, eliminate.* (74)

ἀποκυέω v. (κῦμα) aor. ἀπεκύησα. *to give birth to, bring into being.* (2)

ἀποκυλίω v. (κυλίω) fut. ἀποκυλίσω; aor. ἀπεκύλισα; pf. pass. ἀποκεκύλισμαι. *to roll away.* (4)

ἀποκύω s. ἀποκυέω (alt. form).

ἀπολαμβάνω v. (λαμβάνω) fut. ἀπολήμψομαι; aor. ἀπέλαβον. *to receive; recover, get back; take aside* (mid.). (10)

ἀπόλαυσις, εως, ἡ n. *enjoyment, pleasure.* (2)

ἀπολέγω v. (λέγω) aor. ἀπεῖπον. *to disown, renounce* (mid. in NT). (1) 2 Cor 4:2

ἀπολείπω v. (λείπω) aor. ἀπέλιπον. *to leave behind; remain* (pass.)*; desert.* (7)

ἀπόλλυμι v. (ὄλεθρος) fut. ἀπολέσω, ἀπολῶ; aor. ἀπώλεσα; pf. ἀπολώλεκα, ἀπόλωλα. *to ruin, destroy, kill, put to death; lose out on; lose;* mid. *perish, be ruined, die, be killed, pass away; lose, be lost.* (90)

Ἀπολλύων, ονος, ὁ n. pers. *Apollyon, Destroyer.* (1) Rev 9:11

Ἀπολλωνία, ας, ἡ n. pla. *Apollonia.* (1) Ac 17:1

Ἀπολλῶς, ῶ, ὁ n. pers. *Apollos.* (10)

ἀπολογέομαι v. (λέγω) aor. ἀπελογησάμην; aor. pass. ἀπελογήθην. *to speak in one's own defense, defend oneself, make a defense.* (10)

ἀπολογία, ας, ἡ n. (λέγω) *defense* (speech)*, reply; defense.* (8)

ἀπολούω v. (λούω) aor. ἀπέλουσα. *to wash oneself, wash away* (mid. in NT). (2)

ἀπολύτρωσις, εως, ἡ n. (λύω) *release; redemption, deliverance, acquittal.* (10)

ἀπολύω v. (λύω) fut. ἀπολύσω; aor. ἀπέλυσα; pf. pass. ἀπολέλυμαι; aor. pass. ἀπελύθην. *to set free, release, pardon; free; let go, send away, dismiss, let die; satisfy; divorce; go away* (mid.). (66)

ἀπολῶ, ἀπόλωλα s. ἀπόλλυμι (fut., 2 pf.).

ἀπομάσσω v. (μαστιγόω) *to wipe off* (mid. in NT). (1) Lk 10:11

ἀπονέμω v. (νόμος) *to assign, show, pay, accord.* (1) 1 Pt 3:7

ἀπονίπτω v. (νίπτω) aor. ἀπένιψα. *to wash off.* (1) Mt 27:24

ἀποπίπτω v. (πίπτω) aor. ἀπέπεσα. *to fall.* (1) Ac 9:18

ἀποπλανάω v. (πλάνη) aor. pass. ἀπεπλανήθην. *to mislead; wander away, go astray* (pass.). (2)

ἀποπλέω v. (πλέω) aor. ἀπέπλευσα. *to sail away.* (4)

ἀποπληρόω v. *to fulfill.* (v.l.)

ἀποπνίγω v. (πνίγω) aor. ἀπέπνιξα; aor. pass. ἀπεπνίγην. *to choke; drown.* (2)

ἀπορέω v. (πορεύομαι) *to be at a loss, be in doubt, be uncertain.* (6)

ἀπορία, ας, ἡ n. (πορεύομαι) *perplexity, anxiety.* (1) Lk 21:25

ἀπορίπτω v. (ῥίπτω) aor. ἀπέριψα. *to throw oneself down, jump.* (1) Ac 27:43

ἀπορφανίζω v. (ὀρφανός) aor. pass. ἀπωρφανίσθην. *to make an orphan (by separation) from.* (1) 1 Th 2:17

ἀποσκίασμα, ατος, τό n. (σκιά) *shadow.* (1) Jas 1:17

ἀποσπάω v. (σπάω) aor. ἀπέσπασα; aor. pass. ἀπεσπάσθην. *to draw out; draw away, attract, proselyte; tear oneself away, withdraw* (pass.). (4)

ἀποσταλῶ, ἀποσταλείς s. ἀποστέλλω (2 aor. pass. subj., 2 aor. pass. ptc.).

ἀποστασία, ας, ἡ n. (ἵστημι) *rebellion, abandonment, apostasy*. (2)

ἀποστάσιον, ου, τό n. (ἵστημι) *notice or certificate of divorce*. (3)

ἀποστεγάζω v. (στέγω) aor. ἀπεστέγασα. *to unroof*. (1) Mk 2:4

ἀποστέλλω v. (στέλλω) fut. ἀποστελῶ; aor. ἀπέστειλα; pf. ἀπέσταλκα; pf. pass. ἀπέσταλμαι; aor. pass. ἀπεστάλην. *to send away, send out; send, have something done*. (132)

ἀποστερέω v. aor. ἀπεστέρησα; pf. pass. ἀπετέρημαι. *to steal, rob, defraud; deprive*. (6)

ἀποστῆναι, ἀποστήσομαι, ἀποστῶ s. ἀφίστημι (2 aor. inf., fut. mid., 2 aor. subj.).

ἀποστολή, ῆς, ἡ n. (στέλλω) *apostleship, office of an apostle*. (4)

ἀπόστολος, ου, ὁ n. (στέλλω) *messenger, envoy; apostle*. (80)

ἀποστοματίζω v. (στόμα) *to question closely, interrogate, quiz*. (1) Lk 11:53

ἀποστρέφω v. (στρέφω) fut. ἀποστρέψω; aor. ἀπέστρεψα; aor. pass. ἀπεστράφην. *to turn away; turn, mislead, cause to revolt; reject, repudiate* (mid. and 2 aor. pass.); *return, put back*. (9)

ἀποστυγέω v. (στυγητός) *to hate strongly, abhor*. (1) Rom 12:9

ἀποσυνάγωγος, ον adj. (ἄγω) *expelled from the synagogue, excommunicated, excluded, put under a curse*. (3)

ἀποτάσσω v. (τάσσω) aor. ἀπέταξα. *to say farewell, take leave; renounce, give up* (mid. in NT). (6)

ἀποτελέω v. (τέλος) aor. pass. ἀπετελέσθην. *to finish, complete; be fully formed* (pass.); *perform*. (2)

ἀποτίθημι v. (τίθημι) aor. ἀπέθηκα. mid. in NT *to take off, lay aside; put away*. (9)

ἀποτινάσσω v. (-τείνω) aor. ἀπετίναξα. *to shake off*. (2)

ἀποτίνω v. (τίνω) fut. ἀποτίσω. *to pay the damages*. (1) Phlm 19

ἀποτολμάω v. (τολμάω) *to be bold*. (1) Rom 10:20

ἀποτομία, ας, ἡ n. (τομός) *severity*. (2)

ἀποτόμως adv. (τομός) *severely, rigorously, sharply*. (2)

ἀποτρέπω v. (τροπή) *to turn away from, avoid* (mid. in NT). (1) 2 Ti 3:5

ἀπουσία, ας, ἡ n. (εἰμί) *absence*. (1) Phil 2:12

ἀποφέρω v. (φέρω) aor. ἀπήνεγκα; aor. pass. ἀπηνέχθην. *to carry away, take away; take, bring; lead off, lead away*. (6)

ἀποφεύγω v. (φεύγω) aor. ἀπέφυγον. *to escape, escape from*. (3)

ἀποφθέγγομαι v. (φθέγγομαι) aor. ἀπεφθεγξάμην. *to speak out, declare*. (3)

ἀποφορτίζομαι v. (φέρω) *to unload*. (1) Ac 21:3

ἀπόχρησις, εως, ἡ n. (χράομαι) *consuming, using up*. (1) Col 2:22

ἀποχωρέω v. (χωρέω) aor. ἀπεχώρησα. *to go away, leave, depart, withdraw*. (3)

ἀποχωρίζω v. (χωρίς) aor. pass. ἀπεχωρίσθην. *to separate; be separated, be split* (pass. in NT). (2)

ἀποψύχω v. (ψύχω) *to faint, breathe one's last, die*. (1) Lk 21:26

Ἀππίου Φόρον n. pla. *Forum of Appius*. (1) Ac 28:15

ἀπρόσιτος, ον adj. (-εἰμί) *unapproachable*. (1) 1 Ti 6:16

ἀπρόσκοπος, ον adj. (κόπτω) *undamaged, blameless, clear; giving no offense*. (3)

ἀπροσωπολήμπτως adv. (ὁράω, λαμβάνω) *impartially*. (1) 1 Pt 1:17

ἄπταιστος, ον adj. (πταίω) *without stumbling*. (1) Jd 24

ἅπτω v. (*) aor. ἧψα. *to kindle, light*; mid. *touch, take hold of, hold, cling to; have contact with, handle; have sexual contact; injure, harm*. (39)

Ἀπφία, ας, ἡ n. pers. *Apphia*. (1) Phlm 2

ἀπωθέω v. (-ὠθέω) aor. ἀπῶσα. mid. in NT *to push aside; reject, repudiate*. (6)

ἀπώλεια, ας, ἡ n. (ὄλεθρος) *waste; annihilation, ruin, destruction*. (18)

ἀπώλεσα s. ἀπόλλυμι (aor.).

ἀπῶσα s. ἀπωθέω (aor.).

ἀρά, ᾶς, ἡ n. (*) *curse*. (1) Rom 3:14

ἄρα part., somet. postpos., infer. *so, then; as a result, consequently; perhaps, conceivably*. (49)

ἆρα part., interrog. implying impatience (untransl.). (3)

Ἀραβία, ας, ἡ n. pla. *Arabia*. (2)

ἆραι s. αἴρω (aor. inf.).

Ἀράμ, ὁ n. pers. *Aram*. (2)

ἄραφος, ον adj. (ῥαφίς) *seamless*. (1) Jn 19:23

Ἄραψ, βος, ὁ n. pla. *an Arab*. (1) Ac 2:11

ἀργέω v. (ἔργον) *to be idle, slack off*. (1) 2 Pt 2:3

ἀργός, ή, όν adj. (ἔργον) *unemployed, idle; lazy; useless, worthless, careless*. (8)

ἀργύριον, ου, τό n. (ἄργυρος) *silver money, silver, money, silver coin*. (20)

ἀργυροκόπος, ου, ὁ n. (ἄργυρος, κόπτω) *silversmith*. (1) Ac 19:24

ἄργυρος, ου, ὁ n. (*) *silver, silver money*. (5)

ἀργυροῦς, ᾶ, οῦν adj. (ἄργυρος) *made of silver, silver*. (3)

Ἄρειος Πάγος, ὁ n. pla. *Areopagus, Hill of Ares*. (2)

Ἀρεοπαγίτης, ου, ὁ n. pla. *Areopagite, member of the court of the Areopagus*. (1) Ac 17:34

ἀρεσκεία, ας, ἡ n. (ἀρέσκω) *desire to please*. (1) Col 1:10

ἀρέσκω v. (*) aor. ἤρεσα. *to win favor, flatter; please, accommodate*. (17)

ἀρεστός, ή, όν adj. (ἀρέσκω) *pleasing, desirable*. (4)

Ἀρέτας, α, ὁ n. pers. *Aretas*. (1) 2 Cor 11:32

ἀρετή, ῆς, ἡ n. (ἀρέσκω) *excellence of character, exceptional civic virtue; miracle, power, divine act*. (5)

ἄρῃ s. αἴρω (aor. subj.).

Ἀρῄ n. pers. alt. form of Ἀρνί. (v.l.)

ἀρήν, ἀρνός, ὁ n. (*) *lamb*. (1) Lk 10:3

ἀριθμέω v. (ἀριθμός) aor. ἠρίθμησα; pf. pass. ἠρίθμημαι. *to count*. (3)

ἀριθμός, οῦ, ὁ n. (*) *number; total*. (18)

Ἀριμαθαία, ας, ἡ n. pla. *Arimathea*. (4)

Ἀρίσταρχος, ου, ὁ n. pers. *Aristarchus*. (5)

ἀριστάω v. (ἄριστον) aor. ἠρίστησα. *to eat breakfast; eat a meal, dine*. (3)

ἀριστερός, ά, όν adj. *left* (opp. to right); *left hand* (subst.). (4)

Ἀριστόβουλος, ου, ὁ n. pers. *Aristobulus*. (1) Rom 16:10

ἄριστον, ου, τό n. (*) *breakfast; noon meal, meal*. (3)

ἀρκετός, ή, όν adj. (ἀρκέω) *enough, sufficient, adequate*. (3)

ἀρκέω v. (*) aor. ἤρκεσα; aor. pass. ἠρκέσθην. *to be enough, be sufficient; be satisfied* or *content* (pass.). (8)

ἄρκος, ου, ὁ, ἡ n. *bear*. (1) Rev 13:2

ἅρμα, ατος, τό n. *carriage, chariot, warchariot*. (4)

Ἁρμαγεδών n. pla. *Armageddon*. (1) Rev 16:16

Ἀρμίν, ὁ n. pers. alt. form of Ἀδμίν. (v.l.)

ἁρμόζω v. (*) aor. ἥρμοσα. *to betroth, join in marriage* (mid. in NT). (1) 2 Cor 11:2

ἁρμός, οῦ, ὁ n. (ἁρμόζω) *joint*. (1) Heb 4:12

ἄρνας s. ἀρήν (acc. pl.).

ἀρνέομαι v. (*) fut. ἀρνήσομαι; aor. ἠρνησάμην; pf. pass. ἤρνημαι. *to refuse; deny; repudiate, disown, reject; disregard, renounce*. (33)

Ἀρνί, ὁ n. pers. *Arni*. (1) Lk 3:33

ἀρνίον, ου, τό n. (ἀρήν) *sheep, lamb*. (30)

ἆρον s. αἴρω (aor. impv.).

ἀροτριάω v. (ἄροτρον) *to plow*. (3)

ἄροτρον, ου, τό n. (*) *plow*. (1) Lk 9:62

ἁρπαγή, ῆς, ἡ n. (ἁρπάζω) *robbery; what has been stolen, plunder; greediness*. (3)

ἁρπαγμός, οῦ, ὁ n. (ἁρπάζω) *something to hold, something claimed, windfall, prize.* (1) Phil 2:6

ἁρπάζω v. (*) fut. ἁρπάσω; aor. ἥρπασα; aor. pass. ἡρπάγην, ἡρπάσθην. *to steal; snatch* or *take away, catch up, seize.* (14)

ἅρπαξ, αγος adj. (ἁρπάζω) *ravenous; swindler, robber* (subst.). (5)

ἀρραβών, ῶνος, ὁ n. Heb. *first installment, deposit, down payment, pledge.* (3)

ἄρρητος, ον adj. (ῥῆμα) *not to be spoken, too sacred to be spoken.* (1) 2 Cor 12:4

ἄρρωστος, ον adj. (ῥώννυμι) *sick, ill.* (5)

ἀρσενοκοίτης, ου, ὁ n. (ἄρσην, κεῖμαι) *male homosexual, pederast.* (2)

ἄρσην, εν adj. (*) *male.* (9)

Ἀρτεμᾶς, ᾶ, ὁ n. pers. *Artemas.* (1) Tit 3:12

Ἄρτεμις, ιδος, ἡ n. pers. *Artemis.* (5)

ἀρτέμων, ωνος, ὁ n. *foresail.* (1) Ac 27:40

ἄρτι adv. (*) *just now, just; at once, immediately, now; at the present time,* ἀπ' ἄρτι *from now on; present* (used as adj.). (36)

ἀρτιγέννητος, ον adj. (ἄρτι, γίνομαι) *newborn.* (1) 1 Pt 2:2

ἄρτιος, α, ον adj. (ἄρτι) *complete, capable, proficient.* (1) 2 Ti 3:17

ἄρτος, ου, ὁ n. *bread, loaf of bread; food.* (97)

ἀρτύω v. fut. ἀρτύσω; pf. pass. ἥρτυμαι; aor. pass. ἡρτύθην. *to season, salt.* (3)

Ἀρφαξάδ, ὁ n. pers. *Arphaxad.* (1) Lk 3:36

ἀρχάγγελος, ου, ὁ n. (ἄρχω, ἄγγελος) *archangel, chief angel.* (2)

ἀρχαῖος, αία, αῖον adj. (ἄρχω) *old, of long standing; ancient; ancients, people of ancient times, what is old* (subst.). (11)

Ἀρχέλαος, ου, ὁ n. pers. *Archelaus.* (1) Mt 2:22

ἀρχή, ῆς, ἡ n. (ἄρχω) *beginning, first, original,* ἀπ' ἀρχῆς *from the beginning,*

origin; first cause, the beginning; corner; elementary; ruler, authority; rule, office, domain. (55)

ἀρχηγός, οῦ, ὁ n. (ἄρχω, ἄγω) *leader, ruler, prince; originator, founder.* (4)

ἀρχιερατικός, όν adj. (ἄρχω, ἱερός) *highpriestly.* (1) Ac 4:6

ἀρχιερεύς, έως, ὁ n. (ἄρχω, ἱερός) *high priest; chief priests, ruling priests, Sanhedrin* (pl.). (122)

ἀρχιποίμην, ενος, ὁ n. (ἄρχω, ποιμήν) *chief shepherd.* (1) 1 Pt 5:4

Ἄρχιππος, ου, ὁ n. pers. *Archippus.* (2)

ἀρχισυνάγωγος, ου, ὁ n. (ἄρχω, ἄγω) *leader* or *president of a synagogue.* (9)

ἀρχιτέκτων, ονος, ὁ n. (ἄρχω, τίκτω) *master builder.* (1) 1 Cor 3:10

ἀρχιτελώνης, ου, ὁ n. (ἄρχω, τέλος) *chief tax collector.* (1) Lk 19:2

ἀρχιτρίκλινος, ου, ὁ n. (ἄρχω, τρεῖς, κλίνω) *head waiter, butler, master of a feast.* (3)

ἄρχω v. (*) fut. ἄρξω; aor. ἦρξα. *to rule; begin* (mid.). (86)

ἄρχων, οντος, ὁ n. (ἄρχω) *ruler, lord, prince; authority, leader, official, judge.* (37)

ἄρωμα, ατος, τό n. *spices, aromatic oils* or *ointments* (pl. in NT). (4)

Ἀσά, ὁ n. pers. alt. form of Ἀσάφ. (v.l.)

ἀσάλευτος, ον adj. (ἅλλομαι) *immovable; unshakeable, enduring.* (2)

Ἀσάφ, ὁ n. pers. *Asaph.* (2)

ἄσβεστος, ον adj. (σβέννυμι) *inextinguishable, unquenchable.* (3)

ἀσέβεια, ας, ἡ n. (σέβω) *impiety.* (6)

ἀσεβέω v. (σέβω) aor. ἠσέβησα. *to act impiously.* (1) Jd 15

ἀσεβής, ές adj. (σέβω) *irreverent, impious, ungodly.* (9)

ἀσέλγεια, ας, ἡ n. *self-abandonment, licentiousness, sensuality.* (10)

ἄσημος, ον adj. (σημεῖον) *insignificant, unimportant, obscure.* (1) Ac 21:39

Ἀσήρ, ὁ n. pers. *Asher.* (2)

ἀσθένεια, ας, ἡ n. (σθενόω) *sickness, disease, ailment; weakness; timidity.* (24)

ἀσθενέω v. (σθενόω) aor. ἠσθένησα; pf. ἠσθένηκα. *to be sick, suffer from; be weak; be in need.* (33)

ἀσθένημα, ατος, τό n. (σθενόω) *weakness.* (1) Rom 15:1

ἀσθενής, ές adj. (σθενόω) *sick, ill; weak, feeble, ineffectual, helpless; weakness, what is weak, one who is weak* (subst.). (26)

Ἀσία, ας, ἡ n. pla. *Asia.* (18)

Ἀσιανός, οῦ, ὁ n. pla. *an Asian.* (1) Ac 20:4

Ἀσιάρχης, ου, ὁ n. oth. *Asiarch.* (1) Ac 19:31

ἀσιτία, ας, ἡ n. (σῖτος) *lack of appetite.* (1) Ac 27:21

ἄσιτος, ον adj. (σῖτος) *without eating, fasting.* (1) Ac 27:33

ἀσκέω v. *to practice, engage in, do one's best.* (1) Ac 24:16

ἀσκός, οῦ, ὁ n. *leather bag, wine-skin.* (12)

ἀσμένως adv. (ἡδονή) *gladly.* (1) Ac 21:17

ἄσοφος, ον adj. (σοφός) *unwise, foolish.* (1) Eph 5:15

ἀσπάζομαι v. (*) aor. ἠσπασάμην. *to greet, welcome, take leave, warmly converse, hail, acclaim, pay respects; greet, send greetings* (impv.). (59)

ἀσπασμός, οῦ, ὁ n. (ἀσπάζομαι) *greeting.* (10)

ἄσπιλος, ον adj. (σπίλος) *spotless; pure, without fault.* (4)

ἀσπίς, ίδος, ἡ n. *asp, snake.* (1) Rom 3:13

ἄσπονδος, ον adj. (σπένδω) *irreconcilable.* (1) 2 Ti 3:3

Ἀσσά, ὁ n. pers. alt. form of Ἀσάφ. (v.l.)

ἀσσάριον, ου, τό n. Lat. *as, assarion* (Roman copper coin, about one-sixteenth of a denarius), *paltry sum.* (2)

ἆσσον adv. *nearer, closer, close.* (1) Ac 27:13

Ἄσσος, ου, ἡ n. pla. *Assos.* (2)

ἀστατέω v. (ἵστημι) *to be unsettled, be homeless.* (1) 1 Cor 4:11

ἀστεῖος, α, ον adj. *handsome, well-bred.* (2)

ἀστήρ, έρος, ὁ n. (*) *star.* (24)

ἀστήρικτος, ον adj. (στηρίζω) *unstable, weak.* (2)

ἄστοργος, ον adj. (-στέργω) *hard-hearted, unfeeling, without regard for others.* (2)

ἀστοχέω v. aor. ἠστόχησα. *to miss the mark, miss, fail, deviate, depart.* (3)

ἀστραπή, ῆς, ἡ n. (*) *lightning; light.* (9)

ἀστράπτω v. (ἀστραπή) *to flash, gleam.* (2)

ἄστρον, ου, τό n. (ἀστήρ) *star, constellation.* (4)

Ἀσύγκριτος, ου, ὁ n. pers. *Asyncritus.* (1) Rom 16:14

ἀσύμφωνος, ον adj. (φωνή) *in disagreement with.* (1) Ac 28:25

ἀσύνετος, ον adj. (-ἵημι) *senseless, foolish, without understanding.* (5)

ἀσύνθετος, ον adj. (τίθημι) *faithless, undutiful.* (1) Rom 1:31

ἀσφάλεια, ας, ἡ n. (-σφάλλω) *safety; certainty, truth; security.* (3)

ἀσφαλής, ές adj. (-σφάλλω) *firm; certain; truth, facts* (subst.)*; safe, secure.* (5)

ἀσφαλίζω v. (-σφάλλω) aor. ἠσφάλισα; aor. pass. ἠσφαλίσθην. *to fasten, secure; make secure.* (4)

ἀσφαλῶς adv. (-σφάλλω) *securely, under guard; assuredly, certainly, beyond a doubt.* (3)

ἀσχημονέω v. (ἔχω) *to behave disgracefully, behave dishonorably, behave indecently.* (2)

ἀσχημοσύνη, ης, ἡ n. (ἔχω) *shameless deed; nakedness* (= genitals). (2)

ἀσχήμων, ον adj. (ἔχω) *shameful, unpresentable; genitals* (pl. subst. in NT). (1) 1 Cor 12:23

ἀσωτία, ας, ἡ n. (σῴζω) *debauchery, dissipation, wild living.* (3)

ἀσώτως adv. (σῴζω) *wastefully, loosely.* (1) Lk 15:13

ἀτακτέω v. (τάσσω) aor. ἠτάκτησα. *to behave inappropriately, to be lazy.* (1) 2 Th 3:7

ἄτακτος, ον adj. (τάσσω) *disorderly, insubordinate, lazy.* (1) 1 Th 5:14

ἀτάκτως adv. (τάσσω) *disorderly, irresponsibly, lazily.* (2)

ἄτεκνος, ον adj. (τίκτω) *childless.* (2)

ἀτενίζω v. (-τείνω) aor. ἠτένισα. *to look intently at, stare.* (14)

ἄτερ prep. *without, apart from* (adv. prep. w. gen. in NT). (2)

ἀτιμάζω v. (τιμή) aor. ἠτίμασα; aor. pass. ἠτιμάσθην. *to dishonor, shame, degrade.* (7)

ἀτιμία, ας, ἡ n. (τιμή) *dishonor, disgrace, shame, humiliation,* εἰς ἀτιμίαν *for ordinary use.* (7)

ἄτιμος, ον adj. (τιμή) *dishonored, despised; insignificant.* (4)

ἀτμίς, ίδος, ἡ n. *vapor, mist.* (2)

ἄτομος, ον adj. (τομός) *indivisible; moment* (subst. in NT). (1) 1 Cor 15:52

ἄτοπος, ον adj. (τόπος) *unusual, surprising; evil, wrong, improper.* (4)

Ἀττάλεια, ας, ἡ n. pla. *Attalia.* (1) Ac 14:25

αὐγάζω v. (αὐγή) aor. ηὔγασα. *to see; shine forth.* (1) 2 Cor 4:4

αὐγή, ῆς, ἡ n. (*) *dawn, daybreak.* (1) Ac 20:11

Αὔγουστος, ου, ὁ n. pers. *Augustus.* (1) Lk 2:1

αὐθάδης, ες adj. (αὐτός, ἡδονή) *self-willed, stubborn, arrogant.* (2)

αὐθαίρετος, ον adj. (αὐτός, αἱρέω) *of one's own accord.* (2)

αὐθεντέω v. (αὐτός) *to give orders to, dictate to.* (1) 1 Ti 2:12

αὐλέω v. (*) aor. ηὔλησα. *to play the flute.* (3)

αὐλή, ῆς, ἡ n. (*) *enclosed open space, courtyard, court, fold; farm, house, palace.* (12)

αὐλητής, οῦ, ὁ n. (αὐλέω) *flutist.* (2)

αὐλίζομαι v. (αὐλή) aor. pass. ηὐλίσθην. *to spend the night.* (2)

αὐλός, οῦ, ὁ n. (αὐλέω) *flute.* (1) 1 Cor 14:7

αὐξάνω and αὔξω v. (*) fut. αὐξήσω; aor. ηὔξησα; aor. pass. ηὐξήθην. *to cause to grow, cause to increase; grow, increase* (pass. and act.). (23)

αὔξησις, εως, ἡ n. (αὐξάνω) *growth, increase.* (2)

αὔξω s. αὐξάνω (alt. form).

αὔριον adv. (*) *next day, tomorrow; soon, in a short time.* (14)

αὐστηρός, ά, όν adj. (*) *strict, punctilious.* (2)

αὐτάρκεια, ας, ἡ n. (αὐτός, ἀρκέω) *sufficiency; contentment, self-sufficiency.* (2)

αὐτάρκης, ες adj. (αὐτός, ἀρκέω) *content, self-sufficient.* (1) Phil 4:11

αὐτοκατάκριτος, ον adj. (αὐτός, κρίνω) *self-condemned.* (1) Tit 3:11

αὐτόματος, η, ον adj. (αὐτός) *by itself.* (2)

αὐτόπτης, ου, ὁ n. (αὐτός, ὁράω) *eyewitness.* (1) Lk 1:2

αὐτός, ή, ό pron. (*) reflex. *self* (w. all persons, genders, numbers, ex. *herself*), *alone, in person, thrown on one's own resources, even, very, same; he, she, it* (used as pers. pron.)*; the same,* τὸ αὐτό *in the same way,* ἐπὶ τὸ αὐτό *together,* κατὰ τὸ αὐτό *at the same time* (w. art.). (5597)

αὐτοῦ adv. (αὐτός) *here, there.* (4)

αὐτόφωρος, ον adj. (αὐτός) *in the act.* (1) Jn 8:4

αὐτόχειρ, ρος adj. (αὐτός, χείρ) *with one's own hand.* (1) Ac 27:19

αὐχέω v. *to boast.* (1) Jas 3:5

αὐχμηρός, ά, όν adj. (αὐστηρός) *dark, gloomy.* (1) 2 Pt 1:19

ἀφ᾽ = ἀπό before rough breathing.

ἀφαιρέω v. (αἱρέω) fut. ἀφελῶ; aor. ἀφεῖλον; aor. pass. ἀφῃρέθην. *to take away, remove, cut off; do away with; take away, remove* (mid. as act.). (10)

ἀφανής, ές adj. (φαίνω) *invisible, hidden.* (1) Heb 4:13

ἀφανίζω v. (φαίνω) aor. pass. ἠφανίσθην. *to destroy, ruin; perish, disappear* (pass.); *render invisible* or *unrecognizable, disfigure.* (5)

ἀφανισμός, οῦ, ὁ n. (φαίνω) *destruction.* (1) Heb 8:13

ἄφαντος, ον adj. (φαίνω) *invisible.* (1) Lk 24:31

ἀφεδρών, ῶνος, ὁ n. (ἑδραῖος) *toilet, latrine.* (2)

ἀφειδία, ας, ἡ n. (φείδομαι) *severe treatment.* (1) Col 2:23

ἀφεῖλον s. ἀφαιρέω (2 aor.).

ἀφεῖναι, ἀφείς, ἀφεῖς s. ἀφίημι (2 aor. inf., 2 aor. ptc., pres. 2 sg.).

ἀφελεῖν s. ἀφαιρέω (2 aor. inf.).

ἀφελότης, ητος, ἡ n. *simplicity.* (1) Ac 2:46

ἄφεσις, εως, ἡ n. (-ἵημι) *release; pardon, cancellation, forgiveness.* (17)

ἄφετε, ἀφέωνται s. ἀφίημι (2 aor. impv. 2 pl., pf. pass. 3 pl.).

ἀφή, ῆς, ἡ n. (ἅπτω) *ligament.* (2)

ἀφῆκα s. ἀφίημι (1 aor.).

ἀφήσω s. ἀφίημι (fut.).

ἀφθαρσία, ας, ἡ n. (φθείρω) *incorruptibility, immorality.* (7)

ἄφθαρτος, ον adj. (φθείρω) *imperishable, incorruptible, immoral; imperishable quality* (subst.). (8)

ἀφθορία, ας, ἡ n. (φθείρω) *soundness.* (1) Tit 2:7

ἀφίδω s. ἀφοράω (2 aor. subj.).

ἀφίημι v. (-ἵημι) fut. ἀφήσω; aor. ἀφῆκα; pf. pass. ἀφέωμαι; aor. pass. ἀφέθην. *to let go, send away, give up, utter, divorce; cancel, remit, pardon, forgive; depart from, abandon, omit; leave standing* or *lying, leave, give; let, let to, allow, tolerate.* (143)

ἀφικνέομαι v. (ἱκανός) aor. ἀφικόμην. *to reach, become known to.* (1) Rom 16:19

ἀφιλάγαθος, ον adj. (φίλος, ἀγαθός) *without interest in the good.* (1) 2 Ti 3:3

ἀφιλάργυρος, ον adj. (φίλος, ἄργυρος) *not loving money, not greedy.* (2)

ἄφιξις, εως, ἡ n. (ἱκανός) *departure.* (1) Ac 20:29

ἀφίστημι v. (ἵστημι) fut. ἀποστήσω; aor. ἀπέστησα, ἀπέστην. *to cause to revolt* or *follow, mislead; go away, withdraw, desert, fall away, keep away, abstain* (incl. mid. as act.). (14)

ἄφνω adv. (*) *suddenly, immediately.* (3)

ἀφόβως adv. (φόβος) *fearlessly, boldly, without reverence, shamelessly.* (4)

ἀφομοιόω v. (ὅμοιος) pf. pass. ἀφωμοίωμαι. *to make like; become like, resemble* (pass. in NT). (1) Heb 7:3

ἀφοράω v. (ὁράω) aor. ἀπεῖδον. *to fix one's eyes on; determine, see.* (2)

ἀφορίζω v. (ὁρίζω) fut. ἀφορίσω, ἀφοριῶ; aor. ἀφώρισα; pf. pass. ἀφώρισμαι; aor. pass. ἀφωρίσθην. *to separate, exclude, excommunicate; set apart, appoint.* (10)

ἀφορμή, ῆς, ἡ n. (ὁρμή) *occasion, opportunity, excuse.* (7)

ἀφρίζω v. (ἀφρός) *to foam at the mouth.* (2)

ἀφρός, οῦ, ὁ n. (*) *foam.* (1) Lk 9:39

ἀφροσύνη, ης, ἡ n. (φρήν) *foolishness, lack of sense.* (4)

ἄφρων, ον adj. (φρήν) *foolish, ignorant.* (11)

ἀφυπνόω v. (ὕπνος) aor. ἀφύπνωσα. *to fall asleep.* (1) Lk 8:23

ἀφυστερέω v. *to withhold.* (v.l.)

ἀφῶ s. ἀφίημι (2 aor. subj.).

ἄφωνος, ον adj. (φωνή) *silent; mute; speechless; without conveying meaning, devoid of meaning.* (4)

Ἀχάζ, ὁ n. pers. *Ahaz.* (2)

Ἀχαΐα, ας, ἡ n. pla. *Achaia.* (10)

Ἀχαϊκός, οῦ, ὁ n. pers. *Achaicus.* (1) 1 Cor 16:17

ἀχάριστος, ον adj. (χαίρω) *ungrateful.* (2)

ἀχειροποίητος, ον adj. (χείρ, ποιέω) *not made by hand(s), spiritual.* (3)

ἀχθῆναι, ἀχθήσομαι s. ἄγω (aor. pass. inf., fut. pass.).

Ἀχίμ, ὁ n. pers. *Achim.* (2)

ἀχλύς, ύος, ἡ n. *mist*. (1) Ac 13:11
ἀχρεῖος, ον adj. (χράομαι) *useless, worthless, profitless; unworthy*. (2)
ἀχρειόω v. (χράομαι) aor. pass. ἠχρεώθην. *to become depraved* or *worthless* (pass. in NT). (1) Rom 3:12
ἄχρηστος, ον adj. (χράομαι) *useless, worthless*. (1) Phlm 11
ἄχρι adv. (ἄκρον) adv. prep. w. gen.

ἄψυχος

until, to, unto; as far as; conj. *until, as long as*. (49)
ἄχρις = ἄχρι before vowels.
ἄχυρον, ου, τό n. *chaff*. (2)
ἀψευδής, ές adj. (ψεύδομαι) *truthful, trustworthy*. (1) Tit 1:2
ἄψινθος, ου, ὁ, ἡ n. *wormwood*. (2)
ἄψυχος, ον adj. (ψύχω) *inanimate, lifeless*. (1) 1 Cor 14:7

B

Βάαλ, ὁ n. pers. *Baal* (w. fem. art. in NT). (1) Rom 11:4

Βαβυλών, ῶνος, ἡ n. pla. *Babylon*. (12)

βαθμός, οῦ, ὁ n. (-βαίνω) *grade, rank*. (1) 1 Ti 3:13

βάθος, ους, τό n. (βαθύς) *depth, deep water; depth* (fig.). (8)

βαθύνω v. (βαθύς) *to make deep, go down deep*. (1) Lk 6:48

βαθύς, εῖα, ύ adj. (*) *deep; deep* (fig.); *profound, at the extreme of, very,* ὄρθρου βαθέως *early in the morning*. (4)

βαΐον, ου, τό n. Cop. *palm branch*. (1) Jn 12:13

Βαλαάμ, ὁ n. pers. *Balaam*. (3)

Βαλάκ, ὁ n. pers. *Balak*. (1) Rev 2:14

βαλλάντιον, ου, τό n. *money-bag, purse*. (4)

βάλλω v. (*) fut. βαλῶ; aor. ἔβαλον, ἔβαλα; pf. βέβληκα; pf. pass. βέβλημαι; aor. pass. ἐβλήθην. *to throw, scatter, spew, cast, throw away, let fall; throw oneself, lie* (pass.); *drive out, expel; put, place, take, pour, swing, lay down; bring; deposit; rush down*. (122)

βαπτίζω v. (βάπτω) fut. βαπτίσω; aor. ἐβάπτισα; pf. pass. βεβάπτισμαι; aor. pass. ἐβαπτίσθην. *to wash, purify; plunge, dip, wash, baptize, administer baptism; have oneself baptized, get baptized* (pass.); *plunge, baptize* (fig.). (77)

βάπτισμα, ατος, τό n. (βάπτω) *plunging, dipping, washing, baptism; baptism* (fig.). (19)

βαπτισμός, οῦ, ὁ n. (βάπτω) *washing, cleansing; baptism*. (4)

βαπτιστής, οῦ, ὁ n. (βάπτω) *Baptist, Baptizer* (used only of John). (12)

βάπτω v. (*) fut. βάψω; aor. ἔβαψα; pf. pass. βέβαμμαι. *to dip, dip in, dye*. (4)

Βαραββᾶς, ᾶ, ὁ n. pers. *Barabbas*. (11)

Βαράκ, ὁ n. pers. *Barak*. (1) Heb 11:32

Βαραχίας, ου, ὁ n. pers. *Barachiah*. (1) Mt 23:35

βάρβαρος, ον adj. *foreign-speaking, of foreign language; non-Greek, foreigner* (subst.). (6)

βαρέω v. (βάρος) pf. pass. βεβάρημαι; aor. pass. ἐβαρήθην. *to weigh down, burden, oppress*. (6)

βαρέως adv. (βάρος) *with difficulty*. (2)

Βαρθολομαῖος, ου, ὁ n. pers. *Bartholomew*. (4)

Βαριησοῦς, οῦ, ὁ n. pers. *Bar-Jesus*. (1) Ac 13:6

Βαριωνᾶ and Βαριωνᾶς, ᾶ, ὁ n. pers. *Bar-Jona*. (1) Mt 16:17

Βαρναβᾶς, ᾶ, ὁ n. pers. *Barnabas*. (28)

βάρος, ους, τό n. (*) *weight, burden; claim of importance; fullness*. (6)

Βαρσαββᾶς, ᾶ, ὁ n. pers. *Barsabbas*. (2)

Βαρτιμαῖος, ου, ὁ n. pers. *Bartimaeus*. (1) Mk 10:46

βαρύς, εῖα, ύ adj. (βάρος) *heavy; severe, difficult; weighty, important, serious; fierce, savage*. (6)

βαρύτιμος, ον adj. (βάρος) *very expensive, very precious*. (1) Mt 26:7

βασανίζω v. (βάσανος) aor. ἐβασάνισα; aor. pass. ἐβασανίσθην. *to torment, harass, strain*. (12)

βασανισμός, οῦ, ὁ n. (βάσανος) *tormenting; torment*. (6)

βασανιστής, οῦ, ὁ n. (βάσανος) *oppressive jailer*. (1) Mt 18:34

βάσανος, ου, ἡ n. (*) *torture, torment; severe pain*. (3)

βασιλεία, ας, ἡ n. (βασιλεύς) *kingship, royal power, royal rule, royal reign; kingdom.* (162)

βασίλειος, ον adj. (βασιλεύς) *royal; palace* (pl. subst.). (2)

βασιλεύς, έως, ὁ n. (*) *king.* (115)

βασιλεύω v. (βασιλεύς) fut. βασιλεύσω; aor. ἐβασίλευσα. *to be king, rule, reign; become king.* (21)

βασιλικός, ή, όν adj. (βασιλεύς) *royal; royal official, member of the royal family* (subst.). (5)

βασίλισσα, ης, ἡ n. (βασιλεύς) *queen.* (4)

βάσις, εως, ἡ n. (-βαίνω) *foot.* (1) Ac 3:7

βασκαίνω v. aor. ἐβάσκανα. *to bewitch.* (1) Gal 3:1

βαστάζω v. (*) fut. βαστάσω; aor. ἐβάστασα. *to pick up, take up; carry, bear, support, endure, put up with; carry away, remove, steal.* (27)

βάτος, ου, ὁ, ἡ n. *thorn-bush.* (5)

βάτος, ου, ὁ n. Heb. *bath, jug* (Hebrew liquid measure, about 34 liters or quarts). (1) Lk 16:6

βάτραχος, ου, ὁ n. *frog.* (1) Rev 16:13

βατταλογέω v. (λέγω) aor. ἐβαττα-λόγησα. *to use the same words again and again, speak without thinking, babble.* (1) Mt 6:7

βδέλυγμα, ατος, τό n. (βδελύσσομαι) *loathsome* or *detestable thing; abomination, pollutant,* τὸ βδέλυγμα τῆς ἐρημώσεως *the desolating sacrilege.* (6)

βδελυκτός, ή, όν adj. (βδελύσσομαι) *abhorrent, detestable.* (1) Tit 1:16

βδελύσσομαι v. (*) pf. pass. ἐβδέλυγμαι. *to abhor, detest; detestable* (pf. pass. ptc.). (2)

βέβαιος, α, ον adj. (-βαίνω) *reliable, unshifting, firm; abiding, constant, steadfast; in force, valid.* (8)

βεβαιόω v. (-βαίνω) fut. βεβαιώσω; aor. ἐβεβαίωσα; aor. pass. ἐβεβαιώθην. *to confirm, establish, fulfill; be ratified, be guaranteed* (pass.); *strengthen, make firm.* (8)

βεβαίωσις, εως, ἡ n. (-βαίνω) *confirmation, validation, establishment.* (2)

βέβαμμαι s. βάπτω (pf. pass.).

βέβηλος, ον adj. (-βαίνω) *pointless, worthless; totally worldly.* (5)

βεβηλόω v. (-βαίνω) aor. ἐβεβήλωσα. *to desecrate, profane, violate sanctity.* (2)

βέβληκα, βέβλημαι s. βάλλω (pf., pf. pass.).

βέβρωκα s. βιβρώσκω (pf.).

Βεελζεβούλ, ὁ n. pers. *Beelzebul.* (7)

Βελιάρ, ὁ n. pers. *Beliar.* (1) 2 Cor 6:15

βελόνη, ης, ἡ n. (βάλλω) *needle.* (1) Lk 18:25

βέλος, ους, τό n. (βάλλω) *arrow.* (1) Eph 6:16

βελτίων, ον adj. *better; very well* (neut. as adv. in NT). (1) 2 Ti 1:18

Βενιαμίν, ὁ n. pers. *Benjamin.* (4)

Βερνίκη, ης, ἡ n. pers. *Bernice.* (3)

Βέροια, ας, ἡ n. pla. *Beroea.* (2)

Βεροιαῖος, α, ον adj. pla. *Beroean; a Beroean* (subst. in NT). (1) Ac 20:4

Βέρος, ου, ὁ n. pers. *Berus.* (v.l.)

Βεωορσόρ, ὁ n. pers. alt. form of Βεώρ. (v.l.)

Βεώρ, ὁ n. pers. *Beor.* (v.l.)

Βηθαβαρά, ἡ n. pla. *Bethabara.* (v.l.)

Βηθανία, ας, ἡ n. pla. *Bethany.* (12)

Βηθεσδά, ἡ n. pla. *Bethesda.* (v.l.)

Βηθζαθά, ἡ n. pla. *Bethzatha.* (1) Jn 5:2

Βηθλέεμ, ἡ n. pla. *Bethlehem.* (8)

Βηθσαϊδά, ἡ n. pla. *Bethsaida.* (7)

Βηθφαγή, ἡ n. pla. *Bethphage.* (3)

βῆμα, ατος, τό n. (-βαίνω) *step; tribunal, judicial bench.* (12)

Βηρεύς, έως, ὁ n. pers. *Bereus.* (v.l.)

βήρυλλος, ου, ὁ, ἡ n. *beryl.* (1) Rev 21:20

βία, ας, ἡ n. (*) *force, use of force, press.* (3)

βιάζομαι v. (βία) *to dominate, constrain, treat violently, oppress, suffer violence* (if pass.); *use force, take by force, enter by force* (if mid.). (2)

βίαιος, α, ον adj. (βία) *violent, forcible, strong.* (1) Ac 2:2

βιαστής, οῦ, ὁ n. (βία) *violent or impetuous person.* (1) Mt 11:12

βιβλαρίδιον, ου, τό n. (βίβλος,) *little scroll or roll.* (3)

βιβλίον, ου, τό n. (βίβλος,) *document, certificate; scroll, book.* (34)

βίβλος, ου, ἡ n. (*) *book; record-book.* (10)

βιβρώσκω v. (*) pf. βέβρωκα. *to eat, consume.* (1) Jn 6:13

Βιθυνία, ας, ἡ n. pla. *Bithynia.* (2)

βίος, ου, ὁ n. (*) *life, everyday life; means of subsistence, property, goods.* (10)

βιόω v. (βίος) aor. ἐβίωσα. *to live.* (1) 1 Pt 4:2

βίωσις, εως, ἡ n. (βίος) *manner of life.* (1) Ac 26:4

βιωτικός, ή, όν adj. (βίος) *belonging to daily life.* (3)

βλαβερός, ά, όν adj. (βλάπτω) *harmful.* (1) 1 Ti 6:9

βλάπτω v. (*) aor. ἔβλαψα. *to harm, injure, hurt.* (2)

βλαστάνω and βλαστάω v. aor. ἐβλάστησα. *to produce; bud, sprout.* (4)

Βλάστος, ου, ὁ n. pers. *Blastus.* (1) Ac 12:20

βλασφημέω v. (-βλάξ, φημί) aor. ἐβλασφήμησα; aor. pass. ἐβλασφημήθην. *to slander, revile, defame, speak irreverently of, blaspheme.* (34)

βλασφημία, ας, ἡ n. (-βλάξ, φημί) *reviling, denigration, disrespect, slander, blasphemy.* (18)

βλάσφημος, ον adj. (-βλάξ, φημί) *defaming, denigrating, demeaning, blasphemous; slanderer, blasphemer* (subst.). (4)

βλέμμα, ατος, τό n. (βλέπω) *seeing, what is seen.* (1) 2 Pt 2:8

βλέπω v. (*) fut. βλέψω; aor. ἔβλεψα. *to see, look on, watch, look; be able to see; look at, observe; notice, mark; look to, beware (of), look out; consider, note, keep one's eyes open; perceive,*

feel, discover, find; look in the direction of, face. (133)

βληθήσομαι s. βάλλω (fut. pass.).

βλητέος, α, ον adj. (βάλλω) *must be put.* (1) Lk 5:38

Βοανηργές n. pers. *Boanerges.* (1) Mk 3:17

βοάω v. (βοή) aor. ἐβόησα. *to call, shout, cry out.* (12)

Βόες, ὁ n. pers. *Boaz.* (2)

βοή, ῆς, ἡ n. (*) *outcry, shout.* (1) Jas 5:4

βοήθεια, ας, ἡ n. (βοή) *help; aid, support.* (2)

βοηθέω v. (βοή) aor. ἐβοήθησα. *to furnish aid, help.* (8)

βοηθός, όν adj. (βοή) *helpful; helper* (subst. in NT). (1) Heb 13:6

βόησον s. βοάω (aor. impv.).

βόθυνος, ου, ὁ n. *pit.* (3)

βολή, ῆς, ἡ n. (βάλλω) *throw.* (1) Lk 22:41

βολίζω v. (βάλλω) aor. ἐβόλισα. *to take a sounding, heave the lead.* (2)

Βόος, ὁ n. pers. *Boaz.* (1) Lk 3:32

βόρβορος, ου, ὁ n. *slime, mud, mire.* (1) 2 Pt 2:22

βορρᾶς, ᾶ, ὁ n. *the north.* (2)

βόσκω v. (*) *to herd, tend,* ὁ βόσκων *herdsman; graze, feed* (pass.). (9)

Βοσόρ, ὁ n. pers. *Bosor.* (1) 2 Pt 2:15

βοτάνη, ης, ἡ n. (βόσκω) *herb, plant, vegetation.* (1) Heb 6:7

βότρυς, υος, ὁ n. *bunch of grapes.* (1) Rev 14:18

βουλευτής, οῦ, ὁ n. (βούλομαι) *council member.* (2)

βουλεύω v. (βούλομαι) fut. βουλεύσω; aor. ἐβούλευσα. *to deliberate, resolve, decide* (mid. in NT). (6)

βουλή, ῆς, ἡ n. (βούλομαι) *plan, purpose, intention, motive; resolution, decision, resolve.* (12)

βούλημα, ατος, τό n. (βούλομαι) *intention, purpose, desire.* (3)

βούλομαι v. (*) aor. pass. ἐβουλήθην. *to wish, want, desire; intend, plan, will, want.* (37)

βουνός, οῦ, ὁ n. *hill.* (2)

βοῦς, βοός, ὁ, ἡ n. *head of cattle, ox* (masc.), *cow* (fem.). (8)

βραβεῖον, ου, τό n. (βραβεύω) *prize, award*. (2)

βραβεύω v. (*) *to be judge, decide, rule, control*. (1) Col 3:15

βραδύνω v. (βραδύς) *to hesitate, delay, hold back*. (2)

βραδυπλοέω v. (βραδύς, πλέω) *to sail slowly*. (1) Ac 27:7

βραδύς, εῖα, ύ adj. (*) *slow*. (3)

βραδύτης, ητος, ἡ n. (βραδύς) *slowness*. (1) 2 Pt 3:9

βραχίων, ονος, ὁ n. *arm*. (3)

βραχύς, εῖα, ύ adj. *short; brief*, βραχύ τι *for a short time*, μετὰ βραχύ *a little later; little, small, few*, βραχύ τι *a small amount*, διὰ βραχέων *briefly*. (7)

βρέφος, ους, τό n. *fetus, child; baby, infant, childhood*. (8)

βρέχω v. (*) aor. ἔβρεξα. *to wet; send rain; it rains* (impers.). (7)

βροντή, ῆς, ἡ n. *thunder*. (12)

βροχή, ῆς, ἡ n. (βρέχω) *rain*. (2)

βρόχος, ου, ὁ n. *noose; restriction* (fig. in NT). (1) 1 Cor 7:35

βρυγμός, οῦ, ὁ n. (βρύχω) *gnashing, chattering*. (7)

βρύχω v. (*) *to gnash*. (1) Ac 7:54

βρύω v. *to pour forth*. (1) Jas 3:11

βρῶμα, ατος, τό n. (βιβρώσκω) *food, solid food*. (17)

βρώσιμος, ον adj. (βιβρώσκω) *eatable*, τι βρώσιμον *anything to eat*. (1) Lk 24:41

βρῶσις, εως, ἡ n. (βιβρώσκω) *eating; consuming; food*. (11)

βυθίζω v. (βυθός) *to sink; plunge, expose to* (fig.). (2)

βυθός, οῦ, ὁ n. (*) *sea, deep water*. (1) 2 Cor 11:25

βυρσεύς, έως, ὁ n. *tanner*. (3)

βύσσινος, η, ον adj. (βύσσος) *made of fine linen; fine linen, linen garment* (subst.). (5)

βύσσος, ου, ἡ n. (*) Heb. *fine linen*. (1) Lk 16:19

βωμός, οῦ, ὁ n. (-βαίνω) *altar*. (1) Ac 17:23

Γ

Γαββαθᾶ n. pla. *Gabbatha.* (1) Jn 19:13
Γαβριήλ, ὁ n. pers. *Gabriel.* (2)
γάγγραινα, ης, ἡ n. *gangrene, cancer.* (1) 2 Ti 2:17
Γάδ, ὁ n. pers. *Gad.* (1) Rev 7:5
Γαδαρηνός, ή, όν adj. pla. *from Gadara; a Gadarene* (subst. in NT). (1) Mt 8:28
Γάζα, ης, ἡ n. pla. *Gaza.* (1) Ac 8:26
γάζα, ης, ἡ n. (*) Per. *treasury.* (1) Ac 8:27
γαζοφυλάκιον, ου, τό n. (γάζα, φυλάσσω) Per. *treasure room, treasury; contribution box.* (5)
Γάϊος, ου, ὁ n. pers. *Gaius.* (5)
γάλα, γάλακτος, τό n. *milk.* (5)
Γαλάτης, ου, ὁ n. pla. *a Galatian.* (1) Gal 3:1
Γαλατία, ας, ἡ n. pla. *Galatia.* (4)
Γαλατικός, ή, όν adj. pla. *Galatian.* (2)
γαλήνη, ης, ἡ n. *calm* (of a body of water). (3)
Γαλιλαία, ας, ἡ n. pla. *Galilee.* (61)
Γαλιλαῖος, α, ον adj. pla. *Galilean; a Galilean* (subst.). (11)
Γαλλία, ας, ἡ n. pla. *Gaul.* (v.l.)
Γαλλίων, ωνος, ὁ n. pers. *Gallio.* (3)
Γαμαλιήλ, ὁ n. pers. *Gamaliel.* (2)
γαμέω v. (γάμος) aor. ἐγάμησα, ἔγημα; pf. γεγάμηκα; aor. pass. ἐγαμήθην. *to marry; get married, be married* (pass.). (28)
γαμίζω v. (γάμος) *to give (a woman) in marriage; marry.* (7)
γαμίσκω v. (γάμος) *to give in marriage.* (1) Lk 20:34
γάμος, ου, ὁ n. (*) *wedding, wedding celebration, wedding banquet; marriage; wedding hall.* (16)
γάρ conj. (*) postpos. *for; you see;*

certainly, by all means, so, then, indeed. (1041)
γαστήρ, τρός, ἡ n. *belly, glutton; womb,* ἐν γαστρὶ ἔχω *be pregnant.* (9)
Γαύδη n. pla. alt. form of Καῦδα. (v.l.)
γέ part. (*) encl., postpos. *at least, even, indeed, yet.* (25)
γέγονα s. γίνομαι (2 pf.).
Γεδεών, ὁ n. pers. *Gideon.* (1) Heb 11:32
γέεννα, ης, ἡ n. Ara. *Gehenna, hell.* (12)
Γεθσημανί n. pla. *Gethsemane.* (2)
γείτων, ονος, ὁ, ἡ n. *neighbor.* (4)
γελάω v. (*) fut. γελάσω. *to laugh.* (2)
γέλως, ωτος, ὁ n. (γελάω) *laughter.* (1) Jas 4:9
γεμίζω v. (γέμω) aor. ἐγέμισα; aor. pass. ἐγεμίσθην. *to fill.* (8)
γέμω v. (*) *to be full, be covered with.* (11)
γενεά, ᾶς, ἡ n. (γίνομαι) *race, kind; generation, contemporaries; age, period of time; family history.* (43)
γενεαλογέω v. (γίνομαι, λέγω) *to trace descent; be descended from* (pass. in NT). (1) Heb 7:6
γενεαλογία, ας, ἡ n. (γίνομαι, λέγω) *genealogy.* (2)
γενέσθαι s. γίνομαι (2 aor. mid. inf.).
γενέσια, ων, τά n. (γίνομαι) *birthday celebration* (pl. from subst. adj.). (2)
γένεσις, εως, ἡ n. (γίνομαι) *birth; existence, life, human experience; history, life; lineage, family line.* (5)
γενετή, ῆς, ἡ n. (γίνομαι) *birth.* (1) Jn 9:1
γένημα, ατος, τό n. (γίνομαι) *product, fruit, yield, harvest.* (4)
γεννάω v. (γίνομαι) fut. γεννήσω; aor. ἐγέννησα; pf. γεγέννηκα; pf. pass. γεγέννημαι; aor. pass. ἐγεννήθην.

to beget, become the father of; be
fathered, be conceived, be born (pass.);
bear, give birth; produce, cause. (97)
γέννημα, ατος, τό n. (γίνομαι) child,
offspring, brood. (4)
Γεννησαρέτ, ἡ n. pla. Gennesaret. (3)
γέννησις, εως, ἡ n. birth. (v.l.)
γεννητός, ή, όν adj. (γίνομαι) born,
γεννητοὶ γυναικῶν those born of
women (= humans). (2)
γένος, ους, τό n. (γίνομαι) descendant, descent; family, relatives; nation,
people; class, kind. (20)
Γερασηνός, ή, όν adj. pla. from Gerasene; a Gerasene (subst. in NT). (3)
Γεργεσηνός, ή, όν adj. pla. from
Gergesa; a Gergesene (subst.). (v.l.)
γερουσία, ας, ἡ n. (γῆρας) council of
elders (Sanhedrin). (1) Ac 5:21
γέρων, οντος, ὁ n. (γῆρας) elderly or old
man. (1) Jn 3:4
γεύομαι v. fut. γεύσομαι; aor. ἐγευ-
σάμην. to taste, partake of, eat; come
to know, obtain, experience (fig.).
(15)
γεωργέω v. (γῆ, ἔργον) to cultivate, till.
(1) Heb 6:7
γεώργιον, ου, τό n. (γῆ, ἔργον) cultivated land, field. (1) 1 Cor 3:9
γεωργός, οῦ, ὁ n. (γῆ, ἔργον) farmer;
vine-dresser, tenant farmer. (19)
γῆ, γῆς, ἡ n. (*) earth; people, humanity; region, country; land; ground, soil.
(250)
γῆρας, ως and ους, τό n. (*) old age. (1)
Lk 1:36
γηράσκω v. (γῆρας) aor. ἐγήρασα. to
grow old. (2)
γίνομαι v. (*) fut. γενήσομαι; aor.
ἐγενόμην; pf. γέγονα; pf. pass.
γεγένημαι; aor. pass. ἐγενήθην. to be
born, be produced; be made, be created, be performed, be done, be carried out, be granted, be established;
arise, come about, develop, come, arrive, grow; happen, turn out, take
place, occur, do, come upon, befall,
have, receive, μὴ γένοιτο by no means;

become, turn into; move, reach, come,
go, be at, go or break out, arrive,
spread, be given, join; be, prove to be,
turn out to be; be there, exist, appear,
live; belong to; be in. (669)
γινώσκω v. (*) fut. γνώσομαι; aor.
ἔγνων; pf. ἔγνωκα; pf. pass. ἔγνωσμαι;
aor. pass. ἐγνώσθην. to know, know
about, make acquaintance of; learn
(of), ascertain, find out; understand,
comprehend; perceive, notice, realize,
feel; have sex or marital relations with;
have come to know; acknowledge, recognize. (222)
γλεῦκος, ους, τό n. (γλυκύς) sweet new
wine. (1) Ac 2:13
γλυκύς, εῖα, ύ adj. (*) sweet. (4)
γλῶσσα, ης, ἡ n. (*) tongue; language;
ecstatic language or speech. (50)
γλωσσόκομον, ου, τό n. (γλῶσσα,
κόσμος) money-box, purse. (2)
γναφεύς, έως, ὁ n. (*) cloth refiner. (1)
Mk 9:3
γνήσιος, α, ον adj. (γίνομαι) legitimate,
true; genuine; genuineness, sincerity
(subst.). (4)
γνησίως adv. (γίνομαι) sincerely, gen-
uinely. (1) Phil 2:20
γνούς s. γινώσκω (2 aor. ptc.).
γνόφος, ου, ὁ n. darkness. (1) Heb 12:18
γνώμη, ης, ἡ n. (γινώσκω) purpose, intention, mind; opinion, judgment; approval, consent; declaration, decision.
(9)
γνωρίζω v. (γινώσκω) fut. γνωρίσω; aor.
ἐγνώρισα; aor. pass. ἐγνωρίσθην. to
make known, reveal; know. (25)
γνῶσις, εως, ἡ n. (γινώσκω) knowledge,
comprehension, κατὰ γνῶσιν knowl-
edgeably; what is known; knowledge
(dissident). (29)
γνώστης, ου, ὁ n. (γινώσκω) one acquainted with, expert in. (1) Ac 26:3
γνωστός, ή, όν adj. (γινώσκω) known,
remarkable; capable of being known,
intelligible; acquaintance, friend
(subst.). (15)
γογγύζω v. (*) aor. ἐγόγγυσα. to

grumble, murmur, complain; speak secretly, whisper. (8)

γογγυσμός, οῦ, ὁ n. (γογγύζω) complaint, displeasure, complaining, secret talk, whispering. (4)

γογγυστής, οῦ, ὁ n. (γογγύζω) grumbler. (1) Jd 16

γόης, ητος, ὁ n. swindler, cheat, impostor. (1) 2 Ti 3:13

Γολγοθᾶ, ἡ n. pla. Golgotha. (3)

Γόμορρα, ων, τά and **Γόμορρας, ἡ** n. pla. Gomorrah. (4)

γόμος, ου, ὁ n. (γέμω) load, freight, cargo. (3)

γονεύς, έως, ὁ n. (γίνομαι) parent; parents (pl. in NT). (20)

γόνυ, ατος, τό n. (*) knee. (12)

γονυπετέω v. (γόνυ, πίπτω) aor. ἐγονυπέτησα. to kneel down. (4)

γράμμα, ατος, τό n. (γράφω) letter (of the alphabet); document, letter, epistle, promissory note, writing, book (predom. pl.); learning, knowledge (pl.). (14)

γραμματεύς, έως, ὁ n. (γράφω) secretary, clerk; expert in the law, scribe, scholar, instructor. (63)

γραπτός, ή, όν adj. (γράφω) written. (1) Rom 2:15

γραφή, ῆς, ἡ n. (γράφω) scripture passage, scripture; scriptures, writings (pl.). (50)

γράφω v. (*) fut. γράψω; aor. ἔγραψα;

pf. γέγραφα; pf. pass. γέγραμμαι; aor. pass. ἐγράφην. to inscribe, sign; write, write down, record, cover with writing, write about, write to, compose, give in writing. (191)

γραώδης, ες adj. (εἶδος) characteristic of an old woman. (1) 1 Ti 4:7

γρηγορέω v. (ἐγείρω) aor. ἐγρηγόρησα. to be watchful; be on the alert, be wide awake; be alive. (22)

γυμνάζω v. (γυμνός) pf. pass. γεγύμνασμαι. to train, undergo discipline. (4)

γυμνασία, ας, ἡ n. (γυμνός) training. (1) 1 Ti 4:8

γυμνιτεύω v. (γυμνός) to be poorly clothed. (1) 1 Cor 4:11

γυμνός, ή, όν adj. (*) naked, stripped, bare, uncovered; poorly dressed; without an outer garment. (15)

γυμνότης, ητος, ἡ n. (γυμνός) nakedness; destitution, lack of sufficient clothing. (3)

γυναικάριον, ου, τό n. (γυνή) idle, foolish or weak woman. (1) 2 Ti 3:6

γυναικεῖος, α, ον adj. (γυνή) feminine, female; woman, wife (subst. in NT). (1) 1 Pt 3:7

γυνή, αικός, ἡ n. (*) woman; wife; bride. (215)

Γώγ, ὁ n. pers. Gog. (1) Rev 20:8

γωνία, ας, ἡ n. (*) corner, κεφαλὴ γωνίας corner-stone, keystone. (9)

δ' = δέ before vowels.

δαιμονίζομαι v. (δαιμόνιον) aor. pass. ἐδαιμονίσθην. *to be possessed by a hostile spirit* or *demon*. (13)

δαιμόνιον, ου, τό n. (*) *deity, a divinity; spirit, power, hostile divinity, evil spirit.* (63)

δαιμονιώδης, ες adj. (δαιμόνιον, εἶδος) *demonic, infernal.* (1) Jas 3:15

δαίμων, ονος, ὁ n. (δαιμόνιον) *evil spirit, demon.* (1) Mt 8:31

δάκνω v. *to bite; harm* (fig. in NT). (1) Gal 5:15

δάκρυον, ου, τό n. (*) *tear; weeping* (pl.). (10)

δακρύω v. (δάκρυον) aor. ἐδάκρυσα. *to weep, burst into tears.* (1) Jn 11:35

δακτύλιος, ου, ὁ n. (δείκνυμι) *ring* (for a finger). (1) Lk 15:22

δάκτυλος, ου, ὁ n. (δείκνυμι) *finger.* (8)

Δαλμανουθά, ἡ n. pla. *Dalmanutha.* (1) Mk 8:10

Δαλματία, ας, ἡ n. pla. *Dalmatia.* (1) 2 Ti 4:10

δαμάζω v. (*) aor. ἐδάμασα; pf. pass. δεδάμασμαι. *to subdue, tame, control.* (4)

δάμαλις, εως, ἡ n. (δαμάζω) *heifer, young cow.* (1) Heb 9:13

Δάμαρις, ιδος, ἡ n. pers. *Damaris.* (1) Ac 17:34

Δαμασκηνός, ή, όν adj. pla. *from Damascus; a Damascene* (subst. in NT). (1) 2 Cor 11:32

Δαμασκός, οῦ, ἡ n. pla. *Damascus.* (15)

δάνειον, ου, τό n. (δανίζω) *loan.* (1) Mt 18:27

δανίζω v. (*) aor. ἐδάνισα. *to lend* (money)*; borrow* (mid.). (4)

Δανιήλ, ὁ n. pers. *Daniel.* (1) Mt 24:15

δανιστής, οῦ, ὁ n. (δανίζω) *moneylender, creditor.* (1) Lk 7:41

δαπανάω v. (δαπάνη) fut. δαπανήσω; aor. ἐδαπάνησα. *to spend, spend freely, waste.* (5)

δαπάνη, ης, ἡ n. (*) *cost, expense.* (1) Lk 14:28

Δαυίδ, ὁ n. pers. *David.* (59)

δέ part. (*) postpos. *but, on the other hand, rather; and, as for; now, then, so, that is; at the same time;* δὲ καί *but also, so also, similarly, likewise, too;* μέν... δέ s. μέν. (2792)

δεδώκειν s. δίδωμι (plpf.).

δέησις, εως, ἡ n. (δέομαι) *prayer.* (18)

δεῖ v. (δέω) impers. *it is necessary, one must, one has to; one ought* or *should; had to, should* or *ought to have* (impf.). (101)

δεῖγμα, ατος, τό n. (δείκνυμι) *example.* (1) Jd 7

δειγματίζω v. (δείκνυμι) aor. ἐδειγμάτισα. *to expose, make an example of, disgrace, mock.* (2)

δείκνυμι v. (*) fut. δείξω; aor. ἔδειξα; pf. δέδειχα; aor. pass. ἐδείχθην. *to point out, show, make known; explain, prove.* (33)

δειλία, ας, ἡ n. (δέος) *cowardice.* (1) 2 Ti 1:7

δειλιάω v. (δέος) *to be cowardly, be afraid.* (1) Jn 14:27

δειλός, ή, όν adj. (δέος) *cowardly, timid.* (3)

δεῖνα, ὁ, ἡ, τό n. *so-and-so, somebody; a certain man* (masc. in NT). (1) Mt 26:18

δεινός, ή, όν adj. *fearful, terrible,* ἄλλα δεινά *other afflictions.* (v.l.)

δεινῶς adv. (δέος) *terribly, with hostility.* (2)

δειπνέω v. (δεῖπνον) fut. δειπνήσω; aor. ἐδείπνησα. *to eat, dine.* (4)

δεῖπνον, ου, τό n. (*) *dinner, feast, meal* (main), *supper.* (16)

δεισιδαιμονία, ας, ἡ n. (δαιμόνιον) *religion.* (1) Ac 25:19

δεισιδαίμων, ον adj. (δαιμόνιον) *devout, religious; very devout* (comp. in NT). (1) Ac 17:22

δέκα adj. (*) *ten.* (25)

δεκαοκτώ adj. (δέκα, ὀκτώ) *eighteen.* (2)

δεκαπέντε adj. (δέκα, πέντε) *fifteen.* (3)

Δεκάπολις, εως, ἡ n. pla. *Decapolis.* (3)

δεκατέσσαρες adj. (δέκα, τέσσαρες) *fourteen.* (5)

δέκατος, η, ον adj. (δέκα) *tenth; tenth part, tithe* (subst.). (7)

δεκατόω v. (δέκα) pf. δεδεκάτωκα; pf. pass. δεδεκάτωμαι. *to collect or receive tithes; pay tithes* (pass.). (2)

δεκτός, ή, όν adj. (δέχομαι) *acceptable, welcome; pleasing; favorable.* (5)

δελεάζω v. (δόλος) *to lure, entice.* (3)

δένδρον, ου, τό n. *tree.* (25)

δεξιολάβος, ου, ὁ n. (δεξιός, λαμβάνω) *bowman, slinger, spearman.* (1) Ac 23:23

δεξιός, ά, όν adj. (*) *right* (opp. left); *right hand, right side, the right* (subst.). (54)

δέομαι v. (*) aor. pass. ἐδεήθην. *to ask, request, beg* (somet. = *please*), *pray.* (22)

δέον s. δεῖ (pres. ptc.).

δέος, ους, τό n. (*) *awe, reverence.* (1) Heb 12:28

Δερβαῖος, α, ον adj. pla. *from Derbe; a Derbean* (subst. in NT). (1) Ac 20:4

Δέρβη, ης, ἡ n. pla. *Derbe.* (3)

δέρμα, ατος, τό n. (δέρω) *skin, hide.* (1) Heb 11:37

δερμάτινος, η, ον adj. (δέρω) *(made of) leather.* (2)

δέρω v. (*) aor. ἔδειρα; aor. pass.

ἐδάρην. *to skin; beat, whip, strike* (fig. in NT). (15)

δεσμεύω v. (δέω) *to bind, tie up.* (3)

δέσμη, ης, ἡ n. (δέω) *bundle.* (1) Mt 13:30

δέσμιος, ου, ὁ n. (δέω) *prisoner.* (16)

δεσμός, οῦ, ὁ n. (δέω) *bond, fetter; bonds, imprisonment, prison* (pl.). (18)

δεσμοφύλαξ, ακος, ὁ n. (δέω, φυλάσσω) *jailer, keeper of the prison.* (3)

δεσμωτήριον, ου, τό n. (δέω) *prison, jail.* (4)

δεσμώτης, ου, ὁ n. (δέω) *prisoner.* (2)

δεσπότης, ου, ὁ n. (δέω) *lord, master* (esp. of God and Christ); *owner.* (10)

δεῦρο adv. (*) *come, come here, go; until now,* ἄχρι τοῦ δεῦρο *thus far.* (9)

δεῦτε adv. (δεῦρο) *come, come here, come on* (serves as pl. of δεῦρο). (12)

δευτεραῖος, α, ον adj. (δύο) *on the second day.* (1) Ac 28:13

δευτερόπρωτος, ον adj. *the one after the next.* (v.l.)

δεύτερος, α, ον adj. (δύο) *second; (for) the second time, secondly* (neut. subst. used as adv.). (43)

δέχομαι v. (*) aor. ἐδεξάμην; pf. pass. δέδεγμαι; aor. pass. ἐδέχθην. *to take, receive; grasp; receive* (as a guest), *welcome; put up with, tolerate; be open to, approve, accept.* (56)

δέω v. (*) aor. ἔδησα; pf. δέδεκα; pf. pass. δέδεμαι; aor. pass. ἐδέθην. *to bind, tie; be a prisoner, be imprisoned* (pass.); *tie to; bind* (in marriage); *forbid* (poss.). (43)

δή part. (*) *indeed; now, then, therefore.* (5)

δῆλος, η, ον adj. (*) *clear, plain, evident,* w. ποιέω *to reveal,* w. ὅτι *it is clear that.* (3)

δηλόω v. (δῆλος) fut. δηλώσω; aor. ἐδήλωσα; aor. pass. ἐδηλώθην. *to reveal, make clear, show, give information; explain, clarify, indicate.* (7)

Δημᾶς, ᾶ, ὁ n. pers. *Demas.* (3)

δημηγορέω v. (δῆμος, ἀγοράζω) *to deliver a public address.* (1) Ac 12:21

Δημήτριος, ου ὁ n. pers. *Demetrius*. (3)

δημιουργός, οῦ, ὁ n. (δῆμος, ἔργον) *craftsworker, builder, maker, creator.* (1) Heb 11:10

δῆμος, ου, ὁ n. (*) *people, populace, crowd; (popular) assembly.* (4)

δημόσιος, α, ον adj. (δῆμος) *public; in public, publicly* (δημοσίᾳ used as adv.). (4)

δηνάριον, ου, τό n. Lat. *denarius* (Roman silver coin). (16)

δήποτε adv. *at any time*, w. οἴῳ *whatever.* (v.l.)

δήπου adv. (δή, ποῦ) *of course, surely.* (1) Heb 2:16

δι᾽ = διά before vowels.

διά prep. (*) w. gen. *through, via, out of; throughout, during, at, within, after,* διὰ παντός *always, continually, constantly; by, through, via, with, in, by virtue of* (instr.)*; through, by, by means of, represented by, in the presence of* (pers. agency)*; because of*; w. acc. *through; because of, for the sake of, for, on account of, in the interest of, on the basis of, by, out of;* διὰ τί *why?* διὰ τοῦτο *therefore, because* (w. inf.). (667)

διαβαίνω v. (-βαίνω) aor. διέβην. *to go through, cross, come over.* (3)

διαβάλλω v. (βάλλω) aor. pass. διεβλήθην. *to bring charges, inform.* (1) Lk 16:1

διαβεβαιόομαι v. (-βαίνω) *to speak confidently, insist.* (2)

διαβλέπω v. (βλέπω) fut. διαβλέψω; aor. διέβλεψα. *to look intently; see clearly.* (3)

διάβολος, ον adj. (βάλλω) *slanderous; the devil* (subst.). (37)

διαγγέλλω v. (ἄγγελος) aor. pass. διηγγέλην. *to proclaim, spread the news about; announce, report.* (3)

διαγίνομαι v. (γίνομαι) aor. διεγενόμην. *to pass, elapse* (of time). (3)

διαγινώσκω v. (γινώσκω) fut. διαγνώσομαι. *to determine, examine; decide* or *hear (a case).* (2)

διάγνωσις, εως, ἡ n. (γινώσκω) *decision.* (1) Ac 25:21

διαγογγύζω v. (γογγύζω) *to complain, grumble.* (2)

διαγρηγορέω v. (ἐγείρω) aor. διεγρηγόρησα. *to keep awake; awake fully* (pref.). (1) Lk 9:32

διάγω v. (ἄγω) *to spend one's life, live.* (2)

διαδέχομαι v. (δέχομαι) aor. διεδεξάμην. *to receive in turn, succeed to.* (1) Ac 7:45

διάδημα, ατος, τό n. (δέω) *crown, royal headband, diadem.* (3)

διαδίδωμι v. (δίδωμι) aor. διέδωκα. *to distribute, give.* (4)

διάδοχος, ου, ὁ n. (δέχομαι) *successor.* (1) Ac 24:27

διαζώννυμι v. (ζώννυμι) aor. διέζωσα; pf. pass. διέζωσμαι. *to tie around; put on* (mid.). (3)

διαθήκη, ης, ἡ n. (τίθημι) *last will and testament, will; covenant, ordinance, decree, assurance.* (33)

διαίρεσις, εως, ἡ n. (αἱρέω) *apportionment, division; difference, variety.* (3)

διαιρέω v. (αἱρέω) aor. διεῖλον. *to distribute, divide, apportion.* (2)

διακαθαίρω v. (καθαρός) aor. διεκάθαρα. *to thoroughly purge, clean out.* (1) Lk 3:17

διακαθαρίζω v. (καθαρός) fut. διακαθαριῶ. *to clean out.* (1) Mt 3:12

διακατελέγχομαι v. (ἐλέγχω) *to confute, overwhelm in argument.* (1) Ac 18:28

διακονέω v. (διάκονος) fut. διακονήσω; aor. διηκόνησα; aor. pass. διηκονήθην. *to act as agent, be at one's service, transmit, deliver; perform duties, render assistance, serve, wait on someone at table; help; minister; care for, take care of, look after.* (37)

διακονία, ας, ἡ n. (διάκονος) *mediation, assignment, embassy; service, preparations; office, ministry, responsibility; aid, support; service as assistant* or *deacon.* (34)

διάκονος, ου, ὁ, ἡ n. (*) *agent, intermediary, courier; assistant, attendant, aide, deacon* (masc.), *deaconess* (fem.). (29)

διακόσιοι, αι, α adj. (δύο) *two hundred.* (8)

διακούω v. (ἀκούω) fut. διακούσομαι. *to give a hearing* (in court). (1) Ac 23:35

διακρίνω v. (κρίνω) aor. διέκρινα; aor. pass. διεκρίθην. *to make a distinction, differentiate, distinguish, consider superior; evaluate, judge; decide*; mid. w. aor. pass. *dispute, take issue, criticize; doubt, waver, hesitate.* (19)

διάκρισις, εως, ἡ n. (κρίνω) *distinguishing, differentiation, ability to discriminate; quarrel.* (3)

διακωλύω v. (κωλύω) *to prevent.* (1) Mt 3:14

διαλαλέω v. (λαλέω) *to discuss, talk about.* (2)

διαλέγομαι v. (λέγω) aor. διελεξάμην; aor. pass. διελέχθην. *to converse, discuss, argue; inform, instruct.* (13)

διαλείπω v. (λείπω) aor. διέλιπον. *to stop, cease.* (1) Lk 7:45

διάλεκτος, ου, ἡ n. (λέγω) *language.* (6)

διαλιμπάνω v. *to stop, cease.* (v.l.)

διαλλάσσομαι v. (ἄλλος) aor. pass. διηλλάγην. *to become reconciled.* (1) Mt 5:24

διαλογίζομαι v. (λέγω) *to consider, ponder, reason; argue.* (16)

διαλογισμός, οῦ, ὁ n. (λέγω) *reasoning; thought, opinion, design; dispute, argument; doubt.* (14)

διαλύω v. (λύω) aor. pass. διελύθην. *to disperse, scatter.* (1) Ac 5:36

διαμαρτύρομαι v. (μάρτυς) aor. διεμαρτυράμην. *to testify of, bear witness to; solemnly urge, exhort, warn, charge.* (15)

διαμάχομαι v. (μάχη) *to contend sharply.* (1) Ac 23:9

διαμένω v. (μένω) aor. διέμεινα; pf. διαμεμένηκα. *to remain; live on; remain continually with, stand by.* (5)

διαμερίζω v. (μέρος) aor. διεμέρισα; pf. pass. διαμεμέρισμαι; aor. pass. διεμερίσθην. *to divide, separate; distribute, share; be divided* (pass.). (11)

διαμερισμός, οῦ, ὁ n. (μέρος) *dissension, disunity.* (1) Lk 12:51

διανέμω v. (νόμος) aor. pass. διενεμήθην. *to distribute, spread.* (1) Ac 4:17

διανεύω v. (νεύω) *to give a sign.* (1) Lk 1:22

διανόημα, ατος, τό n. (νίπτω) *thought.* (1) Lk 11:17

διάνοια, ας, ἡ n. (νίπτω) *understanding, intelligence, mind, insight; disposition, thought, attitude; sense, impulse.* (12)

διανοίγω v. (ἀνοίγω) aor. διήνοιξα; pf. pass. διήνοιγμαι; aor. pass. διηνοίχθην. *to open; explain, interpret.* (8)

διανυκτερεύω v. (νύξ) *to spend the whole night.* (1) Lk 6:12

διανύω v. (διά, ἀνά) aor. διήνυσα. *to complete, continue.* (1) Ac 21:7

διαπαρατριβή, ῆς, ἡ n. (τρίβος) *wrangling; frictional wranglings* (pl.). (1) 1 Ti 6:5

διαπεράω v. (πέραν) aor. διεπέρασα. *to cross over.* (6)

διαπλέω v. (πλέω) aor. διέπλευσα. *to sail through.* (1) Ac 27:5

διαπονέομαι v. (πόνος) aor. pass. διεπονήθην. *to be greatly disturbed* or *annoyed.* (2)

διαπορεύομαι v. (πορεύομαι) *to go through, walk through; pass through, go by.* (5)

διαπορέω v. (πορεύομαι) *to be greatly perplexed, be at a loss.* (4)

διαπραγματεύομαι v. (πράσσω) aor. διεπραγματευσάμην. *to gain by trading, earn.* (1) Lk 19:15

διαπρίω v. (πρίζω) *to be infuriated, cut to the quick* (pass. in NT). (2)

διαρπάζω v. (ἁρπάζω) fut. διαρπάσω; aor. διήρπασα. *to plunder thoroughly, rob.* (3)

διαρρήγνυμι and διαρήσσω v. (ῥήγνυμι) aor. διέρρηξα. *to tear, break; tear, burst* (pass.). (5)

διασαφέω v. aor. διεσάφησα. *to explain; tell plainly* or *in detail, report.* (2)

διασείω v. (σείω) aor. διέσεισα. *to extort.* (1) Lk 3:14

διασκορπίζω v. (σκορπίζω) aor. διεσκόρπισα; pf. pass. διεσκόρπισμαι; aor. pass. διεσκορπίσθην. *to scatter, disperse; waste, squander.* (9)

διασπάω v. (σπάω) pf. pass. διέσπασμαι; aor. pass. διεσπάσθην. *to tear apart, tear up.* (2)

διασπείρω v. (σπείρω) aor. pass. διεσπάρην. *to scatter.* (3)

διασπορά, ᾶς, ἡ n. (σπείρω) *dispersion; diaspora.* (3)

διαστέλλω v. (στέλλω) aor. διέστειλα. *to order, give orders* (mid.); *the command* (pass. ptc.). (8)

διάστημα, ατος, τό n. (ἵστημι) *interval.* (1) Ac 5:7

διαστολή, ῆς, ἡ n. (στέλλω) *difference, distinction.* (3)

διαστρέφω v. (στρέφω) aor. διέστρεψα; pf. pass. διέστραμμαι. *to make crooked, pervert, deprave; mislead, turn away.* (7)

διασώζω v. (σώζω) aor. διέσωσα; aor. pass. διεσώθην. *to bring safely through, save, rescue, cure.* (8)

διαταγή, ῆς, ἡ n. (τάσσω) *ordinance, direction.* (2)

διάταγμα, ατος, τό n. (τάσσω) *edict, command.* (1) Heb 11:23

διαταράσσω v. (ταράσσω) aor. pass. διεταράχθην. *to be confused, greatly perplexed* (pass. in NT). (1) Lk 1:29

διατάσσω v. (τάσσω) fut. διατάξω; aor. διέταξα; pf. διατέταχα; pf. pass. διατέταγμαι; aor. pass. διετάχθην, διετάγην. *to make arrangements, arrange; order, command, direct, make a rule, give instructions* (mid. as act.). (16)

διατελέω v. (τέλος) *to continue, remain.* (1) Ac 27:33

διατηρέω v. (τηρέω) *to keep, treasure; keep free of* or *from.* (2)

διατίθημι v. (τίθημι) fut. διαθήσω; aor. διέθηκα. mid. in NT *to decree, ordain; arrange, confer; make a will; the testator* (ptc.). (7)

διατρίβω v. (τρίβος) aor. διέτριψα. *to spend time, stay, remain.* (9)

διατροφή, ῆς, ἡ n. (τρέφω) *support; means of subsistence, food* (pl. in NT). (1) 1 Ti 6:8

διαυγάζω v. (αὐγή) aor. διαυγάψα. *to dawn, break.* (1) 2 Pt 1:19

διαυγής, ές adj. (αὐγή) *transparent, pure.* (1) Rev 21:21

διαφέρω v. (φέρω) aor. διήνεγκα. *to carry through, spread; drive about; differ, be different,* οὐδέν μοι διαφέρει *it makes no difference to me; be worth more than, be superior to; the things that really matter* (neut. pl. ptc.). (13)

διαφεύγω v. (φεύγω) aor. διέφυγον. *to escape.* (1) Ac 27:42

διαφημίζω v. (φημί) aor. διεφήμισα; aor. pass. διεφημίσθην. *to make generally known, spread widely, disseminate, advertise.* (3)

διαφθείρω v. (φθείρω) aor. διέφθειρα; pf. pass. διέφθαρμαι; aor. pass. διεφθάρην. *to spoil, destroy; deprave, ruin.* (6)

διαφθορά, ᾶς, ἡ n. (φθείρω) *destruction, corruption, decay.* (6)

διάφορος, ον adj. (φέρω) *different; outstanding, excellent.* (4)

διαφυλάσσω v. (φυλάσσω) aor. διεφύλαξα. *to guard, protect.* (1) Lk 4:10

διαχειρίζω v. (χείρ) aor. διεχείρισα. *to lay violent hands on, kill, murder* (mid. in NT). (2)

διαχλευάζω v. (χλευάζω) *to jeer, sneer.* (1) Ac 2:13

διαχωρίζω v. (χωρίς) *to separate; be separated, part, go away* (mid. in NT). (1) Lk 9:33

διδακτικός, ή, όν adj. (διδάσκω) *skillful in teaching.* (2)

διδακτός, ή, όν adj. (διδάσκω) *taught, instructed; imparted.* (3)

διδασκαλία, ας, ἡ n. (διδάσκω) *teaching, instruction* (act); *teaching, instruction* (content). (21)

διδάσκαλος, ου, ὁ n. (διδάσκω) *teacher.* (59)

διδάσκω v. (*) fut. διδάξω; aor. ἐδίδαξα; aor. pass. ἐδιδάχθην. *to tell; teach, instruct.* (97)

διδαχή, ῆς, ἡ n. (διδάσκω) *teaching, instruction* (act); *teaching* (content). (30)

δίδραχμον, ου, τό n. (δύο, δράσσομαι) *a double drachma, two-drachma piece* (Greek silver coin). (2)

Δίδυμος, ου, ὁ n. pers. *Didymus* (lit. *twin*). (3)

δίδωμι and διδῶ v. (*) fut. δώσω; aor. ἔδωκα; pf. δέδωκα; pf. pass. δέδομαι; aor. pass. ἐδόθην. *to give, donate; bestow, put; bring; produce, make, cause; entrust; pay, pay out,* λόγον δίδωμι *render account, place, deposit; appoint, make; yield; give up, sacrifice; go, venture somewhere; draw* or *cast lots; grant, allow, permit, order; give back; extend, offer, hold out; take, impose, send, inflict.* (415)

διέβην s. διαβαίνω (2 aor.).

διεγείρω v. (ἐγείρω) aor. διήγειρα; aor. pass. διηγέρθην. *to wake up, arouse, stir up; awaken* (pass.). (6)

διεῖλον s. διαιρέω (2 aor.).

διελέχθην s. διαλέγομαι (aor. pass.).

διενέγκω s. διαφέρω (2 aor. subj.).

διενθυμέομαι v. (θυμός) *to ponder.* (1) Ac 10:19

διέξοδος, ου, ἡ n. (ὁδός) *outlet, way out of town* (used of streets). (1) Mt 22:9

διερμηνευτής, οῦ, ὁ n. (ἑρμηνεύω) *interpreter, translator.* (1) 1 Cor 14:28

διερμηνεύω v. (ἑρμηνεύω) aor. διερμήνευσα. *to translate; explain, interpret.* (6)

διέρχομαι v. (ἔρχομαι) fut. διελεύσομαι; aor. διῆλθον; pf. διελήλυθα. *to go through, spread, go about, travel through, come, go, cross over, go on; penetrate, pierce, pass.* (43)

διερωτάω v. (ἐρωτάω) aor. διηρώτησα. *to ask about, find by inquiry.* (1) Ac 10:17

διεσπάρην s. διασπείρω (2 aor. pass).

διέστειλα s. διαστέλλω (aor.).

διέστην s. διΐστημι (2 aor.).

διέστραμμαι s. διαστρέφω (pf. pass.).

διεταράχθην s. διαταράσσω (aor. pass.).

διετής, ές adj. (δύο, ἔτος) *two years old.* (1) Mt 2:16

διετία, ας, ἡ n. (δύο, ἔτος) *two years.* (2)

διεφθάρην, διέφθαρμαι s. διαφθείρω (2 aor. pass., pf. pass.).

διήγειρα s. διεγείρω (aor.).

διηγέομαι v. (ἄγω) fut. διηγήσομαι; aor. διηγησάμην. *to tell, relate, describe.* (8)

διήγησις, εως, ἡ n. (ἄγω) *narrative, account.* (1) Lk 1:1

διηνεκής, ές adj. (φέρω) *without interruption, always;* εἰς τὸ διηνεκές *for all time, constantly* (all NT uses). (4)

διθάλασσος, ον adj. (δύο, ἅλας) *with the sea on both sides;* τόπος διθάλασσος *a point, reef, sandbank.* (1) Ac 27:41

διϊκνέομαι v. (ἱκανός) *to pierce, penetrate.* (1) Heb 4:12

διΐστημι v. (ἵστημι) aor. διέστησα, διέστην. *to go away, part; go on, sail farther; pass.* (3)

διϊσχυρίζομαι v. (ἰσχύς) *to insist, maintain firmly.* (2)

δικαιοκρισία, ας, ἡ n. (δίκη) *just or fair verdict.* (1) Rom 2:5

δίκαιος, α, ον adj. (δίκη) *upright, just, fair, righteous, honorable, good, innocent; right, equitable* (neut.). (79)

δικαιοσύνη, ης, ἡ n. (δίκη) *justice, equitableness, fairness; righteousness; uprightness, what is right, act of charity, mercy, charitableness.* (92)

δικαιόω v. (δίκη) fut. δικαιώσω; aor. ἐδικαίωσα; pf. pass. δεδικαίωμαι;

aor. pass. ἐδικαιώθην. *to justify, vindicate, treat as just, affirm someone's uprightness;* pass. *be found to be right, be free of charges, be acquitted, be pronounced and treated as righteous; be set free, be made pure; be proved to be right.* (39)

δικαίωμα, ατος, τό n. (δίκη) *regulation, requirement, commandment; righteous deed, sentence of condemnation* (poss.)*; justification, acquittal.* (10)

δικαίως adv. (δίκη) *justly, uprightly, fairly; correctly, rightly, as one ought.* (5)

δικαίωσις, εως, ἡ n. (δίκη) *justification, vindication, acquittal.* (2)

δικαστής, οῦ, ὁ n. (δίκη) *judge.* (2)

δίκη, ης, ἡ n. (*) *penalty, punishment; Justice* (personif.). (3)

δίκτυον, ου, τό n. *fishnet.* (12)

δίλογος, ον adj. (δύο, λέγω) *double-tongued, insincere.* (1) 1 Ti 3:8

διό conj. (ὅς) infer. *therefore, for this reason.* (53)

διοδεύω v. (ὁδός) aor. διώδευσα. *to go* or *travel through; go about.* (2)

Διονύσιος, ου, ὁ n. pers. *Dionysius.* (1) Ac 17:34

διόπερ conj. (ὅς, -πέρ) infer. *therefore, for this very reason.* (2)

διοπετής, ές adj. (Ζεύς, πίπτω) *fallen from heaven.* (1) Ac 19:35

διόρθωμα, ατος, τό n. (ὀρθός) *improvement, reform.* (1) Ac 24:2

διόρθωσις, εως, ἡ n. (ὀρθός) *improvement, reformation, new order.* (1) Heb 9:10

διορύσσω v. (ὀρύσσω) aor. pass. διωρύχθην. *to dig* or *break through, break in.* (4)

Διός s. Ζεύς (gen.).

Διόσκουροι, ων, οἱ n. pers. *the Dioscuri* (twin sons of Zeus). (1) Ac 28:11

διότι conj. (ὅς) *because; therefore; for.* (23)

Διοτρέφης, ους, ὁ n. pers. *Diotrephes.* (1) 3 Jn 9

διπλοῦς, ῆ, οῦν adj. (δύο) *double, twofold,* διπλόω τὰ διπλᾶ *pay back double; twice as much* (neut. comp. as adv.). (4)

διπλόω v. (δύο) aor. ἐδίπλωσα. *to double,* διπλόω τὰ διπλᾶ *pay back double.* (1) Rev 18:6

δίς adv. (δύο) *twice,* ἅπαξ καὶ δίς *again and again, more than once.* (6)

δισμυριάς, άδος, ἡ n. (δύο, μυρίος) *double myriad, twenty thousand.* (1) Rev 9:16

διστάζω v. (δύο) aor. ἐδίστασα. *to doubt, waver; hesitate.* (2)

δίστομος, ον adj. (δύο, στόμα) *double-edged.* (3)

δισχίλιοι, αι, α adj. (δύο, χίλιοι) *two thousand.* (1) Mk 5:13

διϋλίζω v. (ὕλη) *to filter out, strain out.* (1) Mt 23:24

διχάζω v. (δύο) aor. ἐδίχασα. *to divide in two, separate, turn against.* (1) Mt 10:35

διχοστασία, ας, ἡ n. (δύο, ἵστημι) *dissension.* (2)

διχοτομέω v. (δύο, τομός) fut. διχοτομήσω; *to cut in two; punish severely* (poss.). (2)

διψάω v. (δίψος) fut. διψήσω; aor. ἐδίψησα. *to be thirsty; thirst, long for.* (16)

δίψος, ους, τό n. (*) *thirst.* (1) 2 Cor 11:27

δίψυχος, ον adj. (δύο, ψύχω) *double-minded* (lit.)*, doubting, hesitating.* (2)

διωγμός, οῦ, ὁ n. (διώκω) *persecution.* (10)

διώκτης, ου, ὁ n. (διώκω) *persecutor.* (1) 1 Ti 1:13

διώκω v. (*) fut. διώξω; aor. ἐδίωξα; pf. pass. δεδίωγμαι; aor. pass. ἐδιώχθην. *to hasten, run, press on; persecute; drive away, drive out; run after, pursue, strive for, seek after, aspire to.* (45)

δόγμα, ατος, τό n. (δοκέω) *ordinance, decision, command, requirement, decree.* (5)

δογματίζω v. (δοκέω) *to submit to rules and regulations* (pass. in NT). (1) Col 2:20

δοθείς s. δίδωμι (aor. pass. ptc.).

δοῖ s. δίδωμι (2 aor. subj.).

δοκέω v. (*) fut. δόξω; aor. ἔδοξα. *to think, believe, suppose, consider, be disposed; seem, be recognized as, have a reputation, be influential, have the appearance, decide, resolve,* δοκεῖ μοι *it seems to me,* τί σοι (ὑμῖν) δοκεῖ *what do you think?* (62)

δοκιμάζω v. (δέχομαι) fut. δοκιμάσω; aor. ἐδοκίμασα; pf. pass. δεδοκίμασμαι. *to put to the test, examine, try to learn; prove (by testing), approve, accept as proved, see fit, find worthy.* (22)

δοκιμασία, ας, ἡ n. (δέχομαι) *testing, test, examination.* (1) Heb 3:9

δοκιμή, ῆς, ἡ n. (δέχομαι) *test, ordeal, standing a test, character, attitude, proof, evidence.* (7)

δοκίμιον, ου, τό n. (δέχομαι) *testing, means of testing; genuineness* (neut. subst. adj.). (2)

δόκιμος, ον adj. (δέχομαι) *approved, genuine, tried and true; respected, esteemed.* (7)

δοκός, οῦ, ἡ n. *beam of wood.* (6)

δόλιος, α, ον adj. (δόλος) *deceitful, treacherous, dishonest.* (1) 2 Cor 11:13

δολιόω v. (δόλος) *to deceive.* (1) Rom 3:13

δόλος, ου, ὁ n. (*) *deceit, treachery, cunning, something false, underhandedness.* (11)

δολόω v. (δόλος) *to falsify, adulterate.* (1) 2 Cor 4:2

δόμα, ατος, τό n. (δίδωμι) *gift.* (4)

δόξα, ης, ἡ n. (δοκέω) *brightness, radiance, glory, majesty, sublimity, power, might, reflection; greatness, splendor; fame, recognition, renown, honor, prestige, praise; majestic (heavenly) being.* (166)

δοξάζω v. (δοκέω) fut. δοξάσω; aor. ἐδόξασα; pf. pass. δεδόξασμαι; aor. pass. ἐδοξάσθην. *to praise, honor, extol, take pride in; clothe in splendor, glorify.* (61)

Δορκάς, άδος, ἡ n. pers. *Dorcas.* (2)

δόσις, εως, ἡ n. (δίδωμι) *gift; giving.* (2)

δότης, ου, ὁ n. (δίδωμι) *giver, one who gives.* (1) 2 Cor 9:7

Δουβέριος, α, ον adj. pla. *from Doberus; a Doberean* (subst.). (v.l.)

δουλαγωγέω v. (δοῦλος, ἄγω) *to enslave, subjugate.* (1) 1 Cor 9:27

δουλεία, ας, ἡ n. (δοῦλος) *slavery, servility.* (5)

δουλεύω v. (δοῦλος) fut. δουλεύσω; aor. ἐδούλευσα; pf. δεδούλευκα. *to be a slave, be subjected; perform the duties of a slave, serve, obey.* (25)

δούλη, ης, ἡ n. (δοῦλος) *female slave, bondwoman.* (3)

δοῦλος, η, ον adj. (δοῦλος) *slavish, servile, subject.* (2)

δοῦλος, ου, ὁ n. (*) *slave; slave* (fig.), *subject, minister.* (124)

δουλόω v. (δοῦλος) fut. δουλώσω; aor. ἐδούλωσα; pf. pass. δεδούλωμαι; aor. pass. ἐδουλώθην. *to enslave; cause to be like a slave; be a slave, be bound* (pass.). (8)

δοῦναι, δούς s. δίδωμι (2 aor. inf., 2 aor. ptc.).

δοχή, ῆς, ἡ n. (δέχομαι) *reception, banquet.* (2)

δράκων, οντος, ὁ n. *dragon, serpent.* (13)

δράσσομαι v. (*) *to catch, seize.* (1) 1 Cor 3:19

δραχμή, ῆς, ἡ n. (δράσσομαι) *drachma* (Greek silver coin). (3)

δρέπανον, ου, τό n. *sickle.* (8)

δρόμος, ου, ὁ n. (τρέχω) *course; course of life, mission.* (3)

Δρούσιλλα, ης, ἡ n. pers. *Drusilla.* (1) Ac 24:24

δύναμαι v. (*) fut. δυνήσομαι; aor. pass. ἠδυνήθην. *I can, to be able, be capable of, be in a position to, be strong enough.* (210)

δύναμις, εως, ἡ n. (δύναμαι) *power, might, strength, force, capability, the Power* (God), *potency, function,* *effectiveness; ability; deed of power, miracle, wonder; resource, wealth, army; power* (supernatural); *meaning.* (119)

δυναμόω v. (δύναμαι) aor. pass. ἐδυναμώθην. *to enable, endow,* ἐδυναμώθησαν ἀπὸ ἀσθενείας *pass from weakness to strength.* (2)

δυνάστης, ου, ὁ n. (δύναμαι) *ruler, sovereign; court official.* (3)

δυνατέω v. (δύναμαι) *to be effective, be able.* (3)

δυνατός, ή, όν adj. (δύναμαι) *able, capable, powerful, competent, strong, well-versed; possible* (neut.); subst. *Mighty One* (masc.); *power* (neut.). (32)

δύνω v. (*) aor. ἔδυν. *to go down, set* (of the sun). (2)

δύο adj. (*) *two,* εἰς δύο *in two,* ἀνὰ δύο *two apiece,* (ἀνὰ) δύο δύο *two by two,* κατὰ δύο *two at a time.* (135)

δυσβάστακτος, ον adj. (βαστάζω) *hard to bear.* (2)

δυσεντέριον, ου, τό n. (ἐν) *dysentery.* (1) Ac 28:8

δυσερμήνευτος, ον adj. (ἑρμηνεύω) *hard to explain.* (1) Heb 5:11

δύσις, εως, ἡ n. (δύνω) *west* (direction of the setting sun). (1) Mk 16:8+

δύσκολος, ον adj. (κωλύω) *hard, difficult.* (1) Mk 10:24

δυσκόλως adv. (κωλύω) *hardly, with difficulty.* (3)

δυσμή, ῆς, ἡ n. (δύνω) *going down, setting* (of the sun), *west* (pl. in NT). (5)

δυσνόητος, ον adj. (νίπτω) *hard to understand.* (1) 2 Pt 3:16

δυσφημέω v. (φημί) *to slander, defame.* (1) 1 Cor 4:13

δυσφημία, ας, ἡ n. (φημί) *defamation, slander, calumny.* (1) 2 Cor 6:8

δῷ, δώσῃ s. δίδωμι (2 aor. subj. 3 sg., 1 aor. subj. 3 sg.).

δώδεκα adj. (δύο, δέκα) *twelve; the twelve* (subst.). (75)

δωδέκατος, η, ον adj. (δύο, δέκα) *twelfth.* (1) Rev 21:20

δωδεκάφυλος, ον adj. (δύο, δέκα, φύω) *of twelve tribes; the twelve tribes* (subst. in NT). (1) Ac 26:7

δῷη, δώῃ s. δίδωμι (2 aor. opt., 2 aor. subj.).

δῶμα, ατος, τό n. (*) *roof, housetop.* (7)

δωρεά, ᾶς, ἡ n. (δίδωμι) *gift, bounty.* (11)

δωρεάν adv. (δίδωμι) *as a gift, without payment; undeservedly, without reason; in vain, to no purpose.* (9)

δωρέομαι v. (δίδωμι) aor. ἐδωρησάμην; pf. pass. δεδώρημαι. *to present, bestow, give.* (3)

δώρημα, ατος, τό n. (δίδωμι) *gift, present.* (2)

δῶρον, ου, τό n. (δίδωμι) *gift, present, offering.* (19)

δωροφορία, ας, ἡ n. *bringing of a gift.* (v.l.)

E

ἔα interj. (ἐάω) *ah! ha!* (poss. pres. impv. of ἐάω *let alone!*). (1) Lk 4:34

ἐάν conj. (εἰ, ἄν) *if,* ἐὰν καί *even if,* ἐὰν δὲ καί *but if,* ἐὰν μή *unless,* ἐάν τε *whether; whenever, when; ever* (instead of ἄν). (351)

ἐάνπερ conj. (εἰ, ἄν, -πέρ) *if indeed, if only, supposing that.* (3)

ἑαυτοῦ, ῆς, οῦ pron. (αὐτός) reflex. *self (oneself, himself, herself, itself); each other, one another; his, her.* (319)

ἐάω v. (*) fut. ἐάσω; aor. εἴασα. *to let, permit; let go, leave alone,* ἐᾶτε ἕως τούτου *no more of this; leave.* (11)

ἑβδομήκοντα adj. (ἑπτά) *seventy.* (5)

ἑβδομηκοντάκις adv. (ἑπτά) *seventy times,* ἑβδομηκοντάκις ἑπτά *seventy-seven times.* (1) Mt 18:22

ἕβδομος, η, ον adj. (ἑπτά) *seventh; the seventh* (subst.). (9)

ἐβεβλήμην s. βάλλω (plpf. pass.).

Ἔβερ, ὁ n. pers. *Eber.* (1) Lk 3:35

Ἑβραϊκός, ή, όν adj. oth. *Hebrew.* (v.l.)

Ἑβραῖος, ου, ὁ n. oth. *a Hebrew; a Hebrew* or *Aramaic-speaking Israelite.* (4)

Ἑβραΐς, ΐδος, ἡ n. oth. *Hebrew language (Aramaic).* (3)

Ἑβραϊστί adv. oth. *in Hebrew or Aramaic.* (7)

ἐγγίζω v. (ἐγγύς) fut. ἐγγιῶ; aor. ἤγγισα; pf. ἤγγικα. *to draw near, come near, approach (of space or time).* (42)

ἐγγράφω v. (γράφω) pf. pass. ἐγγέγραμμαι. *to write in, record; write down, inscribe.* (3)

ἔγγυος, ου, ὁ n. *guarantee.* (1) Heb 7:22

ἐγγύς adv. (*) *near, close to* (of space and time); *near, close to* (adv. prep. w. gen. and dat.). (31)

ἐγεγόνειν s. γίνομαι (plpf.).

ἐγείρω v. (*) fut. ἐγερῶ; aor. ἤγειρα; pf. pass. ἐγήγερμαι; aor. pass. ἠγέρθην. *to wake, rouse; raise, help to rise; raise up, bring into being, give, cause; raise up (the dead); raise up (from sickness); restore, erect; lift up* or *out;* pass. *wake up, awaken; rise, get up; be raised (from the dead), rise; rise up in arms; appear;* impv. *get up! come!* (144)

ἔγερσις, εως, ἡ n. (ἐγείρω) *resurrection.* (1) Mt 27:53

ἐγκάθετος, ον adj. (-ἵημι) *hired to lie in wait; spy* (subst. in NT). (1) Lk 20:20

ἐγκαίνια, ων, τά n. (καινός) *Festival of Rededication, Feast of Lights, Hanukkah.* (1) Jn 10:22

ἐγκαινίζω v. (καινός) aor. ἐνεκαίνισα; pf. pass. ἐγκεκαίνισμαι. *to ratify, inaugurate, dedicate, open.* (2)

ἐγκακέω v. (κακός) aor. ἐνεκάκησα. *to lose enthusiasm* or *heart, be discouraged, be disappointed; be afraid.* (6)

ἐγκαλέω v. (καλέω) fut. ἐγκαλέσω. *to accuse, bring charges against.* (7)

ἐγκαταλείπω v. (λείπω) fut. ἐγκαταλείψω; aor. ἐγκατέλιπον; aor. pass. ἐγκατελείφθην. *to leave* (of posterity); *forsake, abandon, desert, cease, allow to remain.* (10)

ἐγκατοικέω v. (οἶκος) *to live, reside.* (1) 2 Pt 2:8

ἐγκαυχάομαι v. (καυχάομαι) *to boast.* (1) 2 Th 1:4

ἐγκεντρίζω v. (κέντρον) aor. ἐνεκέντρισα; aor. pass. ἐνεκεντρίσθην. *to graft.* (6)

ἔγκλημα, ατος, τό n. (καλέω) *charge, accusation.* (2)

ἐγκομβόομαι v. aor. ἐνεκομβωσάμην. *to put on, clothe oneself*. (1) 1 Pt 5:5

ἐγκοπή, ῆς, ἡ n. (κόπτω) *hindrance*. (1) 1 Cor 9:12

ἐγκόπτω v. (κόπτω) aor. ἐνέκοψα. *to hinder, thwart, prevent, weary*. (5)

ἐγκράτεια, ας, ἡ n. (κράτος) *self-control*. (4)

ἐγκρατεύομαι v. (κράτος) *to control oneself, abstain, exercise self-control*. (2)

ἐγκρατής, ές adj. (κράτος) *self-controlled, disciplined*. (1) Tit 1:8

ἐγκρίνω v. (κρίνω) aor. ἐνέκρινα. *to class*. (1) 2 Cor 10:12

ἐγκρύπτω v. (κρύπτω) aor. ἐνέκρυψα. *to hide, put into*. (2)

ἔγκυος, ον adj. (κύμα) *pregnant*. (1) Lk 2:5

ἔγνωκα, ἔγνων, ἔγνωσμαι s. γινώσκω (pf., 2 aor., pf. pass.).

ἐγχρίω v. (χρίω) aor. ἐνέχρισα. *to smear on, anoint*. (1) Rev 3:18

ἐγώ, ἐμοῦ; ἡμεῖς, ἡμῶν pron. (*) encl. forms μου, μοι, με *I; we*; τί ἐμοὶ καὶ σοί *what have I to do with you? leave me alone!* (2666)

ἐδαφίζω v. (ἔδαφος) fut. ἐδαφιῶ. *to dash or raze to the ground*. (1) Lk 19:44

ἔδαφος, ους, τό n. (*) *ground*. (1) Ac 22:7

ἑδραῖος, α, ον adj. (*) *firm, steadfast*. (3)

ἑδραίωμα, ατος, τό n. (ἑδραῖος) *foundation, mainstay* (poss.). (1) 1 Ti 3:15

ἔδραμον s. τρέχω (2 aor.).

Ἐζεκίας, ου, ὁ n. pers. *Hezekiah*. (2)

ἔζην s. ζάω (impf.).

ἐθελοθρησκία, ας, ἡ n. (θέλω, θρησκός) *self-made religion, idiosyncratic religion, would-be religion* (poss.). (1) Col 2:23

ἐθέμην, ἔθηκα s. τίθημι (2 aor. mid., 1 aor.).

ἐθίζω v. (ἔθος) pf. pass. εἴθισμαι. *to accustom; the custom* (pf. pass. ptc.). (1) Lk 2:27

ἐθνάρχης, ου, ὁ n. (ἔθνος, ἄρχω) *ethnic head* or *leader*. (1) 2 Cor 11:32

ἐθνικός, ή, όν adj. (ἔθνος) *unbelieving; a non-Israelite, a gentile* (subst. in NT). (4)

ἐθνικῶς adv. (ἔθνος) *in the manner of the nations, like (the rest of) the world, like a gentile*. (1) Gal 2:14

ἔθνος, ους, τό n. (*) *nation, people*; (τὰ) ἔθνη *the nations, gentiles, unbelievers, non-Israelite* or *gentile Christians*. (162)

ἔθος, ους, τό n. (*) *habit, usage; custom*. (12)

ἔθρεψα s. τρέφω (aor.).

εἰ part. (*) *if; that; since; if only, certainly not; whether*; εἰ ἄρα *if indeed, in the hope that*, εἴ γε *if indeed*, εἰ δὲ καί *but if*, εἰ δὲ μή (γε) *if not, otherwise*, εἰ καί *even if, although*, εἰ μὲν γάρ *for if*, εἰ μὲν οὖ *if then*, εἰ μέντοι *if on the other hand*, εἰ μή *but, in general*, εἰ μήτι *unless indeed*, εἰ οὖν *if therefore*, εἰ δέ που *if perchance*, εἴ πως *if perhaps*; εἴ τις (τι) *whoever (whatever)*. (502)

εἴασα s. ἐάω (aor.).

εἶδα s. ὁράω (aor.).

εἰδέα, ας, ἡ n. (εἶδος) *appearance, face* (poss.). (1) Mt 28:3

εἰδέναι, εἰδήσω s. οἶδα (2 pf. inf., fut.).

εἶδος, ους, τό n. (*) *form, outward appearance; kind; seeing, sight*. (5)

εἰδυῖα, εἰδῶ s. οἶδα (2 pf. ptc. fem., 2 pf. subj.).

εἰδωλεῖον, ου, τό n. (εἶδος) *idol's temple*. (1) 1 Cor 8:10

εἰδωλόθυτος, ον adj. (εἶδος, θύω) *food sacrificed to idols, sacrificial meat* (subst. in NT). (9)

εἰδωλολάτρης, ου, ὁ n. (εἶδος, λατρεύω) *image-worshiper, idolater*. (7)

εἰδωλολατρία, ας, ἡ n. (εἶδος, λατρεύω) *image-worship, idolatry*. (4)

εἴδωλον, ου, τό n. (εἶδος) *image, representation; idol, imaged deity*. (11)

εἰδώς s. οἶδα (2 pf. ptc.).

εἴθισμαι s. ἐθίζω (pf. pass.).

εἰκῇ adv. *without cause; to no avail; to no purpose; without due consideration, in a haphazard manner.* (6)

εἴκοσι adj. *twenty.* (11)

εἴκω v. (*) aor. εἶξα. *to yield.* (1) Gal 2:5

εἰκών, όνος, ἡ n. (*) *likeness, portrait, image; living image; form, appearance.* (23)

εἰλάμην s. αἱρέω (1 aor. mid.).

εἰλικρίνεια, ας, ἡ n. (ἥλιος, κρίνω) *sincerity, purity of motive.* (3)

εἰλικρινής, ές adj. (ἥλιος, κρίνω) *pure, sincere.* (2)

εἷλκον, εἵλκυσα s. ἕλκω (impf., aor.).

εἵλκωμαι s. ἑλκόω (pf. pass.).

εἰμί v. (*) fut. ἔσομαι. encl. forms εἰμι, ἐστι(ν), ἐσμεν, ἐστε, εἰσι(ν) *to be, exist, be on hand, be present, come, be available,* ἦν (ἔστι, εἰσί) *there was (is, are); be (copula), mean; be* (w. ref. to place, people, condition, or time); *live; be* (a certain time); *take place, occur, become, be in; it is possible, one can* (impers.); *be or come from; belong to; rely on, do with; an aux.* w. a ptc. (2462)

εἵνεκεν = ἕνεκα.

εἶξα s. εἴκω (aor.).

εἶπα, εἶπον s. λέγω (1 aor., 2 aor.).

εἴπερ part. (εἰ, -πέρ) *if indeed, if after all, since.* (6)

εἰργασάμην, εἴγασμαι s. ἐργάζομαι (aor. mid., pf. pass.).

εἴρηκα, εἰρήκειν, εἴρημαι s. λέγω (pf., plpf., pf. pass.).

εἰρηνεύω v. (εἰρήνη) *to keep the peace.* (4)

εἰρήνη, ης, ἡ n. (*) *peace, harmony, good order; peace* (greeting). (92)

εἰρηνικός, ή, όν adj. (εἰρήνη) *peaceable, peaceful.* (2)

εἰρηνοποιέω v. (εἰρήνη, ποιέω) aor. εἰρηνοποίησα. *to make peace.* (1) Col 1:20

εἰρηνοποιός, ον adj. (εἰρήνη, ποιέω) *making peace; peacemaker* (subst. in NT). (1) Mt 5:9

εἰς prep. (*) w. acc. *into, in, toward, to, on, near, among, at; until, throughout; up to,* εἰς τέλος *completely; against, as, for, so that, in order to,* εἰς τοῦτο *for this reason; with respect to, with reference to; by;* somet. untransl. w. pred. nom. and acc.; *with; in the face of.* (1767)

εἷς, μία, ἕν adj. (*) *one; one* (subst.); *one (and the same), (a) single, only one, alone; a, someone, anyone* (= τὶς); *the first;* εἷς…εἷς *one…the other,* ὁ εἷς…ὁ ἕτερος *the one…the other,* εἷς ἕκαστος *every single,* καθ᾽ ἕν *one by one.* (345)

εἰσάγω v. (ἄγω) aor. εἰσήγαγον. *to bring in* or *into, lead in* or *into.* (11)

εἰσακούω v. (ἀκούω) fut. εἰσακούσομαι; aor. pass. εἰσηκούσθην. *to obey; hear.* (5)

εἰσδέχομαι v. (δέχομαι) fut. εἰσδέξομαι. *to receive, welcome.* (1) 2 Cor 6:17

εἴσειμι v. (-εἶμι) *to go in* or *into.* (4)

εἰσέρχομαι v. (ἔρχομαι) fut. εἰσελεύσομαι; aor. εἰσῆλθον; pf. εἰσελήλυθα. *to enter, come* or *go (into, in, or to); enter into, share in, come to enjoy, attain; happen, develop, arise, reach into.* (194)

εἰσῄειν s. εἴσειμι (impf.)

εἰσήνεγκα, εἰσήνεγκον s. εἰσφέρω (1 aor., 2 aor.).

εἰσιέναι s. εἴσειμι (pres. inf.).

εἰσκαλέομαι v. (καλέω) aor. εἰσεκαλεσάμην. *to invite in.* (1) Ac 10:23

εἴσοδος, ου, ἡ n. (ὁδός) *entrance, access, coming; acceptance, welcome.* (5)

εἰσπηδάω v. (-πηδάω) aor. εἰσεπήδησα. *to leap in, rush in.* (1) Ac 16:29

εἰσπορεύομαι v. (πορεύομαι) *to go into* or *in, enter, come to.* (18)

εἰστήκειν s. ἵστημι (plpf.).

εἰστρέχω v. (τρέχω) aor. εἰσέδραμον. *to run in.* (1) Ac 12:14

εἰσφέρω v. (φέρω) aor. εἰσήνεγκα, εἰσήνεγκον. *to bring in* or *into, drag in; lead into, bring to.* (8)

εἶτα adv. (*) *then, next; furthermore.* (15)

εἴτε part. (εἰ, τέ) *if, whether;* εἴτε...
εἴτε *if... if, whether... or.* (65)

εἶχον s. ἔχω (impf.).

εἴωθα v. pf. εἴωθα. pf. used as pres. *to
be accustomed,* τὸ εἰωθός *custom.* (4)

εἴων s. ἐάω (impf.).

ἐκ prep. (*) w. gen. *from, out of, away
from; to, at, on; of, by, because of, by
reason of, as a result of, with, by means
of, according to, in accordance with,
on the basis of; of* (as partitive gen.),
for (as gen. of price); *from, for* (temp.);
against. (914)

ἕκαστος, η, ον pron. (*) distr. *each,
every* (adj.); *each one, every one*
(subst.). (82)

ἑκάστοτε adv. (ἕκαστος, ὅς, τέ) *at any
time, always.* (1) 2 Pt 1:15

ἑκατόν adj. (*) *one hundred,* κατὰ
ἑκατόν *by hundreds.* (17)

ἑκατονταετής, ές adj. (ἑκατόν, ἔτος) *a
hundred years old.* (1) Rom 4:19

ἑκατονταπλασίων, ον adj. (ἑκατόν) *a
hundred times as much, a hundredfold*
(neut. pl. as adv.). (3)

ἑκατοντάρχης and ἑκατόνταρχος,
ου, ὁ n. (ἑκατόν, ἄρχω) *centurion,
captain.* (20)

ἐκβαίνω v. (-βαίνω) aor. ἐξέβην. *to go
out, come from.* (1) Heb 11:15

ἐκβάλλω v. (βάλλω) fut. ἐκβαλῶ; aor.
ἐξέβαλον; pf. ἐκβέβληκα; aor. pass.
ἐξεβλήθην. *to drive out, expel, throw
out, disdain, spurn; send out or away,
release, bring out, lead out; take out,
remove; disregard, leave out; cause to
happen, bring, lead.* (81)

ἔκβασις, εως, ἡ n. (-βαίνω) *end; outcome; way out.* (2)

ἐκβολή, ῆς, ἡ n. (βάλλω) *jettisoning,
throwing out.* (1) Ac 27:18

ἔκγονος, ον adj. (γίνομαι) *born of; descendants, grandchildren* (pl. subst. in
NT). (1) 1 Ti 5:4

ἐκδαπανάω v. (δαπάνη) aor. pass.
ἐξεδαπανήθην. *to spend, exhaust.* (1)
2 Cor 12:15

ἐκδέχομαι v. (δέχομαι) *to expect, wait.*
(6)

ἔκδηλος, ον adj. (δῆλος) *quite evident,
plain.* (1) 2 Ti 3:9

ἐκδημέω v. (δῆμος) aor. ἐξεδήμησα. *to
leave, get away; be away.* (3)

ἐκδίδωμι v. (δίδωμι) fut. ἐκδώσω; aor.
ἐξέδωκα. *to let out for hire, lease* (mid.
in NT). (4)

ἐκδιηγέομαι v. (ἄγω) *to tell (in detail).*
(2)

ἐκδικέω v. (δίκη) fut. ἐκδικήσω; aor.
ἐξεδίκησα. *to grant justice, avenge;
punish, take vengeance for.* (6)

ἐκδίκησις, εως, ἡ n. (δίκη) *giving of
justice; vengeance; punishment.* (9)

ἔκδικος, ον adj. (δίκη) *punishing; one
who punishes* (subst. in NT). (2)

ἐκδιώκω v. (διώκω) aor. ἐξεδίωξα. *to
drive out; persecute severely.* (1) 1 Th
2:15

ἔκδοτος, ον adj. (δίδωμι) *given up,
delivered up.* (1) Ac 2:23

ἐκδοχή, ῆς, ἡ n. (δέχομαι) *expectation.*
(1) Heb 10:27

ἐκδύω v. (δύνω) aor. ἐξέδυσα. *to strip,
take off; strip or undress oneself* (mid.).
(6)

ἐκεῖ adv. (*) *there, in that place; to that
place.* (105)

ἐκεῖθεν adv. (ἐκεῖ) *from there.* (37)

ἐκεῖνος, η, ο pron. (ἐκεῖ) demonstr. *that
person or thing, that, he, she, it* (abs.);
that (as adj.); ἐκείνης *there* (adv. gen.).
(265)

ἐκεῖσε adv. (ἐκεῖ) *there, to that place;
at that place.* (2)

ἐκέκραξα s. κράζω (aor.).

ἐκέρασα s. κεράννυμι (aor.).

ἐκέρδησα s. κερδαίνω (aor.).

ἐκζητέω v. (ζητέω) aor. ἐξεζήτησα;
aor. pass. ἐξεζητήθην. *to seek out,
search for; look for, seek, charge with.*
(7)

ἐκζήτησις, εως, ἡ n. (ζητέω) *useless
speculation.* (1) 1 Ti 1:4

ἐκθαμβέω v. (θάμβος) aor. pass. ἐξε-
θαμβήθην. *to be very excited, be*

overwhelmed, be alarmed, be distressed (pass. in NT). (4)

ἔκθαμβος, ον adj. (θάμβος) utterly astonished. (1) Ac 3:11

ἐκθαυμάζω v. (θαυμάζω) to be utterly amazed. (1) Mk 12:17

ἔκθετος, ον adj. (τίθημι) exposed, abandoned. (1) Ac 7:19

ἐκκαθαίρω v. (καθαρός) aor. ἐξεκάθαρα. to clean out; cleanse. (2)

ἐκκαίω v. (καίω) aor. pass. ἐξεκαύθην. be inflamed (pass. in NT). (1) Rom 1: 27

ἐκκεντέω v. (κέντρον) aor. ἐξεκέντησα. to pierce. (2)

ἐκκλάω v. (κλάω) aor. pass. ἐξεκλάσθην. to break off. (3)

ἐκκλείω v. (κλείω) aor. ἐξέκλεισα; aor. pass. ἐξεκλείσθην. to shut out; exclude. (2)

ἐκκλησία, ας, ἡ n. (καλέω) assembly; gathering; community, congregation, church (local and universal). (114)

ἐκκλίνω v. (κλίνω) aor. ἐξέκλινα. to steer clear of, stay away from, avoid, turn aside from; cease. (3)

ἐκκολυμβάω v. (κολυμβάω) aor. ἐξεκολύμβησα. to swim away. (1) Ac 27: 42

ἐκκομίζω v. (κόσμος) to carry out (for burial). (1) Lk 7:12

ἐκκόπτω v. (κόπτω) fut. ἐκκόψω; aor. ἐξέκοψα; aor. pass. ἐξεκόπην. to cut off or down; exterminate, remove. (10)

ἐκκρεμάννυμι v. (κρεμάννυμι) to hang on, hang upon (mid. in NT). (1) Lk 19:48

ἐκλαλέω v. (λαλέω) aor. ἐξελάλησα. to tell. (1) Ac 23:22

ἐκλάμπω v. (λάμπω) fut. ἐκλάμψω. to shine (out). (1) Mt 13:43

ἐκλανθάνομαι v. (λανθάνω) pf. pass. ἐκλέλησμαι. to forget (altogether). (1) Heb 12:5

ἐκλέγομαι v. (λέγω) aor. ἐξελεξάμην; pf. pass. ἐκλέλεγμαι. to choose; select. (22)

ἐκλείπω v. (λείπω) fut. ἐκλείψω; aor. ἐξέλιπον. to fail, give out, be gone; depart; die out, cease to shine. (4)

ἐκλεκτός, ή, όν adj. (λέγω) chosen; elect; choice, excellent, picked, elite. (22)

ἐκλέλεγμαι s. ἐκλέγομαι (pf. pass.).

ἐκλέλησμαι s. ἐκλανθάνομαι (pf. pass.).

ἐκλήθην s. καλέω (aor. pass.).

ἐκλογή, ῆς, ἡ n. (λέγω) selection, choice, election, choosing; what is chosen or selected. (7)

ἐκλύω v. (λύω) aor. pass. ἐξελύθην. to become weary, give out, lose heart (pass. in NT). (5)

ἐκμάσσω v. (μαστιγόω) aor. ἐξέμαξα. to wipe, dry. (5)

ἐκμυκτηρίζω v. (μυκτηρίζω) to ridicule, sneer. (2)

ἐκνεύω v. (νεύω) aor. ἐξένευσα. to turn aside, withdraw. (1) Jn 5:13

ἐκνήφω v. (νήφω) aor. ἐξένηψα. to come to one's senses. (1) 1 Cor 15:34

ἐκούσιος, α, ον adj. (ἐκών) voluntary, κατὰ ἑκούσιον of one's own free will. (1) Phlm 14

ἐκουσίως adv. (ἑκών) willingly, deliberately, intentionally. (2)

ἔκπαλαι adv. (πάλαι) long ago; for a long time. (2)

ἐκπειράζω v. (πεῖρα) fut. ἐκπειράσω. to test; entrap; tempt. (4)

ἐκπέμπω v. (πέμπω) aor. ἐξέπεμψα; aor. pass. ἐξεπέμφθην. to send out, send away. (2)

ἐκπέπτωκα s. ἐκπίπτω (pf.).

ἐκπερισσῶς adv. (ἐκ, περί) extraordinarily, with great emphasis. (1) Mk 14:31

ἐκπεσεῖν s. ἐκπίπτω (2 aor. inf.).

ἐκπετάννυμι v. (πέτομαι) aor. ἐξεπέτασα. to spread or hold out. (1) Rom 10:21

ἐκπηδάω v. (-πηδάω) aor. ἐξεπήδησα. to rush out. (1) Ac 14:14

ἐκπίπτω v. (πίπτω) aor. ἐξέπεσον, ἐξέπεσα; pf. ἐκπέπτωκα. to fall; drift off *course, run aground; lose; fail, weaken.* (10)

ἐκπλέω v. (πλέω) aor. ἐξέπλευσα. *to sail away* or *back.* (3)

ἐκπληρόω v. (πληρόω) pf. ἐκπεπλήρωκα. *to fulfill.* (1) Ac 13:33

ἐκπλήρωσις, εως, ἡ n. (πληρόω) *completion.* (1) Ac 21:26

ἐκπλήσσω v. (πλήσσω) aor. pass. ἐξεπλάγην. *to be amazed, be overwhelmed, be shocked, be dumbfounded* (pass. in NT). (13)

ἐκπνέω v. (πνέω) aor. ἐξέπνευσα. *to expire, die.* (3)

ἐκπορεύομαι v. (πορεύομαι) fut. ἐκπορεύσομαι. *to go, come* or *go out, proceed, set out; flow out, project, spread.* (33)

ἐκπορνεύω v. (πόρνη) aor. ἐξεπόρνευσα. *to engage in illicit sex, debauchery.* (1) Jd 7

ἐκπτύω v. (πτύω) aor. ἐξέπτυσα. *to disdain.* (1) Gal 4:14

ἐκριζόω v. (ρίζα) aor. ἐξερίζωσα; aor. pass. ἐξεριζώθην. *to uproot.* (4)

ἔκστασις, εως, ἡ n. (ἵστημι) *amazement, astonishment; trance, ecstasy.* (7)

ἐκστρέφω v. (στρέφω) pf. pass. ἐξέστραμμαι. *to be perverted* (pass. in NT). (1) Tit 3:11

ἐκσῴζω v. *to bring safely.* (v.l.)

ἐκταράσσω v. (ταράσσω) *to agitate, cause trouble to, throw into confusion.* (1) Ac 16:20

ἐκτείνω v. (-τείνω) fut. ἐκτενῶ; aor. ἐξέτεινα. *to stretch out, put out, extend, lay on.* (16)

ἐκτελέω v. (τέλος) aor. ἐξετέλεσα. *to finish.* (2)

ἐκτένεια, ας, ἡ n. (-τείνω) *perseverance, earnestness.* (1) Ac 26:7

ἐκτενής, ές adj. (-τείνω) *eager, earnest, constant.* (1) 1 Pt 4:8

ἐκτενῶς adv. (-τείνω) *eagerly, fervently, constantly;* ἐκτενέστερον *very fervently* (neut. comp. of ἐκτενής). (3)

ἐκτίθημι v. (τίθημι) aor. ἐξέθηκα; aor. pass. ἐξετέθην. *to expose, abandon; explain* (mid.). (4)

ἐκτινάσσω v. (-τείνω) aor. ἐξετίναξα. *to shake off; shake out.* (4)

ἕκτος, η, ον adj. (ἕξ) *sixth.* (14)

ἐκτός adv. (ἐκ) τὸ ἐκτός *the outside;* ἐκτὸς εἰ μή *except, unless;* adv. prep. w. gen. *outside; except.* (8)

ἐκτρέπω v. (τροπή) aor. pass. ἐξετράπην. pass. in NT *to turn, turn away, avoid; be dislocated.* (5)

ἐκτρέφω v. (τρέφω) *to nourish; bring up, rear.* (2)

ἔκτρωμα, ατος, τό n. (τραῦμα) *untimely birth, miscarriage.* (1) 1 Cor 15:8

ἐκφέρω v. (φέρω) fut. ἐξοίσω; aor. ἐξήνεγκα, ἐξήνεγκον. *to carry* or *bring out; bring* or *lead out; produce.* (8)

ἐκφεύγω v. (φεύγω) fut. ἐκφεύξομαι; aor. ἐξέφυγον; pf. ἐκπέφευγα. *to run away; escape.* (8)

ἐκφοβέω v. (φόβος) *to frighten, terrify.* (1) 2 Cor 10:9

ἔκφοβος, ον adj. (φόβος) *terrified.* (2)

ἐκφύω v. (φύω) *to put forth.* (2)

ἐκχέω v. (-χέω) fut. ἐκχεῶ; aor. ἐξέχεα; pf. pass. ἐκκέχυμαι; aor. pass. ἐξεχύθην. *to pour out* (lit. and fig.), *shed, spill, scatter; give oneself to, dedicate oneself* (pass.). (27)

ἐκχωρέω v. (χωρέω) *to go out, go away, depart.* (1) Lk 21:21

ἐκψύχω v. (ψύχω) aor. ἐξέψυξα. *to breathe one's last, die.* (3)

ἑκών, οῦσα, όν adj. (*) *willing(ly), glad(ly), of one's own free will.* (2)

ἔλαθον s. λανθάνω (2 aor.).

ἐλαία, ας, ἡ n. (*) *olive tree,* τὸ Ὄρος τῶν Ἐλαιῶν *the Mount of Olives; olive.* (13)

ἔλαιον, ου, τό n. (ἐλαία) *olive oil, oil; olive orchard.* (11)

ἐλαιών, ῶνος, ὁ n. (ἐλαία) *olive grove, olive orchard,* ἀπὸ ὄρους τοῦ καλουμένου Ἐλαιῶνος *from the hill called The Olive Grove* (= *the Mount of Olives*). (3)

Ἐλαμίτης, ου, ὁ n. pla. *an Elamite*. (1) Ac 2:9

ἐλάσσων, ον adj. (*) *less; inferior; younger*. (4)

ἐλαττονέω v. (ἐλάσσων) aor. ἠλαττόνησα. *to have less, have too little*. (1) 2 Cor 8:15

ἐλαττόω v. (ἐλάσσων) aor. ἠλάττωσα; pf. pass. ἠλάττωμαι. *to make lower, inferior; diminish, become less* (pass.). (3)

ἐλάττων alt. form of ἐλάσσων.

ἐλαύνω v. (*) pf. ἐλήλακα. *to drive, advance, row*. (5)

ἐλαφρία, ας, ἡ n. (ἐλαφρός) *vacillation, levity*. (1) 2 Cor 1:17

ἐλαφρός, ά, όν adj. (*) *light, insignificant*. (2)

ἐλάχιστος, η, ον adj. (ἐλάσσων) *least, smallest, unimportant; very least* (comp.); *very small; insignificant, trivial, very little*. (14)

ἔλαχον s. λαγχάνω (2 aor.).

Ἐλεάζαρ, ὁ n. pers. *Eleazar*. (2)

ἐλεάω v. (ἔλεος) *to have mercy on*. (3)

ἐλεγμός, οῦ, ὁ n. (ἐλέγχω) *reproach, rebuke, reproof*. (1) 2 Ti 3:16

ἔλεγξις, εως, ἡ n. (ἐλέγχω) *reproach, rebuke, reproof*. (1) 2 Pt 2:16

ἔλεγχος, ου, ὁ n. (ἐλέγχω) *proof, proving, conviction*. (1) Heb 11:1

ἐλέγχω v. (*) fut. ἐλέγξω; aor. ἤλεγξα; aor. pass. ἠλέγχθην. *to bring to light, expose, set forth; convict, convince; reprove, correct, show one's fault; punish, discipline*. (17)

ἐλεεινός, ή, όν adj. (ἔλεος) *miserable, pitiable*. (2)

ἐλεέω v. (ἔλεος) fut. ἐλεήσω; aor. ἠλέησα; pf. pass. ἠλέημαι; aor. pass. ἠλεήθην. *to have compassion, have mercy, have pity, show mercy, help, do acts of compassion; find mercy, be shown mercy* (pass.). (29)

ἐλεημοσύνη, ης, ἡ n. (ἔλεος) *alms (giving), charitable giving; alms*. (13)

ἐλεήμων, ον adj. (ἔλεος) *merciful, sympathetic, compassionate*. (2)

ἔλεος, ους, τό n. (*) *mercy, compassion, pity, clemency, good, kindness*. (27)

ἐλευθερία, ας, ἡ n. (ἐλεύθερος) *freedom, liberty*. (11)

ἐλεύθερος, α, ον adj. (*) *free; free person* (subst.); *independent, not bound, exempt*. (23)

ἐλευθερόω v. (ἐλεύθερος) fut. ἐλευθερώσω; aor. ἠλευθέρωσα; aor. pass. ἠλευθερώθην. *to free, set free*. (7)

ἔλευσις, εως, ἡ n. (ἔρχομαι) *coming, arrival*. (1) Ac 7:52

ἐλεύσομαι s. ἔρχομαι (fut. mid.).

ἐλεφάντινος, η, ον adj. *(made) of ivory*. (1) Rev 18:12

ἐλήλακα s. ἐλαύνω (pf.).

ἐλήλυθα, ἐλθεῖν s. ἔρχομαι (2 pf., 2 aor. inf.).

Ἐλιακίμ, ὁ n. pers. *Eliakim*. (3)

ἔλιγμα, ατος, τό n. *package, roll*. (v.l.)

Ἐλιέζερ, ὁ n. pers. *Eliezer*. (1) Lk 3:29

Ἐλιούδ, ὁ n. pers. *Eliud*. (2)

Ἐλισάβετ, ἡ n. pers. *Elizabeth*. (9)

Ἐλισαῖος, ου, ὁ n. pers. *Elisha*. (1) Lk 4:27

ἐλίσσω v. fut. ἑλίξω. *to roll up*. (2)

ἕλκος, ους, τό n. (*) *sore, abscess, ulcer*. (3)

ἑλκόω v. (ἕλκος) pf. pass. εἵλκωμαι. *be covered with sores* (pass. in NT). (1) Lk 16:20

ἑλκύσω s. ἕλκω (fut.).

ἕλκω v. (*) fut. ἑλκύσω; aor. εἵλκυσα. *to draw, haul, drag, hale; draw* (fig.), *attract*. (8)

Ἑλλάς, άδος, ἡ n. pla. *Greece*. (1) Ac 20:2

Ἕλλην, ηνος, ὁ n. pla. *a Greek; gentile, polytheist, Greco-Roman*. (25)

Ἑλληνικός, ή, όν adj. pla. *Greek (language)*. (1) Rev 9:11

Ἑλληνίς, ίδος, ἡ n. pla. *Greek* (as adj.); *Greek or gentile woman*. (2)

Ἑλληνιστής, οῦ, ὁ n. pla. *a Hellenist, a Greek-speaking Israelite*. (3)

Ἑλληνιστί adv. pla. *in the Greek language, in Greek*. (2)

ἐλλογέω and ἐλλογάω v. (λέγω) *to charge to someone's account.* (2)

Ἐλμαδάμ, ὁ n. pers. *Elmadam.* (1) Lk 3:28

ἐλόμενος s. αἱρέω (2 aor. mid. ptc.).

ἐλπίζω v. (ἐλπίς) fut. ἐλπιῶ; aor. ἤλπισα; pf. ἤλπικα. *to hope, hope for, put one's hope in; expect.* (31)

ἐλπίς, ίδος, ἡ n. (*) *hope, expectation; basis of hope; something hoped for.* (53)

Ἐλύμας, α, ὁ n. pers. *Elymas.* (1) Ac 13:8

ελωι Ara. *my God.* (2)

ἔμαθον s. μανθάνω (2 aor.).

ἐμαυτοῦ, ῆς pron. (ἐγώ, αὐτός) reflex. *myself, my own, ἀπ᾽ ἐμαυτοῦ on my own authority.* (37)

ἐμβαίνω v. (-βαίνω) aor. ἐνέβην. *to step or get into, embark.* (16)

ἐμβάλλω v. (βάλλω) aor. ἐνέβαλον. *to throw (in or into).* (1) Lk 12:5

ἐμβάπτω v. (βάπτω) aor. ἐνέβαψα. *to dip (in or into).* (2)

ἐμβατεύω v. (-βαίνω) poss. mngs. *to enter, visit; acquire; enter into, go into detail; take one's stand on.* (1) Col 2:18

ἐμβιβάζω v. (-βαίνω) aor. ἐνεβίβασα. *to put in, put on board.* (1) Ac 27:6

ἐμβλέπω v. (βλέπω) aor. ἐνέβλεψα. *to look at, gaze on, be able to see; consider.* (12)

ἐμβριμάομαι v. aor. ἐνεβριμησάμην; aor. pass. ἐνεβριμήθην. *to warn sternly; scold, censure; be deeply moved.* (5)

ἐμέω v. aor. ἤμεσα. *to vomit, throw up, spew out.* (1) Rev 3:16

ἐμμαίνομαι v. (μαίνομαι) *to be enraged.* (1) Ac 26:11

Ἐμμανουήλ, ὁ n. pers. *Emmanuel.* (1) Mt 1:23

Ἐμμαοῦς, ἡ n. pla. *Emmaus.* (1) Lk 24:13

ἐμμένω v. (μένω) aor. ἐνέμεινα. *to stay, remain; persevere in, stand by, abide by.* (4)

Ἑμμώρ, ὁ n. pers. *Hamor.* (1) Ac 7:16

ἐμνήσθην s. μιμνήσκομαι (aor. pass.).

ἐμός, ή, όν adj. (ἐγώ) *my, mine; τὸ ἐμόν my property.* (76)

ἐμπαιγμονή, ῆς, ἡ n. (παῖς) *mocking.* (1) 2 Pt 3:3

ἐμπαιγμός, οῦ, ὁ n. (παῖς) *scorn, mocking.* (1) Heb 11:36

ἐμπαίζω v. (παῖς) fut. ἐμπαίξω; aor. ἐνέπαιξα; aor. pass. ἐνεπαίχθην. *to ridicule, make fun of, mock; deceive, trick.* (13)

ἐμπαίκτης, ου, ὁ n. (παῖς) *mocker.* (2)

ἐμπέπλησμαι s. ἐμπίμπλημι (pf. pass.).

ἐμπεριπατέω v. (πατέω) fut. ἐμπεριπατήσω. *to walk about, move.* (1) 2 Cor 6:16

ἐμπίμπλημι and ἐμπιπλάω v. (πίμπλημι) aor. ἐνέπλησα; pf. pass. ἐμπέπλησμαι; aor. pass. ἐνεπλήσθην. *to fill; satisfy; have plenty to eat (pass.); enjoy.* (5)

ἐμπίμπρημι v. (πίμπρημι) aor. ἐνέπρησα. *to set on fire, burn.* (1) Mt 22:7

ἐμπίπτω v. (πίπτω) fut. ἐμπεσοῦμαι; aor. ἐνέπεσον. *to fall in or into; fall among.* (7)

ἐμπλέκω v. (πλέκω) aor. pass. ἐνεπλάκην. *to be involved in, be entangled (pass. in NT).* (2)

ἐμπλοκή, ῆς, ἡ n. (πλέκω) *braiding (elaborate), braid.* (1) 1 Pt 3:3

ἐμπνέω v. (πνέω) *to breathe.* (1) Ac 9:1

ἐμπορεύομαι v. (πορεύομαι) fut. ἐμπορεύσομαι. *to be in or carry on business; buy and sell, trade in, exploit.* (2)

ἐμπορία, ας, ἡ n. (πορεύομαι) *business, trade.* (1) Mt 22:5

ἐμπόριον, ου, τό n. (πορεύομαι) *market, marketplace.* (1) Jn 2:16

ἔμπορος, ου, ὁ n. (πορεύομαι) *merchant, wholesale dealer.* (5)

ἔμπροσθεν adv. (ἐν, πρός) *in front, ahead, forward; τὸ ἔμπροσθεν the front; in front of, before, at, in the presence of, in the face of, to, ahead of (adv. prep. w. gen.).* (48)

ἐμπτύω v. (πτύω) fut. ἐμπτύσω; aor.

ἐνέπτυσα; aor. pass. ἐνεπτύσθην. *to spit on* or *at*. (6)

ἐμφανής, ές adj. (φαίνω) *visible; known, revealed*. (2)

ἐμφανίζω v. (φαίνω) fut. ἐμφανίσω; aor. ἐνεφάνισα; aor. pass. ἐνεφανίσθην. *to make visible; make clear, explain, inform, make a report, reveal; present evidence, bring charges*. (10)

ἔμφοβος, ον adj. (φόβος) *afraid, startled, terrified*. (5)

ἐμφυσάω v. (φύω) aor. ἐνεφύσησα. *to breathe on*. (1) Jn 20:22

ἔμφυτος, ον adj. (φύω) *implanted*. (1) Jas 1:21

ἐν prep. (*) w. dat. *in, among, on, at, near, before, in the presence of, to; into; in association with, under the control* or *influence of, in communion with, under the impulsion* or *domination of, in a state of, in the power of, subject to; with; with the help of, through;* ἐν τῷ *whereby, whereas, in the sphere of; by, in connection with, in the case of; because of, on account of; while, when, within, during, in the course of; when, while* (ἐν τῷ w. inf.); *according to; consisting in, amounting to*. (2752)

ἐναγκαλίζομαι v. (ἀγκάλη) aor. ἐνηγκαλίσμην. *to take in one's arms, hug*. (2)

ἐνάλιος, ον adj. (ἅλας) *belong to the sea; sea creature* (subst. in NT). (1) Jas 3:7

ἔναντι adv. (ἐν, ἀντί) adv. prep. w. gen. in NT *opposite, before; in the eyes* or *judgment of*. (2)

ἐναντίον adv. (ἐν, ἀντί) *in the sight* or *judgment of, before* (adv. prep. w. gen.); τοὐναντίον (= τὸ ἐναντίον) *on the other hand*. (8)

ἐναντιόομαι v. *to oppose*. (v.l.)

ἐναντίος, α, ον adj. (ἐν, ἀντί) *opposite, against, contrary; opposed*, ὁ ἐξ ἐναντίας *the opponent*. (8)

ἐνάρχομαι v. (ἄρχω) aor. ἐνηρξάμην. *to begin, make a beginning*. (2)

ἔνατος, η, ον adj. (ἐννέα) *ninth*. (10)

ἐνγ- s. ἐγγ-.

ἐνδεής, ές adj. (δέομαι) *poor, impoverished*. (1) Ac 4:34

ἔνδειγμα, ατος, τό n. (δείκνυμι) *evidence, plain indication*. (1) 2 Th 1:5

ἐνδείκνυμι v. (δείκνυμι) aor. ἐνέδειξα. *to show, demonstrate, give proof; accord, do to* (mid. in NT). (11)

ἔνδειξις, εως, ἡ n. (δείκνυμι) *sign, omen; demonstration, proof*. (4)

ἔνδεκα adj. (εἷς, δέκα) *eleven*. (6)

ἐνδέκατος, η, ον adj. (εἷς, δέκα) *eleventh*. (3)

ἐνδέχομαι v. (δέχομαι) *it is possible* (impers. in NT). (1) Lk 13:33

ἐνδημέω v. (δῆμος) aor. ἐνεδήμησα. *to be at home* (fig. in NT). (3)

ἐνδιδύσκω v. (δύνω) *to dress, put on; dress oneself in* (mid.). (2)

ἔνδικος, ον adj. (δίκη) *just, deserved*. (2)

ἐνδοξάζομαι v. (δοκέω) aor. pass. ἐνεδοξάσθην. *to be glorified, be honored*. (2)

ἔνδοξος, ον adj. (δοκέω) *honored, distinguished, eminent; glorious, splendid*. (4)

ἔνδυμα, ατος, τό n. (δύνω) *garment, clothing; covering*. (8)

ἐνδυναμόω v. (δύναμαι) aor. ἐνεδυνάμωσα; aor. pass. ἐνεδυναμώθην. *to strengthen; become* or *grow strong, be strong* (pass.). (7)

ἐνδύνω v. (δύνω) *to slip in, worm into*. (1) 2 Ti 3:6

ἔνδυσις, εως, ἡ n. (δύνω) *putting on* (clothing). (1) 1 Pt 3:3

ἐνδύω v. (δύνω) aor. ἐνέδυσα; pf. pass. ἐνδέδυμαι. *to dress, clothe; clothe oneself in, put on, wear, be clothed* (mid.). (27)

ἐνδώμησις, εως, ἡ n. (δῶμα) *construction, material*. (1) Rev 21: 18

ἐνέδρα, ας, ἡ n. (ἑδραῖος) *ambush*. (2)

ἐνεδρεύω v. (ἑδραῖος) *to lie in wait; plot*. (2)

ἐνειλέω v. (-εἴλω) aor. ἐνείλησα. *to wrap in*. (1) Mk 15:46

ἔνειμι v. (εἰμί) *to be in* or *inside*. (1) Lk 11:41

ἕνεκα, ἕνεκεν, and εἵνεκεν prep. *because of, on account of, for the sake of* (adv. prep. w. gen.); *in order that*. (26)

ἐνέκρυψα s. ἐγκρύπτω (aor.).

ἐνέμεινα s. ἐμμένω (aor.).

ἐνενήκοντα adj. (ἐννέα) *ninety*. (4)

ἐνεός, ά, όν adj. *speechless*. (1) Ac 9:7

ἐνέπαιξα, ἐνεπαίχθην s. ἐμπαίζω (aor., aor. pass.).

ἐνέπεσον s. ἐμπίπτω (2 aor.).

ἐνέπλησα, ἐνεπλήσθην s. ἐμπίμπλημι (aor., aor. pass.).

ἐνέπρησα s. ἐμπίμπρημι (aor.).

ἐνέργεια, ας, ἡ n. (ἔργον) *working, operation, action, influence, power, activity*. (8)

ἐνεργέω v. (ἔργον) aor. ἐνήργησα. *to work, be at work, be active, operate, be effective* (act. and mid.); *produce, effect*. (21)

ἐνέργημα, ατος, τό n. (ἔργον) *activity*. (2)

ἐνεργής, ές adj. (ἔργον) *effective, active, powerful*. (3)

ἐνευλογέω v. (λέγω) aor. pass. ἐνευλογήθην. *to act kindly, bless*. (2)

ἐνεχθείς s. φέρω (aor. pass. ptc.).

ἐνέχω v. (ἔχω) *to bear ill-will; be subject to, be loaded down with* (pass.). (3)

ἐνθάδε adv. (ἐν) *here, in* or *to this place*. (8)

ἔνθεν adv. (ἐν) *from there, from here*. (2)

ἐνθυμέομαι v. (θυμός) aor. pass. ἐνεθυμήθην. *to reflect on, consider, think*. (2)

ἐνθύμησις, εως, ἡ n. (θυμός) *thought, reflection, idea*. (4)

ἔνι v. (εἰμί) impers. and w. neg. in NT *there is* (= ἔνεστιν). (6)

ἐνιαυτός, οῦ, ὁ n. (αὐτός) *year* (lit. and fig.), κατ᾽ ἐνιαυτόν *annually*. (14)

ἐνίστημι v. (ἵστημι) fut. ἐνστήσω; pf. ἐνέστηκα. *to be here, be at hand, arrive, come, be present, have come;* ptc. *present; impending*. (7)

ἐνισχύω v. (ἰσχύς) aor. ἐνίσχυσα. *to* *grow strong, regain one's strength; strengthen*. (2)

ἐνκ- s. ἐγκ-.

ἐννέα adj. (*) *nine*. (5)

ἐννεύω v. (νεύω) *to nod, make signals*. (1) Lk 1:62

ἔννοια, ας, ἡ n. (νίπτω) *thought, knowledge, insight, way of thinking*. (2)

ἔννομος, ον adj. (νόμος) *legal, lawful, subject to the law*. (2)

ἔννυχος, ον adj. (νύξ) *at night-time* (acc. neut. pl. as adv. in NT). (1) Mk 1:35

ἐνοικέω v. (οἶκος) fut. ἐνοικήσω; aor. ἐνῴκησα. *to live, dwell (in)*. (5)

ἐνορκίζω v. (ὅρκος) *to adjure, cause to swear* (an oath). (1) 1 Th 5:27

ἑνότης, ητος, ἡ n. (εἷς) *unity*. (2)

ἐνοχλέω v. (ὄχλος) *to trouble, annoy, cause trouble*. (2)

ἔνοχος, ον adj. (ἔχω) *subject to, held in; liable, answerable, guilty, deserving, guilty of sin against*. (10)

ἐνπ- s. ἐμπ-.

ἔνταλμα, ατος, τό n. (ἐντολή) *commandment*. (3)

ἐνταφιάζω v. (θάπτω) aor. ἐνεταφίασα. *to prepare for burial, bury*. (2)

ἐνταφιασμός, οῦ, ὁ n. (θάπτω) *preparation for burial, burial*. (2)

ἐντέλλομαι v. (ἐντολή) fut. ἐντελοῦμαι; aor. ἐνετειλάμην; pf. pass. ἐντέταλμαι. *to command, order, give orders, ordain*. (15)

ἐντεῦθεν adv. (ἐν) *from here*, ἐντεῦθεν καὶ ἐντεῦθεν *on each side; from this*. (10)

ἔντευξις, εως, ἡ n. (τυγχάνω) *intercessory prayer, prayer (of thanksgiving)*. (2)

ἔντιμος, ον adj. (τιμή) *honored, respected, distinguished, esteemed; valuable, precious*. (5)

ἐντολή, ῆς, ἡ n. (*) *writ, warrant; command, commandment, law, standard, legal right*. (67)

ἐντόπιος, α, ον adj. (τόπος) *local; local resident* (subst. in NT). (1) Ac 21:12

ἐντός adv. (ἐν) adv. prep. w. gen. in NT

inside, within, among, in one's midst; τὸ ἐντός what is inside, contents. (2)

ἐντρέπω v. (τροπή) aor. pass. ἐνετράπην. to shame, make ashamed; pass. be ashamed; have regard for, respect; show deference to. (9)

ἐντρέφω v. (τρέφω) to train in. (1) 1 Ti 4:6

ἔντρομος, ον adj. (τρέμω) trembling. (3)

ἐντροπή, ῆς, ἡ n. (τροπή) shame, humiliation. (2)

ἐντρυφάω v. (τρυφή) to revel, carouse, cavort. (1) 2 Pt 2:13

ἐντυγχάνω v. (τυγχάνω) aor. ἐνέτυχον. to approach, appeal, plead. (5)

ἐντυλίσσω v. aor. ἐνετύλιξα; pf. pass. ἐντετύλιγμαι. to wrap (up); fold up. (3)

ἐντυπόω v. (τύπος) pf. pass. ἐντετύπωμαι. to carve, impress. (1) 2 Cor 3:7

ἐνυβρίζω v. (ὕβρις) aor. ἐνύβρισα. to insult, outrage. (1) Heb 10:29

ἐνυπνιάζομαι v. (ὕπνος) aor. pass. ἐνυπνιάσθην. to dream, have visions. (2)

ἐνύπνιον, ου, τό n. (ὕπνος) dream. (1) Ac 2:17

ἐνών s. ἔνειμι (pres. ptc.).

ἐνώπιον adv. (ὁράω) adv. prep. w. gen. in NT before; in the sight or presence of, among; in the opinion or judgment of; in relation to, against, by the authority of, on behalf of. (94)

Ἐνώς, ὁ n. pers. Enos. (1) Lk 3:38

ἐνωτίζομαι v. (οὖς) aor. ἐνωτισάμην. to give ear, pay attention. (1) Ac 2:14

Ἐνώχ, ὁ n. pers. Enoch. (3)

ἐξ = ἐκ before vowels.

ἕξ adj. (*) six. (13)

ἐξαγγέλλω v. (ἄγγελος) aor. ἐξήγγειλα. to proclaim, report. (2)

ἐξαγοράζω v. (ἀγοράζω) aor. ἐξηγόρασα. to deliver, liberate; make the most of (mid.). (4)

ἐξάγω v. (ἄγω) aor. ἐξήγαγον. to lead out, bring out. (12)

ἐξαιρέω v. (αἱρέω) aor. ἐξεῖλον. to take out, tear out; set free, deliver, rescue, save (mid.). (8)

ἐξαίρω v. (αἴρω) aor. ἐξῆρα. to remove, drive away or out. (1) 1 Cor 5:13

ἐξαιτέω v. (αἰτέω) aor. ἐξῄτησα. to ask for, demand (mid. in NT). (1) Lk 22:31

ἐξαίφνης adv. (ἄφνω) suddenly, unexpectedly. (5)

ἐξακολουθέω v. (ἀκολουθέω) fut. ἐξακολουθήσω; aor. ἐξηκολούθησα. to follow, obey; pursue. (3)

ἐξακόσιοι, αι, α adj. (ἕξ) six hundred. (2)

ἐξαλείφω v. (ἀλείφω) fut. ἐξαλείψω; aor. ἐξήλειψα; aor. pass. ἐξηλείφθην. to wipe away, wipe out, erase; remove, destroy, obliterate. (5)

ἐξάλλομαι v. (ἅλλομαι) to leap up. (1) Ac 3:8

ἐξανάστασις, εως, ἡ n. (ἵστημι) resurrection. (1) Phil 3:11

ἐξανατέλλω v. (ἀνατολή) aor. ἐξανέτειλα. to spring up. (2)

ἐξανίστημι v. (ἵστημι) aor. ἐξανέστησα, ἐξανέστην. to raise up offspring; stand up. (3)

ἐξαπατάω v. (ἀπάτη) aor. ἐξηπάτησα; aor. pass. ἐξηπατήθην. to deceive, cheat, lead astray. (6)

ἐξάπινα adv. (ἄφνω) suddenly. (1) Mk 9:8

ἐξαπορέομαι v. (πορεύομαι) aor. pass. ἐξηπορήθην. to be in great difficulty or doubt, despair. (2)

ἐξαποστέλλω v. (στέλλω) fut. ἐξαποστελῶ; aor. ἐξαπέστειλα. to send out, send off; send away; send, dispatch. (13)

ἐξαρτίζω v. (ἄρτι) aor. ἐξήρτισα; pf. pass. ἐξήρτισμαι. to finish, complete; equip, furnish. (2)

ἐξαστράπτω v. (ἀστραπή) to flash or gleam like lightning. (1) Lk 9:29

ἐξαυτῆς adv. (αὐτός) at once, immediately, soon thereafter. (6)

ἐξέβαλον s. ἐκβάλλω (2 aor.).

ἐξέβην s. ἐκβαίνω (2 aor.).

ἐξεγείρω v. (ἐγείρω) fut. ἐξεγερῶ; aor. ἐξήγειρα. to raise; bring into being; elevate. (2)

ἐξεδόμην s. ἐκδίδωμι (2 aor. mid.).

ἐξεῖλον s. ἐξαιρέω (2 aor.).

ἔξειμι v. (-εῖμι) *to go out, go away, go on a journey, get to.* (4)

ἔξελε, ἐξελέσθαι s. ἐξαιρέω (2 aor. impv., 2 aor. mid. inf.).

ἐξελήλυθα s. ἐξέρχομαι (2 pf.).

ἐξέλκω v. (ἕλκω) *to drag away, take in tow.* (1) Jas 1:14

ἐξέμαξα s. ἐκμάσσω (aor.).

ἐξέπεσα, ἐξέπεσον s. ἐκπίπτω (1 aor., 2 aor.).

ἐξεπέτασα s. ἐκπετάννυμι (aor.).

ἐξεπλάγην s. ἐκπλήσσω (2 aor. pass.).

ἐξέπλευσα s. ἐκπλέω (aor.).

ἐξέπνευσα s. ἐκπνέω (aor.).

ἐξέραμα, ατος, τό n. *vomit.* (1) 2 Pt 2:22

ἐξεραυνάω v. (ἐρωτάω) aor. ἐξηραύνησα. *to inquire carefully, try to find out.* (1) 1 Pt 1:10

ἐξέρχομαι v. (ἔρχομαι) fut. ἐξελεύσομαι; aor. ἐξῆλθον; pf. ἐξελήλυθα. *to go out, come out, go away, retire, get out, leave* (w. ἀπό), *release, disembark, appear, step out, flow out, ring out, originate, be gone, disappear; die* (w. ἐκ τοῦ κόσμου); *proceed; depart; escape.* (218)

ἐξέστηκα s. ἐξίστημι (pf.).

ἔξεστιν v. (εἰμί) impers. *it is right, is authorized, is permitted, is proper* (v. and ptc. ἐξόν); *it is possible* (ptc.). (31)

ἐξετάζω v. (-ἐτάζω) aor. ἐξήτασα. *to scrutinize, examine, inquire, make a careful search; question.* (3)

ἐξεχύθην s. ἐκχέω (aor. pass.).

ἐξηγέομαι v. (ἄγω) aor. ἐξηγησάμην. *to tell, report, describe, relate; expound, make known, bring news of.* (6)

ἐξῄειν, ἐξήεσαν s. ἔξειμι (impf., impf. 3 pl.).

ἐξήκοντα adj. (ἕξ) *sixty.* (9)

ἐξῆρα s. ἐξαίρω (aor.).

ἐξῆς adv. (ἔχω) *on the next (day)*, ἐν τῷ ἐξῆς *soon afterward.* (5)

ἐξηχέω v. (ἦχος) pf. pass. ἐξήχημαι. *to ring out, sound forth* (pass. in NT). (1) 1 Th 1:8

ἕξις, εως, ἡ n. (ἔχω) *maturity; exercise, practice* (poss.). (1) Heb 5:14

ἐξίστημι and ἐξιστάνω v. (ἵστημι) aor. ἐξέστησα, ἐξέστην; pf. ἐξέστηκα. *to confuse, amaze, astound; lose one's mind, be out of one's senses, be amazed, be astonished, be astounded* (2 aor., pf. act., and all mid.). (17)

ἐξισχύω v. (ἰσχύς) aor. ἐξίσχυσα. *to be able, be strong enough, be in a position.* (1) Eph 3:18

ἔξοδος, ου, ἡ n. (ὁδός) *the Exodus; departure, death.* (3)

ἐξοίσω s. ἐκφέρω (fut.).

ἐξολεθρεύω v. (ὄλεθρος) aor. pass. ἐξωλεθρεύθην. *to destroy utterly, root out.* (1) Ac 3:23

ἐξομολογέω v. (ὅμοιος, λέγω) fut. ἐξομολογήσω; aor. ἐξωμολόγησα. *to promise, consent*; mid. *confess, admit; profess, acknowledge; praise.* (10)

ἐξόν s. ἔξεστιν (pres. ptc. neut.).

ἐξορκίζω v. (ὅρκος) *to put under oath, adjure.* (1) Mt 26:63

ἐξορκιστής, οῦ, ὁ n. (ὅρκος) *exorcist.* (1) Ac 19:13

ἐξορύσσω v. (ὀρύσσω) aor. ἐξώρυξα. *to tear out; dig through.* (2)

ἐξουδενέω v. (οὐ, εἷς) aor. pass. ἐξουδενήθην. *to treat with contempt* or *scorn.* (1) Mk 9:12

ἐξουθενέω v. (οὐ, εἷς) aor. ἐξουθένησα; pf. pass. ἐξουθένημαι; aor. pass. ἐξουθενήθην. *to disdain, count as nothing; reject disdainfully; treat with contempt.* (11)

ἐξουσία, ας, ἡ n. (εἰμί) *freedom of choice, right, liberty, disposal; capability, might, power, control; authority, absolute power, warrant; ruling* or *official power; official, government, (spirit) power; domain, jurisdiction; means of exercising power.* (102)

ἐξουσιάζω v. (εἰμί) aor. pass. ἐξουσιάσθην. *to have the right* or *power, be in authority; be mastered* (pass.). (4)

ἐξουσιαστικός, ή, όν adj. *authoritative.* (v.l.)

ἐξοχή, ῆς, ἡ n. (ἔχω) *prominence; κατ᾽ ἐξοχήν prominent.* (1) Ac 25:23

ἐξυπνίζω v. (ὕπνος) fut. ἐξυπνίσω. *to wake up, arouse.* (1) Jn 11:11

ἔξυπνος, ον adj. (ὕπνος) *awake, aroused.* (1) Ac 16:27

ἔξω adv. (ἐκ) *outside; outer, outside, foreign* (as adj.)*; out; outsider* (w. art.)*;* adv. prep. w. gen. *outside; out, out of.* (63)

ἔξωθεν adv. (ἐκ) *from the outside; outside; outward, out; as adj. having to do with the outside, external,* τὸ ἔξωθεν *the outside;* οἱ ἔξωθεν *those on the outside;* adv. prep. w. gen. *from outside.* (13)

ἐξωθέω v. (-ωθέω) aor. ἐξῶσα. *to push out, expel; beach, run ashore.* (2)

ἐξώτερος, α, ον adj. (ἐκ) *farthest, extreme.* (3)

ἔοικα v. (εἰκών) pf. ἔοικα. pf. used as pres. *to be like, resemble.* (2)

ἑορτάζω v. (ἑορτη) *to celebrate a festival.* (1) 1 Cor 5:8

ἑορτή, ῆς, ἡ n. (*) *festival, celebration, feast.* (25)

ἐπ᾽ = ἐπί before smooth breathing.

ἐπαγγελία, ας, ἡ n. (ἄγγελος) *promise, pledge, offer, what was promised; assurance of agreement.* (52)

ἐπαγγέλλομαι v. (ἄγγελος) aor. ἐπηγγειλάμην; pf. pass. ἐπήγγελμαι. *to promise, offer, make a promise; profess, lay claim to.* (15)

ἐπάγγελμα, ατος, τό n. (ἄγγελος) *promise; thing promised.* (2)

ἐπάγω v. (ἄγω) aor. ἐπήγαγον, ἔπηξα. *to bring on, bring upon.* (3)

ἐπαγωνίζομαι v. (ἀγών) *to contend.* (1) Jd 3

ἐπαθροίζω v. (θροέω) *to increase* (pass. in NT). (1) Lk 11:29

Ἐπαίνετος, ου, ὁ n. pers. *Epaenetus.* (1) Rom 16:5

ἐπαινέω v. (αἶνος) fut. ἐπαινέσω; aor. ἐπήνεσα. *to praise, approve of.* (6)

ἔπαινος, ου, ὁ n. (αἶνος) *praise,*

approval, recognition, fame; thing worthy of praise. (11)

ἐπαίρω v. (αἴρω) aor. ἐπῆρα; aor. pass. ἐπήρθην. *to lift up, hold up, raise;* pass. *be taken up; be in opposition, rise up; be presumptuous, put on airs.* (19)

ἐπαισχύνομαι v. (αἰσχρός) aor. pass. ἐπαισχύνθην. *to be ashamed.* (11)

ἐπαιτέω v. (αἰτέω) *to beg.* (2)

ἐπακολουθέω v. (ἀκολουθέω) aor. ἐπηκολούθησα. *to follow; accompany, authenticate; follow after, devote oneself to.* (4)

ἐπακούω v. (ἀκούω) aor. ἐπήκουσα. *to hear, listen to.* (1) 2 Cor 6:2

ἐπακροάομαι v. (ἀκροατής) *to listen to.* (1) Ac 16:25

ἐπάν conj. (ἄν) *when, as soon as* (w. subj.). (3)

ἐπάναγκες adv. (ἀνάγκη) *of a necessary nature,* τὰ ἐπάναγκες *the necessary things.* (1) Ac 15:28

ἐπανάγω v. (ἄγω) aor. ἐπανήγαγον. *to go out, push off, put out* (to sea)*; return.* (3)

ἐπαναμιμνῄσκω v. (μιμνῄσκομαι) *to remind (again).* (1) Rom 15:15

ἐπαναπαύομαι v. (παύω) aor. pass. ἐπανεπάην. *to rest (upon); find rest or support, rely on.* (2)

ἐπανέρχομαι v. (ἔρχομαι) aor. ἐπανῆλθον. *to return.* (2)

ἐπανίστημι v. (ἵστημι) fut. ἐπαναστήσω. *to rise up, rise in rebellion* (mid. in NT). (2)

ἐπανόρθωσις, εως, ἡ n. (ὀρθός) *improvement.* (1) 2 Ti 3:16

ἐπάνω adv. (ἐπί, ἀνά) *above, over* (lit. and fig.)*; more than* (w. numbers)*; above, over* (adv. prep. w. gen.). (19)

ἐπάξας s. ἐπάγω (aor. ptc.).

ἐπάραι, ἔπαρον, ἐπάρας s. ἐπαίρω (aor. inf., aor. impv., aor. ptc.).

ἐπάρατος, ον adj. (ἀρά) *accursed.* (1) Jn 7:49

ἐπαρκέω v. (ἀρκέω) aor. ἐπήρκεσα. *to help, aid, provide for.* (3)

ἐπαρχεία, ας, ἡ n. (ἄρχω) *province*. (2)

ἔπαυλις, εως, ἡ n. (αὐλή) *farm, homestead, residence*. (1) Ac 1:20

ἐπαύριον adv. (αὔριον) *tomorrow*, τῇ ἐπαύριον *on the next day*. (17)

Ἐπαφρᾶς, ᾶ, ὁ n. pers. *Epaphras*. (3)

ἐπαφρίζω v. (ἀφρός) *to cause to foam; cast up like foam*. (1) Jd 13

Ἐπαφρόδιτος, ου, ὁ n. pers. *Epaphraditus*. (2)

ἐπεγείρω v. (ἐγείρω) aor. ἐπήγειρα. *to arouse, excite, stir up*. (2)

ἐπεί conj. (ἐπί) *because, since, for, then, for otherwise*. (26)

ἐπειδή conj. (δή) *when, after; because, since*. (10)

ἐπειδήπερ conj. (δή, -πέρ) *inasmuch as, since*. (1) Lk 1:1

ἔπειμι v. (-εῖμι) *to come upon, come near; next, next day* (fem. ptc. in NT). (5)

ἐπεισαγωγή, ῆς, ἡ n. (ἄγω) *bringing in, introduction*. (1) Heb 7:19

ἐπεισέρχομαι v. (ἔρχομαι) fut. ἐπεισελεύσομαι. *to come (upon)*. (1) Lk 21:35

ἔπειτα adv. (εἶτα) *then, thereupon, next* (of time); *then, next* (of list items). (16)

ἐπέκεινα adv. (ἐκεῖ) adv. prep. w. gen. in NT *farther on, beyond*. (1) Ac 7:43

ἐπεκλήθην s. ἐπικαλέω (aor. pass.).

ἐπεκτείνομαι v. (-τείνω) *to stretch out* or *strain toward*. (1) Phil 3:13

ἐπελαβόμην s. ἐπιλαμβάνομαι (2 aor. mid.).

ἐπελαθόμην s. ἐπιλανθάνομαι (2 aor. mid.).

ἐπελεύσομαι s. ἐπέρχομαι (fut. mid.).

ἐπέμεινα s. ἐπιμένω (aor.).

ἐπενδύομαι v. (δύνω) aor. ἐπενεδυσάμην. *to put on (in addition)*. (2)

ἐπενδύτης, ου, ὁ n. (δύνω) *outer garment, coat*. (1) Jn 21:7

ἐπενεγκεῖν s. ἐπιφέρω (2 aor. inf.).

ἐπεποίθειν s. πείθω (plpf.).

ἐπέρχομαι v. (ἔρχομαι) fut. ἐπελεύσομαι; aor. ἐπῆλθον. *to come, arrive, come upon; happen, come about; attack*. (9)

ἐπερωτάω v. (ἐρωτάω) fut. ἐπερωτήσω; aor. ἐπηρώτησα; aor. pass. ἐπηρωτήθην. *to ask, ask about, inquire after; ask for*. (56)

ἐπερώτημα, ατος, τό n. (ἐρωτάω) *appeal*. (1) 1 Pt 3:21

ἔπεσα, ἔπεσον s. πίπτω (1 aor., 2 aor.).

ἐπέστειλα s. ἐπιστέλλω (aor.).

ἐπέστην s. ἐφίστημι (2 aor.).

ἐπεστράφην s. ἐπιστρέφω (2 aor. pass.).

ἐπετίθην s. ἐπιτίθημι (impf.).

ἐπετράπην s. ἐπιτρέπω (2 aor. pass.).

ἐπέτυχον s. ἐπιτυγχάνω (2 aor.).

ἐπεφάνην s. ἐπιφαίνω (2 aor. pass.).

ἐπέχω v. (ἔχω) aor. ἐπέσχον. *to hold fast; hold toward, aim at, notice, fix one's attention on, take pains with; stop, stay*. (5)

ἐπηγγειλάμην, ἐπήγγελμαι s. ἐπαγγέλλομαι (aor. mid., pf. pass.).

ἐπήγειρα s. ἐπεγείρω (aor.).

ἐπῆλθον s. ἐπέρχομαι (2 aor.).

ἐπήνεσα s. ἐπαινέω (aor.).

ἔπηξα s. πήγνυμι (aor.).

ἐπῆρα s. ἐπαίρω (aor.).

ἐπηρεάζω v. *to threaten, mistreat, abuse, malign*. (2)

ἐπήρθην s. ἐπαίρω (aor. pass.).

ἐπί prep. (*) w. gen. *on, upon, near; at; before, in the presence of; toward, in the direction of; in consideration of, in regard to, on the basis of, concerning, about, on the evidence of, to, of, in the case of; over, in charge of; in* or *at the time of, for*; w. dat. *on, in, above, upon; at, near (by), among*; ἐπ᾽ εὐλογίαις *generously; depending on, reflecting on, on the basis of, with, because of, from; to, in addition to; over; against; about; for; in* or *at the time of, during*; w. acc. *on, over, upon, beside, at, to*, ἐπὶ τὸ αὐτό *together, by, near, among, for; toward, after, in the direction of, across, up to, in the neighborhood of; above; before; for* (purpose); *against; times* (w.

numbers), ἐπὶ πλεῖον *to a greater extent*, ἐφ᾽ ὅσον *to the degree that; about; in; over a period of.* (890)

ἐπιβαίνω v. (-βαίνω) aor. ἐπέβην; pf. ἐπιβέβηκα. *to go up* or *upon, mount, go on board, embark, set foot in.* (6)

ἐπιβάλλω v. (βάλλω) fut. ἐπιβαλῶ; aor. ἐπέβαλον. *to throw over, lay on, put on; throw oneself* or *beat upon, break over; begin, break down* (poss.); *fall to, belong to.* (18)

ἐπιβαρέω v. (βάρος) aor. ἐπεβάρησα. *to weigh down, burden;* poss. *exaggerate; be too severe with.* (3)

ἐπιβιβάζω v. (-βαίνω) aor. ἐπεβίβασα. *to put on, load upon.* (3)

ἐπιβλέπω v. (βλέπω) aor. ἐπέβλεψα. *to show special respect for, gaze upon; look upon, take a look at.* (3)

ἐπίβλημα, ατος, τό n. (βάλλω) *patch.* (4)

ἐπιβουλή, ῆς, ἡ n. (βούλομαι) *plot.* (4)

ἐπιγαμβρεύω v. (γάμος) fut. ἐπιγαμβρεύσω. *to marry as next of kin.* (1) Mt 22:24

ἐπίγειος, ον adj. (γῆ) *earthly, human;* subst. *earthly things, on earth; worldly things.* (7)

ἐπιγίνομαι v. (γίνομαι) aor. ἐπεγενόμην. *to come to pass, come up.* (1) Ac 28:13

ἐπιγινώσκω v. (γινώσκω) fut. ἐπιγνώσομαι; aor. ἐπέγνων; pf. ἐπέγνωκα; aor. pass. ἐπεγνώσθην. *to know, know completely; learn, find out, learn to know, notice, perceive, learn of, ascertain; acknowledge acquaintance with, recognize, know again; acknowledge, give recognition to; understand.* (44)

ἐπίγνωσις, εως, ἡ n. (γινώσκω) *knowledge, recognition, consciousness.* (20)

ἐπιγραφή, ῆς, ἡ n. (γράφω) *inscription, superscription.* (5)

ἐπιγράφω v. (γράφω) pf. pass. ἐπιγέγραμμαι. *to write on* or *in, place over.* (5)

ἔπιδε s. ἐφοράω (2 aor. impv.).

ἐπιδείκνυμι v. (δείκνυμι) aor. ἐπέδει-ξα. *to show, point out; show on oneself* (mid.); *demonstrate, give proof.* (7)

ἐπιδέχομαι v. (δέχομαι) *to receive, welcome; accept.* (2)

ἐπιδημέω v. (δῆμος) *to be in town, visit, stay.* (2)

ἐπιδιατάσσομαι v. (τάσσω) *to add a codicil* (to a will). (1) Gal 3:15

ἐπιδίδωμι v. (δίδωμι) fut. ἐπιδώσω; pf. ἐπιδέδωκα; aor. pass. ἐπεδόθην. *to give, hand over, deliver; give up* or *over, surrender.* (9)

ἐπιδιορθόω v. (ὀρθός) aor. ἐπεδιόρ-θωσα. *to set right* or *correct in addition.* (1) Tit 1:5

ἐπιδύω v. (δύνω) *to sink down, set* (of the sun). (1) Eph 4:26

ἐπιείκεια, ας, ἡ n. (εἰκών) *clemency, gentleness, graciousness, courtesy, indulgence, tolerance.* (2)

ἐπιεικής, ές adj. (εἰκών) *yielding, gentle, kind, courteous, tolerant,* τὸ ἐπιεικές *forbearing spirit.* (5)

ἐπιζητέω v. (ζητέω) aor. ἐπεζήτησα. *to search for, seek after, inquire, want to know; wish (for), desire, want.* (13)

ἐπιθανάτιος, ον adj. (θνήσκω) *sentenced to death.* (1) 1 Cor 4:9

ἐπιθεῖναι, ἐπιθείς, ἐπίθες s. ἐπιτί-θημι (2 aor. inf., 2 aor. ptc., 2 aor. impv.).

ἐπίθεσις, εως, ἡ n. (τίθημι) *laying on* (of hands). (4)

ἐπιθυμέω v. (θυμός) fut. ἐπιθυμήσω; aor. ἐπεθύμησα. *to desire, long for; lust for.* (16)

ἐπιθυμητής, οῦ, ὁ n. (θυμός) *one who desires.* (1) 1 Cor 10:6

ἐπιθυμία, ας, ἡ n. (θυμός) *desire, longing; craving, lust, passion.* (38)

ἐπικαθίζω v. (καθίζω) aor. ἐπεκάθισα. *to sit* or *sit down (on).* (1) Mt 21:7

ἐπικαλέω v. (καλέω) aor. ἐπεκάλεσα; pf. pass. ἐπικέκλημαι; aor. pass. ἐπεκλήθην. *to call, give a surname; mid. call upon* or *on, call out, invoke* *for; appeal; call on someone as a witness.* (30)

ἐπικάλυμμα, ατος, τό n. (καλύπτω) *cover, veil, covering.* (1) 1 Pt 2:16

ἐπικαλύπτω v. (καλύπτω) aor. pass. ἐπεκαλύφθην. *to cover up, put out of sight.* (1) Rom 4:7

ἐπικατάρατος, ον adj. (ἀρά) *cursed.* (2)

ἐπίκειμαι v. (κεῖμαι) *to lie upon* or *on; press around* or *upon, confront; be imposed, be incumbent; be urgent about.* (7)

ἐπικέλλω v. (κελεύω) aor. ἐπέκειλα. *to run aground.* (1) Ac 27:41

Ἐπικούρειος, ου, ὁ n. oth. *an Epicurean.* (1) Ac 17:18

ἐπικουρία, ας, ἡ n. (κείρω) *help.* (1) Ac 26:22

ἐπικρίνω v. (κρίνω) aor. ἐπέκρινα. *to decide, determine.* (1) Lk 23:24

ἐπιλαμβάνομαι v. (λαμβάνω) aor. ἐπελαβόμην. *to take hold of, grasp, press into service; arrest; catch; take hold of; take an interest in, help.* (19)

ἐπιλανθάνομαι v. (λανθάνω) aor. ἐπελαθόμην; pf. pass. ἐπιλέλησμαι. *to forget; neglect, overlook, care nothing about, disregard.* (8)

ἐπιλέγω v. (λέγω) aor. ἐπέλεξα. *to call, name; choose, select* (mid.). (2)

ἐπιλείπω v. (λείπω) fut. ἐπιλείψω. *to fail.* (1) Heb 11:32

ἐπιλείχω v. *to lick.* (1) Lk 16:21

ἐπιλέλησμαι s. ἐπιλανθάνομαι (pf. pass.).

ἐπιλησμονή, ῆς, ἡ n. (λανθάνω) *forgetfulness.* (1) Jas 1:25

ἐπίλοιπος, ον adj. (λείπω) *left, remaining.* (1) 1 Pt 4:2

ἐπίλυσις, εως, ἡ n. (λύω) *explanation, interpretation.* (1) 2 Pt 1:20

ἐπιλύω v. (λύω) aor. pass. ἐπελύθην. *to explain, interpret; settle, resolve, decide.* (2)

ἐπιμαρτυρέω v. (μάρτυς) *to bear witness, attest.* (1) 1 Pt 5:12

ἐπιμέλεια, ας, ἡ n. (μέλει) *care, attention.* (1) Ac 27:3

ἐπιμελέομαι v. (μέλει) fut. ἐπιμελήσομαι; aor. pass. ἐπεμελήθην. *to care for, take care of.* (3)

ἐπιμελῶς adv. (μέλει) *carefully, diligently.* (1) Lk 15:8

ἐπιμένω v. (μένω) fut. ἐπιμενῶ; aor. ἐπέμεινα. *to stay, remain; continue, persist (in), persevere, keep on.* (16)

ἐπινεύω v. (νεύω) aor. ἐπένευσα. *to give consent.* (1) Ac 18:20

ἐπίνοια, ας, ἡ n. (νίπτω) *thought, conception, intent.* (1) Ac 8:22

ἐπιορκέω v. (ὅρκος) fut. ἐπιορκήσω. *to swear falsely, perjure oneself; break one's oath.* (1) Mt 5:33

ἐπίορκος, ον adj. (ὅρκος) *perjured; perjurer* (subst. in NT). (1) 1 Ti 1:10

ἐπιοῦσα s. ἔπειμι (pres. ptc. fem.).

ἐπιούσιος, ον adj. (εἰμί) poss. mngs. *necessary for existence; for the current day, for today; for the following day; for the future, that belongs to it, next, that comes* or *is coming.* (2)

ἐπιπίπτω v. (πίπτω) aor. ἐπέπεσον; pf. ἐπιπέπτωκα. *to fall on, press (about), approach eagerly, throw oneself upon,* ἐπιπίπτω ἐπὶ τὸν τράχηλον *embrace; befall, come upon.* (11)

ἐπιπλήσσω v. (πλήσσω) aor. ἐπέπληξα. *to rebuke, reprove.* (1) 1 Ti 5:1

ἐπιποθέω v. (*) aor. ἐπεπόθησα. *to long for, desire, yearn over.* (9)

ἐπιπόθησις, εως, ἡ n. (ἐπιποθέω) *longing.* (2)

ἐπιπόθητος, ον adj. (ἐπιποθέω) *longed for, desired.* (1) Phil 4:1

ἐπιποθία, ας, ἡ n. (ἐπιποθέω) *longing, desire.* (1) Rom 15:23

ἐπιπορεύομαι v. (πορεύομαι) *to go* or *journey to.* (1) Lk 8:4

ἐπιράπτω v. (ῥαφίς) *to sew on.* (1) Mk 2:21

ἐπιρίπτω v. (ῥίπτω) aor. ἐπέριψα. *to throw on; cast upon* (fig.). (2)

ἐπισείω v. *to urge on, incite.* (v.l.)

ἐπίσημος, ον adj. (σημεῖον) *splendid, prominent, outstanding; notorious.* (2)

ἐπισιτισμός, οῦ, ὁ n. (σῖτος) *provisions (of food)*. (1) Lk 9:12

ἐπισκέπτομαι v. (σκοπός) fut. ἐπισκέψομαι; aor. ἐπεσκεψάμην. *to look at, examine, inspect, look for; select; visit; look after, make an appearance to help, be concerned about.* (11)

ἐπισκευάζομαι v. (σκεῦος) aor. ἐπεσκευασάμην. *to get ready.* (1) Ac 21:15

ἐπισκηνόω v. (σκηνή) aor. ἐπεσκήνωσα. *to take up quarters, take up one's abode, dwell in.* (1) 2 Cor 12:9

ἐπισκιάζω v. (σκιά) fut. ἐπισκιάσω; aor. ἐπεσκίασα. *to overshadow, cast a shadow; cover.* (5)

ἐπισκοπεύω v. alt. form of ἐπισκοπέω. (v.l.)

ἐπισκοπέω v. (σκοπός) *to look at, take care, see to it; oversee, care for.* (2)

ἐπισκοπή, ῆς, ἡ n. (σκοπός) *visitation; position, assignment, work; supervision.* (4)

ἐπίσκοπος, ου, ὁ n. (σκοπός) *guardian; overseer, supervisor.* (5)

ἐπισπάω v. (σπάω) *to pull over the foreskin, conceal circumcision* (mid. in NT). (1) 1 Cor 7:18

ἐπισπείρω v. (σπείρω) *to sow afterward.* (1) Mt 13:25

ἐπίσταμαι v. (ἵστημι) *to understand; know, be acquainted with, know about.* (14)

ἐπιστάς s. ἐφίστημι (aor. ptc.).

ἐπίστασις, εως, ἡ n. (ἵστημι) *pressure* (prob. mng.)*; care, attention, superintendence, delay* (poss. mngs.)*; stopping,* ἐπίστασις ποιέω ὄχλου *stir up a crowd.* (2)

ἐπιστάτης, ου, ὁ n. (ἵστημι) *master (of Jesus).* (7)

ἐπιστέλλω v. (στέλλω) aor. ἐπέστειλα. *to inform* or *instruct by letter; write.* (3)

ἐπίστηθι s. ἐφίστημι (2 aor. impv.).

ἐπιστήμων, ον adj. (ἵστημι) *expert, learned, understanding.* (1) Jas 3:13

ἐπιστηρίζω v. (στηρίζω) aor. ἐπεστήριξα. *to strengthen.* (4)

ἐπιστολή, ῆς, ἡ n. (στέλλω) *letter, epistle.* (24)

ἐπιστομίζω v. (στόμα) *to silence.* (1) Tit 1:11

ἐπιστρέφω v. (στρέφω) fut. ἐπιστρέψω; aor. ἐπέστρεψα; aor. pass. ἐπεστράφην. *to turn around, go back; turn; return;* aor. pass. as act. *return; turn around; turn.* (36)

ἐπιστροφή, ῆς, ἡ n. (στρέφω) *conversion.* (1) Ac 15:3

ἐπισυνάγω v. (ἄγω) fut. ἐπισυνάξω; aor. ἐπισυνήγαγον, ἐπισυνῆξα; pf. pass. ἐπισυνήγμαι; aor. pass. ἐπισυνήχθην. *to gather (together).* (8)

ἐπισυναγωγή, ῆς, ἡ n. (ἄγω) *meeting; assembling.* (2)

ἐπισυντρέχω v. (τρέχω) *to run together.* (1) Mk 9:25

ἐπισφαλής, ές adj. (-σφάλλω) *unsafe, dangerous.* (1) Ac 27:9

ἐπισχύω v. (ἰσχύς) *to grow strong, persist, insist.* (1) Lk 23:5

ἐπισωρεύω v. (σωρεύω) fut. ἐπισωρεύσω. *to heap up, accumulate.* (1) 2 Ti 4:3

ἐπιταγή, ῆς, ἡ n. (τάσσω) *command, order, injunction; authority.* (7)

ἐπιτάσσω v. (τάσσω) aor. ἐπέταξα. *to order, command, give orders.* (10)

ἐπιτελέω v. (τέλος) aor. ἐπετέλεσα. *to end, bring to an end, finish; complete, accomplish, perform, bring about, erect; fulfill, lay upon, accomplish.* (10)

ἐπιτήδειος, α, ον adj. *fit for, necessary.* (1) Jas 2:16

ἐπιτίθημι v. (τίθημι) fut. ἐπιθήσω; aor. ἐπέθηκα, ἐπέθην. *to lay* or *put upon, place on, put above, inflict upon, bring upon, give* (of a surname)*, add;* mid. *give, put on board; attack, lay a hand on.* (39)

ἐπιτιμάω v. (τιμή) aor. ἐπετίμησα. *to rebuke, reprove, censure, speak seriously, warn.* (29)

ἐπιτιμία, ας, ἡ n. (τιμή) *punishment.* (1) 2 Cor 2:6

ἐπιτρέπω v. (τροπή) aor. ἐπέτρεψα; aor. pass. ἐπετράπην. *to allow, permit, give permission.* (18)

ἐπιτροπή, ῆς, ἡ n. (τροπή) *permission, commission, full power.* (1) Ac 26:12

ἐπίτροπος, ου, ὁ n. (τροπή) *manager, foreman, steward; guardian.* (3)

ἐπιτυγχάνω v. (τυγχάνω) aor. ἐπέτυχον. *to obtain, attain to, reach.* (5)

ἐπιφαίνω v. (φαίνω) aor. ἐπέφανα; aor. pass. ἐπεφάνην. *to give light to; become apparent; show oneself, make an appearance* (pass.). (4)

ἐπιφάνεια, ας, ἡ n. (φαίνω) *appearance* (of Jesus). (6)

ἐπιφανής, ές adj. (φαίνω) *splendid, glorious, remarkable.* (1) Ac 2:20

ἐπιφαύσκω v. (φαίνω) fut. ἐπιφαύσω. *to arise, appear, shine.* (1) Eph 5:14

ἐπιφέρω v. (φέρω) aor. ἐπήνεγκον. *to bring on* or *about, inflict; bring, pronounce.* (2)

ἐπιφωνέω v. (φωνή) *to cry out (loudly).* (4)

ἐπιφώσκω v. (φαίνω) *to shine forth, dawn, break, draw on* or *near.* (2)

ἐπιχειρέω v. (χείρ) aor. ἐπεχείρησα. *to endeavor, try, attempt.* (3)

ἐπιχέω v. (-χέω) *to pour on* or *over, apply.* (1) Lk 10:34

ἐπιχορηγέω v. (χορός) aor. ἐπεχορήγησα; aor. pass. ἐπεχορηγήθην. *to give, grant; supply, furnish; support.* (5)

ἐπιχορηγία, ας, ἡ n. (χορός) *assistance, support.* (2)

ἐπιχρίω v. (χρίω) aor. ἐπέχρισα. *to anoint, spread* or *smear (on).* (2)

ἔπλησα s. πίμπλημι (aor.).

ἐποικοδομέω v. (οἶκος, δῶμα) aor. ἐποικοδόμησα; aor. pass. ἐποικοδομήθην. *to build on* or *upon; edify, build up* or *on.* (7)

ἐπονομάζω v. (ὄνομα) *to call, name; call oneself* (pass. in NT). (1) Rom 2:17

ἐποπτεύω v. (ὁράω) aor. ἐπώπτευσα. *to watch, observe, see.* (2)

ἐπόπτης, ου, ὁ n. (ὁράω) *eyewitness.* (1) 2 Pt 1:16

ἔπος, ους, τό n. *word,* ὡς ἔπος εἰπεῖν *so to speak.* (1) Heb 7:9

ἐπουράνιος, ον adj. (οὐρανός) *celestial; heavenly, in heaven;* neut. pl. subst. *heaven, heavenly things;* masc. pl. subst. *heavenly beings.* (19)

ἐπράθην s. πιπράσκω (aor. pass.).

ἐπρίσθην s. πρίζω (aor. pass.).

ἑπτά adj. (*) *seven.* (88)

ἑπτάκις adv. (ἑπτά) *seven times.* (4)

ἑπτακισχίλιοι, αι, α adj. (ἑπτά, χίλιοι) *seven thousand.* (1) Rom 11:4

ἑπταπλασίων, ον adj. *sevenfold.* (v.l.)

Ἔραστος, ου, ὁ n. pers. *Erastus.* (3)

ἐραυνάω v. (ἐρωτάω) aor. ἠραύνησα. *to search, examine, investigate, fathom.* (6)

ἐργάζομαι v. (ἔργον) aor. ἠργασάμην, εἰργασάμην; pf. pass. εἴργασμαι. *to work, be busy, do business, trade; do, accomplish, carry out, perform, practice, officiate at, bring about, give rise to, work on, work for* (of food). (41)

ἐργασία, ας, ἡ n. (ἔργον) *practice, pursuit; trade, business; profit, gain; pains, effort.* (6)

ἐργάτης, ου, ὁ n. (ἔργον) *workman, laborer; doer,* ἐργάτης ἀδικίας *evildoer.* (16)

ἔργον, ου, τό n. (*) *deed, action, manifestation, practical proof, accomplishment; work, occupation, task; product, undertaking, enterprise; thing, matter.* (169)

ἐρεθίζω v. aor. ἠρέθισα. *to arouse, provoke, irritate, embitter.* (2)

ἐρείδω v. aor. ἤρεισα. *to jam fast, become fixed.* (1) Ac 27:41

ἐρεύγομαι v. fut. ἐρεύξομαι. *to utter, proclaim.* (1) Mt 13:35

ἐρημία, ας, ἡ n. (ἔρημος) *desert.* (4)

ἔρημος, ον adj. (*) *isolated, desolate, deserted, unfrequented, abandoned, empty, lonely; desert, grassland, wilderness, lonely place, steppe* (fem. subst.). (48)

ἐρημόω v. (ἔρημος) pf. pass. ἠρήμωμαι; aor. pass. ἠρημώθην. *to lay waste; be laid waste, be depopulated, be ruined* (pass. in NT). (5)

ἐρήμωσις, εως, ἡ n. (ἔρημος) *devastation, destruction, depopulation.* (3)

ἐρίζω v. (ἔρις) fut. ἐρίσω. *to quarrel, wrangle.* (1) Mt 12:19

ἐριθεία, ας, ἡ n. *strife, contentiousness, selfishness, selfish ambition; disputes, outbreaks of selfishness* (pl.). (7)

ἔριον, ου, τό n. *wool.* (2)

ἔρις, ιδος, ἡ n. (*) *strife, discord, contention; quarrels* (pl.). (9)

ἐρίφιον, ου, τό n. (ἔριφος) *goat.* (1) Mt 25:33

ἔριφος, ου, ὁ n. (*) *kid, he-goat; goats* (pl.). (2)

Ἑρμᾶς, ᾶ, ὁ n. pers. *Hermas.* (1) Rom 16:14

ἑρμηνεία, ας, ἡ n. (ἑρμηνεύω) *translation, interpretation.* (2)

ἑρμηνεύω v. (*) *to translate; be translated* (pass. in NT). (3)

Ἑρμῆς, οῦ, ὁ n. pers. *Hermes.* (2)

Ἑρμογένης, ους, ὁ n. pers. *Hermogenes.* (1) 2 Ti 1:15

ἑρπετόν, οῦ, τό n. *reptile.* (4)

ἐρρέθην s. λέγω (aor. pass.).

ἔρρηξα s. ῥήγνυμι (aor.).

ἐρρίζωμαι s. ῥιζόω (pf. pass.).

ἔρριμμαι s. ῥίπτω (pf. pass.).

ἐρρυσάμην, ἐρρύσθην s. ῥύομαι (aor. mid., aor. pass.).

ἔρρωμαι s. ῥώννυμι (pf. pass.).

ἐρυθρός, ά, όν adj. *red,* ἡ ἐρυθρὰ θάλασσα *the Red Sea.* (2)

ἔρχομαι v. (*) fut. ἐλεύσομαι; aor. ἦλθον, ἦλθα; pf. ἐλήλυθα. *to come, come back, return, appear (in public); go; be brought; submit; result in, deal with.* (634)

ἐρῶ s. λέγω (fut.).

ἐρωτάω v. (*) fut. ἐρωτήσω; aor. ἠρώτησα. *to ask, ask a question; request, beseech.* (63)

ἔσβεσα s. σβέννυμι (aor.).

ἐσήμανα s. σημαίνω (aor.).

ἐσθής, ῆτος, ἡ n. (ἱμάτιον) *clothing.* (8)

ἐσθίω and ἔσθω v. (*) fut. φάγομαι; aor.

ἔφαγον. *to eat, get sustenance; consume, devour.* (158)

Ἐσλί, ὁ n. pers. *Esli.* (1) Lk 3:25

ἐσόμενος s. εἰμί (fut. mid. ptc.).

ἔσοπτρον, ου, τό n. (ὁράω) *mirror.* (2)

ἑσπέρα, ας, ἡ n. *evening.* (3)

Ἑσρώμ, ὁ n. pers. *Hezron.* (3)

ἑσσόομαι v. (ἥσσων) aor. pass. ἡσσώθην. *to be inferior, be worse off, be made to feel less important.* (1) 2 Cor 12:13

ἐστάθην, ἑστάναι, ἕστηκα, ἔστην, ἔστησα s. ἵστημι (aor. pass., pf. inf., pf., 2 aor., 1 aor.).

ἐστράφην s. στρέφω (2 aor. pass.).

ἐστρωμένος, ἔστωσα s. στρωννύω (pf. pass. ptc., aor.).

ἔστω s. εἰμί (pres. impv. 3 sg.).

ἑστώς s. ἵστημι (2 pf. ptc.).

ἔστωσαν s. εἰμί (pres. impv. 3 pl.).

ἐσφάγην s. σφάζω (2 aor. pass.).

ἔσχατος, η, ον adj. (ἐκ) *farthest,* τὸ ἔσχατον *the end; last,* τὰ ἔσχατα *the last state,* ἔσχατον πάντων *last of all; least, most insignificant, poorest.* (52)

ἐσχάτως adv. (ἐκ) *finally,* ἐσχάτως ἔχω *to be at the point of death.* (1) Mk 5:23

ἔσω adv. (εἰς) *inside, in, into; into, inside* (adv. prep. w. gen.); *within, inner; those within* (pl. subst.). (9)

ἔσωθεν adv. (εἰς) *from inside, from within; inside, within,* τὸ ἔσωθεν *inner nature.* (12)

ἐσώτερος, α, ον adj. (εἰς) *inner;* ἐσώτερον *inside* (neut. as adv. prep. w. gen.). (2)

ἑταῖρος, ου, ὁ n. *comrade, companion, friend.* (3)

ἐταράχθην s. ταράσσω (aor. pass.).

ἐτάφην s. θάπτω (2 aor. pass.).

ἐτέθην s. τίθημι (aor. pass.).

ἔτεκον s. τίκτω (2 aor.).

ἑτερόγλωσσος, ον adj. (ἕτερος, γλῶσσα) *speaking a foreign or strange language.* (1) 1 Cor 14:21

ἑτεροδιδασκαλέω v. (ἕτερος, διδάσκω) *to give divergent or divisive instruction.* (2)

ἑτεροζυγέω v. (ἕτερος, ζυγός) *to be unevenly yoked, mismated.* (1) 2 Cor 6:14

ἕτερος, α, ον adj. (*) *other, another; some, third* (in lists); *different, foreign;* subst. *someone else, (the) others* (pl.), *one's neighbor,* τῇ ἑτέρᾳ *on the next day,* ἐν ἑτέρῳ *in another place; stranger.* (98)

ἑτέρως adv. (ἕτερος) *differently, otherwise.* (1) Phil 3:15

ἔτι adv. (*) *still, yet, again,* οὐδὲ ἔτι νῦν *not even yet,* οὐκ ἔτι *no longer,* οὐ μὴ ἔτι *never again, (any) further, longer, before; in addition, more, also, other, farther; then.* (93)

ἑτοιμάζω v. (ἕτοιμος) aor. ἡτοίμασα; pf. ἡτοίμακα; pf. pass. ἡτοίμασμαι; aor. pass. ἡτοιμάσθην. *to prepare, put or keep in readiness, make preparations; be ready* (pass.). (40)

ἑτοιμασία, ας, ἡ n. (ἕτοιμος) *readiness, preparation, equipment.* (1) Eph 6:15

ἕτοιμος, η, ον adj. (*) *ready, put in readiness,* τὰ ἕτοιμα *what has been accomplished, here, prepared.* (17)

ἑτοίμως adv. (ἕτοιμος) *readily,* ἑτοίμως ἔχω *to be ready.* (3)

ἔτος, ους, τό n. (*) *year,* ἔτη ἔχω *to be ... years old,* ὡς *or* ὡσεὶ ἐτῶν *about ... years old,* κατ᾽ ἔτος *every year.* (49)

εὖ adv. *well; well done! excellent!* (5)

Εὕα, ας, ἡ n. pers. *Eve.* (2)

εὐαγγελίζω v. (ἄγγελος) aor. εὐηγγέλισα; pf. pass. εὐηγγέλισμαι; aor. pass. εὐηγγελίσθην. act. and mid. *to bring good news, announce good news; proclaim the gospel, proclaim, preach;* pass. *be proclaimed, have good news announced to someone.* (54)

εὐαγγέλιον, ου, τό n. (ἄγγελος) *good news, gospel.* (76)

εὐαγγελιστής, οῦ, ὁ n. (ἄγγελος) *one who proclaims the gospel, evangelist.* (3)

εὐαρεστέω v. (ἀρέσκω) aor. εὐηρέστησα; pf. εὐηρέστηκα. *to please, be pleasing; be pleased, take delight, be satisfied* (pass.). (3)

εὐάρεστος, ον adj. (ἀρέσκω) *pleasing, acceptable,* εὐαρέστους εἶναι *give satisfaction; what is acceptable* (subst.). (9)

εὐαρέστως adv. (ἀρέσκω) *in an acceptable manner.* (1) Heb 12:28

Εὔβουλος, ου, ὁ n. pers. *Eubulus.* (1) 2 Ti 4:21

εὖγε adv. (γέ) *well done! excellent!* (1) Lk 19:17

εὐγενής, ές adj. (γίνομαι) *well-born, high-born; noble-minded, open-minded.* (3)

εὐδία, ας, ἡ n. (Ζεύς) *fair weather.* (1) Mt 16:2

εὐδοκέω v. (δοκέω) aor. εὐδόκησα. *to consent, determine, resolve, will, wish; be well pleased, take delight, like, approve.* (21)

εὐδοκία, ας, ἡ n. (δοκέω) *good will; favor, good pleasure; wish, desire.* (9)

εὐεργεσία, ας, ἡ n. (ἔργον) *doing good, service; good deed, benefit, a kindness.* (2)

εὐεργετέω v. (ἔργον) *to do good to, benefit.* (1) Ac 10:38

εὐεργέτης, ου, ὁ n. (ἔργον) *benefactor.* (1) Lk 22:25

εὔθετος, ον adj. (τίθημι) *fit, suitable, usable, convenient.* (3)

εὐθέως adv. (εὐθύς) *immediately, at once.* (36)

εὐθυδρομέω v. (εὐθύς, τρέχω) aor. εὐθυδρόμησα. *to run a straight course.* (2)

εὐθυμέω v. (θυμός) *to be cheerful, cheer up, keep up one's courage.* (3)

εὔθυμος, ον adj. (θυμός) *cheerful, in good spirits, encouraged.* (1) Ac 27:36

εὐθύμως adv. (θυμός) *cheerfully.* (1) Ac 24:10

εὐθύνω v. (εὐθύς) aor. εὔθυνα. *to straighten, make straight; guide straight, steer; a pilot* (ptc.). (2)

εὐθύς, εῖα, ύ adj. (*) *straight; proper, right, upright.* (51)

εὐθύς adv. (εὐθύς) *immediately, at once; then, so then.* (8)

εὐθύτης, ητος, ἡ n. (εὐθύς) *righteousness, uprightness.* (1) Heb 1:8

εὐκαιρέω v. (καιρός) aor. εὐκαίρησα. *to have time, have opportunity, spend one's time.* (3)

εὐκαιρία, ας, ἡ n. (καιρός) *favorable opportunity, right moment.* (2)

εὔκαιρος, ον adj. (καιρός) *well-timed, suitable, time of need.* (2)

εὐκαίρως adv. (καιρός) *conveniently, in season, when it is convenient.* (2)

εὔκοπος, ον adj. (κόπτω) *easy;* εὐκοπώτερόν ἐστιν *it is easier* (comp. in NT). (7)

εὐλάβεια, ας, ἡ n. (λαμβάνω) *awe, fear (of God), piety, anxiety.* (2)

εὐλαβέομαι v. (λαμβάνω) aor. pass. ηὐλαβήθην. *to be concerned, be anxious, become apprehensive, take care.* (1) Heb 11:7

εὐλαβής, ές adj. (λαμβάνω) *devout, God-fearing.* (4)

εὐλογέω v. (λέγω) fut. εὐλογήσω; aor. εὐλόγησα; pf. εὐλόγηκα; pf. pass. εὐλόγημαι. *to speak well of, praise; bless, consecrate; provide with benefits.* (42)

εὐλογητός, ή, όν adj. (λέγω) *blessed, praised,* ὁ εὐλογητός *the Blessed One* (of God). (8)

εὐλογία, ας, ἡ n. (λέγω) *praise; false eloquence, flattery, blessing; generous gift, bounty.* (16)

εὐμετάδοτος, ον adj. (δίδωμι) *generous.* (1) 1 Ti 6:18

Εὐνίκη, ης, ἡ n. pers. *Eunice.* (1) 2 Ti 1:5

εὐνοέω v. (νίπτω) *to be well-disposed, make friends.* (1) Mt 5:25

εὔνοια, ας, ἡ n. (νίπτω) *good attitude, willingness.* (1) Eph 6:7

εὐνουχίζω v. (ἔχω) aor. εὐνούχισα; aor. pass. εὐνουχίσθην. *to castrate, emasculate, make a eunuch of.* (2)

εὐνοῦχος, ου, ὁ n. (ἔχω) *eunuch, impotent male, a celibate.* (8)

Εὐοδία, ας, ἡ n. pers. *Euodia.* (1) Phil 4:2

εὐοδόω v. (ὁδός) aor. pass. εὐοδώθην. *to prosper, succeed, have things go well, be well, gain, earn* (pass. in NT). (4)

εὐπάρεδρος, ον adj. (ἑδραῖος) *constant; devotion* (subst. in NT). (1) 1 Cor 7:35

εὐπειθής, ές adj. (πείθω) *compliant, obedient.* (1) Jas 3:17

εὐπερίσπαστος, ον adj. *easily distracting.* (v.l.)

εὐπερίστατος, ον adj. (ἵστημι) *easily ensnaring, obstructing,* or *constricting.* (1) Heb 12:1

εὐποιΐα, ας, ἡ n. (ποιέω) *well-doing.* (1) Heb 13:16

εὐπορέω v. (πορεύομαι) *to have plenty, be well off, be (financially) able* (mid. in NT). (1) Ac 11:29

εὐπορία, ας, ἡ n. (πορεύομαι) *prosperity.* (1) Ac 19:25

εὐπρέπεια, ας, ἡ n. (πρέπω) *fine appearance, beauty.* (1) Jas 1:11

εὐπρόσδεκτος, ον adj. (δέχομαι) *acceptable; favorable.* (5)

εὐπροσωπέω v. (ὁράω) aor. εὐπροσώπησα. *to make a good showing.* (1) Gal 6:12

Εὐρακύλων, ωνος, ὁ n. pla. *the northeaster* (wind). (1) Ac 27:14

εὑρίσκω v. (*) fut. εὑρήσω; aor. εὗρον, εὗρα; pf. εὕρηκα; aor. pass. εὑρέθην. *to find, come upon; discover;* pass. *be found, find oneself; appear, prove;* mid. *find for oneself, obtain, have an opportunity, maintain.* (176)

Εὐροκλύδων, ωνος, ὁ n. pla. *the southeaster* (wind). (v.l.)

εὐρύχωρος, ον adj. (χωρέω) *broad, spacious, roomy.* (1) Mt 7:13

εὐσέβεια, ας, ἡ n. (σέβω) *devoutness, piety, godliness, respect for deity, devotion; godly acts* (pl.). (15)

εὐσεβέω v. (σέβω) *to show profound respect for, show exceptional devotion to, worship.* (2)

εὐσεβής, ές adj. (σέβω) *devout, godly, pious, reverent.* (3)

εὐσεβῶς adv. (σέβω) *in a godly manner.* (2)

εὔσημος, ον adj. (σημεῖον) *clear, distinct, intelligible.* (1) 1 Cor 14:9

εὔσπλαγχος, ον adj. (σπλάγχνον) *tender-hearted, compassionate, good-hearted.* (2)

εὐσχημόνως adv. (ἔχω) *decently, becomingly; correctly, in the right way.* (3)

εὐσχημοσύνη, ης, ἡ n. (ἔχω) *propriety, decorum, presentability.* (1) 1 Cor 12:23

εὐσχήμων, ον adj. (ἔχω) *proper, presentable,* τὸ εὔσχημον *good order; prominent, of high standing, noble.* (5)

εὐτόνως adv. (-τείνω) *vigorously, vehemently.* (2)

εὐτραπελία, ας, ἡ n. (τροπή) *coarse jesting, risqué wit.* (1) Eph 5:4

Εὔτυχος, ου, ὁ n. pers. *Eutychus.* (1) Ac 20:9

εὐφημία, ας, ἡ n. (φημί) *good report* or *repute.* (1) 2 Cor 6:8

εὔφημος, ον adj. (φημί) *praiseworthy, commendable.* (1) Phil 4:8

εὐφορέω v. (φέρω) aor. εὐφόρησα. *to bear good crops, yield well, be fruitful.* (1) Lk 12:16

εὐφραίνω v. (φρήν) aor. pass. ηὐφράνθην. *to gladden, cheer up, make glad;* pass. *be glad, enjoy oneself, rejoice, be merry; celebrate.* (14)

Εὐφράτης, ου, ὁ n. pla. *Euphrates.* (2)

εὐφροσύνη, ης, ἡ n. (φρήν) *joy, gladness, cheerfulness.* (2)

εὐχαριστέω v. (χαίρω) aor. εὐχαρίστησα; aor. pass. εὐχαριστήθην. *to be thankful, feel obligated to thank; give, express, render,* or *return thanks, offer a prayer of thanksgiving,* εὐχαριστῶ τῷ θεῷ *thanks be to God.* (38)

εὐχαριστία, ας, ἡ n. (χαίρω) *thankfulness, gratitude; the rendering of thanks, thanksgiving, prayer of thanksgiving.* (15)

εὐχάριστος, ον adj. (χαίρω) *thankful.* (1) Col 3:15

εὐχή, ῆς, ἡ n. (εὔχομαι) *prayer; vow.* (3)

εὔχομαι v. (*) aor. εὐξάμην. *to pray; wish.* (7)

εὔχρηστος, ον adj. (χράομαι) *useful, serviceable.* (3)

εὐψυχέω v. (ψύχω) *to be glad, have courage.* (1) Phil 2:19

εὐωδία, ας, ἡ n. (ὄζω) *aroma, fragrance, fragrant odor.* (3)

εὐώνυμος, ον adj. (ὄνομα) *left* (opp. right). (9)

ἐφ' = ἐπί before rough breathing.

ἔφαγον s. ἐσθίω (2 aor.).

ἐφάλλομαι v. (ἄλλομαι) *to leap upon.* (1) Ac 19:16

ἐφάπαξ adv. (ἅπαξ) *at once; once for all, once and never again.* (5)

Ἐφέσιος, α, ον adj. pla. *Ephesian; an Ephesian* (subst.). (5)

Ἔφεσος, ου, ἡ n. pla. *Ephesus.* (16)

ἐφευρετής, οῦ, ὁ n. (εὑρίσκω) *inventor, contriver.* (1) Rom 1:30

ἐφημερία, ας, ἡ n. (ἡμέρα) *division* (of priests). (2)

ἐφήμερος, ον adj. (ἡμέρα) *for the day, daily.* (1) Jas 2:15

ἐφικνέομαι v. (ἱκανός) aor. ἐφικόμην. *to come to, reach.* (2)

ἐφίστημι v. (ἵστημι) aor. ἐπέστην; pf. ἐφέστηκα. *to stand at* or *near; happen to, overtake, befall; attack; begin, come on; fix one's mind on, be attentive to, be ready, be on hand, be persistent;* pf. *stand by, be present; be imminent.* (21)

ἐφοράω v. (ὁράω) aor. ἐπεῖδον. *to gaze upon, look at, concern oneself with.* (2)

Ἐφραίμ, ὁ n. pla. *Ephraim.* (1) Jn 11:54

εφφαθα Ara. *be opened.* (1) Mk 7:34

ἐχθές adv. *yesterday* (day preceding today); *yesterday* (past time). (3)

ἔχθρα, ας, ἡ n. (ἐχθρός) *enmity.* (6)

ἐχθρός, ά, όν adj. (*) *hated; hating, hostile; enemy* (subst.). (32)

ἔχιδνα, ης, ἡ n. *snake, viper.* (5)
ἔχω v. (*) fut. ἕξω; aor. ἔσχον; pf. ἔσχηκα. *to have, own, possess, hold,* ἐν γαστρὶ ἔχω *be pregnant; have* (in close relationship), *have as, take; hold (to), grip, keep safe, seize; have on, wear; be able; consider, look upon, think; be possessed by, to have been granted, be under, one must; bring about, cause; meet,* ἔχω ὁδόν *be situated* (a certain distance) *away; it is, the situation is* (impers.)*; be* (in a certain way)*; next (to), belonging to, immediately* *following,* τῇ ἐχομένῃ *on the next day* (mid. ptc.). (708)
ἕως conj. *till, until; as long as, while;* adv. prep. w. gen. *until,* ἕως οὗ or ὅτου *until,* ἕως πότε *how long;* ἕως οὗ *while* (w. subj)*; as far as, to,* ἕως ἄνω *to the brim,* ἕως ἔσω *right into,* ἕως κάτω *to the bottom,* ἕως ὧδε *as far as this place,* ἕως πρός *as far as,* ἕως καὶ εἰς *even into,* ἕως ἔξω *outside,* ἕως ἐπί *to; up to; to the point of, as many as, even, unto,* ἐᾶτε ἕως τούτου *no more of this!* (146)

Ζαβουλών, ὁ n. pers. *Zebulun.* (3)
Ζακχαῖος, ου, ὁ n. pers. *Zacchaeus.* (3)
Ζάρα, ὁ n. pers. *Zerah.* (1) Mt 1:3
Ζαχαρίας, ου, ὁ n. pers. *Zechariah.* (11)
ζάω v. (*) fut. ζήσομαι, ζήσω; aor. ἔζησα. *to live, become alive again, be well, recover, live on, remain alive; be lively; meaning life, living* (ptc.). (140)
Ζεβεδαῖος, ου, ὁ n. pers. *Zebedee.* (12)
ζεστός, ή, όν adj. (ζέω) *hot.* (3)
ζεῦγος, ους, τό n. (ζυγός) *yoke, team; pair.* (2)
ζευκτηρία, ας, ἡ n. (ζυγός) *bands, ropes.* (1) Ac 27:40
Ζεύς, Διός, ὁ n. (*) pers. *Zeus.* (2)
ζέω v. (*) *to be enthusiastic, excited,* or *on fire.* (2)
ζηλεύω v. (ζέω) *to be eager, be earnest.* (1) Rev 3:19
ζῆλος, ου, ὁ and **ζῆλος, ους, τό** n. (ζέω) *zeal, ardor; jealousy, envy.* (16)
ζηλόω v. (ζέω) aor. ἐζήλωσα. *to strive, exert oneself earnestly, be dedicated, be deeply interested in, court someone's favor; be filled with jealousy or envy.* (11)
ζηλωτής, οῦ, ὁ n. (ζέω) *enthusiast, adherent, loyalist, one who is eager; patriot, zealot.* (8)
ζημία, ας, ἡ n. (*) *damage, disadvantage, loss, forfeit.* (4)
ζημιόω v. (ζημία) aor. pass. ἐζημιώθην. pass. in NT *to suffer damage* or *loss, forfeit, sustain injury, lose; be punished.* (6)
Ζηνᾶς, ὁ n. pers. *Zenas.* (1) Tit 3:13

ζητέω v. (*) fut. ζητήσω; aor. ἐζήτησα; aor. pass. ἐζητήθην. *to seek, look for, search for; investigate, examine, consider, deliberate; strive for, aim at, try to obtain, desire, wish for, want; ask for, request, demand, require.* (117)
ζήτημα, ατος, τό n. (ζητέω) *(controversial) question, issue, argument.* (5)
ζήτησις, εως, ἡ n. (ζητέω) *investigation; controversial question, controversy; discussion, debate.* (7)
ζιζάνιον, ου, τό n. Sem. *darnel; weeds* (pl. in NT). (8)
Ζοροβαβέλ, ὁ n. pers. *Zerubbabel.* (3)
ζόφος, ου, ὁ n. *darkness; gloom, hell.* (5)
ζυγός, οῦ, ὁ n. (*) *yoke; scale.* (6)
ζύμη, ης, ἡ n. (ζέω) *leaven* (lit. and fig.). (13)
ζυμόω v. (ζέω) aor. pass. ἐζυμώθην. *to ferment, leaven.* (4)
ζωγρέω v. (ζάω, ἄγρα) pf. pass. ἐζώγρημαι. *to capture alive, catch.* (2)
ζωή, ῆς, ἡ n. (ζάω) *life,* ψυχὴ ζωῆς *living thing.* (135)
ζώνη, ης, ἡ n. (ζώννυμι) *belt, girdle.* (8)
ζώννυμι and **ζωννύω** v. (*) fut. ζώσω; aor. ἔζωσα. *to gird.* (3)
ζωογονέω v. (ζάω, γίνομαι) fut. ζωογονήσω. *to give life to, make alive; keep alive.* (3)
ζῷον, ου, τό n. (ζάω) *animal; living thing* or *being.* (23)
ζωοποιέω v. (ζάω, ποιέω) fut. ζωοποιήσω; aor. ἐζωοποίησα; aor. pass. ἐζωοποιήθην. *to make alive, give life to.* (11)

H

ἤ part. (*) *or,* ἤ...ἤ *either...or; nor, or* (w. neg.)*; than, rather than,* πρὶν ἤ *before.* (343)

ἤγαγον s. ἄγω (2 aor.).

ἡγεμονεύω v. (ἄγω) *to be leader, command, rule, order, be governor, be procurator or prefect.* (2)

ἡγεμονία, ας, ἡ n. (ἄγω) *chief command, direction, management, reign, government.* (1) Lk 3:1

ἡγεμών, όνος, ὁ n. (ἄγω) *ruler; governor, procurator, prefect.* (20)

ἡγέομαι v. (ἄγω) aor. ἡγησάμην; pf. pass. ἥγημαι. *to think, consider, regard, deem, esteem, respect; ruler, leader, leading men, chief* (pres. ptc.). (28)

ᾔδειν s. οἶδα (2 plpf.).

ἡδέως adv. (ἡδονή) *gladly; very gladly* (superl. ἥδιστα). (5)

ἤδη adv. *now, already, by this time;* ἤδη ποτέ *now at length, now at last; in fact; really.* (61)

ἥδιστα s. ἡδέως (superl.).

ἡδονή, ῆς, ἡ n. (*) *pleasure, delight, enjoyment, (illicit) desire.* (5)

ἡδύοσμον, ου, τό n. (ἡδονή) *mint* (plant). (2)

ἦθος, ους, τό n. (ἔθος) *custom, usage, habit.* (1) 1 Cor 15:33

ἥκω v. (*) fut. ἥξω; aor. ἧξα. *to have come, be present, be here; come.* (26)

ἡλάμην s. ἄλλομαι (aor. mid.).

ἠλέγχθην s. ἐλέγχω (aor. pass.).

ἦλθα, ἦλθον s. ἔρχομαι (1 aor., 2 aor.).

ηλι Heb. *my God.* (2)

Ἡλί, ὁ n. pers. *Eli (Heli).* (1) Lk 3:23

Ἡλίας, ου, ὁ n. pers. *Elijah.* (29)

ἡλικία, ας, ἡ n. (*) *age, time of life, years; maturity; (bodily) stature.* (8)

ἡλίκος, η, ον adj. (ἡλικία) *how great, how large, how small.* (3)

ἥλιος, ου, ὁ n. (*) *the sun.* (32)

ἧλος, ου, ὁ n. (*) *nail.* (2)

ἡμεῖς s. ἐγώ (pl.).

ἡμέρα, ας, ἡ n. (*) *day* (opp. night)*, daylight; day* (24-hour period)*; day* (as in day of judgment)*; time.* (389)

ἡμέτερος, α, ον adj. (ἐγω) *our.* (7)

ἡμιθανής, ές adj. (ἥμισυς, θνήσκω) *half dead.* (1) Lk 10:30

ἥμισυς, εια, υ adj. (*) *half; one half* (neut. subst. in NT). (5)

ἡμίωρον, ου, τό n. (ἥμισυς, ὥρα) *a half hour.* (1) Rev 8:1

ἤνεγκα s. φέρω (aor.).

ἠνέῳγμαι, ἠνεῴχθην s. ἀνοίγω (pf. pass., aor. pass.).

ἡνίκα part. *when, at the time when,* ἡνίκα ἄν *whenever,* ἡνίκα ἐάν *when.* (2)

ἤπερ part. (ἤ, -πέρ) *than.* (1) Jn 12:43

ἤπιος, α, ον adj. *gentle, kind.* (1) 2 Ti 2:24

Ἤρ, ὁ n. pers. *Er.* (1) Lk 3:28

ἦρα s. αἴρω (aor.).

ἤρεμος, ον adj. *quiet, tranquil.* (1) 1 Ti 2:2

ἤρθην s. αἴρω (aor. pass.).

Ἡρῴδης, ου, ὁ n. pers. *Herod.* (43)

Ἡρῳδιανοί, ῶν, οἱ n. oth. *Herodians.* (3)

Ἡρῳδιάς, άδος, ἡ n. pers. *Herodias.* (6)

Ἡρῳδίων, ωνος, ὁ n. pers. *Herodion.* (1) Rom 16:11

Ἡσαΐας, ου, ὁ n. pers. *Isaiah.* (22)

Ἡσαῦ, ὁ n. pers. *Esau.* (3)

ἦσθα s. εἰμί (impf. 2 sg.).

ἥσσων, ον adj. (*) *lesser,* τὸ ἧσσον *worse; less* (neut. as adv.). (2)

ἡσυχάζω v. (ἡσύχιος) aor. ἡσύχασα. *to rest, abstain from work; be peaceable* or *orderly; be quiet, remain silent.* (5)

ἡσυχία, ας, ἡ n. (ἡσύχιος) *quietness, rest; silence.* (4)

ἡσύχιος, ον adj. (*) *quiet, well-ordered, without turmoil.* (2)

ἥτις s. ὅστις (fem.).

ἤτοι part. (ἤ, -τοί) *or,* ἤτοι . . . ἤ *either . . . or.* (1) Rom 6:16

ἡττάομαι v. (ἥσσων) pf. pass. ἥττημαι. *to be defeated, succumb.* (2)

ἥττημα, ατος, τό n. (ἥσσων) *loss.* (2)

ἤτω s. εἰμί (pres. impv. 3 sg.).

ηὐξήθην, ηὔξησα s. αὐξάνω (aor. pass., aor.).

ηὐφράνθην s. εὐφραίνω (aor. pass).

ἤφιε s. ἀφίημι (impf. 3 sg.).

ἠχέω v. (ἦχος) *to sound, ring out.* (1) 1 Cor 13:1

ἦχος, ου, ὁ n. (*) *sound, tone, noise; report, news.* (3)

ἦχος, ους, τό n. (ἦχος) *sound, tone, noise, roar.* (1) Lk 21:25

Θαδαῖος n. pers. alt. form of Θαδδαῖος. (v.l.)

Θαδδαῖος, ου, ὁ n. pers. *Thaddaeus*. (2)

θάλασσα, ης, ἡ n. (ἅλας) *sea; lake*. (91)

θάλπω v. *to cherish, comfort*. (2)

Θαμάρ, ἡ n. pers. *Tamar*. (1) Mt 1:3

θαμβέω v. (θάμβος) aor. pass. ἐθαμβήθην. *to be astounded* or *amazed* (pass. in NT). (3)

θάμβος, ους, τό n. (*) *amazement, awe*. (3)

θανάσιμος, ον adj. (θνήσκω) *deadly; deadly thing* (subst. in NT). (1) Mk 16:18

θανατηφόρος, ον adj. (θνήσκω, φέρω) *death-dealing, deadly*. (1) Jas 3:8

θάνατος, ου, ὁ n. (θνήσκω) *death*, θάνατοι *danger(s) of death; death* (spiritual or eternal); *fatal illness, pestilence*. (120)

θανατόω v. (θνήσκω) fut. θανατώσω; aor. ἐθανάτωσα; aor. pass. ἐθανατώθην. *to put to death, kill, have someone put to death, be in danger of death; extirpate; bring death*. (11)

θάπτω v. (*) aor. ἔθαψα; aor. pass. ἐτάφην. *to bury*. (11)

Θάρα, ὁ n. pers. *Terah*. (1) Lk 3:34

θαρρέω v. (θάρσος) aor. ἐθάρρησα. *to be confident, be courageous, be able to depend on, be bold*. (6)

θαρσέω v. (θάρσος) *to be courageous; have courage! don't be afraid!* (impv. in NT). (7)

θάρσος, ους, τό n. (*) *courage*. (1) Ac 28:15

θαῦμα, ατος, τό n. (θαυμάζω) *wonder, marvel; amazement*. (2)

θαυμάζω v. (*) aor. ἐθαύμασα; aor. pass.

ἐθαυμάσθην. *to wonder, marvel, be astonished* (intr.); *admire, wonder at, respect* (trans.); *wonder, be amazed* (pass.). (43)

θαυμάσιος, α, ον adj. (θαυμάζω) *wonderful; wonderful things* (neut. pl. subst. in NT). (1) Mt 21:15

θαυμαστός, ή, όν adj. (θαυμάζω) *wonderful, marvelous, remarkable*. (6)

θεά, ᾶς, ἡ n. (θεός) *goddess*. (1) Ac 19:27

θεάομαι v. (*) aor. ἐθεασάμην; pf. pass. τεθέαμαι; aor. pass. ἐθεάθην. *to see, look at; be seen, be noticed, attract attention* (pass.); *come* or *go to see, visit; behold*. (22)

θεατρίζω v. (θεάομαι) *to put to shame, expose publicly*. (1) Heb 10:33

θέατρον, ου, τό n. (θεάομαι) *theater; a play, spectacle*. (3)

θεῖον, ου, τό n. (*) *sulfur*. (7)

θεῖος, α, ον adj. (θεός) *divine; divine being, divinity* (neut. subst.). (3)

θειότης, ητος, ἡ n. (θεός) *divinity, divine nature, divineness*. (1) Rom 1:20

θειώδης, ες adj. (θεῖον) *sulfurous*. (1) Rev 9:17

θέλημα, ατος, τό n. (θέλω) *what is willed, will*, τὰ θελήματα *desires; will* (act), *desire*. (62)

θέλησις, εως, ἡ n. (θέλω) *will*. (1) Heb 2:4

θέλω v. (*) aor. ἠθέλησα. *to wish (to have), desire; will, want, be ready, prefer; like, take pleasure; maintain;* τί θέλει τοῦτο εἶναι *what can this mean?* (208)

θεμέλιον, ου, τό n. (τίθημι) *foundation, basis*. (1) Ac 16:26

θεμέλιος, ου, ὁ n. (τίθημι) *foundation* (stone); *foundation* (fig.), *treasure, reserve.* (15)

θεμελιόω v. (τίθημι) fut. θεμελιώσω; aor. ἐθεμελίωσα; pf. pass. τεθεμελίωμαι. *to lay a foundation, found; establish, strengthen.* (5)

θεοδίδακτος, ον adj. (θεός, διδάσκω) *taught* or *instructed by God.* (1) 1 Th 4:9

θεομάχος, ον adj. (θεός, μάχη) *fighting against God.* (1) Ac 5:39

θεόπνευστος, ον adj. (θεός, πνέω) *inspired by God.* (1) 2 Ti 3:16

θεός, οῦ, ὁ, ἡ n. (*) *deity, god, goddess; God* (of Christ); *God* (in Israelite and Christian contexts); *god* (of humans and of the belly); *god* (of the devil). (1317)

θεοσέβεια, ας, ἡ n. (θεός, σέβω) *piety, godliness.* (1) 1 Ti 2:10

θεοσεβής, ές adj. (θεός, σέβω) *god-fearing, devout.* (1) Jn 9:31

θεοστυγής, ές adj. (θεός, στυγητός) *hating God.* (1) Rom 1:30

θεότης, ητος, ἡ n. (θεός) *divine character* or *nature, deity, divinity.* (1) Col 2:9

Θεόφιλος, ου, ὁ n. pers. *Theophilus.* (2)

θεραπεία, ας, ἡ n. (θεράπων) *treatment, healing; servants.* (3)

θεραπεύω v. (θεράπων) fut. θεραπεύσω; aor. ἐθεράπευσα; pf. pass. τεθεράπευμαι; aor. pass. ἐθεραπεύθην. *to serve; heal, restore, cure.* (43)

θεράπων, οντος, ὁ n. (*) *servant.* (1) Heb 3:5

θερίζω v. (θέρμη) fut. θερίσω; aor. ἐθέρισα; aor. pass. ἐθερίσθην. *to harvest; reap.* (21)

θερισμός, οῦ, ὁ n. (θέρμη) *harvest* (process and time); *harvest* (crop). (13)

θεριστής, οῦ, ὁ n. (θέρμη) *reaper, harvester.* (2)

θερμαίνω v. (θέρμη) *to warm oneself* (mid. in NT). (6)

θέρμη, ης, ἡ n. (*) *heat.* (1) Ac 28:3

θέρος, ους, τό n. (θέρμη) *summer.* (3)

Θεσσαλονικεύς, έως, ὁ n. pla. *a Thessalonian.* (4)

Θεσσαλονίκη, ης, ἡ n. pla. *Thessalonica.* (5)

Θευδᾶς, ᾶ, ὁ n. pers. *Theudas.* (1) Ac 5:36

θεωρέω v. (θεάομαι) fut. θεώρησω; aor. ἐθεώρησα. *to be a spectator, look at, observe, see, catch sight of; notice, perceive, find, undergo, experience.* (58)

θεωρία, ας, ἡ n. (θεάομαι) *spectacle, sight.* (1) Lk 23:48

θήκη, ης, ἡ n. (τίθημι) *sheath* (for a sword). (1) Jn 18:11

θηλάζω v. (*) aor. ἐθήλασα. *to nurse* (of a woman); *suck, nurse* (of a child). (5)

θῆλυς, εια, υ adj. (θηλάζω) *female; woman* (subst.). (5)

θήρα, ας, ἡ n. (θηρίον) *net, trap.* (1) Rom 11:9

θηρεύω v. (θηρίον) aor. ἐθήρευσα. *to catch, hunt.* (1) Lk 11:54

θηριομαχέω v. (θηρίον, μάχη) aor. ἐθηριομάχησα. *to fight with wild animals; struggle* or *contend with* (fig.). (1) 1 Cor 15:32

θηρίον, ου, τό n. (*) *animal, beast, snake; monster* (fig.). (46)

θησαυρίζω v. (τίθημι) aor. ἐθησαύρισα; pf. pass. τεθησαύρισμαι. *to lay up, store up, gather, save; reserve.* (8)

θησαυρός, οῦ, ὁ n. (τίθημι) *repository, treasure box* or *chest, storehouse, storeroom; treasure.* (17)

θιγγάνω v. aor. ἔθιγον. *to touch.* (3)

θλίβω v. (*) pf. pass. τέθλιμμαι. *to press upon, crowd; press together, make narrow; oppress, afflict;* pass. *narrow* (pf. ptc.), *be afflicted* or *oppressed.* (10)

θλῖψις, εως, ἡ n. (θλίβω) *oppression, affliction, tribulation, difficult circumstances, distress; trouble.* (45)

θνήσκω v. (*) pf. τέθνηκα. *to die;* pf. in NT *have died, be dead; be dead* (fig.). (9)

θνητός, ή, όν adj. (θνήσκω) *mortal; the mortal* (subst.). (6)

θορυβάζω v. (θόρυβος) *to be troubled* or *distracted* (pass. in NT). (1) Lk 10: 41

θορυβέω v. (θόρυβος) *to throw into disorder; be troubled, distressed,* or *aroused, be in disorder* (pass.). (4)

θόρυβος, ου, ὁ n. (*) *noise, clamor; turmoil, excitement, uproar, disturbance.* (7)

θραύω v. pf. pass. τέθραυσμαι. *to break, weaken, oppress, tread down.* (1) Lk 4:18

θρέμμα, ατος, τό n. (τρέφω) *(domesticated) animal; flocks* (pl. in NT). (1) Jn 4:12

θρηνέω v. (θροέω) fut. θρηνήσω; aor. ἐθρήνησα. *to mourn, lament; sing a dirge; mourn for.* (4)

θρησκεία, ας, ἡ n. (θρησκός) *worship, religion.* (4)

θρησκός, όν adj. (*) *religious.* (1) Jas 1:26

θριαμβεύω v. aor. ἐθριάμβευσα. poss. mngs. *to lead in triumphal procession; to lead in triumph, cause to triumph, triumph over, expose to shame; display, publicize, make known.* (2)

θρίξ, τριχός, ἡ n. (*) *hair.* (15)

θροέω v. (*) *to be inwardly aroused, be disturbed* or *frightened* (pass. in NT). (3)

θρόμβος, ου, ὁ n. (τρέφω) *drop* or *clot* (of blood). (1) Lk 22:44

θρόνος, ου, ὁ n. *throne, the enthroned.* (62)

θρύπτω v. *to break in (small) pieces.* (v.l.)

Θυάτειρα, ων, τά n. pla. *Thyatira.* (4)

θυγάτηρ, τρός, ἡ n. (*) *daughter* (lit.); *daughter* (gen. as a girl or woman);

female descendant; daughter (as inhabitant). (28)

θυγάτριον, ου, τό n. (θυγάτηρ) *little daughter.* (2)

θύελλα, ης, ἡ n. (θυμός) *storm, whirlwind.* (1) Heb 12:18

θύϊνος, η, ον adj. (θύω) *from the citron tree, scented.* (1) Rev 18:12

θυμίαμα, ατος, τό n. (θύω) *incense; incense burning* or *offering.* (6)

θυμιατήριον, ου, τό n. (θύω) *altar of incense.* (1) Heb 9:4

θυμιάω v. (θύω) aor. ἐθυμίασα. *to make an incense offering.* (1) Lk 1:9

θυμομαχέω v. (θυμός, μάχη) *to be very angry.* (1) Ac 12:20

θυμός, οῦ, ὁ n. (*) *passion, passionate longing; anger, rage, wrath, indignation.* (18)

θυμόω v. (θυμός) aor. pass. ἐθυμώθην. *to make angry; become angry* (pass. in NT). (1) Mt 2:16

θύρα, ας, ἡ n. (*) *door* (lit. and fig.), *opportunity; gate, entrance, doorway.* (39)

θυρεός, οῦ, ὁ n. (θύρα) *shield.* (1) Eph 6:16

θυρίς, ίδος, ἡ n. (θύρα) *window.* (2)

θυρωρός, οῦ, ὁ, ἡ n. (θύρα) *doorkeeper, gatekeeper.* (4)

θυσία, ας, ἡ n. (θύω) *offering* (act); *sacrifice, offering.* (28)

θυσιαστήριον, ου, τό n. (θύω) *altar; sanctuary.* (23)

θύω v. (*) aor. ἔθυσα; pf. pass. τέθυμαι; aor. pass. ἐτύθην. *to sacrifice; kill, slaughter, kill; slaughter sacrificially; celebrate.* (14)

θῶ s. τίθημι (aor. subj.).

Θωμᾶς, ᾶ, ὁ n. pers. *Thomas.* (11)

θώραξ, ακος, ὁ n. *breastplate, chest.* (5)

Ἰάϊρος, ου, ὁ n. pers. *Jairus.* (2)
Ἰακώβ, ὁ n. pers. *Jacob.* (27)
Ἰάκωβος, ου, ὁ n. pers. *James.* (42)
ἴαμα, ατος, τό n. (ἰάομαι) *healing.* (3)
Ἰαμβρῆς, ὁ n. pers. *Jambres.* (1) 2 Ti 3:8
Ἰανναί, ὁ n. pers. *Jannai.* (1) Lk 3:24
Ἰάννης, ὁ n. pers. *Jannes.* (1) 2 Ti 3:8
ἰάομαι v. (*) fut. ἰάσομαι; aor. ἰασάμην; pf. pass. ἴαμαι; aor. pass. ἰάθην. *to heal, cure; restore.* (26)
Ἰάρετ, ὁ n. pers. *Jared.* (1) Lk 3:37
ἴασις, εως, ἡ n. (ἰάομαι) *healing.* (3)
ἴασπις, ιδος, ἡ n. *jasper.* (4)
Ἰάσων, ονος, ὁ n. pers. *Jason.* (5)
ἰατρός, οῦ, ὁ n. (ἰάομαι) *physician.* (7)
ἴδε part. (εἶδος) *look! see! take notice; here is (are); pay attention! here.* (29)
ἴδιος, α, ον adj. (*) *one's own, private, belonging to one; own* (w. emph.)*; own* (for a pron)*;* οἱ ἴδιοι *associates, relations, relatives;* τὰ ἴδια *home, possessions, property, affairs, business;* ἰδίᾳ *and* κατ᾽ ἰδίαν *by oneself, privately.* (114)
ἰδιώτης, ου, ὁ n. (ἴδιος) *layperson, amateur, unskilled* or *untrained person; one not in the know, outsider.* (5)
ἰδού part. (εἶδος) *behold, look, see, yet, remember, consider; see! here* or *there is (are), here* or *there was (were), there comes (came).* (200)
Ἰδουμαία, ας, ἡ n. pla. *Idumea.* (1) Mk 3:8
ἱδρώς, ῶτος, ὁ n. *sweat, perspiration.* (1) Lk 22:44
Ἰεζάβελ, ἡ n. pers. *Jezebel.* (1) Rev 2:20
Ἱεράπολις, εως, ἡ n. pla. *Hierapolis.* (1) Col 4:13
ἱερατεία, ας, ἡ n. (ἱερός) *priestly office* or *service.* (2)

ἱεράτευμα, ατος, τό n. (ἱερός) *priesthood.* (2)
ἱερατεύω v. (ἱερός) *to hold the office of a priest, perform the service of a priest.* (1) Lk 1:8
Ἰερεμίας, ου, ὁ n. pers. *Jeremiah.* (3)
ἱερεύς, έως, ὁ n. (ἱερός) *priest* (lit. and fig.). (31)
Ἰεριχώ, ἡ n. pla. *Jericho.* (7)
ἱερόθυτος, ον adj. (ἱερός, θύω) *devoted* or *sacrificed to a divinity; meat sacrificed to idols* (neut. subst. in NT). (1) 1 Cor 10:28
ἱερόν, οῦ, τό n. (ἱερός) *temple, sanctuary.* (71)
ἱεροπρεπής, ές adj. (ἱερός, πρέπω) *reverent, venerable.* (1) Tit 2:3
ἱερός, ά, όν adj. (*) *holy;* τὰ ἱερά *the holy things.* (3)
Ἱεροσόλυμα, τά, ἡ and **Ἰερουσαλήμ, ἡ** n. pla. *Jerusalem* (lit. and fig.). (139)
Ἱεροσολυμίτης, ου, ὁ n. pla. *inhabitant of Jerusalem.* (2)
ἱεροσυλέω v. (ἱερός, συλάω) *to rob temples; commit sacrilege.* (1) Rom 2:22
ἱερόσυλος, ον adj. (ἱερός, συλάω) *temple robber; sacrilegious person* (subst. in NT). (1) Ac 19:37
ἱερουργέω v. (ἱερός, ἔργον) *to perform holy service, act as a priest.* (1) Rom 15:16
ἱερωσύνη, ης, ἡ n. (ἱερός) *priestly office, priesthood.* (3)
Ἰεσσαί, ὁ n. pers. *Jesse.* (5)
Ἰεφθάε, ὁ n. pers. *Jephthah.* (1) Heb 11:32
Ἰεχονίας, ου, ὁ n. pers. *Jechoniah.* (2)
Ἰησοῦς, οῦ, ὁ n. pers. *Jesus, Joshua.* (917)

ἱκανός, ή, όν adj. (*) sufficient, adequate, (large) enough, τὸ ἱκανόν ποιῶ to satisfy, τὸ ἱκανόν bail; fit, appropriate, competent, qualified, able, worthy, good enough; considerable, large, loud, bright, severe enough, large sum, ἐφ' ἱκανόν for a long time, long; many, quite a few. (39)

ἱκανότης, ητος, ή n. (ἱκανός) fitness, capability, qualification. (1) 2 Cor 3:5

ἱκανόω v. (ἱκανός) aor. ἱκάνωσα. to make sufficient, qualify, empower, authorize. (2)

ἱκετηρία, ας, ή n. (ἱκανός) supplication, prayer. (1) Heb 5:7

ἱκμάς, άδος, ή n. moisture. (1) Lk 8:6

Ἰκόνιον, ου, τό n. pla. Iconium. (6)

ἱλαρός, ά, όν adj. (ἵλεως) cheerful, glad, happy. (1) 2 Cor 9:7

ἱλαρότης, ητος, ή n. (ἵλεως) cheerfulness, gladness, wholeheartedness, graciousness. (1) Rom 12:8

ἱλάσκομαι v. (ἵλεως) aor. pass. ἱλάσθην. to expiate, wipe out, make atonement for; be merciful or gracious (pass.). (2)

ἱλασμός, οῦ, ὁ n. (ἵλεως) expiation. (2)

ἱλαστήριον, ου, τό n. (ἵλεως) means of expiation; place of propitiation, mercyseat. (2)

ἵλεως, ων adj. (*) gracious, merciful, ἵλεώς σοι God forbid! (2)

Ἰλλυρικόν, οῦ, τό n. pla. Illyricum. (1) Rom 15:19

ἱμάς, άντος, ὁ n. strap, thong, whip. (4)

ἱματίζω v. (ἱμάτιον) pf. pass. ἱμάτισμαι. to dress, clothe. (2)

ἱμάτιον, ου, τό n. (*) clothing, apparel; cloak, coat, robe; clothes (pl.). (60)

ἱματισμός, οῦ, ὁ n. (ἱμάτιον) clothing, apparel. (5)

ἵνα conj. (*) in order that; that, (somet. with subj. for impv.); so that; that (for emph.). (663)

ἱνατί conj. (ἵνα, τίς) why? for what reason? (6)

Ἰόππη, ης, ή n. pla. Joppa. (10)

Ἰορδάνης, ου, ὁ n. pla. Jordan (River). (15)

ἰός, οῦ, ὁ n. (*) poison, venom; corrosion, rust. (3)

Ἰουδαία, ας, ή n. pla. Judea (region in southern Palestine); Judea (all Palestine). (43)

ἰουδαΐζω v. to live in a Jewish (or Judean) fashion. (1) Gal 2:14

Ἰουδαϊκός, ή, όν adj. pla. Jewish (or Judean). (1) Tit 1:14

Ἰουδαϊκῶς adv. pla. in a Jewish (or Judean) manner. (1) Gal 2:14

Ἰουδαῖος, α, ον adj. pla. Jewish (or Judean); subst. a Jew or Jewess (or a Judean). (195)

Ἰουδαϊσμός, οῦ, ὁ n. oth. Judaism (or Judeanism). (2)

Ἰούδας, α, ὁ n. pers. Judah (persons, tribe, and territory); Judas; Jude. (44)

Ἰουλία, ας, ή n. pers. Julia. (1) Rom 16:15

Ἰούλιος, ου, ὁ n. pers. Julius. (2)

Ἰουνία, ας, ή n. pers. Junia. (1) Rom 16:7

Ἰουνιᾶς, ᾶ, ὁ n. pers. Junias. (v.l.)

Ἰοῦστος, ου, ὁ n. pers. Justus. (3)

ἱππεύς, έως, ὁ n. (ἵππος) horse rider, cavalryman. (2)

ἱππικός, ή, όν adj. (ἵππος) pertaining to a horse rider; cavalry (subst. in NT). (1) Rev 9:16

ἵππος, ου, ὁ n. (*) horse, steed. (17)

ἶρις, ιδος, ή n. rainbow; halo, radiance. (2)

Ἰσαάκ, ὁ n. pers. Isaac. (20)

ἰσάγγελος, ον adj. (ἴσος, ἄγγελος) like an angel. (1) Lk 20:36

ἴσθι s. εἰμί (pres. impv.).

Ἰσκαριώθ, ὁ and Ἰσκαριώτης, ου, ὁ n. pers. Iscariot. (11)

ἴσος, η, ον adj. (*) equal, same, consistent, τὰ ἴσα an equal amount; equally, equal (neut. pl. as adv.). (8)

ἰσότης, ητος, ή n. (ἴσος) equality, fairness. (3)

ἰσότιμος, ον adj. (ἴσος, τιμή) equal,

like, of the same kind or value. (1) 2
Pt 1:1

ἰσόψυχος, ον adj. (ἴσος, ψύχω) of like
soul or mind. (1) Phil 2:20

Ἰσραήλ, ὁ n. pla. Israel (person, nation,
and fig. of Christians). (68)

Ἰσραηλίτης, ου, ὁ n. pla. an Israelite.
(9)

Ἰσσαχάρ, ὁ n. pers. Issachar. (1) Rev
7:7

ἴστε s. οἶδα (2 pf. ind. or impv. 2 pl.).

ἵστημι and **ἱστάνω** v. (*) fut. στήσω;
aor. ἔστησα, ἔστην; pf. ἔστηκα; aor.
pass. ἐστάθην. trans. (pres., fut., 1 aor.
act.) set, place, bring, allow to come;
put forward, propose; establish, hold
against; reinforce validity of, up-
hold, maintain, validate; make someone stand; set or fix a time, determine a
monetary amount, pay; intr. (2 aor. act.,
fut. mid. and pass., aor. pass.) stand
(still), stop, come to an end; come up,
stand, appear; resist; stand firm or still,
hold one's ground; stand up; intr. (pf.,
plpf.) stand; stand (there), be (there),
stand around idle; attend upon, be the
servant of; stand firm; stand or be in.
(155)

ἱστορέω v. aor. ἱστόρησα. to visit, to
make the acquaintance of. (1) Gal 1:18

ἰσχυρός, ά, όν adj. (ἰσχύς) strong; violent, loud, severe, mighty, strong. (29)

ἰσχύς, ύος, ἡ n. (*) strength, might,
power. (10)

ἰσχύω v. (ἰσχύς) fut. ἰσχύσω; aor.
ἴσχυσα. to be in good health, be
healthy; have power, be competent, be

able, εἰς οὐδὲν ἰσχύω be good for
nothing, be strong enough; be mighty,
win out, prevail; be valid, be in force,
mean. (28)

ἴσως adv. (ἴσος) perhaps, probably. (1)
Lk 20:13

Ἰταλία, ας, ἡ n. pla. Italy. (4)

Ἰταλικός, ή, όν adj. pla. Italian. (1) Ac
10:1

Ἰτουραῖος, α, ον adj. pla. Ituraean. (1)
Lk 3:1

ἰχθύδιον, ου, τό n. (ἰχθύς) little fish. (2)

ἰχθύς, ύος, ὁ n. (*) fish. (20)

ἴχνος, ους, τό n. (*) footprint, footstep
(fig. in NT). (3)

Ἰωαθάμ, ὁ n. pers. Jotham. (2)

Ἰωακίμ, ὁ and **Ἰωακείμ, ὁ** n. pers.
Joachim (= Jehoiakim). (v.l.)

Ἰωανάν, ὁ n. pers. Joanan. (1) Lk 3:27

Ἰωάννα, ας, ἡ n. pers. Joanna. (2)

Ἰωάννης, ου, ὁ n. pers. John. (135)

Ἰώβ, ὁ n. pers. Job. (1) Jas 5:11

Ἰωβήδ, ὁ n. pers. Obed. (3)

Ἰωδά, ὁ n. pers. Joda. (1) Lk 3:26

Ἰωήλ, ὁ n. pers. Joel. (1) Ac 2:16

Ἰωνάθας, ου, ὁ n. pers. Jonathas. (v.l.)

Ἰωνάμ, ὁ n. pers. Jonam. (1) Lk 3:30

Ἰωνᾶς, ᾶ, ὁ n. pers. Jonah. (9)

Ἰωράμ, ὁ n. pers. Joram. (2)

Ἰωρίμ, ὁ n. pers. Jorim. (1) Lk 3:29

Ἰωσαφάτ, ὁ n. pers. Josaphat (= Jeho-
shaphat). (2)

Ἰωσῆς, ῆτος, ὁ n. pers. Joses. (3)

Ἰωσήφ, ὁ n. pers. Joseph. (35)

Ἰωσήχ, ὁ n. pers. Josech. (1) Lk 3:26

Ἰωσίας, ου, ὁ n. pers. Josiah. (2)

ἰῶτα, τό n. iota. (1) Mt 5:18

K

κἀγώ (καί, ἐγώ) = καὶ ἐγώ *and I, as I; but I; I also, I too, I for my part, I in turn; I in particular, I for instance; if I.* (84)

καθ᾽ = κατά before rough breathing.

καθά conj. or adv. (ὅς) *just as.* (1) Mt 27:10

καθαίρεσις, εως, ἡ n. (αἱρέω) *tearing down, destruction; disabling.* (3)

καθαιρέω v. (αἱρέω) fut. καθελῶ; aor. καθεῖλον. *to take* or *bring down, lower; tear down, destroy, overpower, conquer; suffer the loss of* (pass.). (9)

καθαίρω v. (καθαρός) *to clear, prune.* (1) Jn 15:2

καθάπερ conj. or adv. (ὅς, -πέρ) *just as.* (13)

καθάπτω v. (ἅπτω) aor. καθῆψα. *to take hold of, seize, fasten on.* (1) Ac 28:3

καθαρίζω v. (καθαρός) fut. καθαριῶ; aor. ἐκαθάρισα. *to make clean; heal; declare clean, cleanse, purify.* (31)

καθαρισμός, οῦ, ὁ n. (καθαρός) *purification; purity.* (7)

καθαρός, ά, όν adj. (*) *clean, clear; ritually pure; free* (from sin), *guiltless; pure.* (27)

καθαρότης, ητος, ἡ n. (καθαρός) *purity.* (1) Heb 9:13

καθέδρα, ας, ἡ n. (ἑδραῖος) *chair; seat.* (3)

καθέζομαι v. (ἑδραῖος) *to sit, remain, be, be situated; sit down.* (7)

καθεῖλον, καθελῶ s. καθαιρέω (2 aor., fut.).

καθεξῆς adv. (ἔχω) *in order, one after the other, in orderly sequence, point by point,* οἱ καθεξῆς *the successors,* τὸ καθεξῆς *afterward.* (5)

καθεύδω v. *to sleep; be indifferent; sleep* (= *be dead*). (22)

καθηγητής, οῦ, ὁ n. (ἄγω) *teacher.* (2)

καθῆκα s. καθίημι (aor.).

καθήκω v. (ἥκω) *it comes (to someone), it is fitting,* τὰ μὴ καθήκοντα *what is improper* (impers. in NT). (2)

κάθημαι v. (ἑδραῖος) fut. καθήσομαι. *to sit, sit there, sit quietly, be enthroned; stay, be, live, reside, settle; sit down.* (91)

καθημερινός, ή, όν adj. (ἡμέρα) *daily.* (1) Ac 6:1

καθίζω v. (*) fut. καθίσω; aor. ἐκάθισα; pf. κεκάθικα. trans. *to seat, set; appoint, install, authorize;* intr. *sit down, rest upon; reside, settle, stay, live.* (46)

καθίημι v. (-ἵημι) aor. καθῆκα. *to let down.* (4)

καθίστημι and καθιστάνω v. (ἵστημι) fut. καταστήσω; aor. κατέστησα; aor. pass. κατεστάθην. *to bring, conduct, take; appoint, put in charge, authorize; make, cause; be made, become* (pass.). (21)

καθό adv. (ὅς) *as; in so far as, to the degree that.* (4)

καθόλου adv. (ὅλος) *entirely, completely,* καθόλου μή *not at all.* (1) Ac 4:18

καθοπλίζω v. (ὅπλον) pf. pass. καθώπλισμαι. *to arm* or *equip oneself; in his armor, fully armed* (mid. ptc. in NT). (1) Lk 11:21

καθοράω v. (ὁράω) *to perceive, notice.* (1) Rom 1:20

καθότι conj. (ὅς) *as, to the degree that; because, in view of the fact that.* (6)

καθώς adv. (ὡς) *just as, as; to the degree that; since, in so far as; when; how* (indirect discourse). (182)

καθώσπερ adv. (ὡς, -πέρ) *just as, as*. (1) Heb 5:4

καί conj. (*) *and, when, and then, and so, and yet, nevertheless, but, who? how? that is, namely, indeed;* καί ... καί *both ... and, not only ... but also; also, likewise, even, so also, so, at all, still,* καί γάρ *for,* καί γε *indeed*. (9161)

Καϊάφας, α, ὁ n. pers. *Caiaphas*. (9)

Κάϊν, ὁ n. pers. *Cain*. (3)

Καϊνάμ, ὁ n. pers. *Cainan*. (2)

καινός, ή, όν adj. (*) *new* (in quality), *unused; unknown, strange, remarkable; new* (in time). (42)

καινότης, ητος, ἡ n. (καινός) *newness; new* (= adj. in NT). (2)

καίπερ conj. (καί, -πέρ) *although*. (5)

καιρός, οῦ, ὁ n. (*) *time, period, season,* ἄχρι καιροῦ *for a while,* πρὸς καιρόν *for a limited* or *short time, right* or *proper time, opportunity; definite* or *fixed time, festal season,* κατὰ καιρόν *from time to time* or *at the right time,* καιρῷ ἰδίῳ *in due time;* καιροῖς ἰδίοις *at the right time; present (time),* ἐν αὐτῷ τῷ καιρῷ *just at that time, time of crisis, last times, endtime*. (85)

Καῖσαρ, αρος, ὁ n. pers. *emperor, Caesar*. (29)

Καισάρεια, ας, ἡ n. pla. *Caesarea*. (17)

καίτοι conj. (καί, -τοί) *yet, on the other hand*. (2)

καίτοιγε conj. (καί, -τοί, γέ) *although*. (1) Jn 4:2

καίω v. (*) pf. pass. κεκαύμαι. *to light, have* or *keep burning; burn (up);* pass. *be lit, burn; be burned*. (12)

κἀκεῖ adv. (καί, ἐκεῖ) = καὶ ἐκεῖ *and there; there also*. (10)

κἀκεῖθεν adv. (καί, ἐκεῖ) = καὶ ἐκεῖθεν *and from there; and then*. (10)

κἀκεῖνος, η, ο (καί, ἐκεῖ) = καὶ ἐκεῖνος *and that (one* or *thing) he, that one* or *he also*. (22)

κακία, ας, ἡ n. (κακός) *badness, depravity, wickedness, vice; malice, ill-will, malignity; trouble, misfortune*. (11)

κακοήθεια, ας, ἡ n. (κακός, ἔθος) *meanspiritedness, malice, malignity, craftiness*. (1) Rom 1:29

κακολογέω v. (κακός, λέγω) aor. ἐκακολόγησα. *to speak evil of, revile, insult*. (4)

κακοπαθέω v. (κακός, πάσχω) aor. ἐκακοπάθησα. *to suffer misfortune; bear hardship patiently*. (3)

κακοπαθία, ας, ἡ n. (κακός, πάσχω) *suffering, strenuous effort, perseverance*. (1) Jas 5:10

κακοποιέω v. (κακός, ποιέω) aor. ἐκακοποίησα. *to do wrong, be an evildoer* or *criminal; harm, injure*. (4)

κακοποιός, όν adj. (κακός, ποιέω) *doing evil; evildoer, criminal, sorcerer* (subst. in NT). (3)

κακός, ή, όν adj. (*) *bad, evil, base; injurious, dangerous, pernicious;* neut. subst. *evil, wrong, evil deed; misfortune, harm*. (50)

κακοῦργος, ον adj. (κακός, ἔργον) *evil doing; criminal, evildoer* (subst. in NT). (4)

κακουχέω v. (κακός, ἔχω) *to mistreat, torment; be mistreated* or *tormented* (pass. in NT). (2)

κακόω v. (κακός) fut. κακώσω; aor. ἐκάκωσα. *to harm, mistreat; make angry, embitter, poison*. (6)

κακῶς adv. (κακός) *bad, badly, severely,* κακῶς ἔχω *to be sick; wrongly, wickedly, with wrong motives*. (16)

κάκωσις, εως, ἡ n. (κακός) *mistreatment, oppression*. (1) Ac 7:34

καλάμη, ης, ἡ n. (*) *stalk, straw, stubble*. (1) 1 Cor 3:12

κάλαμος, ου, ὁ n. (καλάμη) *reed; stalk, staff; measuring rod; reed pen*. (12)

καλέω v. (*) fut. καλέσω; aor. ἐκάλεσα; pf. κέκληκα; pf. pass. κέκλημαι; aor. pass. ἐκλήθην. *to call, call by name, address as, designate as, name, provide with a name; invite,* ὁ κεκληκώς

the host; summon, call together, call in;
call (to something); pass. *be called, be*
named, have as a name, be; be invited;
be called (to something). (148)
καλλιέλαιος, ου, ἡ n. (καλός, ἐλαία)
cultivated olive tree. (1) Rom 11:24
κάλλιον s. καλῶς (comp.).
καλοδιδάσκαλος, ον adj. (καλός,
διδάσκω) *teaching what is good.* (1)
Tit 2:3
Καλοὶ Λιμένες, Καλῶν Λιμένων, οἱ
n. pla. *Fair Havens.* (1) Ac 27:8
καλοποιέω v. (καλός, ποιέω) *to do what*
is right or *good.* (1) 2 Th 3:13
καλός, ἡ, όν adj. (*) *beautiful, hand-*
some; good, useful, free from defects,
fine, precious, noble, praiseworthy,
morally unobjectionable, blameless,
excellent, full measure, pleasant, desir-
able, advantageous, pleasing to God,
better, τὸ καλόν *what passes the test.*
(100)
κάλυμμα, ατος, τό n. (καλύπτω) *head-*
covering, covering, veil (lit. and fig.).
(4)
καλύπτω v. (*) fut. καλύψω; aor.
ἐκάλυψα; pf. pass. κεκάλυμμαι. *to*
cover (up); hide, conceal, keep secret,
remove from sight. (8)
καλῶς adv. (καλός) *fitly, appropriately,*
in the right way, splendidly, well,
please, well enough; commendably, in
a manner free from objection; in a man-
ner that is beneficial or acceptable,
καλῶς ἔχω *be well or in good health;*
rightly, quite right!, well said! cor-
rectly; καλῶς ποιέω *do what is right,*
act rightly, do well, be kind; κάλλιον
very well (comp.). (37)
κάμηλος, ου, ὁ, ἡ n. *camel.* (6)
κάμιλος, ου, ὁ n. *rope, ship's cable.*
(v.l.)
κάμινος, ου, ἡ n. (καίω) *oven, furnace.*
(4)
καμμύω v. (-μύω) aor. ἐκάμμυσα. *to*
close (of eyes). (2)
κάμνω v. aor. ἔκαμον. *to be weary, be*
fatigued; be ill; die (poss.). (2)

κάμπτω v. (*) fut. κάμψω; aor. ἔκαμψα.
to bend, bow; bend (itself). (4)
κἄν (καί, εἰ, ἄν) = καὶ ἐάν *and if,*
whether; even if, even though; (even)
if only, at least, just. (17)
Κανά, ἡ n. pla. *Cana.* (4)
Καναναῖος, ου, ὁ n. pla. *a Cananaean,*
zealot. (2)
Κανανίτης, ου, ὁ n. pla. *a Cananite.*
(v.l.)
Κανδάκη, ης, ἡ n. pers. *Candace.* (1) Ac
8:27
κανών, όνος, ὁ n. *rule, standard; assign-*
ment, formulation. (4)
καπηλεύω v. *to trade in, peddle, huck-*
ster. (1) 2 Cor 2:17
καπνός, οῦ, ὁ n. *smoke.* (13)
Καππαδοκία, ας, ἡ n. pla. *Cappadocia.*
(2)
καρδία, ας, ἡ n. (*) *heart, inner self,*
mind, desire; interior, center. (156)
καρδιογνώστης, ου, ὁ n. (καρδία,
γινώσκω) *knower of hearts, one who*
knows the hearts. (2)
Κάρπος, ου, ὁ n. pers. *Carpus.* (1) 2 Ti
4:13
καρπός, οῦ, ὁ n. (*) *fruit, crop(s), re-*
sult, outcome, product, deed; advan-
tage, gain, profit. (66)
καρποφορέω v. (καρπός, φέρω) fut.
καρποφορήσω; aor. ἐκαρποφόρησα. *to*
bear fruit or *crops; bear fruit* (fig.). (8)
καρποφόρος, ον adj. (καρπός, φέρω)
fruitbearing, fruitful. (1) Ac 14:17
καρτερέω v. (κράτος) aor. ἐκαρτέρησα.
to be strong, be steadfast, hold, out,
endure, persevere. (1) Heb 11:27
κάρφος, ους, τό n. *speck, splinter, chip.*
(6)
κατ' = κατά *before smooth breathing.*
κατά prep. (*) w. gen. *down (from), into,*
throughout; down upon or *toward, by,*
against, in contradiction to; w. acc.
along, over, through, in, upon, toward,
to, up to, κατὰ πρόσωπον *face to face,*
κατ' οἶκον *from house to house* (ex.
of distr. use: place); *at, on, during,*
about, κατ' ἡμέραν *daily* (ex. of distr.

use: time); *at a time, in detail; for the purpose of, for; according to, in accordance with, in conformity with, because of, on the basis of, just as, with; with respect to, in relation to;* οἱ κατὰ φύσιν κλάδοι *the natural branches* (ex. of use like an adj.), ἡ καθ᾽ ὑμᾶς πίστις *your faith* (ex. of posses. use), ἡ κατὰ πίστιν δικαιοσύνη *the righteousness of faith* (ex. of a gen. w. a n.). (473)

καταβαίνω v. (-βαίνω) fut. καταβήσομαι; aor. κατέβην; pf. καταβέβηκα. *to come, go,* or *climb down, get out, descend, fall down; be brought down.* (81)

καταβάλλω v. (βάλλω) *to throw down, strike down;* mid. *found, lay (a foundation).* (2)

καταβαρέω v. (βάρος) aor. κατεβάρησα. *to burden, be a burden.* (1) 2 Cor 12:16

καταβαρύνω v. (βάρος) *to weigh down; be heavy* (pass. in NT). (1) Mk 14:40

κατάβασις, εως, ἡ n. (-βαίνω) *descent, slope, declivity.* (1) Lk 19:37

καταβιβάζω v. *bring down, drive down.* (v.l.)

καταβολή, ῆς, ἡ n. (βάλλω) *foundation, beginning;* εἰς καταβολὴν σπέρματος *to establish a posterity* or *to become a father.* (11)

καταβραβεύω v. (βραβεύω) *to rob of a prize, condemn.* (1) Col 2:18

καταγγελεύς, έως, ὁ n. (ἄγγελος) *proclaimer, preacher.* (1) Ac 17:18

καταγγέλλω v. (ἄγγελος) aor. κατήγγειλα; aor. pass. κατηγγέλην. *to proclaim, announce, make known.* (18)

καταγελάω v. (γελάω) *to laugh at, ridicule.* (3)

καταγινώσκω v. (γινώσκω) pf. pass. κατέγνωσμαι. *to condemn, convict.* (3)

κατάγνυμι v. (ἀξίνη) fut. κατεάξω; aor. κατέαξα; aor. pass. κατεάγην. *to break.* (4)

καταγράφω v. (γράφω) *to write, draw figures.* (1) Jn 8:6

κατάγω v. (ἄγω) aor. κατήγαγον; aor. pass. κατήχθην. *to lead* or *bring down; put in* (pass.). (9)

καταγωνίζομαι v. (ἀγών) aor. κατηγωνισάμην. *to conquer, defeat, overcome.* (1) Heb 11:33

καταδέω v. (δέω) aor. κατέδησα. *to bind up, bandage.* (1) Lk 10:34

κατάδηλος, ον adj. (δῆλος) *very clear, quite plain.* (1) Heb 7:15

καταδικάζω v. (δίκη) aor. κατεδίκασα. *to condemn, find* or *pronounce guilty.* (5)

καταδίκη, ης, ἡ n. (δίκη) *(sentence of) condemnation, conviction, guilty verdict.* (1) Ac 25:15

καταδιώκω v. (διώκω) aor. κατεδίωξα. *to search for eagerly, hunt for.* (1) Mk 1:36

καταδουλόω v. (δοῦλος) fut. καταδουλώσω. *to enslave, reduce to slavery* (fig. in NT). (2)

καταδυναστεύω v. (δύναμαι) *to oppress, exploit, dominate.* (2)

κατάθεμα, ατος, τό n. (τίθημι) *something cursed.* (1) Rev 22:3

καταθεματίζω v. (τίθημι) *to curse.* (1) Mt 26:74

καταισχύνω v. (αἰσχρός) aor. pass. κατῃσχύνθην. *to dishonor, disgrace; put to shame, disappoint; be disappointed* (pass.). (13)

κατακαίω v. (καίω) fut. κατακαύσω; aor. κατέκαυσα; aor. pass. κατεκαύθην, κατεκάην. *to burn (down), burn up, consume.* (12)

κατακαλύπτω v. (καλύπτω) *to cover, veil; cover oneself* (mid. in NT). (3)

κατακαυχάομαι v. (καυχάομαι) *to boast against, brag, exult over; triumph over.* (4)

κατάκειμαι v. (κεῖμαι) *to lie down* (of sick people); *recline for a meal, dine.* (12)

κατακλάω v. (κλάω) aor. κατέκλασα. *to break in pieces.* (2)

κατακλείω v. (κλείω) aor. κατέκλεισα. *to shut up, lock up.* (2)

κατακληρονομέω v. (κλῆρος, νόμος) aor. κατεκληρονόμησα. *to give as rightful possession.* (1) Ac 13:19

κατακλίνω v. (κλίνω) aor. κατέκλινα; aor. pass. κατεκλίθην. *to cause to lie or sit down; recline at table* (pass.). (5)

κατακλύζω v. (κλύδων) aor. pass. κατεκλύσθην. *to flood, inundate.* (1) 2 Pt 3:6

κατακλυσμός, οῦ, ὁ n. (κλύδων) *flood, deluge.* (4)

κατακολουθέω v. (ἀκολουθέω) aor. κατηκολούθησα. *to follow.* (2)

κατακόπτω v. (κόπτω) *to lacerate, cut, beat.* (1) Mk 5:5

κατακρημνίζω v. (κρεμάννυμι) aor. κατεκρήμνισα. *to throw down from a cliff.* (1) Lk 4:29

κατάκριμα, ατος, τό n. (κρίνω) *condemnation, punishment, penalty, death-sentence, doom.* (3)

κατακρίνω v. (κρίνω) fut. κατακρινῶ; aor. κατέκρινα; pf. pass. κατακέκριμαι; aor. pass. κατεκρίθην. *to pronounce a sentence on, sentence, condemn, adjudge; be under a sentence* (pass.). (18)

κατάκρισις, εως, ἡ n. (κρίνω) *condemnation.* (2)

κατακύπτω v. (κύπτω) aor. κατέκυψα. *to bend down.* (1) Jn 8:8

κατακυριεύω v. (κύριος) aor. κατεκυρίευσα. *to become master, gain dominion over, subdue; be master, lord it (over), rule.* (4)

καταλαλέω v. (λαλέω) *to speak degradingly of, speak evil of, speak against, defame, slander.* (5)

καταλαλιά, ᾶς, ἡ n. (λαλέω) *evil speech, slander, defamation, detraction.* (2)

κατάλαλος, ον adj. (λαλέω) *slanderous; slanderer* (subst. in NT). (1) Rom 1:30

καταλαμβάνω v. (λαμβάνω) aor. κατέλαβον; pf. κατείληφα; pf. pass. κατείλημμαι; aor. pass. κατελήμφθην. *to win, attain, make one's own; catch*

up with, seize, overtake; catch, detect; grasp, find, understand (mid.). (15)

καταλέγω v. (λέγω) *to select, enroll.* (1) 1 Ti 5:9

καταλείπω v. (λείπω) fut. καταλείψω; aor. κατέλιπον; pf. pass. καταλέλειμμαι; aor. pass. κατελείφθην. *to leave (behind); leave; leave over; leave without help; give up, neglect; remain (behind)* (pass.). (24)

καταλιθάζω v. (λίθος) fut. καταλιθάσω. *to stone to death.* (1) Lk 20:6

καταλλαγή, ῆς, ἡ n. (ἄλλος) *reconciliation.* (4)

καταλλάσσω v. (ἄλλος) aor. κατήλλαξα; aor. pass. κατηλλάγην. *to reconcile.* (6)

κατάλοιπος, ον adj. (λείπω) *left, remaining.* (1) Ac 15:17

κατάλυμα, ατος, τό n. (λύω) *lodging place, guest-room, dining-room.* (3)

καταλύω v. (λύω) fut. καταλύσω; aor. κατέλυσα; aor. pass. κατελύθην. *to throw down, detach; destroy, demolish, dismantle, tear down; put an end to, abolish, do away with, repeal, ruin, suppress, stop; halt, rest, find lodging.* (17)

καταμανθάνω v. (μανθάνω) aor. κατέμαθον. *to observe (well), notice, learn.* (1) Mt 6:28

καταμαρτυρέω v. (μάρτυς) *to bear witness against, testify against.* (3)

καταμένω v. (μένω) *to stay, live.* (1) Ac 1:13

καταναλίσκω v. (ἄλωσις) *to consume.* (1) Heb 12:29

καταναρκάω v. fut. καταναρκήσω; aor. κατενάρκησα. *to burden, be a burden to.* (3)

κατανεύω v. (νεύω) aor. κατένευσα. *to signal.* (1) Lk 5:7

κατανοέω v. (νίπτω) aor. κατενόησα. *to notice, observe, consider, contemplate, look at; envisage, think about, see through.* (14)

καταντάω v. (κατά, ἀντί) aor. κατήντησα; pf. κατήντηκα. *to come (to),* arrive (at), reach; arrive at, attain, meet. (13)

κατάνυξις, εως, ἡ n. (νύσσω) *stupefaction, stupor.* (1) Rom 11:8

κατανύσσομαι v. (νύσσω) aor. pass. κατενύγην. *to be pierced, be stabbed.* (1) Ac 2:37

καταξιόω v. (ἄξιος) aor. pass. κατηξιώθην. *to consider worthy.* (3)

καταπατέω v. (πατέω) fut. καταπατήσω; aor. κατεπάτησα; aor. pass. κατεπατήθην. *to trample (under foot), tread upon; treat with disdain.* (5)

κατάπαυσις, εως, ἡ n. (παύω) *rest, place of rest.* (9)

καταπαύω v. (παύω) aor. κατέπαυσα. *to cause to rest, restrain; stop, rest* (intr.). (4)

καταπέτασμα, ατος, τό n. (πέτομαι) *curtain.* (6)

καταπίμπρημι v. *to burn to ashes.* (v.l.)

καταπίνω v. (πίνω) aor. κατέπιον; aor. pass. κατεπόθην. *to swallow (up); devour;* pass. *be drowned, be overwhelmed; be swallowed up.* (7)

καταπίπτω v. (πίπτω) aor. κατέπεσον. *to fall (down).* (3)

καταπλέω v. (πλέω) aor. κατέπλευσα. *to sail (down).* (1) Lk 8:26

καταπονέω v. (πόνος) *to subdue, wear out, oppress, torment, mistreat.* (2)

καταποντίζω v. aor. pass. κατεποντίσθην. *to drown; be sunk, be drowned, sink* (pass. in NT). (2)

κατάρα, ας, ἡ n. (ἀρά) *curse, imprecation, object of a curse.* (6)

καταράομαι v. (ἀρά) aor. κατηρασάμην; pf. pass. κατήραμαι. *to curse, execrate.* (5)

καταργέω v. (ἔργον) fut. καταργήσω; aor. κατήργησα; pf. κατήργηκα; pf. pass. κατήργημαι; aor. pass. κατηργήθην. *to use up, exhaust, waste; invalidate, make powerless, nullify; abolish, wipe out, set aside, do away with, bring to an end, break the power of, destroy;* pass. *cease, pass away,*

doom to perish, be transitory; be discharged, be released. (27)

καταριθμέω v. (ἀριθμός) pf. pass. κατηρίθμημαι. *to count among; belong to* (pass. in NT). (1) Ac 1:17

καταρτίζω v. (ἄρτι) fut. καταρτίσω; aor. κατήρτισα; pf. pass. κατήρτισμαι. *to put in order, restore, adjust, (make) complete, prepare, make, create, outfit;* pass. *mend one's ways, be fully trained; be created, be designed.* (13)

κατάρτισις, εως, ἡ n. (ἄρτι) *maturation.* (1) 2 Cor 13:9

καταρτισμός, οῦ, ὁ n. (ἄρτι) *equipment, equipping, training, discipline.* (1) Eph 4:12

κατασείω v. (σείω) aor. κατέσεισα. *to shake, wave; make a sign, motion.* (4)

κατασκάπτω v. (σκάπτω) aor. κατέσκαψα; pf. pass. κατέσκαμμαι. *to tear down, raze to the ground.* (2)

κατασκευάζω v. (σκεῦος) fut. κατασκευάσω; aor. κατεσκεύασα; pf. pass. κατεσκεύασμαι; aor. pass. κατεσκευάσθην. *to make ready, prepare; build, construct, erect, create; furnish, equip.* (11)

κατασκηνόω v. (σκηνή) fut. κατασκηνώσω; aor. κατεσκήνωσα. *to live, settle, nest, dwell.* (4)

κατασκήνωσις, εως, ἡ n. (σκηνή) *a place to live, nest.* (2)

κατασκιάζω v. (σκιά) *to overshadow.* (1) Heb 9:5

κατασκοπέω v. (σκοπός) aor. κατεσκόπησα. *to spy out, lie in wait for.* (1) Gal 2:4

κατάσκοπος, ου, ὁ n. (σκοπός) *spy.* (1) Heb 11:31

κατασοφίζομαι v. (σοφός) aor. κατεσοφισάμην. *to get the better of, take advantage of by cunning* or *trickery.* (1) Ac 7:19

καταστέλλω v. (στέλλω) aor. κατέστειλα; pf. pass. κατέσταλμαι. *to restrain, quiet, calm.* (2)

κατάστημα, ατος, τό n. (ἵστημι) *behavior, demeanor.* (1) Tit 2:3

καταστολή, ῆς, ἡ n. (στέλλω) *attire, clothing.* (1) 1 Ti 2:9

καταστρέφω v. (στρέφω) aor. κατέστρεψα. *to upset, overturn.* (2)

καταστρηνιάω v. (στρῆνος) aor. κατεστρηνίασα. *to be governed by strong physical desire, feel sensuous impulses that alienate.* (1) 1 Ti 5:11

καταστροφή, ῆς, ἡ n. (στρέφω) *destruction; ruin.* (2)

καταστρώννυμι v. (στρωννύω) aor. pass. κατεστρώθην. *to lay low, kill.* (1) 1 Cor 10:5

κατασύρω v. (σύρω) *to drag (away by force).* (1) Lk 12:58

κατασφάζω v. (σφάζω) aor. κατέσφαξα. *to slaughter, strike down.* (1) Lk 19: 27

κατασφραγίζω v. (σφραγίς) pf. pass. κατεσφράγισμαι. *to seal (up).* (1) Rev 5:1

κατάσχεσις, εως, ἡ n. (ἔχω) *possession, taking into possession.* (2)

κατάσχω s. κατέχω (2 aor. subj.).

κατατίθημι v. (τίθημι) aor. κατέθηκα. *to place; grant, give, do* (mid. in NT). (2)

κατατομή, ῆς, ἡ n. (τομός) *mutilation, cutting in pieces.* (1) Phil 3:2

κατατρέχω v. (τρέχω) aor. κατέδραμον. *to run down.* (1) Ac 21:32

καταφέρω v. (φέρω) aor. κατήνεγκα; aor. pass. κατηνέχθην. *to cast against* (of votes), *bring* (of charges)*; be brought into, sink into, be overcome* (pass.). (4)

καταφεύγω v. (φεύγω) aor. κατέφυγον. *to flee; take refuge.* (2)

καταφθείρω v. (φθείρω) pf. pass. κατέφθαρμαι. *to ruin, corrupt, deprave.* (1) 2 Ti 3:8

καταφιλέω v. (φίλος) aor. κατεφίλησα. *to kiss.* (6)

καταφρονέω v. (φρήν) fut. καταφρονήσω; aor. κατεφρόνησα. *to look down on, despise, scorn, treat with contempt; care nothing for, disregard, be unafraid of.* (9)

καταφρονητής, οῦ, ὁ n. (φρήν) *despiser, scoffer.* (1) Ac 13:41

καταχέω v. (-χέω) aor. κατέχεα. *to pour out* or *down over.* (2)

καταχθόνιος, ον adj. *under the earth, subterranean.* (1) Phil 2:10

καταχράομαι v. (χράομαι) aor. κατεχρησάμην. *to use, make use of.* (2)

καταψύχω v. (ψύχω) aor. κατέψυξα. *to cool off, refresh.* (1) Lk 16:24

κατεάγην, κατέαξα, κατέαξω s. κατάγνυμι (2 aor. pass., aor., fut.).

κατέβην s. καταβαίνω (2 aor.).

κατεγέλων s. καταγελάω (impf.).

κατέγνωσμαι s. καταγινώσκω (pf. pass.).

κατέδραμον s. κατατρέχω (2 aor.).

κατείδωλος, ον adj. (εἶδος) *full of cult-images* or *idols.* (1) Ac 17:16

κατείλημμαι, κατείληφα s. καταλαμβάνω (pf. pass., 2 pf.).

κατεκάην s. κατακαίω (2 aor. pass.).

κατεκρίθην s. κατακρίνω (aor. pass.).

κατέλαβον, κατελήμφθην s. καταλαμβάνω (2 aor., aor. pass.).

κατελθεῖν s. κατέρχομαι (2 aor. inf.).

κατέλιπον s. καταλείπω (2 aor.).

κατέναντι adv. (κατά, ἐν, ἀντί) *opposite;* adv. prep. w. gen. *opposite; in the sight of, before.* (8)

κατενεχθείς s. καταφέρω (aor. pass. ptc.).

κατενύγην s. κατανύσσομαι (2 aor. pass.).

κατενώπιον adv. (ὁράω) adv. prep. w. gen. in NT *opposite, in the presence of; before.* (3)

κατεξουσιάζω v. (εἰμί) *to exercise authority, tyrannize.* (2)

κατέπεσον s. καταπίπτω (2 aor.).

κατεπέστην s. κατεφίσταμαι (2 aor.).

κατέπιον s. καταπίνω (2 aor.).

κατέπλευσα s. καταπλέω (aor.).

κατεπόθην s. καταπίνω (aor. pass.).

κατεργάζομαι v. (ἔργον) aor. κατειργασάμην; pf. pass. κατείργασμαι; aor. pass. κατειργάσθην. *to do, achieve, accomplish, commit; bring about, produce, create, call forth, work out; prepare; conquer, overpower, subdue.* (22)

κατέρχομαι v. (ἔρχομαι) aor. κατῆλθον. *to come down; arrive, put in.* (16)

κατεσθίω v. (ἐσθίω) fut. καταφάγομαι; aor. κατέφαγον. *to eat up, consume, devour, swallow; destroy, tear to pieces, exploit.* (14)

κατευθύνω v. (εὐθύς) aor. κατεύθυνα. *to lead, direct.* (3)

κατευλογέω v. (λέγω) *to bless.* (1) Mk 10:16

κατεφίσταμαι v. (ἵστημι) aor. κατεπέστην. *to rise up.* (1) Ac 18:12

κατέχω v. (ἔχω) aor. κατέσχον. *to prevent, hinder, restrain, hold back, keep, hold down, suppress, stifle, check, delay; hold to, hold fast, retain; possess; confine, bind; take into one's possession, occupy; lay claim to; hold course, head for.* (17)

κατηγορέω v. (ἄγω) fut. κατηγορήσω; aor. κατηγόρησα. *to bring charges against; accuse, reproach.* (23)

κατηγορία, ας, ἡ n. (ἄγω) *accusation, charge.* (3)

κατήγορος, ου, ὁ n. (ἄγω) *accuser.* (4)

κατήγωρ, ορος, ὁ n. (ἄγω) *accuser.* (1) Rev 12:10

κατήφεια, ας, ἡ n. (φαίνω) *gloominess, dejection.* (1) Jas 4:9

κατηχέω v. (ἦχος) aor. κατήχησα; pf. pass. κατήχημαι; aor. pass. κατηχήθην. *to report, inform; teach, instruct.* (8)

κατήχθην s. κατάγω (aor. pass.).

κατιόω v. (ἰός) pf. pass. κατίωμαι. *to rust over; become rusty, tarnished, or corroded* (pass. in NT). (1) Jas 5:3

κατισχύω v. (ἰσχύς) fut. κατισχύσω; aor. κατίσχυσα. *to be dominant, prevail, be able; win a victory over.* (3)

κατοικέω v. (οἶκος) aor. κατῴκησα. *to live, dwell, reside, settle (down); inhabit, dwell in* (trans.). (44)

κατοίκησις, εως, ἡ n. (οἶκος) *living quarters, dwelling,* κατοίκησιν ἔχω *to live.* (1) Mk 5:3

κατοικητήριον, ου, τό n. (οἶκος) *dwelling-place.* (2)

κατοικία, ας, ἡ n. (οἶκος) *dwelling-place, habitation.* (1) Ac 17:26

κατοικίζω v. (οἶκος) aor. κατῴκισα. *to cause to dwell* or *live, establish, settle.* (1) Jas 4:5

κατοπτρίζω v. (ὁράω) *to produce a reflection; contemplate, reflect* (mid. in NT). (1) 2 Cor 3:18

κάτω adv. (κατά) *below,* τὰ κάτω *this world; downwards, down, bottom.* (9)

κατώτερος, α, ον adj. (κατά) *lower.* (1) Eph 4:9

κατωτέρω adv. (κατά) *lower, below, under.* (1) Mt 2:16

Καῦδα n. pla. *Cauda.* (1) Ac 27:16

καῦμα, ατος, τό n. (καίω) *burning, heat.* (2)

καυματίζω v. (καίω) aor. ἐκαυμάτισα; aor. pass. ἐκαυματίσθην. *to burn up, scorch.* (4)

καῦσις, εως, ἡ n. (καίω) *burning.* (1) Heb 6:8

καυσόω v. (καίω) *to suffer from burning heat; be consumed by heat, burn up* (pass. in NT). (2)

καυστηριάζω v. (καίω) pf. pass. κεκαυστηρίασμαι. *to sear.* (1) 1 Ti 4:2

καύσων, ωνος, ὁ n. (καίω) *heat, burning (sun), hot day, scorching heat.* (3)

καυχάομαι v. (*) fut. καυχήσομαι; aor. ἐκαυχησάμην; pf. pass. κεκαύχημαι. *to boast, glory, pride oneself, brag; boast about, be proud of* (trans.). (37)

καύχημα, ατος, τό n. (καυχάομαι) *boast, object of boasting, pride; what is said in boasting* or *praise.* (11)

καύχησις, εως, ἡ n. (καυχάομαι) *boasting, pride; object of boasting, reason for boasting.* (11)

Καφαρναούμ, ἡ n. pla. *Capernaum.* (16)

Κεγχρεαί, ῶν, αἱ n. pla. *Cenchreae.* (2)

Κεδρών, ὁ n. pla. *Kidron.* (1) Jn 18:1

κεῖμαι v. (*) *to lie, recline; stand, be laid, be stored; be appointed, be set,* be destined, be given, exist, be valid, find oneself, be. (24)

κειρία, ας, ἡ n. (κείρω) binding material. (1) Jn 11:44

κείρω v. (*) aor. ἔκειρα. to shear; cut one's hair, have one's hair cut (mid.). (4)

κέλευσμα, ατος, τό n. (κελεύω) signal, cry of command. (1) 1 Th 4:16

κελεύω v. (*) aor. ἐκέλευσα. to command, order, urge. (25)

κενοδοξία, ας, ἡ n. (κενός, δοκέω) vanity, conceit, excessive ambition. (1) Phil 2:3

κενόδοξος, ον adj. (κενός, δοκέω) conceited, boastful. (1) Gal 5:26

κενός, ή, όν adj. (*) empty, emptyhanded; without content, truth, or power, without any basis, foolish, senseless; vain, εἰς κενόν in vain, to no purpose. (18)

κενοφωνία, ας, ἡ n. (κενός, φωνή) empty talk, chatter. (2)

κενόω v. (κενός) fut. κενώσω; aor. ἐκένωσα; pf. pass. κεκένωμαι; aor. pass. ἐκενώθην. to empty, divest of prestige; destroy, render void, make invalid. (5)

κέντρον, ου, τό n. (*) sting; goad. (4)

κεντυρίων, ωνος, ὁ n. Lat. centurion. (3)

κενῶς adv. (κενός) in an empty manner, idly, in vain. (1) Jas 4:5

κεραία, ας, ἡ n. (κέρας) projection, hook, serif (part of a letter). (2)

κεραμεύς, έως, ὁ n. (κέραμος) potter. (3)

κεραμικός, ή, όν adj. (κέραμος) belonging to the potter, made of clay. (1) Rev 2:27

κεράμιον, ου, τό n. (κέραμος) earthenware vessel, jar. (2)

κέραμος, ου, ὁ n. (*) roof tile. (1) Lk 5:19

κεράννυμι v. (*) aor. ἐκέρασα; pf. pass. κεκέρασμαι. to mix, pour. (3)

κέρας, ατος, τό n. (*) horn; corner, end, extension; horn (of power). (11)

κεράτιον, ου, τό n. (κέρας) carob pod. (1) Lk 15:16

κερδαίνω v. (κέρδος) fut. κερδήσω; aor. ἐκέρδησα; aor. pass. ἐκερδήθην. to gain, profit; spare oneself, avoid. (17)

κέρδος, ους, τό n. (*) gain, profit. (3)

κέρμα, ατος, τό n. (κείρω) piece of money, coin, (small) change. (1) Jn 2:15

κερματιστής, οῦ, ὁ n. (κείρω) money-changer. (1) Jn 2:14

κεφάλαιον, ου, τό n. (κεφαλή) main thing, main point; sum of money. (2)

κεφαλή, ῆς, ἡ n. (*) head, κατὰ κεφαλῆς ἔχω to have on the head; head (of superior rank), uppermost part, extremity, end, point, κεφαλὴ γωνίας cornerstone. (75)

κεφαλιόω v. (κεφαλή) aor. ἐκεφαλίωσα. to strike on the head. (1) Mk 12:4

κεφαλίς, ίδος, ἡ n. (κεφαλή) roll (of a book). (1) Heb 10:7

κέχρημαι s. χράομαι (pf. pass.).

κημόω v. fut. κημώσω. to muzzle. (1) 1 Cor 9:9

κῆνσος, ου, ὁ n. Lat. tax, poll-tax. (4)

κῆπος, ου, ὁ n. (*) garden. (5)

κηπουρός, οῦ, ὁ n. (κῆπος) gardener. (1) Jn 20:15

κηρίον, ου, τό n. wax, honey-comb. (v.l.)

κήρυγμα, ατος, τό n. (κηρύσσω) something proclaimed aloud, (gospel) proclamation. (9)

κῆρυξ, υκος, ὁ n. (κηρύσσω) herald, proclaimer. (3)

κηρύσσω v. (*) aor. ἐκήρυξα; aor. pass. ἐκηρύχθην. to announce, make known; proclaim (aloud), speak of, mention publicly, spread, preach, publicize. (61)

κῆτος, ους, τό n. sea-monster. (1) Mt 12:40

Κηφᾶς, ᾶ, ὁ n. pers. Cephas. (9)

κιβωτός, οῦ, ἡ n. boat, ark; κιβωτός τῆς διαθήκης covenant chest. (6)

κιθάρα, ας, ἡ n. (*) lyre, harp. (4)

κιθαρίζω v. (κιθάρα) to play the lyre or harp. (2)

κιθαρῳδός, οῦ, ὁ n. (κιθάρα, ᾠδη) *lyre-player, harpist*. (2)

Κιλικία, ας, ἡ n. pla. *Cilicia*. (8)

κινδυνεύω v. (κίνδυνος) *to be in danger, run a risk; there is a danger* (impers.). (4)

κίνδυνος, ου, ὁ n. (*) *danger, risk*. (9)

κινέω v. (*) fut. κινήσω; aor. ἐκίνησα; aor. pass. ἐκινήθην. *to move away, remove; move, set in motion, shake, arouse; move around, exist* (pass.); *cause, bring about*. (8)

κίνησις, εως, ἡ n. *motion*. (v.l.)

κιννάμωμον, ου, τό n. Sem. *cinnamon*. (1) Rev 18:13

Κίς, ὁ n. pers. *Kish*. (1) Ac 13:21

κίχρημι v. (χράομαι) aor. ἔχρησα. *to lend*. (1) Lk 11:5

κλάδος, ου, ὁ n. (κλάω) *branch*. (11)

κλαίω v. (*) fut. κλαύσω; aor. ἔκλαυσα. *to weep, cry; weep for, bewail* (trans.). (40)

κλάσις, εως, ἡ n. (κλάω) *breaking (of bread)*. (2)

κλάσμα, ατος, τό n. (κλάω) *fragment, piece, crumb*. (9)

Κλαῦδα n. pla. *Clauda* (alt. form of Καῦδα). (v.l.)

Κλαυδία, ας, ἡ n. pers. *Claudia*. (1) 2 Ti 4:21

Κλαύδιος, ου, ὁ n. pers. *Claudius*. (3)

κλαυθμός, οῦ, ὁ n. (*) *weeping, crying*. (9)

κλάω v. (*) aor. ἔκλασα. *to break (of bread)*. (14)

κλείς, κλειδός, ἡ n. (κλείω) *key*. (6)

κλείω v. (*) fut. κλείσω; aor. ἔκλεισα; pf. pass. κέκλεισμαι; aor. pass. ἐκλείσθην. *to shut, lock, bar; close*. (16)

κλέμμα, ατος, τό n. (κλέπτω) *stealing, theft*. (1) Rev 9:21

Κλεοπᾶς, ᾶ, ὁ n. pers. *Cleopas*. (1) Lk 24:18

κλέος, ους, τό n. *fame, glory, credit*. (1) 1 Pt 2:20

κλέπτης, ου, ὁ n. (κλέπτω) *thief*. (16)

κλέπτω v. (*) fut. κλέψω; aor. ἔκλεψα. *to steal*. (13)

κλῆμα, ατος, τό n. (κλάω) *branch*. (4)

Κλήμης, εντος, ὁ n. pers. *Clement*. (1) Phil 4:3

κληρονομέω v. (κλῆρος, νόμος) fut. κληρονομήσω; aor. ἐκληρονόμησα; pf. κεκληρονόμηκα. *to inherit, be an heir; acquire, obtain, come into possession of, receive, share in*. (18)

κληρονομία, ας, ἡ n. (κλῆρος, νόμος) *inheritance; possession, property; salvation, share*. (14)

κληρονόμος, ου, ὁ n. (κλῆρος, νόμος) *heir; beneficiary*. (15)

κλῆρος, ου, ὁ n. (*) *lot; portion, share, place, inheritance*, οἱ κλῆροι *those in one's care*. (11)

κληρόω v. (κλῆρος) aor. pass. ἐκληρώθην. *to appoint by lot, choose; obtain an inheritance*. (1) Eph 1:11

κλῆσις, εως, ἡ n. (καλέω) *call, calling, invitation; position, condition*. (11)

κλητός, ή, όν adj. (καλέω) *called, invited*. (10)

κλίβανος, ου, ὁ n. *oven, furnace*. (2)

κλίμα, ατος, τό n. (κλίνω) *district, region*. (3)

κλινάριον, ου, τό n. (κλίνω) *bed, cot*. (1) Ac 5:15

κλίνη, ης, ἡ n. (κλίνω) *bed, couch, pallet, stretcher, sickbed; dining couch*. (9)

κλινίδιον, ου, τό n. (κλίνω) *small bed, pallet, stretcher*. (2)

κλίνω v. (*) aor. ἔκλινα; pf. κέκλικα. *to incline, bow; lay (down); cause to fall, turn to flight; decline, be far spent* (intr.). (7)

κλισία, ας, ἡ n. (κλίνω) *group (of people eating)*. (1) Lk 9:14

κλοπή, ῆς, ἡ n. (κλέπτω) *theft, stealing*. (2)

κλύδων, ωνος, ὁ n. (*) *rough water, surf*. (2)

κλυδωνίζομαι v. (κλύδων) *to be tossed about by waves*. (1) Eph 4:14

Κλωπᾶς, ᾶ, ὁ n. pers. *Clopas*. (1) Jn 19:25

κνήθω v. (γναφεύς) *to itch; feel an itching* (pass. in NT). (1) 2 Ti 4:3

Κνίδος, ου, ἡ n. pla. *Cnidus.* (1) Ac 27:7

κοδράντης, ου, ὁ n. Lat. *quadrans, penny* (Roman copper coin, 1/64 of a denarius). (2)

κοιλία, ας, ἡ n. *belly, stomach; womb, uterus,* ἐκ κοιλίας *from birth; heart.* (22)

κοιμάω v. (κεῖμαι) pf. pass. κεκοίμημαι; aor. pass. ἐκοιμήθην. *to sleep, fall asleep; die, pass away* (pass. in NT). (18)

κοίμησις, εως, ἡ n. (κεῖμαι) *lying down to sleep, sleep.* (1) Jn 11:13

κοινός, ή, όν adj. (*) *communal, (in) common; common, ordinary, profane, impure, unclean.* (14)

κοινόω v. (κοινός) aor. ἐκοίνωσα; pf. κεκοίνωκα; pf. pass. κεκοίνωμαι. *to make common* or *impure, defile, desecrate; consider* or *declare unclean.* (14)

κοινωνέω v. (κοινός) aor. ἐκοινώνησα. *to share, have a share, participate, take an interest in; give a share, make one a partner.* (8)

κοινωνία, ας, ἡ n. (κοινός) *fellowship, association, communion, close relationship, unity; generosity, fellow-feeling, altruism; sign of fellowship, gift, contribution; participation, sharing, taking part, common possession.* (19)

κοινωνικός, ή, όν adj. (κοινός) *liberal, generous.* (1) 1 Ti 6:18

κοινωνός, οῦ, ὁ, ἡ n. (κοινός) *companion, partner, sharer.* (10)

κοίτη, ης, ἡ n. (κεῖμαι) *bed, marriage-bed; sexual intercourse, sexual excesses* (pl.), *semen,* κοίτην ἔχω *to conceive.* (4)

κοιτών, ῶνος, ὁ n. (κεῖμαι) *bedroom.* (1) Ac 12:20

κόκκινος, η, ον adj. (κόκκος) *red, scarlet; scarlet cloth, scarlet garment* (neut. subst.). (6)

κόκκος, ου, ὁ n. (*) *seed, grain.* (7)

κολάζω v. (κωλύω) aor. ἐκόλασα. *to penalize, punish.* (2)

κολακεία, ας, ἡ n. *flattery.* (1) 1 Th 2:5

κόλασις, εως, ἡ n. (κωλύω) *punishment.* (2)

κολαφίζω v. aor. ἐκολάφισα. *to strike with the fist, beat, cuff, treat roughly; torment.* (5)

κολλάω v. (*) aor. pass. ἐκολλήθην. *to unite; cling to, attach to, touch, join (oneself to), associate with, become a follower* or *disciple of, hire oneself out to, be attached* or *devoted to* (pass. in NT). (12)

κολλούριον, ου, τό n. *eye-salve.* (1) Rev 3:18

κολλυβιστής, οῦ, ὁ n. *money-changer.* (3)

κολοβόω v. (κωλύω) aor. ἐκολόβωσα; aor. pass. ἐκολοβώθην. *to shorten.* (4)

Κολοσσαί, ῶν, αἱ n. pla. *Colossae.* (1) Col 1:2

κόλπος, ου, ὁ n. *bosom, breast, chest; fold (of a garment); bay.* (6)

κολυμβάω v. (*) *to swim.* (1) Ac 27:43

κολυμβήθρα, ας, ἡ n. (κολυμβάω) *pool, swimming-pool.* (3)

κολωνία, ας, ἡ n. Lat. *colony.* (1) Ac 16:12

κομάω v. (κόμη) *to wear long hair, let one's hair grow long.* (2)

κόμη, ης, ἡ n. (*) *(long) hair.* (1) 1 Cor 11:15

κομίζω v. (κόσμος) fut. κομίσω, κομιῶ; aor. ἐκόμισα. *to bring;* mid. *get back, recover; carry off, get (for oneself), receive, obtain.* (10)

κομψότερον adv. (κόσμος) *better,* κομψότερον ἔχω *to recover* (from illness). (1) Jn 4:52

κονιάω v. (*) pf. pass. κεκονίαμαι. *to whitewash.* (2)

κονιορτός, οῦ, ὁ n. (κονιάω, ὁρμή) *dust.* (5)

κοπάζω v. (κόπτω) aor. ἐκόπασα. *to stop, abate, cease, rest, fall.* (3)

κοπετός, οῦ, ὁ n. (κόπτω) *mourning, lamentation.* (1) Ac 8:2

κοπή, ῆς, ἡ n. (κόπτω) *cutting down, slaughter, defeat.* (1) Heb 7:1

κοπιάω v. (κόπτω) aor. ἐκοπίασα; pf. κεκοπίακα. *to become tired* or *weary; work hard, toil, strive, struggle, labor.* (23)

κόπος, ου, ὁ n. (κόπτω) *trouble, difficulty; work, labor, toil.* (18)

κοπρία, ας, ἡ n. (κόπριον) *manure pile.* (1) Lk 14:35

κόπριον, ου, τό n. (*) *dung, manure.* (1) Lk 13:8

κόπτω v. (*) fut. κόψω; aor. ἔκοψα. *to cut off; mourn* (mid.). (8)

κόραξ, ακος, ὁ n. *crow, raven.* (1) Lk 12:24

κοράσιον, ου, τό n. (κείρω) *girl.* (8)

κορβᾶν (*) Heb. *gift to God, corban.* (1) Mk 7:11

κορβανᾶς, ᾶ, ὁ n. (κορβᾶν) Ara. *temple treasury.* (1) Mt 27:6

Κόρε, ὁ n. pers. *Korah.* (1) Jd 11

κορέννυμι v. pf. pass. κεκόρεσμαι; aor. pass. ἐκορέσθην. *to satiate; be satiated* or *full, have (eaten) enough* (pass. in NT). (2)

Κορίνθιος, ου, ὁ n. pla. *a Corinthian.* (2)

Κόρινθος, ου, ἡ n. pla. *Corinth.* (6)

Κορνήλιος, ου, ὁ n. pers. *Cornelius.* (8)

κόρος, ου, ὁ n. Heb. *cor, kor, measure* (Hebrew dry measure, about 393 liters or quarts). (1) Lk 16:7

κοσμέω v. (κόσμος) aor. ἐκόσμησα; pf. pass. κεκόσμημαι. *to make neat* or *tidy, trim, fix up, put in order; adorn, decorate, make beautiful, do credit to.* (10)

κοσμικός, ή, όν adj. (κόσμος) *earthly, worldly.* (2)

κόσμιος, ον adj. (κόσμος) *respectable, honorable; appropriate, modest.* (2)

κοσμοκράτωρ, ορος, ὁ n. (κόσμος, κράτος) *world-ruler.* (1) Eph 6:12

κόσμος, ου, ὁ n. (*) *adornment, adorning, (orderly) universe; world; earth; humankind, humanity; totality, sum total.* (186)

Κούαρτος, ου, ὁ n. pers. *Quartus.* (1) Rom 16:23

κουμ Ara. *stand up.* (1) Mk 5:41

κουστωδία, ας, ἡ n. Lat. *guard* (of soldiers). (3)

κουφίζω v. *to make light, lighten.* (1) Ac 27:38

κόφινος, ου, ὁ n. *basket.* (6)

κράβαττος, ου, ὁ n. *mattress, pallet, bed.* (11)

κράζω v. (*) fut. κράξω; aor. ἔκραξα, ἐκέκραξα; pf. κέκραγα. *to cry out, scream, shriek; call (out), cry.* (56)

κραιπάλη, ης, ἡ n. *drinking bout, dissipation.* (1) Lk 21:34

κρανίον, ου, τό n. (*) *skull.* (4)

κράσπεδον, ου, τό n. *edge, border, hem, tassel.* (5)

κραταιός, ά, όν adj. (κράτος) *powerful, mighty.* (1) 1 Pt 5:6

κραταιόω v. (κράτος) aor. pass. ἐκραταιώθην. *to strengthen; become strong, grow strong* (pass. in NT). (4)

κρατέω v. (κράτος) fut. κρατήσω; aor. ἐκράτησα; pf. κεκράτηκα; pf. pass. κεκράτημαι. *to attain; hold; seize, control, arrest, apprehend, take hold of, grasp; hold back, restrain from, hinder in, prevent; hold fast, keep; hold in place, hold unforgiven.* (47)

κράτιστος, η, ον adj. (κράτος) *most noble, most excellent.* (4)

κράτος, ους, τό n. (*) *might, working; κατὰ κράτος mightily; mighty deed; power, sovereignty, rule.* (12)

κραυγάζω v. (κράζω) fut. κραυγάσω; aor. ἐκραύγασα. *to cry out, cry for help, scream.* (9)

κραυγή, ῆς, ἡ n. (κράζω) *shout(ing), clamor, outcry, loud cry(ing); wailing, crying.* (6)

κρέας, κρέως, τό n. *meat.* (2)

κρείττων and **κρείσσων, ον** adj. (κράτος) *more prominent, better, higher in rank, preferable, superior; more useful* or *advantageous; better* (neut. acc. sg. as adv.). (19)

κρεμάννυμι v. (*) aor. ἐκρέμασα; aor. pass. ἐκρεμάσθην. *to hang, crucify* (trans.); κρέμαμαι *hang, depend* (mid.). (7)

κρημνός, οῦ, ὁ n. (κρεμάννυμι) *steep slope* or *bank, cliff*. (3)

Κρής, ητός, ὁ n. pla. *a Cretan*. (2)

Κρήσκης, εντος, ὁ n. pers. *Crescens*. (1) 2 Ti 4:10

Κρήτη, ης, ἡ n. pla. *Crete*. (5)

κριθή, ῆς, ἡ n. (*) *barley*. (1) Rev 6:6

κρίθινος, η, ον adj. (κριθή) *made of barley flour*. (2)

κρίμα, ατος, τό n. (κρίνω) *dispute, lawsuit; decision, degree; judging, judgment, authority to judge; judicial verdict, condemnation, punishment, sentence*. (27)

κρίνον, ου, τό n. *lily, beautiful flower*. (2)

κρίνω v. (*) fut. κρινῶ; aor. ἔκρινα; pf. κέκρικα; pf. pass. κέκριμαι; aor. pass. ἐκρίθην. *to select, prefer, recognize, approve; judge, pass judgment upon, express an opinion about, pass an unfavorable judgment upon, criticize, find fault with, condemn; think, consider, look upon; reach a decision, decide, propose, intend; hale before court, hand over for judicial punishment, punish, administer justice, sit in judgment, rule; be on trial, go to law, be judged* (mid. and pass.). (114)

κρίσις, εως, ἡ n. (κρίνω) *judging, judgment, condemnation, sentence, punishment, evaluation; court; right, justice*. (47)

Κρίσπος, ου, ὁ n. pers. *Crispus*. (2)

κριτήριον, ου, τό n. (κρίνω) *lawcourt, tribunal*. (3)

κριτής, οῦ, ὁ n. (κρίνω) *judge; ruler*. (19)

κριτικός, ή, όν adj. (κρίνω) *able to discern* or *judge*. (1) Heb 4:12

κρούω v. aor. ἔκρουσα. *to strike, knock* (at a door). (9)

κρυβῆναι s. κρύπτω (2 aor. pass. inf.).

κρύπτη, ης, ἡ n. (κρύπτω) *dark and hidden place, cellar*. (1) Lk 11:33

κρυπτός, ή, όν adj. (κρύπτω) *hidden, secret; hidden* or *secret thing, hidden* or *secret place*, ἐν κρυπτῷ *privately* (neut. subst.). (17)

κρύπτω v. (*) aor. ἔκρυψα; pf. pass. κέκρυμμαι; aor. pass. ἐκρύβην. *to hide, keep secret; conceal*. (18)

κρυσταλλίζω v. (κρύσταλλος) *to shine like crystal, be as transparent as crystal*. (1) Rev 21:11

κρύσταλλος, ου, ὁ n. (*) *rock-crystal, ice*. (2)

κρυφαῖος, α, ον adj. (κρύπτω) *hidden, private*. (2)

κρυφῇ adv. (κρύπτω) *in secret*. (1) Eph 5:12

κτάομαι v. (*) aor. ἐκτησάμην. *to procure for oneself, get, acquire, secure, take, win*. (7)

κτῆμα, ατος, τό n. (κτάομαι) *property, possession; landed property, field, piece of land*. (4)

κτῆνος, ους, τό n. (κτάομαι) *domesticated animal, pet, pack-animal, animal used for riding; cattle* (pl.). (4)

κτήτωρ, ορος, ὁ n. (κτάομαι) *owner*. (1) Ac 4:34

κτίζω v. (*) aor. ἔκτισα; pf. pass. ἔκτισμαι; aor. pass. ἐκτίσθην. *to create, make*, ὁ κτίσας *the Creator*. (15)

κτίσις, εως, ἡ n. (κτίζω) *creation, creature, world; that which is created; governance* or *authority system*. (19)

κτίσμα, ατος, τό n. (κτίζω) *that which is created, creature*. (4)

κτίστης, ου, ὁ n. (κτίζω) *Creator*. (1) 1 Pt 4:19

κυβεία, ας, ἡ n. *trickery, craftiness*. (1) Eph 4:14

κυβέρνησις, εως, ἡ n. (*) *administration*. (1) 1 Cor 12:28

κυβερνήτης, ου, ὁ n. (κυβέρνησις) *shipmaster*. (2)

κυκλεύω v. (κυκλόω) aor. ἐκύκλευσα. *to surround*. (1) Rev 20:9

κυκλόθεν adv. (κυκλόω) *around; around* (adv. prep. w. gen.). (3)

κυκλόω v. (*) aor. ἐκύκλωσα; aor. pass. ἐκυκλώθην. *to surround, encircle; go* or *march around, circle round*. (4)

κύκλῳ adv. (κυκλόω) *around; around, nearby* (adj.); *around* (adv. prep. w. gen.). (8)

κυλισμός, οῦ, ὁ n. (κυλίω) *rolling, wallowing.* (1) 2 Pt 2:22

κυλίω v. (*) *to roll; roll (oneself), roll about* (pass. in NT). (1) Mk 9:20

κυλλός, ή, όν adj. *crippled, deformed, injured.* (4)

κῦμα, ατος, τό n. (*) *wave.* (5)

κύμβαλον, ου, τό n. *cymbal.* (1) 1 Cor 13:1

κύμινον, ου, τό n. Sem. *cummin.* (1) Mt 23:23

κυνάριον, ου, τό n. (κύων) *little dog, dog.* (4)

Κύπριος, ου, ὁ n. pla. *a Cypriot.* (3)

Κύπρος, ου, ἡ n. pla. *Cyprus.* (5)

κύπτω v. (*) aor. ἔκυψα. *to bend (oneself) down.* (2)

Κυρηναῖος, ου, ὁ n. pla. *a Cyrenian.* (6)

Κυρήνη, ης, ἡ n. pla. *Cyrene.* (1) Ac 2:10

Κυρήνιος, ου, ὁ n. pers. *Quirinius.* (1) Lk 2:2

κυρία, ας, ἡ n. (κύριος) *lady, mistress; congregation* (fig.). (2)

κυριακός, ή, όν adj. (κύριος) *belonging to the Lord, Lord's.* (2)

κυριεύω v. (κύριος) fut. κυριεύσω; aor. ἐκυρίευσα. *to rule, lord it over; be master of, dominate.* (7)

κύριος, ου, ὁ n. (*) *owner; lord* (of men or supernatural beings), *master, sir, Lord* (of God or Jesus). (717)

κυριότης, ητος, ἡ n. (κύριος) *lordship, dominion, ruling power.* (4)

κυρόω v. (κύριος) aor. ἐκύρωσα; pf. pass. κεκύρωμαι. *to confirm, ratify, validate, make legally binding; conclude, decide in favor of, make valid, affirm, reaffirm.* (2)

κύων, κυνός, ὁ n. (*) *dog;* fig. *unqualified person; dog* (as an infamous person). (5)

κῶλον, ου, τό n. *dead body, corpse.* (1) Heb 3:17

κωλύω v. (*) aor. ἐκώλυσα; aor. pass. ἐκωλύθην. *to hinder, prevent, forbid, restrain; refuse, deny, withhold, keep back.* (23)

κώμη, ης, ἡ n. (*) *village, small town; inhabitants of a village.* (27)

κωμόπολις, εως, ἡ n. (κώμη, πόλις) *market-town.* (1) Mk 1:38

κῶμος, ου, ὁ n. (κώμη) *excessive feasting, carousing, revelry.* (3)

κώνωψ, ωπος, ὁ n. *gnat, mosquito.* (1) Mt 23:24

Κώς, Κῶ, ἡ n. pla. *Cos.* (1) Ac 21:1

Κωσάμ, ὁ n. pers. *Cosam.* (1) Lk 3:28

κωφός, ή, όν adj. (κόπτω) *mute; deaf.* (14)

λαγχάνω v. aor. ἔλαχον. *to receive, obtain; be appointed* or *chosen by lot; cast lots.* (4)

Λάζαρος, ου, ὁ n. pers. *Lazarus.* (15)

λάθρᾳ adv. (λανθάνω) *secretly.* (4)

λαῖλαψ, απος, ἡ n. *whirlwind, hurricane, fierce gust.* (3)

λακάω v. aor. ἐλάκησα. *to burst open* or *apart.* (1) Ac 1:18

λακτίζω v. *to kick.* (1) Ac 26:14

λαλέω v. (*) fut. λαλήσω; aor. ἐλάλησα; pf. λελάληκα; pf. pass. λελάλημαι; aor. pass. ἐλαλήθην. *to sound, give forth sounds; talk, speak, express oneself, assert, proclaim, say, report, discourse, whisper.* (296)

λαλιά, ᾶς, ἡ n. (λαλέω) *speech, speaking, what one said; form of speech, way of speaking, accent.* (3)

λαμβάνω v. (*) fut. λήμψομαι; aor. ἔλαβον; pf. εἴληφα. *to take, take hold of, grasp, take in hand, draw, put on; remove; acquire, seize, take advantage of; accept, collect; take up; choose, select, come upon, catch; receive; make one's own, apprehend;* λαμβάνω πρόσωπον *show partiality,* συμβούλιον λαμβάνω *consult; get, obtain, bring.* (258)

Λάμεχ, ὁ n. pers. *Lamech.* (1) Lk 3:36

λαμπάς, άδος, ἡ n. (λάμπω) *torch; lamp.* (9)

λαμπρός, ά, όν adj. (λάμπω) *bright; clear, transparent; shining;* τὰ λαμπρά *splendor.* (9)

λαμπρότης, ητος, ἡ n. (λάμπω) *shining, brightness.* (1) Ac 26:13

λαμπρῶς adv. (λάμπω) *splendidly, sumptuously.* (1) Lk 16:19

λάμπω v. (*) fut. λάμψω; aor. ἔλαμψα. *to shine, flash, shine forth, gleam.* (7)

λανθάνω v. (*) aor. ἔλαθον. *to escape notice, be hidden, be unaware.* (6)

λαξευτός, ή, όν adj. (-λᾶς) *hewn (in rock).* (1) Lk 23:53

Λαοδίκεια, ας, ἡ n. pla. *Laodicea.* (6)

Λαοδικεύς, έως, ὁ n. pla. *a Laodicean.* (1) Col 4:16

λαός, οῦ, ὁ n. (*) *people, populace, crowd; (common) people; people-group; people (of God).* (142)

λάρυγξ, γγος, ὁ n. *throat, gullet.* (1) Rom 3:13

Λασαία, ας, ἡ n. pla. *Lasaea.* (1) Ac 27:8

λατομέω v. (-λᾶς) aor. ἐλατόμησα; pf. pass. λελατόμημαι. *to hew (out of a rock), cut.* (2)

λατρεία, ας, ἡ n. (λατρεύω) *service* or *worship (of God); rites* (pl.). (5)

λατρεύω v. (*) fut. λατρεύσω; aor. ἐλάτρευσα. *to serve, worship.* (21)

λάχανον, ου, τό n. *vegetable, garden herb.* (4)

Λεββαῖος, ου, ὁ n. pers. *Lebbaeus.* (v.l.)

λεγιών, ῶνος, ἡ n. Lat. *legion* (Roman military unit of about 6,000 soldiers). (4)

λέγω v. (*) fut. ἐρῶ; aor. εἶπον, εἶπα; pf. εἴρηκα; pf. pass. εἴρημαι; aor. pass. ἐρρέθην. *to say, utter in words, tell, give expression to, talk, mean; ask, answer, reply, order, command, direct, enjoin, recommend, assure, assert, maintain, declare, proclaim, interpret; speak, report; call, name; conclude; think.* (2354)

λεῖμμα, ατος, τό n. (λείπω) *remnant.* (1) Rom 11:5

λεῖος, α, ον adj. *smooth, level.* (1) Lk 3:5

λείπω v. (*) *to fall short, be inferior; be or do without, be in need (of); lack.* (6)

λειτουργέω v. (λαός, ἔργον) aor. ἐλειτούργησα. *to render service; serve.* (3)

λειτουργία, ας, ἡ n. (λαός, ἔργον) *service (as a priest); help, assistance, service.* (6)

λειτουργικός, ή, όν adj. (λαός, ἔργον) *engaged in special service.* (1) Heb 1:14

λειτουργός, οῦ, ὁ n. (λαός, ἔργον) *servant, minister; aide, assistant.* (5)

λεμα Ara. *why?* (2)

λέντιον, ου, τό n. Lat. *towel.* (2)

λεπίς, ίδος, ἡ n. (*) *scale* (fig. in NT). (1) Ac 9:18

λέπρα, ας, ἡ n. (λεπίς) *serious skin disease.* (4)

λεπρός, ά, όν adj. (λεπίς) *with a bad skin disease; person with a bad skin disease* (subst.). (9)

λεπτός, ή, όν adj. (λεπίς) *small;* subst. in NT *lepton, small copper coin* (Roman coin, 1/128 of a denarius). (3)

Λευί, ὁ and **Λευίς, Λευί, ὁ** n. pers. *Levi.* (8)

Λευίτης, ου, ὁ n. oth. *Levite.* (3)

Λευιτικός, ή, όν adj. oth. *Levitical.* (1) Heb 7:11

λευκαίνω v. (λευκός) aor. ἐλεύκανα. *to make white.* (2)

λευκός, ή, όν adj. (*) *bright, shining, gleaming, brilliant; white.* (25)

λέων, οντος, ὁ n. *lion.* (9)

λήθη, ης, ἡ n. (λανθάνω) *forgetfulness,* λήθην λαμβάνω τινός *forget something.* (1) 2 Pt 1:9

λῆμψις, εως, ἡ n. (λαμβάνω) *receiving.* (1) Phil 4:15

ληνός, οῦ, ἡ n. (*) *wine-press.* (5)

λῆρος, ου, ὁ n. *idle talk, nonsense, humbug.* (1) Lk 24:11

ληστής, οῦ, ὁ n. *bandit, robber, highwayman; revolutionary, insurrectionist, guerrilla.* (15)

λίαν adv. (*) *very (much), exceedingly, vehemently, quite.* (12)

λίβα s. λίψ (acc.).

λίβανος, ου, ὁ n. (*) *frankincense.* (2)

λιβανωτός, οῦ, ὁ n. (λίβανος) *censer.* (2)

Λιβερτῖνος, ου, ὁ n. oth. *Freedperson.* (1) Ac 6:9

Λιβύη, ης, ἡ n. pla. *Libya.* (1) Ac 2:10

λιθάζω v. (λίθος) aor. ἐλίθασα; aor. pass. ἐλιθάσθην. *to stone.* (9)

λίθινος, η, ον adj. (λίθος) *(made of) stone.* (3)

λιθοβολέω v. (λίθος, βάλλω) aor. ἐλιθοβόλησα; aor. pass. ἐλιθοβολήθην. *to throw stones at, stone (to death).* (7)

λίθος, ου, ὁ n. (*) *stone.* (59)

λιθόστρωτος, ον adj. (λίθος, στρωννύω) *paved with stones; stone pavement, mosaic* (neut. subst. in NT). (1) Jn 19:13

λικμάω v. fut. λικμήσω. *to crush.* (2)

λιμήν, ένος, ὁ n. *harbor.* (2)

λίμνη, ης, ἡ n. *lake.* (11)

λιμός, οῦ, ὁ, ἡ n. *hunger; famine.* (12)

λίνον, ου, τό n. *lamp-wick; linen garment.* (2)

Λίνος, ου, ὁ n. pers. *Linus.* (1) 2 Ti 4:21

λιπαρός, ά, όν adj. *bright, rich, costly;* τὰ λιπαρά *luxury* (subst. in NT). (1) Rev 18:14

λίτρα, ας, ἡ n. Lat. *(Roman) pound* (measure of weight, about 327 grams or 11.5 ounces). (2)

λίψ, λιβός, ὁ n. *the southwest.* (1) Ac 27:12

λογεία, ας, ἡ n. (λέγω) *collection* (of money). (2)

λογίζομαι v. (λέγω) aor. ἐλογισάμην; aor. pass. ἐλογίσθην. *to calculate, reckon, count, take into account, credit, evaluate, estimate, consider, look upon as, regard, class; think (about), ponder, let one's mind dwell on, have in mind, propose, reason; think, believe, be of the opinion, imagine, hold.* (40)

λογικός, ή, όν adj. (λέγω) *thoughtful, spiritual.* (2)

λόγιον, ου, τό n. (λέγω) *a saying; sayings, oracles* (pl. in NT). (4)

λόγιος, α, ον adj. (λέγω) *learned, cultured*. (1) Ac 18:24

λογισμός, οῦ, ὁ n. (λέγω) *calculation, reasoning, reflection, thought, sophistry*. (2)

λογομαχέω v. (λέγω, μάχη) *to dispute about words, split hairs*. (1) 2 Ti 2:14

λογομαχία, ας, ἡ n. (λέγω, μάχη) *word-battle, dispute about words*. (1) 1 Ti 6:4

λόγος, ου, ὁ n. (λέγω) *word, what one says, statement, question, prayer, preaching, prophecy, command, report, story, appearance, proverb, proclamation, instruction, teaching, message, a speech, speaking, assertion, declaration, talk, subject, matter, thing, complaint, treatise,* διὰ λόγου *by word of mouth,* ὁ λόγος τοῦ θεοῦ *the gospel* (oft.), πολὺς ἡμῖν ὁ λόγος *much to say to you; computation, reckoning, account, ledger heading, settlement (of an account), reason, ground, motive,* πρὸς ὃν ἡμῖν ὁ λόγος *with whom we have to do; Logos, Word*. (330)

λόγχη, ης, ἡ n. *spear, lance*. (1) Jn 19:34

λοιδορέω v. (λοίδορος) aor. ἐλοιδόρησα. *to revile, abuse*. (4)

λοιδορία, ας, ἡ n. (λοίδορος) *abuse (verbal), reproach, reviling*. (3)

λοίδορος, ου, ὁ n. (*) *reviler, abusive person*. (2)

λοιμός, οῦ, ὁ n. *pestilence, plague, disease; public menace or enemy*. (2)

λοιπός, ή, όν adj. (λείπω) *left, remaining; other, rest (of); from now on, in the future, henceforth, beyond that, in addition, finally, furthermore, therefore* (neut. as adv.). (55)

Λουκᾶς, ᾶ, ὁ n. pers. *Luke*. (3)

Λούκιος, ου, ὁ n. pers. *Lucius*. (2)

λουτρόν, οῦ, τό n. (λούω) *bath, washing*. (2)

λούω v. (*) aor. ἔλουσα; pf. pass. λέλουμαι, λέλουσμαι. *to bathe, wash;* mid. *wash or bathe oneself; wash or bathe oneself, cleanse, bathe, wash for oneself* (cult.). (5)

Λύδδα, ας, ἡ n. pla. *Lydda*. (3)

Λυδία, ας, ἡ n. pers. *Lydia*. (2)

Λυκαονία, ας, ἡ n. pla. *Lycaonia*. (1) Ac 14:6

Λυκαονιστί adv. pla. *in the Lycaonian language*. (1) Ac 14:11

Λυκία, ας, ἡ n. pla. *Lycia*. (1) Ac 27:5

λύκος, ου, ὁ n. *wolf* (lit. and fig.). (6)

λυμαίνω v. *to cause harm to, injure, spoil, ruin, destroy* (mid. in NT). (1) Ac 8:3

λυπέω v. (λύπη) aor. ἐλύπησα; pf. λελύπηκα; aor. pass. ἐλυπήθην. *to vex, irritate, offend, insult, cause pain; be sad or sorrowful, be distressed, grieve* (pass.). (26)

λύπη, ης, ἡ n. (*) *grief, sorrow, affliction, pain,* ἐκ λύπης *reluctantly*. (16)

Λυσανίας, ου, ὁ n. pers. *Lysanias*. (1) Lk 3:1

Λυσίας, ου, ὁ n. pers. *Lysias*. (2)

λύσις, εως, ἡ n. (λύω) *release, separation, divorce*. (1) 1 Cor 7:27

λυσιτελέω v. (λύω, τέλος) *to be advantageous, be better; it is better, it profits* (impers. in NT). (1) Lk 17:2

Λύστρα, ἡ, τά n. pla. *Lystra*. (6)

λύτρον, ου, τό n. (λύω) *price of release, ransom*. (2)

λυτρόω v. (λύω) aor. pass. ἐλυτρώθην. *to set free, redeem, rescue* (mid.); *be ransomed* (pass.). (3)

λύτρωσις, εως, ἡ n. (λύω) *ransoming, releasing, redemption, deliverance*. (3)

λυτρωτής, οῦ, ὁ n. (λύω) *redeemer*. (1) Ac 7:35

λυχνία, ας, ἡ n. (λύχνος) *lampstand*. (12)

λύχνος, ου, ὁ n. (*) *lamp* (lit. and fig.). (14)

λύω v. (*) aor. ἔλυσα; pf. pass. λέλυμαι; aor. pass. ἐλύθην. *to loose; untie, set free, release, unbind, free; destroy, break up; bring to an end, abolish; permit* (poss.). (42)

Λωΐς, ΐδος, ἡ n. pers. *Lois*. (1) 2 Ti 1:5

Λώτ, ὁ n. pers. *Lot*. (4)

Μάαθ, ὁ n. pers. *Maath*. (1) Lk 3:26
Μαγαδάν, ἡ n. pla. *Magadan*. (1) Mt 15:39
Μαγδαλά, ἡ n. pla. *Magdala*. (v.l.)
Μαγδαληνή, ῆς, ἡ n. pers. *Magdalene*. (12)
Μαγεδάλ n. pla. alt. form of Μαγαδάν. (v.l.)
μαγεία, ας, ἡ n. (μάγος) *magic; magic arts* (pl.). (1) Ac 8:11
μαγεύω v. (μάγος) *to practice magic*. (1) Ac 8:9
μάγος, ου, ὁ n. (*) *a Magus, wise man; magician*. (6)
Μαγώγ, ὁ n. pers. *Magog*. (1) Rev 20:8
Μαδιάμ, ὁ n. pla. *Midian*. (1) Ac 7:29
μαθεῖν s. μανθάνω (2 aor. inf.).
μαθητεύω v. (μανθάνω) aor. ἐμαθήτευσα; aor. pass. ἐμαθητεύθην. *to become a disciple* (pass.)*; teach, make a disciple of*. (4)
μαθητής, οῦ, ὁ n. (μανθάνω) *pupil, apprentice; disciple, adherent, Christian*. (261)
μαθήτρια, ας, ἡ n. (μανθάνω) *(female) disciple*. (1) Ac 9:36
Μαθθαῖος, ου, ὁ n. pers. *Matthew*. (5)
Μαθθάτ, ὁ n. pers. *Matthat*. (2)
Μαθθίας, ου, ὁ n. pers. *Matthias*. (2)
Μαθουσαλά, ὁ n. pers. *Methuselah*. (1) Lk 3:37
μαίνομαι v. (*) *to be mad, out of one's mind, crazy*. (5)
μακαρίζω v. (μακάριος) *to call or consider blessed, happy, fortunate*. (2)
μακάριος, α, ον adj. (*) *happy, fortunate, blessed, privileged*. (50)
μακαρισμός, οῦ, ὁ n. (μακάριος) *blessing*. (3)

Μακεδονία, ας, ἡ n. pla. *Macedonia*. (22)
Μακεδών, όνος, ὁ n. pla. *a Macedonian*. (5)
μάκελλον, ου, τό n. *meat market, food market*. (1) 1 Cor 10:25
μακράν adv. (μῆκος) *far (away); in time to come*. (10)
μακρόθεν adv. (μῆκος) *from far away, from a distance; at or from a distance, far away* (predom. w. ἀπό). (14)
μακροθυμέω v. (μῆκος, θυμός) aor. ἐμακροθύμησα. *to have patience, wait patiently; be patient, forbearing; delay*. (10)
μακροθυμία, ας, ἡ n. (μῆκος, θυμός) *patience, steadfastness, endurance; forbearance*. (14)
μακροθύμως adv. (μῆκος, θυμός) *patiently*. (1) Ac 26:3
μακρός, ά, όν adj. (μῆκος) *long; far away, distant*. (4)
μακροχρόνιος, ον adj. (μῆκος, χρόνος) *long-lived*. (1) Eph 6:3
μαλακία, ας, ἡ n. (μαλακός) *debility, weakness, sickness*. (3)
μαλακός, ή, όν adj. (*) *soft; effeminate* (esp. of certain male homosexuals). (4)
Μαλελεήλ, ὁ n. pers. *Maleleel*. (1) Lk 3:37
μάλιστα adv. (μᾶλλον) *most of all, above all, especially, particularly, very greatly, outstandingly*. (12)
μᾶλλον adv. (*) *more*, πολλῷ μᾶλλον *much or even more, even more, now more than ever, still more; all the more, more surely; rather, instead*, οὐχὶ μᾶλλον *not rather*, μᾶλλον δέ *but rather*. (81)

Μάλχος, ου, ὁ n. pers. *Malchus*. (1) Jn 18:10

μάμμη, ης, ἡ n. *grandmother*. (1) 2 Ti 1:5

μαμωνᾶς, ᾶ, ὁ n. Ara. *wealth, property*. (4)

Μαναήν, ὁ n. pers. *Manaen*. (1) Ac 13:1

Μανασσῆς, ῆ, ὁ n. pers. *Manasseh*. (3)

μανθάνω v. (*) aor. ἔμαθον; pf. μεμάθηκα. *to learn, understand; find out, ascertain; appropriate to oneself, realize; hear* (poss.). (25)

μανία, ας, ἡ n. (μαίνομαι) *madness, frenzy, delirium*. (1) Ac 26:24

μάννα, τό n. Heb. *manna*. (4)

μαντεύομαι v. (μαίνομαι) *to prophesy, divine, give an oracle*. (1) Ac 16:16

μαραίνω v. (*) aor. pass. ἐμαράνθην. *to destroy; die out, fade, disappear, wither* (pass. in NT). (1) Jas 1:11

μαρανα θα Ara. *(our) Lord, come!* (1) 1 Cor 16:22

μαργαρίτης, ου, ὁ n. *pearl*. (9)

Μάρθα, ας, ἡ n. pers. *Martha*. (13)

Μαρία, ας, ἡ and **Μαριάμ, ἡ** n. pers. *Mary*. (54)

Μᾶρκος, ου, ὁ n. pers. *Mark*. (8)

μάρμαρος, ου, ὁ n. *marble*. (1) Rev 18:12

μαρτυρέω v. (μάρτυς) fut. μαρτυρήσω; aor. ἐμαρτύρησα; pf. μεμαρτύρηκα; pf. pass. μεμαρτύρημαι; aor. pass. ἐμαρτυρήθην. *to bear witness, be a witness, testify, confirm, declare; testify favorably, speak well of, approve, attest; pass. be witnessed, be testified; be well spoken of, be approved, be praised*. (76)

μαρτυρία, ας, ἡ n. (μάρτυς) *testimony, testifying, attestation; testimony* (legal); *statement of approval*. (37)

μαρτύριον, ου, τό n. (μάρτυς) *testimony, proof*; ἡ σκηνὴ τοῦ μαρτυρίου *tent of testimony*. (19)

μαρτύρομαι v. (μάρτυς) *to testify, bear witness; insist, implore, affirm*. (5)

μάρτυς, υρος, ὁ n. (*) *witness* (legal); *testifier; witness; martyr*. (35)

μασάομαι v. (μαστιγόω) *to bite*. (1) Rev 16:10

μαστιγόω v. (*) fut. μαστιγώσω; aor. ἐμαστίγωσα. *to whip, flog, scourge; punish, chastise*. (7)

μαστίζω v. (μαστιγόω) *to strike with a whip, scourge*. (1) Ac 22:25

μάστιξ, ιγος, ἡ n. (μαστιγόω) *whip, lash; lashing* (pl.); *torment, suffering*. (6)

μαστός, οῦ, ὁ n. *breast, chest* (pl. of males); *breast* (of females). (3)

ματαιολογία, ας, ἡ n. (μάταιος, λέγω) *empty or fruitless talk*. (1) 1 Ti 1:6

ματαιολόγος, ον adj. (μάταιος, λέγω) *talking idly; idle talker, windbag* (subst. in NT). (1) Tit 1:10

μάταιος, α, ον adj. (*) *empty, idle, fruitless, useless, powerless, lacking truth, worthless, foolish, futile; worthless things, idols* (pl. subst.). (6)

ματαιότης, ητος, ἡ n. (μάταιος) *emptiness, futility, purposelessness, worthlessness, frustration*. (3)

ματαιόω v. (μάταιος) aor. pass. ἐματαιώθην. *to render worthless; be given over to worthlessness, think about worthless things, be foolish* (pass. in NT). (1) Rom 1:21

μάτην adv. (μάταιος) *in vain, to no end*. (2)

Ματθάν, ὁ n. pers. *Matthan*. (2)

Ματταθά, ὁ n. pers. *Mattatha*. (1) Lk 3:31

Ματταθίας, ου, ὁ n. pers. *Mattathias*. (2)

μάχαιρα, ης, ἡ n. (μάχη) *sword, dagger; sword* (fig.). (29)

μάχη, ης, ἡ n. (*) *battle; fighting, quarrels, strife, disputes* (pl. in NT). (4)

μάχομαι v. (μάχη) *to fight; quarrel, dispute*. (4)

μεγαλεῖος, α, ον adj. (μέγας) *magnificent; mighty deeds* (neut. pl. subst. in NT). (1) Ac 2:11

μεγαλειότης, ητος, ἡ n. (μέγας) *grandeur, sublimity, majesty; impressiveness*. (3)

μεγαλοπρεπής, ές adj. (μέγας, πρέπω) *magnificent, sublime, majestic, impressive*. (1) 2 Pt 1:17

μεγαλύνω v. (μέγας) aor. pass. ἐμεγαλύνθην. *to make large* or *long, make great; exalt, glorify, magnify, speak highly of, praise, extol*; pass. *increase, grow; be glorified*. (8)

μεγάλως adv. (μέγας) *greatly, very (much)*. (1) Phil 4:10

μεγαλωσύνη, ης, ἡ n. (μέγας) *majesty, Majesty* (= God). (3)

μέγας, μεγάλη, μέγα adj. (*) *large, long, spacious, wide, old; rich; loud, strong, deep, bright, intense, mighty, severe, high, fierce, profound, firm; great, sublime, important; surprising*; pl. subst. *great ones* (masc.); *great things, proud words* (neut.). (243)

μέγεθος, ους, τό n. (μέγας) *greatness*. (1) Eph 1:19

μεγιστάν, ᾶνος, ὁ n. (μέγας) *great person, courtier, magnate*. (3)

μέγιστος s. μέγας (superl.).

μεθ᾽ = μετά before rough breathing.

μεθερμηνεύω v. (ἑρμηνεύω) *to translate*. (8)

μέθη, ης, ἡ n. (μεθύω) *drunkenness, drinking-bout* (poss.). (3)

μεθίστημι v. (ἵστημι) aor. μετέστησα; aor. pass. μετεστάθην. *to remove, transfer, depose, discharge; turn away, mislead*. (5)

μεθοδεία, ας, ἡ n. (ὁδός) *scheming, craftiness; wiles, stratagems* (pl.). (2)

μεθύσκω v. (μεθύω) aor. pass. ἐμεθύσθην. *to cause to become drunk; to get drunk, become intoxicated* (pass. in NT). (5)

μέθυσος, ου, ὁ n. (μεθύω) *drunkard*. (2)

μεθύω v. (*) *to be drunk*. (5)

μειζότερος s. μέγας (comp.).

μείζων s. μέγας (comp. somet. used as superl.).

μέλας, αινα, αν adj. *black; ink* (neut. subst.). (6)

Μελεά, ὁ n. pers. *Melea*. (1) Lk 3:31

μέλει v. (*) impers. *it is a care* or *concern, is of interest to someone; μή σοι μελέτω never mind*. (10)

μελετάω v. (μέλει) aor. ἐμελέτησα. *to practice, cultivate, take pains with; think about, meditate upon*. (2)

μέλι, ιτος, τό n. *honey*. (4)

μελίσσιος, ον adj. *pertaining to bees*. (v.l.)

Μελίτη, ης, ἡ n. pla. *Malta*. (1) Ac 28:1

μέλλω v. fut. μελλήσω. w. inf. *to be about to, be on the point of, begin, be going, intend, propose; be destined, be inevitable, must; (in the) future, to come* (ptc.); *to delay*. (109)

μέλος, ους, τό n. *member* (of the body), *part, limb; member* (of a whole). (34)

Μελχί, ὁ n. pers. *Melchi*. (2)

Μελχισέδεκ, ὁ n. pers. *Melchizedek*. (8)

μεμβράνα, ης, ἡ n. Lat. *parchment*. (1) 2 Ti 4:13

μεμένηκειν s. μένω (plpf.).

μέμιγμαι s. μίγνυμι (pf. pass.).

μεμίαμαι s. μιαίνω (pf. pass.).

μέμνημαι s. μιμνῄσκομαι (pf. pass.).

μέμφομαι v. (*) *to find fault with, blame*. (2)

μεμψίμοιρος, ον adj. (μέμφομαι) *complaining about one's lot, discontented*. (1) Jd 16

μέν part. (*) postpos. μὲν ... δέ *to be sure ... but, on the one hand ... on the other hand, one ... other, some ... others*, μὲν ... ἀλλά *to be sure ... but*, μὲν ... πλήν *indeed ... but*, πρῶτον μὲν ... ἔπειτα *in the first place ... then*, τοῦτο μὲν ... τοῦτο δέ *in part ... in part*; μὲν οὖν *so, then*. (179)

Μεννά, ὁ n. pers. *Menna*. (1) Lk 3:31

μενοῦν part. (μέν, οὖν) *rather, on the contrary*. (1) Lk 11:28

μενοῦνγε part. (μέν, οὖν, γέ) somet. postpos. *rather, on the contrary, indeed*, ἀλλὰ μενοῦνγε *more than that*. (3)

μέντοι part. (μέν, -τοί) postpos. *really, actually; though, to be sure, indeed, nevertheless*, ὅμως μέντοι *yet, but*. (8)

μένω v. (*) fut. μενῶ; aor. ἔμεινα; pf. μεμένηκα. *to remain, stay, live, dwell, lodge, continue, abide; last, persist, continue to live, survive, endure,* τὸ μένον *what is permanent; wait for, await* (trans.). (118)

μερίζω v. (μέρος) aor. ἐμέρισα; pf. pass. μεμέρισμαι; aor. pass. ἐμερίσθην. *to divide; distribute, deal out, assign, apportion; share* (mid.). (14)

μέριμνα, ης, ἡ n. (μεριμνάω) *anxiety, worry, care.* (6)

μεριμνάω v. (*) fut. μεριμνήσω; aor. ἐμερίμνησα. *to have anxiety, be anxious, be unduly concerned, worry about; care for, be concerned about.* (19)

μερίς, ίδος, ἡ n. (μέρος) *part, district; share, portion, something in common.* (5)

μερισμός, οῦ, ὁ n. (μέρος) *division, separation; distribution, apportionment.* (2)

μεριστής, οῦ, ὁ n. (μέρος) *divider, arbitrator.* (1) Lk 12:14

μέρος, ους, τό n. (*) *part, piece, party, branch, line of business, matter, affair,* ἀνὰ μέρος *one after the other,* ἀπὸ μέρους *in part,* ἐκ μέρους *individually, in part,* ἐν μέρει *with regard to,* κατὰ μέρος *in detail, point by point,* μέρος τι *partly; region, district, side* (pl.)*; share, place.* (42)

μεσημβρία, ας, ἡ n. (μέσος, ἡμέρα) *midday, noon; south.* (2)

μεσιτεύω v. (μέσος) aor. ἐμεσίτευσα. *to guarantee.* (1) Heb 6:17

μεσίτης, ου, ὁ n. (μέσος) *mediator, arbitrator, intermediary.* (6)

μεσονύκτιον, ου, τό n. (μέσος, νύξ) *midnight.* (4)

Μεσοποταμία, ας, ἡ n. pla. *Mesopotamia.* (2)

μέσος, η, ον adj. (*) *middle, in the middle, between, in two; among;* neut. subst. *the middle,* ἀνὰ μέσον *within, through, between, on the center of,* διὰ μέσου *through (the midst of),* εἰς (τὸ) μέσον *in(to) the middle* or *center,* ἐν (τῷ) μέσῳ *among, before, in(to)* or *through the middle, within, on the center,* κατὰ μέσον *in the middle;* ἀνὰ μέσον *among, in the midst of,* ἐν μέσῳ *among,* ἐκ (τοῦ) μέσου *from among;* neut. as adv. prep. w. gen. *in the middle of, in the midst of.* (58)

μεσότοιχον, ου, τό n. (μέσος, τεῖχος) *dividing wall.* (1) Eph 2:14

μεσουράνημα, ατος, τό n. (μέσος, οὐρανός) *zenith, midheaven.* (3)

μεσόω v. (μέσος) *to be in* or *at the middle, be half over.* (1) Jn 7:14

Μεσσίας, ου, ὁ n. pers. *Messiah, Anointed One.* (2)

μεστός, ή, όν adj. (*) *full; filled with something.* (9)

μεστόω v. (μεστός) pf. pass. μεμέστωμαι. *to fill; be full* (pass. in NT). (1) Ac 2:13

μετ' = μετά *before smooth breathing.*

μετά prep. (*) w. gen. *among, in the midst of; with, in company with, follow, for, on, to, on the side of, against; in, by means of;* w. acc. *behind; after,* μετὰ τοῦτο or ταῦτα *after this, after* (w. inf.). (469)

μεταβαίνω v. (-βαίνω) fut. μεταβήσομαι; aor. μετέβην; pf. μεταβέβηκα. *to go* or *pass (over); pass (on).* (12)

μεταβάλλω v. (βάλλω) *to change one's mind* (mid. in NT). (1) Ac 28:6

μετάγω v. (ἄγω) *to guide, steer.* (2)

μεταδίδωμι v. (δίδωμι) aor. μετέδωκα. *to give (a part of), impart, share.* (5)

μετάθεσις, εως, ἡ n. (τίθημι) *removal, taking up* or *away; change, transformation.* (3)

μεταίρω v. (αἴρω) aor. μετῆρα. *to go away.* (2)

μετακαλέω v. (καλέω) fut. μετακαλέσω; aor. μετεκάλεσα. *to call to oneself, summon* (mid. in NT). (4)

μετακινέω v. (κινέω) *to shift, remove.* (1) Col 1:23

μεταλαμβάνω v. (λαμβάνω) aor. μετέλαβον. *to have a share in, receive* *one's share, share in, take; receive, have*. (7)

μετάλημψις, εως, ἡ n. (λαμβάνω) *sharing, receiving*. (1) 1 Ti 4:3

μεταλλάσσω v. (ἄλλος) aor. μετήλλαξα. *to exchange*. (2)

μεταμέλομαι v. (μέλει) aor. pass. μετεμελήθην. *to be very sorry, regret; change one's mind, have second thoughts*. (6)

μεταμορφόω v. (μορφή) aor. pass. μετεμορφώθην. pass. in NT *to be transfigured; transformed, changed*. (4)

μετανοέω v. (νίπτω) fut. μετανοήσω; aor. μετενόησα. *to repent, feel remorse, be converted*. (34)

μετάνοια, ας, ἡ n. (νίπτω) *repentance, turning about* or *away, conversion*. (22)

μεταξύ adv. (μετά, σύν) *between, in the middle, next, afterward, meanwhile;* adv. prep. w. gen. *in the middle of; between, among*. (9)

μεταπέμπω v. (πέμπω) aor. μετέπεμψα; aor. pass. μετεπέμφθην. *to send for, summon* (mid. and pass. in NT). (9)

μεταστρέφω v. (στρέφω) aor. μετέστρεψα; aor. pass. μετεστράφην. *to change, alter, distort*. (2)

μετασχηματίζω v. (ἔχω) fut. μετασχηματίσω; aor. μετεσχημάτισα. *to change, transform; change* or *disguise oneself* (mid.)*; apply to*. (5)

μετατίθημι v. (τίθημι) aor. μετέθηκα; aor. pass. μετετέθην. *to put in another place, transfer, bring back, take up* or *away; change, alter, pervert; change one's mind, turn away, desert* (mid.). (6)

μετατρέπω v. (τροπή) aor. pass. μετετράπην. *to turn (around)*. (1) Jas 4:9

μετέβην s. μεταβαίνω (2 aor.).

μετέπειτα adv. (εἶτα) *afterwards*. (1) Heb 12:17

μετέχω v. (ἔχω) aor. μετέσχον; pf. μετέσχηκα. *to share, have a share, participate, belong; eat, drink, enjoy, live on*. (8)

μετεωρίζομαι v. *to be anxious, worry*. (1) Lk 12:29

μετῆρα s. μεταίρω (aor.).

μετοικεσία, ας, ἡ n. (οἶκος) *removal to another place of habitation, deportation*. (4)

μετοικίζω v. (οἶκος) fut. μετοικιῶ; aor. μετῴκισα. *to remove (to another place of habitation), resettle, deport*. (2)

μετοχή, ῆς, ἡ n. (ἔχω) *sharing, participation*. (1) 2 Cor 6:14

μέτοχος, ον adj. (ἔχω) *sharing* or *participating in; (business) partner, companion* (subst.). (6)

μετρέω v. (μέτρον) aor. ἐμέτρησα; aor. pass. ἐμετρήθην. *to measure; give out, deal out, apportion*. (11)

μετρητής, οῦ, ὁ n. (μέτρον) *measure* (liquid, about 40 liters or quarts). (1) Jn 2:6

μετριοπαθέω v. (μέτρον, πάσχω) *to deal gently, moderate one's feelings*. (1) Heb 5:2

μετρίως adv. (μέτρον) *moderately, somewhat,* οὐ μετρίως *greatly*. (1) Ac 20:12

μέτρον, ου, τό n. (*) *measure; quantity, number, capacity,* οὐκ ἐκ μέτρου *without measure*. (14)

μέτωπον, ου, τό n. (ὁράω) *forehead*. (8)

μέχρι adv. conj. *until;* adv. prep. w. gen. *as far as; until, to; to the point of*. (17)

μέχρις = μέχρι before vowels.

μή part. (*) *not* (usu. w. non-ind. verbs), εἰ μή *except (that); that (not), lest, so that not* (conj.)*;* used when expecting neg. answers to questions*;* οὐ μή *not at all, by no means* (strong fut. neg.). (1042)

μηδαμῶς adv. (μή, δέ, ἐγώ) *by no means, certainly not, no*. (2)

μηδέ part. (μή, δέ) *and not, but not, nor; not even*. (56)

μηδείς, μηδεμία, μηδέν adj. (μή, δέ, εἷς) *no; no one, nobody, nothing* (subst.)*; in no way* (neut. as adv.). (90)

μηδέποτε adv. (μή, δέ, ποῦ) *never*. (1) 2 Ti 3:7

μηδέπω adv. (μή, δέ, -πω) *not yet*. (1) Heb 11:7

Μῆδος, ου, ὁ n. pla. *a Mede*. (1) Ac 2:9

μηθέν s. μηδείς (= μηδέν).

μηκέτι adv. (μή, ἔτι) *no longer, not from now on*. (22)

μῆκος, ους, τό n. (*) *length*. (3)

μηκύνω v. (μῆκος) *to make long; become long, grow* (mid. in NT). (1) Mk 4:27

μηλωτή, ῆς, ἡ n. *sheepskin*. (1) Heb 11:37

μήν part. (μέν) *surely, certainly*. (1) Heb 6:14

μήν, μηνός, ὁ n. (*) *month*, κατὰ μῆνα ἕκαστον *every month; new moon*. (18)

μηνύω v. aor. ἐμήνυσα; aor. pass. ἐμηνύθην. *to make known, reveal, inform, report*. (4)

μήποτε part. (μή, ποῦ) *never; (in order) that … not* (conj.)*; whether perhaps* (interrog.)*; probably, perhaps*. (25)

μήπω adv. (μή, -πω) *not yet*. (2)

μηρός, οῦ, ὁ n. *thigh*. (1) Rev 19:16

μήτε part. (μή, τέ) *and not, nor*, μήτε … μήτε *neither … nor*. (34)

μήτηρ, τρός, ἡ n. (*) *mother* (lit. and fig.). (83)

μήτι part. (μή, τὶς) used when expecting neg. answers to questions, *perhaps* (used when the questioner is in doubt concerning the answer). (17)

μήτιγε part. (μή, τὶς, γέ) *not to mention, let alone*. (1) 1 Cor 6:3

μήτρα, ας, ἡ n. (μήτηρ) *womb*. (2)

μητρολῴας, ου, ὁ n. (μήτηρ, ἀλοάω) *one who murders one's mother*. (1) 1 Ti 1:9

μιαίνω v. (*) pf. pass. μεμίαμμαι; aor. pass. ἐμιάνθην. *to stain, defile* (ritually or morally). (5)

μίασμα, ατος, τό n. (μιαίνω) *shameful deed, misdeed, crime*. (1) 2 Pt 2:20

μιασμός, οῦ, ὁ n. (μιαίνω) *defilement, corruption*. (1) 2 Pt 2:10

μίγμα, ατος, τό n. (μίγνυμι) *mixture, compound*. (1) Jn 19:39

μίγνυμι v. (*) aor. ἔμιξα; pf. pass. μέμιγμαι. *to mix, mingle*. (4)

μικρός, ά, όν adj. *small, short, little,* *short distance, little way; unimportant, insignificant, humble; little one, child, a little* (subst.)*; short time, little while, for a moment* (neut. as adv.)*;* comp. μικρότερος *smallest; least (important)*. (46)

Μίλητος, ου, ἡ n. pla. *Miletus*. (3)

μίλιον, ου, τό n. Lat. *mile* (Roman measure of distance, about 1480 meters or 1619 yards). (1) Mt 5:41

μιμέομαι v. (*) *to imitate, emulate, follow, copy*. (4)

μιμητής, οῦ, ὁ n. (μιμέομαι) *imitator*. (6)

μιμνήσκομαι v. (*) pf. pass. μέμνημαι; aor. pass. ἐμνήσθην. *to remember, recollect, remind oneself, think of; mention; think of, care for, be concerned about, keep in mind*. (23)

μισέω v. fut. μισήσω; aor. ἐμίσησα; pf. μεμίσηκα; pf. pass. μεμίσημαι. *to hate, detest; disfavor, disregard*. (40)

μισθαποδοσία, ας, ἡ n. (μισθός, δίδωμι) *recompense, reward, punishment, retribution, penalty*. (3)

μισθαποδότης, ου, ὁ n. (μισθός, δίδωμι) *rewarder*. (1) Heb 11:6

μίσθιος, ου, ὁ n. (μισθός) *day laborer, hired worker*. (2)

μισθός, οῦ, ὁ n. (*) *pay, wages, gain; recompense, reward, punishment*. (29)

μισθόω v. (μισθός) aor. ἐμίσθωσα. *to hire, engage* (mid. in NT). (2)

μίσθωμα, ατος, τό n. (μισθός) *what is rented, rented house*. (1) Ac 28:30

μισθωτός, οῦ, ὁ n. (μισθός) *hired worker*. (3)

Μιτυλήνη, ης, ἡ n. pla. *Mitylene*. (1) Ac 20:14

Μιχαήλ, ὁ n. pers. *Michael*. (2)

μνᾶ, μνᾶς, ἡ n. Sem. *mina* (Greek monetary unit, 100 drachmas). (9)

Μνάσων, ωνος, ὁ n. pers. *Mnason*. (1) Ac 21:16

μνεία, ας, ἡ n. (μιμνήσκομαι) *memory, remembrance; mention*. (7)

μνῆμα, ατος, τό n. (μιμνήσκομαι) *grave, tomb*. (8)

μνημεῖον, ου, τό n. (μιμνήσκομαι) monument, memorial; grave, tomb. (40)

μνήμη, ης, ἡ n. (μιμνήσκομαι) recollection, memory. (1) 2 Pt 1:15

μνημονεύω v. (μιμνήσκομαι) aor. ἐμνημόνευσα. to remember, keep in mind, think of, mention. (21)

μνημόσυνον, ου, τό n. (μιμνήσκομαι) memory; memorial offering. (3)

μνηστεύω v. pf. pass. ἐμνήστευμαι; aor. pass. ἐμνηστεύθην. to betroth; be betrothed, become engaged (pass. in NT). (3)

μογιλάλος, ον adj. (μόγις, λαλέω) speaking with difficulty, having a speech impediment; mute, unable to articulate. (1) Mk 7:32

μόγις adv. (*) scarcely, with difficulty. (1) Lk 9:39

μόδιος, ίου, ὁ n. Lat. container (for measuring grain, holds about 8.75 liters or 8 quarts). (3)

μοιχαλίς, ίδος, ἡ n. (μοιχός) adulteress, unfaithful one; adulterous, unfaithful (adj.). (7)

μοιχάω v. (μοιχός) to commit adultery, be an adulterer or adulteress (pass. in NT). (4)

μοιχεία, ας, ἡ n. (μοιχός) adultery. (3)

μοιχεύω v. (μοιχός) fut. μοιχεύσω; aor. ἐμοίχευσα; aor. pass. ἐμοιχεύθην. to commit adultery. (15)

μοιχός, οῦ, ὁ n. (*) adulterer. (3)

μόλις adv. (μόγις) with difficulty; not readily, only rarely. (6)

Μολόχ, ὁ n. pers. Moloch. (1) Ac 7:43

μολύνω v. (*) aor. ἐμόλυνα; aor. pass. ἐμολύνθην. to stain, soil; defile. (3)

μολυσμός, οῦ, ὁ n. (μολύνω) defilement. (1) 2 Cor 7:1

μομφή, ῆς, ἡ n. (μέμφομαι) blame, (cause for) complaint. (1) Col 3:13

μονή, ῆς, ἡ n. (μένω) staying, tarrying, μονὴν ποιῶ to live, stay; dwelling-place, room, abode. (2)

μονογενής, ές adj. (μόνος, γίνομαι) (one and) only; unique (in kind). (9)

μόνος, η, ον adj. (*) only, alone, deserted, helpless, isolated; only, alone, in isolation, solely (neut. as adv.); κατὰ μόνας alone. (114)

μονόφθαλμος, ον adj. (μόνος, ὁράω) one-eyed. (2)

μονόω v. (μόνος) pf. pass. μεμόνωμαι. to make solitary; be left alone (pass. in NT). (1) 1 Ti 5:5

μορφή, ῆς, ἡ n. (*) form, outward appearance, shape. (3)

μορφόω v. (μορφή) aor. pass. ἐμορφώθην. to form, shape; take on form, be formed (pass. in NT). (1) Gal 4:19

μόρφωσις, εως, ἡ n. (μορφή) embodiment, formulation, (outward) form. (2)

μοσχοποιέω v. (μόσχος, ποιέω) aor. ἐμοσχοποίησα. to manufacture a calf. (1) Ac 7:41

μόσχος, ου, ὁ n. (*) calf, young bull or ox. (6)

μουσικός, ή, όν adj. musical; musician (subst. in NT). (1) Rev 18:22

μόχθος, ου, ὁ n. (μόγις) labor, exertion, hardship. (3)

μυελός, οῦ, ὁ n. marrow. (1) Heb 4:12

μυέω v. (-μύω) pf. pass. μεμύημαι. to initiate; learn the secret of (pass. in NT). (1) Phil 4:12

μῦθος, ου, ὁ n. (*) tale, story, legend, myth. (5)

μυκάομαι v. to roar. (1) Rev 10:3

μυκτηρίζω v. (*) to turn up the nose at, treat with contempt, mock. (1) Gal 6:7

μυλικός, ή, όν adj. (μύλος) belonging to a mill, λίθος μυλικός millstone. (1) Lk 17:2

μύλινος, η, ον adj. (μύλος) belonging to a mill; millstone (subst. in NT). (1) Rev 18:21

μύλος, ου, ὁ n. (*) mill; millstone, μύλος ὀνικός great millstone, a millstone worked by a donkey. (4)

Μύρα, ων, τά n. pla. Myra. (1) Ac 27:5

μυριάς, άδος, ἡ n. (μυρίος) myriad, ten thousand; myriads, μυριάδες μυριάδων countless thousands (pl.). (8)

μυρίζω v. (μύρον) aor. ἐμύρισα. *to anoint.* (1) Mk 14:8

μύριοι, αι, α adj. (μυρίος) *ten thousand, zillions.* (1) Mt 18:24

μυρίος, α, ον adj. (*) *innumerable, countless.* (2)

μύρον, ου, τό n. (*) *ointment, perfume.* (14)

Μυσία, ας, ἡ n. pla. *Mysia.* (2)

μυστήριον, ου, τό n. (-μύω) *(God's) secret, mystery, secret truth; transcendent* or *ultimate reality, secret.* (28)

μυωπάζω v. (-μύω, ὁράω) *to be nearsighted.* (1) 2 Pt 1:9

μώλωψ, ωπος, ὁ n. *welt, wale, bruise, wound.* (1) 1 Pt 2:24

μωμάομαι v. (μέμφομαι) aor. ἐμωμησάμην; aor. pass. ἐμωμήθην. *to find fault with, criticize, censure, blame.* (2)

μῶμος, ου, ὁ n. (μέμφομαι) *blemish, defect.* (1) 2 Pt 2:13

μωραίνω v. (μωρός) aor. ἐμώρανα; aor. pass. ἐμωράνθην. *to make foolish, show to be foolish;* pass. *become foolish; become tasteless, insipid.* (4)

μωρία, ας, ἡ n. (μωρός) *foolishness.* (5)

μωρολογία, ας, ἡ n. (μωρός, λέγω) *foolish* or *silly talk.* (1) Eph 5:4

μωρός, ά, όν adj. (*) *foolish, stupid; fool, foolishness* (subst.). (12)

Μωϋσῆς, έως, ὁ n. pers. *Moses.* (80)

N

Ναασσών, ὁ n. pers. *Nahshon.* (3)

Ναγγαί, ὁ n. pers. *Naggai.* (1) Lk 3:25

Ναζαρά, ἡ; Ναζαρέθ, ἡ; and Ναζαρέτ, ἡ n. pla. *Nazareth.* (12)

Ναζαρηνός, ή, όν adj. pla. *from Nazareth; inhabitant of Nazareth, a Nazarene* (subst. in NT). (6)

Ναζωραῖος, ου, ὁ n. pla. *Nazoraean, inhabitant of Nazareth, a Nazarene.* (13)

Ναθάμ, ὁ n. pers. *Nathan.* (1) Lk 3:31

Ναθαναήλ, ὁ n. pers. *Nathanael.* (6)

ναί part. *yes, indeed, certainly, it's true that, of course, quite so, surely.* (33)

Ναιμάν, ὁ n. pers. *Naaman.* (1) Lk 4:27

Ναΐν, ἡ n. pla. *Nain.* (1) Lk 7:11

ναός, οῦ, ὁ n. (*) *temple* (lit. and fig.), *shrine.* (45)

Ναούμ, ὁ n. pers. *Nahum.* (1) Lk 3:25

νάρδος, ου, ἡ n. Sem. *oil of nard, ointment* or *perfume of nard.* (2)

Νάρκισσος, ου, ὁ n. pers. *Narcissus.* (1) Rom 16:11

ναυαγέω v. (ναῦς, ἀξίνη) aor. ἐναυάγησα. *to suffer shipwreck* (lit. and fig.), *come to ruin.* (2)

ναύκληρος, ου, ὁ n. (ναῦς, κλῆρος) *(ship) captain.* (1) Ac 27:11

ναῦς, ὁ n. (*) *ship.* (1) Ac 27:41

ναύτης, ου, ὁ n. (ναῦς) *sailor.* (3)

Ναχώρ, ὁ n. pers. *Nahor.* (1) Lk 3:34

νεανίας, ου, ὁ n. (νέος) *youth, young man.* (3)

νεανίσκος, ου, ὁ n. (νέος) *youth, young man; servant.* (11)

Νέα Πόλις, ἡ n. pla. *Neapolis.* (1) Ac 16:11

νεκρός, ά, όν adj. (*) *dead; dead* (fig.), *useless;* subst. *dead person, dead body, corpse, the dead, realm of the dead; dead person* (fig.). (128)

νεκρόω v. (νεκρός) aor. ἐνέκρωσα; pf. pass. νενέκρωμαι. *to put to death; be as good as dead, worn out, impotent* (pass.). (3)

νέκρωσις, εως, ἡ n. (νεκρός) *death, putting to death; deadness, mortification.* (2)

νεομηνία, ας, ἡ n. (νέος, μήν) *new moon* (festival), *first of the month.* (1) Col 2:16

νέος, α, ον adj. (*) *new, fresh; young,* νεώτερος *younger;* αἱ νέαι *young women,* ὁ νεώτερος *young man, the youngest,* αἱ νεώτεραι *young(er) women* (subst.). (23)

νεότης, ητος, ἡ n. (νέος) *youth.* (4)

νεόφυτος, ον adj. (νέος, φύω) *newly converted.* (1) 1 Ti 3:6

νεύω v. (*) aor. ἔνευσα. *to nod (as a signal).* (2)

νεφέλη, ης, ἡ n. (νέφος) *cloud.* (25)

Νεφθαλίμ, ὁ n. pers. *Naphtali.* (3)

νέφος, ους, τό n. (*) *cloud, host.* (1) Heb 12:1

νεφρός, οῦ, ὁ n. *kidney; mind* (fig. in NT). (1) Rev 2:23

νεωκόρος, ου, ὁ n. (ναός) *honorary temple keeper.* (1) Ac 19:35

νεωτερικός, ή, όν adj. (νέος) *youthful.* (1) 2 Ti 2:22

νεώτερος s. νέος (comp.).

νή part. *yes indeed, by* (w. acc. in oaths). (1) 1 Cor 15:31

νήθω v. *to spin.* (2)

νηπιάζω v. (νήπιος) *to be (as) a child.* (1) 1 Cor 14:20

νήπιος, α, ον adj. (*) subst. in NT *infant, child* (lit. and fig.), *immature person, child-like* or *innocent person; minor, one not yet of age.* (15)

Νηρεύς, εως, ὁ n. pers. *Nereus*. (1) Rom 16:15

Νηρί, ὁ n. pers. *Neri*. (1) Lk 3:27

νησίον, ου, τό n. (νῆσος) *little island*. (1) Ac 27:16

νῆσος, ου, ἡ n. (*) *island*. (9)

νηστεία, ας, ἡ n. (ἐσθίω) *going hungry, hunger; fast, fasting*. (5)

νηστεύω v. (ἐσθίω) fut. νηστεύσω; aor. ἐνήστευσα. *to fast*. (20)

νῆστις, ιδος, ὁ, ἡ n. (ἐσθίω) *not eating, hungry* (used as adj.). (2)

νηφάλιος, α, ον adj. (νήφω) *temperate, sober; level-headed, self-controlled*. (3)

νήφω v. (*) aor. ἔνηψα. *to be well-balanced, self-controlled*. (6)

Νίγερ, ὁ n. pers. *Niger*. (1) Ac 13:1

Νικάνωρ, ορος, ὁ n. pers. *Nicanor*. (1) Ac 6:5

νικάω v. (νίκη) fut. νικήσω; aor. ἐνίκησα; pf. νενίκηκα. *to be victor, conquer, prevail, win* (a verdict); *vanquish, overcome*. (28)

νίκη, ης, ἡ n. (*) *victory*. (1) 1 Jn 5:4

Νικόδημος, ου, ὁ n. pers. *Nicodemus*. (5)

Νικολαΐτης, ου, ὁ n. oth. *Nicolaitan*. (2)

Νικόλαος, ου, ὁ n. pers. *Nicolaus*. (1) Ac 6:5

Νικόπολις, εως, ἡ n. pla. *Nicopolis*. (1) Tit 3:12

νῖκος, ους, τό n. (νίκη) *victory*. (4)

Νινευίτης, ου, ὁ n. pla. *a Ninevite*. (3)

νιπτήρ, ῆρος, ὁ n. (νίπτω) *(wash) basin*. (1) Jn 13:5

νίπτω v. (*) aor. ἔνιψα. *to wash; wash oneself* or *for oneself* (mid.). (17)

νοέω v. (νίπτω) aor. ἐνόησα. *to perceive, apprehend, understand, gain an insight into, comprehend; consider, take note of; think, imagine*. (14)

νόημα, ατος, τό n. (νίπτω) *thought, purpose, design, intention; mind, understanding*. (6)

νόθος, η, ον adj. *illegitimate* (of children). (1) Heb 12:8

νομή, ῆς, ἡ n. *pasture, pasturage; spreading*, νομὴν ἔχω *to spread*. (2)

νομίζω v. (νόμος) aor. ἐνόμισα. *to think, believe, hold, consider, suppose*. (15)

νομικός, ή, όν adj. (νόμος) *about law; legal expert, lawyer, jurist* (subst.). (9)

νομίμως adv. (νόμος) *in accordance with rules* or *law, lawfully*. (2)

νόμισμα, ατος, τό n. (νόμος) *coin*. (1) Mt 22:19

νομοδιδάσκαλος, ου, ὁ n. (νόμος, διδάσκω) *teacher of the law*. (3)

νομοθεσία, ας, ἡ n. (νόμος, τίθημι) *legislation, (giving of the) law*. (1) Rom 9:4

νομοθετέω v. (νόμος, τίθημι) pf. pass. νενομοθέτημαι. pass. in NT *to receive the law; be legally enacted*. (2)

νομοθετης, ου, ὁ n. (νόμος, τίθημι) *lawgiver*. (1) Jas 4:12

νόμος, ου, ὁ n. (*) *custom, rule, principle, norm, system; law, Mosaic law; sacred ordinance, law* (of the Pentateuch and the Hebrew Scriptures). (194)

νοσέω v. (νόσος) *to be ailing with, have a morbid craving for*. (1) 1 Ti 6:4

νόσημα, ατος, τό n. *disease*. (v.l.)

νόσος, ου, ἡ n. (*) *disease, illness*. (11)

νοσσιά, ᾶς, ἡ n. (νέος) *brood*. (1) Lk 13:34

νοσσίον, ου, τό n. (νέος) *the young* (of a bird). (1) Mt 23:37

νοσσός, οῦ, ὁ n. (νέος) *the young* (of a bird), δύο νοσσοὺς περιστερῶν *two young pigeons*. (1) Lk 2:24

νοσφίζω v. aor. ἐνόσφισα. *to keep back* (mid. in NT). (3)

νότος, ου, ὁ n. *south wind, southwest wind; south*. (7)

νουθεσία, ας, ἡ n. (νοῦς, τίθημι) *admonition, instruction, warning, rebuke*. (3)

νουθετέω v. (νοῦς, τίθημι) *to admonish, warn, instruct*. (8)

νουνεχῶς adv. (νοῦς, ἔχω) *wisely, thoughtfully*. (1) Mk 12:34

νοῦς, νοός ὁ n. (*) *intellect, understanding, mind, sensibleness, composure;*

attitude, way of thinking; thought,
opinion, decree. (24)

Νύμφα, ας, ἡ n. pers. Nympha. (1) Col
4:15

νύμφη, ης, ἡ n. (*) bride; daughter-in-
law. (8)

νυμφίος, ου, ὁ n. (νύμφη) bridegroom.
(16)

νυμφών, ῶνος, ὁ n. (νύμφη) bridal cham-
ber, οἱ υἱοὶ τοῦ νυμφῶνος bridegroom's attendants. (3)

νῦν adv. (*) now, at the present time, just
now; present (adj.); as it is, νῦν δέ but
as a matter of fact; subst. present time,
now; the present. (147)

νυνί adv. (νῦν) now; as it is. (20)

νύξ, νυκτός, ἡ n. (*) night (lit. and fig.).
(61)

νύσσω v. (*) aor. ἔνυξα. to prick, stab.
(1) Jn 19:34

νυστάζω v. aor. ἐνύσταξα. to nod, become drowsy, doze, be idle. (2)

νυχθήμερον, ου, τό n. (νύξ, ἡμέρα)
a day and a night. (1) 2 Cor 11:
25

Νῶε, ὁ n. pers. Noah. (8)

νωθρός, ά, όν adj. lazy, sluggish, hard
(of hearing). (2)

νῶτος, ου, ὁ n. back (of the body). (1)
Rom 11:10

Ξ

ξαίνω v. *to comb, card* (of wool). (v.l.)

ξενία, ας, ἡ n. (ξένος) *hospitality, entertainment, guest room, place of lodging.* (2)

ξενίζω v. (ξένος) aor. ἐξένισα; aor. pass. ἐξενίσθην. *to receive as a guest, entertain; surprise, astonish;* pass. *stay; be surprised, wonder.* (10)

ξενοδοχέω v. (ξένος, δέχομαι) aor. ἐξενοδόχησα. *to show hospitality.* (1) 1 Ti 5:10

ξένος, η, ον adj. (*) *strange, foreign, surprising, unheard of; stranger, alien, host* (subst.). (14)

ξέστης, ου, ὁ n. Lat. *pitcher, jug.* (1) Mk 7:4

ξηραίνω v. (ξηρός) aor. ἐξήρανα; pf. pass. ἐξήραμμαι; aor. pass. ἐξηράνθην. *to dry (up);* pass. *become dry, dry up, wither, stop; be paralyzed, wither, become stiff; be ripe.* (15)

ξηρός, ά, όν adj. (*) *dry, dried up; withered, shrunken, paralyzed; dry land* (subst.). (8)

ξύλινος, η, ον adj. (ξύλον) *wooden.* (2)

ξύλον, ου, τό n. (*) *wood* (sg. and pl.); *club, cudgel, stocks, cross; tree.* (20)

ξυράω v. (ξύλον) fut. ξυρήσω; pf. pass. ἐξύρημαι. *to have oneself shaved* (mid.); *be shaved* (pass.). (3)

O

ὁ, ἡ, τό art. (*) *the; this one, that one.*
(19867)

ὀγδοήκοντα adj. (ὀκτώ) *eighty.* (2)

ὄγδοος, η, ον adj. (ὀκτώ) *eighth.* (5)

ὄγκος, ου, ὁ n. (*) *weight, burden, impediment.* (1) Heb 12:1

ὅδε, ἥδε, τόδε pron. (ὁ) demonstr. *this, this one; such and such.* (10)

ὁδεύω v. (ὁδός) *to go, travel, make a trip.* (1) Lk 10:33

ὁδηγέω v. (ὁδός, ἄγω) fut. ὁδηγήσω. *to lead, guide; conduct, instruct.* (5)

ὁδηγός, οῦ, ὁ n. (ὁδός, ἄγω) *leader, guide.* (5)

ὁδοιπορέω v. (ὁδός, πορεύομαι) *to travel, be on the way.* (1) Ac 10:9

ὁδοιπορία, ας, ἡ n. (ὁδός, πορεύομαι) *walking, journey.* (2)

ὁδός, οῦ, ἡ n. (*) *way, road, highway, street; trip, journey; way (of life), conduct, the Way, teaching, religion; toward* (as prep.). (101)

ὀδούς, ὀδόντος, ὁ n. *tooth.* (12)

ὀδυνάω v. (ὀδύνη) *to suffer pain; be pained, distressed, anxious* (pass. in NT). (4)

ὀδύνη, ης, ἡ n. (*) *distress, grief, pang.* (2)

ὀδυρμός, οῦ, ὁ n. *lamentation, mourning.* (2)

Ὀζίας, ου, ὁ n. pers. *Uzziah.* (2)

ὄζω v. (*) *to emit an odor, smell, stink.* (1) Jn 11:39

ὅθεν adv. (ὅς) *from where, whence, from which, where; for which reason, therefore, hence.* (15)

ὀθόνη, ης, ἡ n. (*) *linen cloth, sheet.* (2)

ὀθόνιον, ου, τό n. (ὀθόνη) *(linen) cloth, cloth wrapping.* (5)

οἶδα v. (*) fut. εἰδήσω; pf. οἶδα. pf. used as pres. *to know (about); know, have to do with; can, be able, know or understand how; understand, recognize, come to know, experience; recollect, recall, be aware of; respect, honor.* (318)

οἰκεῖος, α, ον adj. (οἶκος) *member of a household* (subst. in NT). (3)

οἰκετεία, ας, ἡ n. (οἶκος) *household (slaves).* (1) Mt 24:45

οἰκέτης, ου, ὁ n. (οἶκος) *house slave, domestic, slave.* (4)

οἰκέω v. (οἶκος) *to live, dwell; inhabit, dwell in* (trans.). (9)

οἴκημα, ατος, τό n. (οἶκος) *quarters, (prison) cell.* (1) Ac 12:7

οἰκητήριον, ου, τό n. (οἶκος) *dwelling, habitation.* (2)

οἰκία, ας, ἡ n. (οἶκος) *house, home, dwelling; household, family.* (93)

οἰκιακός, οῦ, ὁ n. (οἶκος) *member of a household.* (2)

οἰκοδεσποτέω v. (οἶκος, δέω) *to manage one's household, keep house.* (1) 1 Ti 5:14

οἰκοδεσπότης, ου, ὁ n. (οἶκος, δέω) *master of the house, householder.* (12)

οἰκοδομέω v. (οἶκος, δῶμα) fut. οἰκοδομήσω; aor. ᾠκοδόμησα; pf. pass. οἰκοδόμημαι; aor. pass. οἰκοδομήθην. *to build, erect, build up again, restore; strengthen, build up, make more able, edify, benefit.* (40)

οἰκοδομή, ῆς, ἡ n. (οἶκος, δῶμα) *building (up), construction, edification; building, edifice.* (18)

οἰκοδόμος, ου, ὁ n. (οἶκος, δῶμα) *builder.* (1) Ac 4:11

οἰκονομέω v. (οἶκος, νόμος) *to manage, administer, be manager.* (1) Lk 16:2

οἰκονομία, ας, ἡ n. (οἶκος, νόμος) *management* (of a household), *direction, office, commission, task, administration; arrangement, order, plan; training*. (9)

οἰκονόμος, ου, ὁ n. (οἶκος, νόμος) *(house) steward, manager; treasurer; administrator*. (10)

οἶκος, ου, ὁ n. (*) *house* (lit. and fig.), *dwelling, home, palace, temple, city, habitation,* κατὰ (τοὺς) οἴκους *house to house,* κατ᾽ οἶκον *in private homes; household, family; descendants, nation; property, possessions, estate*. (114)

οἰκουμένη, ης, ἡ n. (οἶκος) *inhabited earth, world; Roman Empire; humankind; age*. (15)

οἰκουργός, όν adj. (οἶκος, ἔργον) *busy at home, carrying out household duties*. (1) Tit 2:5

οἰκτιρμός, οῦ, ὁ n. (οἰκτίρω) *pity, mercy, compassion*. (5)

οἰκτίρμων, ον adj. (οἰκτίρω) *merciful, compassionate*. (3)

οἰκτίρω v. (*) fut. οἰκτιρήσω. *to have compassion*. (2)

οἶμαι contr. of οἴομαι.

οἰνοπότης, ου, ὁ n. (οἶνος, πίνω) *winedrinker, drunkard*. (2)

οἶνος, ου, ὁ n. (*) *wine* (lit. and fig.); *vine, vineyard*. (34)

οἰνοφλυγία, ας, ἡ n. (οἶνος, φλύαρος) *drunkenness*. (1) 1 Pt 4:3

οἴομαι v. (*) contr. οἶμαι *to think, suppose, expect*. (3)

οἷος, α, ον pron. (ὁ, ὅς) rel. *of what sort, (such) as,* οἷος ... τοιοῦτος *as ... so,* οἵους διωγμούς *what persecutions!* (14)

οἴσω s. φέρω (fut.).

ὀκνέω v. (*) aor. ὤκνησα. *to hesitate, delay*. (1) Ac 9:38

ὀκνηρός, ά, όν adj. (ὀκνέω) *idle, lazy, indolent; troublesome*. (3)

ὀκταήμερος, ον adj. (ὀκτώ, ἡμέρα) *on the eighth day*. (1) Phil 3:5

ὀκτώ adj. (*) *eight*. (8)

ὄλεθρος, ου, ὁ n. (*) *destruction* (state and act), *ruin, death*. (4)

ὀλιγοπιστία, ας, ἡ n. (ὀλίγος, πείθω) *littleness* or *poverty of faith*. (1) Mt 17:20

ὀλιγόπιστος, ον adj. (ὀλίγος, πείθω) *of little faith* or *trust*. (5)

ὀλίγος, η, ον adj. (*) pl. *few; (a) few* (subst.); sg. *little, small, short; small amount* (subst.); *in a short time, quickly, a little* (neut. as adv.); *slight, brief*. (40)

ὀλιγόψυχος, ον adj. (ὀλίγος, ψύχω) *faint-hearted, discouraged*. (1) 1 Th 5:14

ὀλιγωρέω v. (ὀλίγος) *to think lightly, make light*. (1) Heb 12:5

ὀλίγως adv. (ὀλίγος) *scarcely, barely*. (1) 2 Pt 2:18

ὀλοθρευτής, οῦ, ὁ n. (ὄλεθρος) *destroyer* (of an angel). (1) 1 Cor 10:10

ὀλοθρεύω v. (ὄλεθρος) *to destroy, ruin,* ὁ ὀλοθρεύων *destroyer* (of an angel). (1) Heb 11:28

ὁλοκαύτωμα, ατος, τό n. (ὅλος, καίω) *whole burnt offering*. (3)

ὁλοκληρία, ας, ἡ n. (ὅλος, κλῆρος) *wholeness, completeness, perfect health*. (1) Ac 3:16

ὁλόκληρος, ον adj. (ὅλος, κλῆρος) *with integrity, whole, complete, undamaged, intact, blameless, sound*. (2)

ὀλολύζω v. *to cry out*. (1) Jas 5:1

ὅλος, η, ον adj. (*) *whole, entire, complete; wholly, completely, altogether,* τοῦτο ὅλον *all this,* δι᾽ ὅλου *throughout* (used as adv.). (109)

ὁλοτελής, ές adj. (ὅλος, τέλος) *in every way complete, quite perfect*. (1) 1 Th 5:23

Ὀλυμπᾶς, ᾶ, ὁ n. pers. *Olympas*. (1) Rom 16:15

ὄλυνθος, ου, ὁ n. *late* or *summer fig*. (1) Rev 6:13

ὅλως adv. (ὅλος) *completely, wholly, everywhere, at all; actually, in fact*. (4)

ὄμβρος, ου, ὁ n. *rainstorm, thunderstorm*. (1) Lk 12:54

ὁμείρομαι v. *to long for.* (1) 1 Th 2:8

ὁμιλέω v. (ὅμοιος, -εΐλω) aor. ὡμίλησα. *to speak, converse, address, talk.* (4)

ὁμιλία, ας, ἡ n. (ὅμοιος, -εΐλω) *association, social intercourse, company.* (1) 1 Cor 15:33

ὅμιλος, ου, ὁ n. *crowd, throng.* (v.l.)

ὁμίχλη, ης, ἡ n. *mist, fog.* (1) 2 Pt 2:17

ὄμμα, ατος, τό n. (ὁράω) *eye.* (2)

ὀμνύω and ὄμνυμι v. (*) aor. ὤμοσα. *to swear, take* or *assure by an oath.* (26)

ὁμοθυμαδόν adv. (ὅμοιος, θυμός) *with one mind, purpose,* or *impulse, together,* γενόμενοι ὁμοθυμαδόν *unanimously.* (11)

ὁμοιάζω v. *to be like, resemble.* (v.l.)

ὁμοιοπαθής, ές adj. (ὅμοιος, πάσχω) *with the same nature.* (2)

ὅμοιος, α, ον adj. (*) *of the same nature, like, similar, a match for, just as great as.* (45)

ὁμοιότης, ητος, ἡ n. (ὅμοιος) *likeness, similarity, agreement,* καθ᾽ ὁμοιότητα *in the same way.* (2)

ὁμοιόω v. (ὅμοιος) fut. ὁμοιώσω; aor. ὡμοίωσα; aor. pass. ὡμοιώθην. *to make like; compare; become like, be like, be in the form of, resemble* (pass.). (15)

ὁμοίωμα, ατος, τό n. (ὅμοιος) *likeness; image, form, copy, appearance.* (6)

ὁμοίως adv. (ὅμοιος) *likewise, so, similarly, in the same way, also.* (30)

ὁμοίωσις, εως, ἡ n. (ὅμοιος) *likeness, resemblance.* (1) Jas 3:9

ὁμολογέω v. (ὅμοιος, λέγω) fut. ὁμολογήσω; aor. ὡμολόγησα. *to promise; agree; confess, grant, admit; acknowledge, claim, profess, praise, say plainly.* (26)

ὁμολογία, ας, ἡ n. (ὅμοιος, λέγω) *professing, confessing; confession, acknowledgment, profession.* (6)

ὁμολογουμένως adv. (ὅμοιος, λέγω) *undeniably, most certainly.* (1) 1 Ti 3:16

ὁμότεχνος, ον adj. (ὅμοιος, τίκτω) *practicing the same trade.* (1) Ac 18:3

ὁμοῦ adv. (ὅμοιος) *together; in company with.* (4)

ὁμόφρων, ον adj. (ὅμοιος, φρήν) *united in spirit, harmonious.* (1) 1 Pt 3:8

ὅμως adv. (ὅμοιος) *all the same, nevertheless, yet, likewise, also.* (3)

ὀναίμην s. ὀνίνημι (2 aor. mid. opt.).

ὄναρ, τό n. *dream,* κατ᾽ ὄναρ *in a dream.* (6)

ὀνάριον, ου, τό n. (ὄνος) *(young) donkey.* (1) Jn 12:14

ὀνειδίζω v. (ὄνειδος) aor. ὠνείδισα. *to reproach, revile, mock, insult, charge; reprimand.* (9)

ὀνειδισμός, οῦ, ὁ n. (ὄνειδος) *reproach, reviling, disgrace, insult.* (5)

ὄνειδος, ους, τό n. (*) *disgrace, reproach, insult.* (1) Lk 1:25

Ὀνήσιμος, ου, ὁ n. pers. *Onesimus.* (2)

Ὀνησίφορος, ου, ὁ n. pers. *Onesiphorus.* (2)

ὀνικός, ή, όν adj. (ὄνος) *pertaining to a donkey,* μύλος ὀνικός *great millstone, a millstone worked by a donkey.* (2)

ὀνίνημι v. aor. ὠνησάμην. *to have benefit of, enjoy* (mid. in NT). (1) Phlm 20

ὄνομα, ατος, τό n. (*) *name,* κατ᾽ ὄνομα *by name,* εἰς τὸ ὄνομα *with regard to* or *thinking of someone; person; title, category; reputation, fame.* (231)

ὀνομάζω v. (ὄνομα) aor. ὠνόμασα; aor. pass. ὠνομάσθην. *to name, call; use a name* or *word, mention, pronounce;* pass. *be called; be named; be known.* (10)

ὄνος, ου, ὁ, ἡ n. (*) *donkey.* (5)

ὄντως adv. (εἰμί) *really, certainly, in truth; real* (adj.). (10)

ὄξος, ους, τό n. (ὀξύς) *sour wine, wine vinegar.* (6)

ὀξύς, εῖα, ύ adj. (*) *sharp; quick, swift.* (8)

ὀπή, ῆς, ἡ n. *opening, hole.* (2)

ὄπισθεν adv. (ὀπίσω) *from behind, to the rear, after; behind, on the back; behind, after* (adv. prep. w. gen.). (7)

ὀπίσω adv. (*) *behind, back,* (τὰ) ὀπίσω *what lies behind* or *home;* adv. prep. w. gen. *behind; after, follow.* (35)

ὁπλίζω v. (ὅπλον) aor. ὥπλισα. *to equip; equip* or *prepare oneself with* (mid. in NT). (1) 1 Pt 4:1

ὅπλον, ου, τό n. (*) *tool; weapon.* (6)

ὁποῖος, α, ον pron. (ποῦ) correl. *of what sort, as.* (5)

ὅπου adv. (ποῦ) *where,* ὅπου ἄν (or ἐάν) *whenever* or *wherever; in so far as, since.* (82)

ὀπτάνομαι v. (ὁράω) *to appear.* (1) Ac 1:3

ὀπτασία, ας, ἡ n. (ὁράω) *a vision, celestial sight.* (4)

ὀπτός, ή, όν adj. *roasted, baked, broiled.* (1) Lk 24:42

ὀπώρα, ας, ἡ n. (*) *fruit.* (1) Rev 18:14

ὅπως adv. (ποῦ) *how, that; (in order) that, (with a view) to* (conj.). (53)

ὅραμα, ατος, τό n. (ὁράω) *something seen, sight; vision.* (12)

ὅρασις, εως, ἡ n. (ὁράω) *appearance, sight; vision.* (4)

ὁρατος, ή, όν adj. (ὁράω) *visible.* (1) Col 1:16

ὁράω v. (*) fut. ὄψομαι; aor. εἶδον, εἶδα, ὦψησα; pf. ἑώρακα, ἑόρακα; aor. pass. ὤφθην. trans. *see, catch sight of, notice, look at; look after, visit, come to know; experience, witness; perceive, understand, note, consider, deliberate; feel;* intr. *look; pay attention, see to it that; see to, take care.* (454)

ὀργή, ῆς, ἡ n. (*) *anger; wrath, indignation, punishment, judgment.* (36)

ὀργίζω v. (ὀργή) aor. pass. ὠργίσθην. *to be angry* (pass. in NT). (8)

ὀργίλος, η, ον adj. (ὀργή) *inclined to anger, quick-tempered.* (1) Tit 1:7

ὀργυιά, ᾶς, ἡ n. (ὀρέγω) *fathom* (nautical measure, about 1.85 meters or 6 feet). (2)

ὀρέγω v. (*) *to aspire to, strive for, desire, long for* (mid. in NT). (3)

ὀρεινός, ή, όν adj. (ὄρος) *mountainous; hill country* (fem. subst. in NT). (2)

ὄρεξις, εως, ἡ n. (ὀρέγω) *longing, desire.* (1) Rom 1:27

ὀρθοποδέω v. (ὀρθός, πούς) *to act rightly, be straightforward, progress* (fig. in NT). (1) Gal 2:14

ὀρθός, ή, όν adj. (*) *straight, upright.* (2)

ὀρθοτομέω v. (ὀρθός, τομός) *to cut straight; guide along a straight path, teach* or *interpret correctly* (fig. in NT). (1) 2 Ti 2:15

ὀρθρίζω v. (ὄρθρος) *to be up* or *get up very early in the morning.* (1) Lk 21:38

ὀρθρινός, ή, όν adj. (ὄρθρος) *early in the morning.* (1) Lk 24:22

ὄρθρος, ου, ὁ n. (*) *dawn, early morning,* ὑπὸ τὸν ὄρθρον *about daybreak.* (3)

ὀρθῶς adv. (ὀρθός) *rightly, correctly.* (4)

ὁρίζω v. (*) aor. ὥρισα; pf. pass. ὥρισμαι; aor. pass. ὡρίσθην. *to appoint, determine, set, designate.* (8)

ὅριον, ου, τό n. (ὁρίζω) *boundary; region, district* (pl. in NT). (12)

ὁρκίζω v. (ὅρκος) *to adjure, implore.* (2)

ὅρκος, ου, ὁ n. (*) *oath.* (10)

ὁρκωμοσία, ας, ἡ n. (ὅρκος, ὀμνύω) *oath-taking, oath.* (4)

ὁρμάω v. (ὁρμή) aor. ὥρμησα. *to rush.* (5)

ὁρμή, ῆς, ἡ n. (*) *impulse, inclination, desire, attempt.* (2)

ὅρμημα, ατος, τό n. (ὁρμή) *violent rush, violence.* (1) Rev 18:21

ὄρνεον, ου, τό n. (ὄρνις) *bird.* (3)

ὄρνις, ιθος, ὁ, ἡ n. (*) *hen.* (2)

ὁροθεσία, ας, ἡ n. (ὁρίζω, τίθημι) *(fixed) boundary.* (1) Ac 17:26

ὄρος, ους, τό n. (*) *mountain, hill, mount.* (63)

ὅρος, ου, ὁ n. *boundary, limit.* (v.l.)

ὀρύσσω v. (*) aor. ὤρυξα. *to dig (up); dig out, prepare by digging.* (3)

ὀρφανός, ή, όν adj. (*) *orphaned; orphan* (subst.). (2)

ὀρχέομαι v. aor. ὠρχησάμην. *to dance.* (4)

ὅς, ἥ, ὅ pron. (*) rel. *who, which, what, that, the one who, so that, what?* ὅ

ἐστιν *which means, ὅς ἄν (ἐάν) whoever, ὅς μέν... ὅς δέ one... another,
ἀνθ᾽ ὧν because or therefore, εἰς ὅ
to this end, ἐν οἷς under which circumstances, ἐφ᾽ ᾧ for or because, οὗ
χάριν therefore, ἀφ᾽ ἧς since, ἀφ᾽ οὗ
since, ἕως οὗ until, μέχρις οὗ until;
this (one), he.* (1398)
ὁσάκις adv. (ὅσος) *as often as.* (3)
ὅσιος, α, ον adj. (*) *devout, pleasing to
God, holy; holy one* (subst.); τὰ ὅσια
divine assurances or *decrees.* (8)
ὁσιότης, ητος, ἡ n. (ὅσιος) *devoutness,
piety, holiness.* (2)
ὁσίως adv. (ὅσιος) *devoutly.* (1) 1 Th
2:10
ὀσμή, ῆς, ἡ n. (ὄζω) *smell; odor, fragrance.* (6)
ὅσος, η, ον pron. (*) correl. *as great,
as far, as long,* (ἐφ᾽) ὅσον χρόνον
as long as, ἔτι μικρὸν ὅσον ὅσον
in a very little while; how much or
many, as much or *many as,* πάντες
(ἅπαντες) ὅσοι *all who,* πάντα ὅσα
everything that, ὅσοι or ὅσα *all that* or
who, ὅσοι ἄν (ἐάν) *whoever;* ὅσον...
μᾶλλον περισσότερον *as much as...
so much the more,* πλείονος... καθ᾽
ὅσον πλείονα *as much more... as,*
καθ᾽ ὅσον... κατὰ τοσοῦτο *to the degree that... to the same degree,* καθ᾽
ὅσον... οὕτως *just as... so,* τοσούτῳ
... ὅσῳ (by) *as much... as,* τοσούτῳ
μᾶλλον... ὅσῳ *all the more... as,* ὅσα
... τοσοῦτον *to the degree that... to
the same degree.* (110)
ὅσπερ, ἥπερ, ὅπερ pron. rel. *who, which.*
(v.l.)
ὀστέον, ου and **ὀστοῦν, οῦ, τό** n. *bone.*
(4)
ὅστις, ἥτις, ὅ τι pron. (ὅς, τίς) rel.
*whoever, every one who; who, one
who;* = ὅς, ἧς, ὅ; ὅτι *why?* (153)
ὀστράκινος, η, ον adj. *made of earth* or
clay. (2)
ὄσφρησις, εως, ἡ n. (ὄζω) *sense of smell,
nose.* (1) 1 Cor 12:17
ὀσφῦς, ύος, ἡ n. *waist, loins; place of the*

genitals, ἐξέρχομαι ἐκ τῆς ὀσφύος *be
someone's descendant(s),* καρπὸς τῆς
ὀσφύος *descendants.* (8)
ὅταν part. (ὅς, ἄν) *at the time that, whenever, when.* (123)
ὅτε part. (ὅς, τέ) *when; while, as long as.*
(103)
ὅτι conj. (ὅς, τίς) *that; in that, concerning this,* τί ὅτι *why?* οὐχ ὅτι *not as
if;* can introduce direct discourse, =
quotation marks; *because, since, for;
so that,* ὡς ὅτι *that* (in the opinion of
the writer). (1296)
οὗ adv. (ὅς) *where, in which, at which, on
which, to which; (in a situation) where.*
(24)
οὐ adv. (*) *not* (usu. w. ind. verbs); used
when expecting pos. answers to questions; οὐ μή *not at all, by no means*
(strong fut. neg.). (1606)
οὔ part. (οὐ) *no.* (17)
οὐά interj. *aha!* (1) Mk 15:29
οὐαί interj. *woe, alas; woe* (subst.); *woe,
calamity* (fem. subst.). (46)
οὐδ᾽ = οὐδέ before vowels.
οὐδαμῶς adv. (οὐ, δέ) *by no means.* (1)
Mt 2:6
οὐδέ conj. (οὐ, δέ) *and not, nor;* οὐδὲ...
οὐδέ *neither... nor; also not, not either, neither; not even.* (143)
οὐδείς, οὐδεμία, οὐδέν adj. (οὐ, δέ,
εἷς) *no; no one, nobody, none,* οὐδέν
nothing, worthless, invalid, in no way
(subst.). (234)
οὐδέποτε adv. (οὐ, δέ, ποῦ) *never.* (16)
οὐδέπω adv. (οὐ, δέ, -πω) *not yet, still
not,* οὐδέπω οὐδείς *no one ever.* (4)
οὐθείς = οὐδείς.
οὐκ = οὐ before smooth breathing.
οὐκέτι adv. (οὐ, ἔτι) *no longer, no more,
no further,* οὐκέτι οὐ μή *never again;
not.* (47)
οὐκοῦν adv. (οὐ, οὖν) *so then, so.* (1) Jn
18:37
οὖν part. (*) postpos. *so, therefore, consequently, accordingly, then* (inference);
so, now, then, well, in reply, in turn
(narrative continuation); *certainly,*

really, to be sure, indeed, of course (poss.)*; but, however* (poss.). (499)

οὔπω adv. (οὐ, -πω) *not yet,* οὐδεὶς οὔπω *no one ever.* (26)

οὐρά, ᾶς, ἡ n. *tail.* (5)

οὐράνιος, ον adj. (οὐρανός) *heavenly.* (9)

οὐρανόθεν adv. (οὐρανός) *from heaven.* (2)

οὐρανός, οῦ, ὁ n. (*) *heaven, sky; heaven* (God's abode)*; God* (fig.). (273)

Οὐρβανός, οῦ, ὁ n. pers. *Urbanus.* (1) Rom 16:9

Οὐρίας, ου, ὁ n. pers. *Uriah.* (1) Mt 1:6

οὖς, ὠτός, τό n. (*) *ear,* πρὸς τὸ οὖς λαλέω *whisper; hearing.* (36)

οὐσία, ας, ἡ n. (εἰμί) *property, wealth.* (2)

οὔτε adv. (οὐ, τέ) *and not,* οὔτε . . . οὔτε *neither . . . nor, no.* (87)

οὗτος, αὕτη, τοῦτο pron. (*) demonstr. *this, this one, he, she, it,* αὐτὸς οὗτος *he himself,* διὰ τοῦτο and ἐν τούτῳ *for this reason,* τοῦτ᾽ ἔστιν *that is; this* (adj.). (1387)

οὕτως and **οὕτω** adv. (οὗτος) *in this manner, thus, so, hence,* οὕτως ὅτι *since,* ὁ μὲν οὕτως, ὁ δὲ οὕτως *the one in one way, the other in another; in this way, as follows; so intense(ly); without further ado, just, simply, accordingly; such* (adj.)*; something like this* (subst.). (208)

οὐχ = οὐ before rough breathing.

οὐχί adv. (οὐ) *not; no, by no means;* used when expecting pos. answers to questions. (54)

ὀφειλέτης, ου, ὁ n. (ὀφείλω) *debtor; one under obligation, one liable for, one who is guilty of a misdeed, sinner.* (7)

ὀφειλή, ῆς, ἡ n. (ὀφείλω) *obligation, debt; duty.* (3)

ὀφείλημα, ατος, τό n. (ὀφείλω) *debt, one's due; sin.* (2)

ὀφείλω v. (*) *to owe, be indebted* (financial sense)*; owe, be indebted* (social or moral sense), *commit a sin; have to, ought.* (35)

ὄφελον part. (ὀφείλω) *O that, would that, I wish.* (4)

ὄφελος, ους, τό n. (ὠφελέω) *benefit, good.* (3)

ὀφθαλμοδουλία, ας, ἡ n. (ὁράω, δοῦλος) *eye-service, service to attract attention.* (2)

ὀφθαλμός, οῦ, ὁ n. (ὁράω) *eye, sight; understanding.* (100)

ὀφθείς, ὀφθήσομαι s. ὁράω (aor. pass. ptc., fut. pass.).

ὄφις, εως, ὁ n. *snake, serpent* (lit. and fig.). (14)

ὀφρῦς, ύος, ἡ n. *brow, edge* (of a hill or cliff). (1) Lk 4:29

ὀχλέω v. (ὄχλος) *to trouble, disturb, torment.* (1) Ac 5:16

ὀχλοποιέω v. (ὄχλος, ποιέω) aor. ὠχλοποίησα. *to form a mob.* (1) Ac 17:5

ὄχλος, ου, ὁ n. (*) *crowd, throng, (common) people, populace, rabble; horde, mass.* (175)

ὀχύρωμα, ατος, τό n. (ἔχω) *fortress.* (1) 2 Cor 10:4

ὀψάριον, ου, τό n. (*) *fish.* (5)

ὀψέ adv. (*) *late in the day, (in the) evening; after* (adv. prep. w. gen.). (3)

ὄψιμος, ον adj. (ὀψέ) *late; late or spring rain* (subst. in NT). (1) Jas 5:7

ὄψιος, α, ον adj. (ὀψέ) *late; evening* (fem. subst.). (15)

ὄψις, εως, ἡ n. (ὁράω) *outward appearance, aspect; face, countenance.* (3)

ὀψώνιον, ου, τό n. (ὀψάριον, ὠνέομαι) *pay, wages, expense, support; compensation.* (4)

Π

παγιδεύω v. (πήγνυμι) aor. ἐπαγίδευσα. *to set a snare* or *trap, entrap*. (1) Mt 22:15

παγίς, ίδος, ἡ n. (πήγνυμι) *trap, snare* (lit. and fig.). (5)

πάγος s. Ἄρειος Πάγος.

παθεῖν, παθών s. πάσχω (2 aor. inf., 2 aor. ptc.).

πάθημα, ατος, τό n. (πάσχω) *suffering, misfortune; feeling, interest, desire*. (16)

παθητός, ή, όν adj. (πάσχω) *subject to suffering*. (1) Ac 26:23

πάθος, ους, τό n. (πάσχω) *passion*. (3)

παιδαγωγός, οῦ, ὁ n. (παῖς, ἄγω) *guardian, leader, guide*. (3)

παιδάριον, ου, τό n. (παῖς) *a youth; young slave* (poss.). (1) Jn 6:9

παιδεία, ας, ἡ n. (παῖς) *upbringing, training, instruction, discipline, correction*. (6)

παιδευτής, οῦ, ὁ n. (παῖς) *instructor, teacher, corrector, one who disciplines*. (2)

παιδεύω v. (παῖς) aor. ἐπαίδευσα; pf. pass. πεπαίδευμαι; aor. pass. ἐπαιδεύθην. *to educate; practice discipline, correct, guide, lead, discipline (by whipping* or *scourging)*. (13)

παιδιόθεν adv. (παῖς) *from childhood*. (1) Mk 9:21

παιδίον, ου, τό n. (παῖς) *child* (lit. and fig.), *infant*. (52)

παιδίσκη, ης, ἡ n. (παῖς) *female slave, slave*. (13)

παίζω v. (παῖς) *to play, amuse oneself*. (1) 1 Cor 10:7

παῖς, παιδός, ὁ, ἡ n. (*) masc. *boy, youth; child, son; slave, servant;* fem. *daughter, girl*. (24)

παίω v. aor. ἔπαισα. *to strike, hit, wound, sting*. (5)

πάλαι adv. (*) *long ago, formerly; for a long time, all along; already*. (7)

παλαιός, ά, όν adj. (πάλαι) *old* (lit. and fig.)*; obsolete*. (19)

παλαιότης, ητος, ἡ n. (πάλαι) *age, obsolescence*. (1) Rom 7:6

παλαιόω v. (πάλαι) pf. πεπαλαίωκα; aor. pass. ἐπαλαιώθην. *to make old, declare* or *treat as obsolete; become old* or *obsolete, wear out* (pass.). (4)

πάλη, ης, ἡ n. *struggle, fight*. (1) Eph 6:12

παλιγγενεσία, ας, ἡ n. (πάλιν, γίνομαι) *renewal, new age* or *world; rebirth, regeneration*. (2)

πάλιν adv. (*) *back; again, once more, anew; also, furthermore, thereupon; on the other hand, in turn*. (141)

παμπληθεί adv. (πᾶς, πίμπλημι) *all together*. (1) Lk 23:18

Παμφυλία, ας, ἡ n. pla. *Pamphylia*. (5)

πανδοχεῖον, ου, τό n. (πᾶς, δέχομαι) *inn*. (1) Lk 10:34

πανδοχεύς, έως, ὁ n. (πᾶς, δέχομαι) *inn-keeper*. (1) Lk 10:35

πανήγυρις, εως, ἡ n. (πᾶς, ἄγω) *festal gathering*. (1) Heb 12:22

πανοικεί adv. (πᾶς, οἶκος) *with one's whole household*. (1) Ac 16:34

πανοπλία, ας, ἡ n. (πᾶς, ὅπλον) *full armor* (lit. and fig.). (3)

πανουργία, ας, ἡ n. (πᾶς, ἔργον) *cunning, craftiness, trickery*. (5)

πανοῦργος, ον adj. (πᾶς, ἔργον) *clever, crafty, sly*. (1) 2 Cor 12:16

πανταχῆ adv. (πᾶς) *everywhere*. (1) Ac 21:28

πανταχοῦ adv. (πᾶς) *everywhere, in all directions.* (7)

παντελής, ές adj. (πᾶς, τέλος) *complete*; w. εἰς τό in NT *completely; forever, for all time.* (2)

πάντῃ adv. (πᾶς) *in every way.* (1) Ac 24:3

πάντοθεν adv. (πᾶς) *from all directions, on all sides, entirely.* (3)

παντοκράτωρ, ορος, ὁ n. (πᾶς, κράτος) *Almighty, All-Powerful, Omnipotent (One).* (10)

πάντοτε adv. (πᾶς, ὅς, τέ) *always, at all times.* (41)

πάντως adv. (πᾶς) *by all means, certainly, probably, doubtless; of course, perhaps; at least; not at all, by no means* (w. οὐ). (8)

παρ' = παρά before vowels.

παρά prep. (*) w. gen. *from (the side of); from (the action* or *command of); from,* ἡ παρ' ἐμοῦ διαθήκη *my covenant,* τὰ παρά τινος *what someone gives,* οἱ παρά τινος *family* or *relatives;* w. dat. *at* or *by (the side of), beside, near, in; in the sight* or *judgment of; at the side of; with; among, before;* w. acc. *by, along, at* or *to the edge of, by* or *to the side of, near, at, on; in comparison to, more than, beyond, instead of, rather than; because of; against, contrary to; less.* (194)

παραβαίνω v. (-βαίνω) aor. παρέβην. *to go* or *turn aside; transgress, break* (trans.). (3)

παραβάλλω v. (βάλλω) aor. παρέβαλον. *to approach, come near.* (1) Ac 20:15

παράβασις, εως, ἡ n. (-βαίνω) *overstepping, transgression, violation.* (7)

παραβάτης, ου, ὁ n. (-βαίνω) *violator, transgressor, sinner.* (5)

παραβιάζομαι v. (βία) aor. παρεβιασάμην. *to urge strongly, prevail upon.* (2)

παραβολεύομαι v. (βάλλω) aor. παρεβολευσάμην. *to expose to danger, risk.* (1) Phil 2:30

παραβολή, ῆς, ἡ n. (βάλλω) *type, figure, symbol; parable, comparison, illustration, proverb, maxim.* (50)

παραγγελία, ας, ἡ n. (ἄγγελος) *order, command, precept, advice, exhortation, instruction.* (5)

παραγγέλλω v. (ἄγγελος) aor. παρήγγειλα; pf. pass. παρήγγελμαι. *to give orders, command, instruct, direct, urge, insist on.* (32)

παραγίνομαι v. (γίνομαι) aor. παρεγενόμην. *to draw near, come, arrive, be present; appear; stand by, come to the aid of.* (37)

παράγω v. (ἄγω) *to go away; pass by; pass away, disappear* (act. and pass.). (10)

παραδειγματίζω v. (δείκνυμι) *to expose, make an example of, hold up to contempt.* (1) Heb 6:6

παράδεισος, ου, ὁ n. Per. *paradise.* (3)

παραδέχομαι v. (δέχομαι) fut. παραδέξομαι; aor. pass. παρεδέχθην. *to accept; receive.* (6)

παραδίδωμι v. (δίδωμι) fut. παραδώσω; aor. παρέδωκα; pf. παραδέδωκα; pf. pass. παραδέδομαι; aor. pass. παρεδόθην. *to hand over, give (over), deliver, entrust, give back, restore, give up, risk, turn over, deliver (into custody), abandon; give over, commend, commit; hand down, pass on transmit, relate, teach; allow, permit.* (119)

παράδοξος, ον adj. (δοκέω) *strange, wonderful, remarkable.* (1) Lk 5:26

παράδοσις, εως, ἡ n. (δίδωμι) *tradition.* (13)

παραζηλόω v. (ζέω) fut. παραζηλώσω; aor. παρεζήλωσα. *to provoke to jealousy, make jealous.* (4)

παραθαλάσσιος, α, ον adj. (ἅλας) *(located) by the sea* or *lake.* (1) Mt 4:13

παραθεωρέω v. (θεάομαι) *to overlook, leave unnoticed, neglect.* (1) Ac 6:1

παραθήκη, ης, ἡ n. (τίθημι) *deposit, what is entrusted to another.* (3)

παράθου, παραθῶσιν s. παρατίθημι (2 aor. mid. impv., 2 aor. subj. 3 pl.).

παραινέω v. (αἶνος) *to recommend, urge.* (2)

παραιτέομαι v. (αἰτέω) aor. παρητησάμην; pf. pass. παρήτημαι. *to ask for, request, intercede for, beg; excuse, decline, reject, refuse, avoid, discharge, dismiss.* (12)

παρακαθέζομαι v. (ἑδραῖος) aor. pass. παρεκαθέσθην. *to sit beside* (mid.); *seat oneself beside* (pass. in NT). (1) Lk 10:39

παρακαλέω v. (καλέω) aor. παρεκάλεσα; pf. pass. παρακέκλημαι; aor. pass. παρεκλήθην. *to call to one's side, summon, invite, call upon for help; appeal to, urge, exhort, impress upon; request, implore, entreat, beg; comfort, encourage, cheer up; invite in, conciliate, be friendly to, speak to in a friendly manner.* (109)

παρακαλύπτω v. (καλύπτω) pf. pass. παρακεκάλυμμαι. *to hide, conceal; be hidden* (pass. in NT). (1) Lk 9: 45

παράκειμαι v. (κεῖμαι) *to be at hand, ready.* (2)

παρακέκλημαι, παρακληθῶ s. παρακαλέω (pf. pass., aor. pass. subj.).

παράκλησις, εως, ἡ n. (καλέω) *encouragement, exhortation; appeal, request; comfort, consolation.* (29)

παράκλητος, ου, ὁ n. (καλέω) *mediator, helper, intercessor.* (5)

παρακοή, ῆς, ἡ n. (ἀκούω) *unwillingness to hear, disobedience.* (3)

παρακολουθέω v. (ἀκολουθέω) fut. παρακολουθήσω; aor. παρηκολούθησα; pf. παρηκολούθηκα. *to follow, accompany, attend; follow faithfully or as a rule; follow a thing or a course of events, take note of.* (4)

παρακούω v. (ἀκούω) aor. παρήκουσα. *to hear what is not intended for one's ears, overhear; ignore, refuse to listen to, disobey.* (3)

παρακύπτω v. (κύπτω) aor. παρέκυψα. *to take a look, stoop to look; look (in or into), steal a glance.* (5)

παραλαμβάνω v. (λαμβάνω) fut. παραλήμψομαι; aor. παρέλαβον; aor. pass. παρελήμφθην. *to take (to oneself), take with* or *along, bring along, take into one's home* (of a wife), παραλαμβάνω τινὰ (κατ᾽ ἰδίαν) *take someone aside; take over, receive, come down, learn; accept.* (49)

παραλέγομαι v. (λέγω) *to coast along.* (2)

παραλημφθήσομαι s. παραλαμβάνω (fut. pass.).

παράλιος, ον adj. (ἅλας) *by the seacoast; seacoast district* (subst. in NT). (1) Lk 6:17

παραλλαγή, ῆς, ἡ n. (ἄλλος) *change, variation.* (1) Jas 1:17

παραλογίζομαι v. (λέγω) *to deceive, delude.* (2)

παραλυτικός, ή, όν adj. (λύω) *lame; lame person, paralytic* (subst. in NT). (10)

παραλύω v. (λύω) pf. pass. παραλέλυμαι. *to weaken; be weakened, paralyzed,* ὁ παραλελυμένος *the paralytic* (pass. in NT). (5)

παραμένω v. (μένω) fut. παραμενῶ; aor. παρέμεινα. *to remain, stay (on); continue in an office, serve.* (4)

παραμυθέομαι v. (μῦθος) aor. παρεμυθησάμην. *to cheer up, console, comfort.* (4)

παραμυθία, ας, ἡ n. (μῦθος) *encouragement, comfort, consolation.* (1) 1 Cor 14:3

παραμύθιον, ου, τό n. (μῦθος) *consolation, means of consolation, alleviation, solace.* (1) Phil 2:1

παρανομέω v. (νόμος) *to break* or *act contrary to the law.* (1) Ac 23:3

παρανομία, ας, ἡ n. (νόμος) *lawlessness, evil-doing.* (1) 2 Pt 2:16

παραπικραίνω v. (πικρός) aor. παρεπίκρανα. *to be disobedient, rebellious.* (1) Heb 3:16

παραπικρασμός, οῦ, ὁ n. (πικρός) *revolt, rebellion.* (2)

παραπίπτω v. (πίπτω) aor. παρέπεσον.

to fall away, commit apostasy. (1) Heb 6:6

παραπλέω v. (πλέω) aor. παρέπλευσα. *to sail past.* (1) Ac 20:16

παραπλήσιος, α, ον adj. (πλησίον) *similar; near, close to,* παραπλήσιον θανάτῳ *nearly died* (neut. as adv. prep. w. dat. in NT). (1) Phil 2:27

παραπλησίως adv. (πλησίον) *similarly, likewise.* (1) Heb 2:14

παραπορεύομαι v. (πορεύομαι) *to go* or *pass by; go (through).* (5)

παράπτωμα, ατος, τό n. (πίπτω) *offense, wrongdoing, sin.* (19)

παραρρέω v. (ῥέω) aor. pass. παρερρύην. *to be washed away, drift away.* (1) Heb 2:1

παράσημος, ον adj. (σημεῖον) *marked.* (1) Ac 28:11

παρασκευάζω v. (σκεῦος) fut. παρασκευάσω; pf. pass. παρεσκεύασμαι. *to prepare; prepare oneself* (mid.)*; be ready* (pf. mid.). (4)

παρασκευή, ῆς, ἡ n. (σκεῦος) *preparation; day of preparation* (in NT). (6)

παρασχών s. παρέχω (2 aor. ptc.).

παρατείνω v. (-τείνω) aor. παρέτεινα. *to extend, prolong.* (1) Ac 20:7

παρατηρέω v. (τηρέω) aor. παρετήρησα. *to watch (maliciously), lie in wait for* (act. and mid.)*; mid. watch, guard; observe scrupulously.* (6)

παρατήρησις, εως, ἡ n. (τηρέω) *observation.* (1) Lk 17:20

παρατίθημι v. (τίθημι) fut. παραθήσω; aor. παρέθηκα. *to set before; put before;* mid. *demonstrate, point out; give over, entrust, commend.* (19)

παρατυγχάνω v. (τυγχάνω) *to happen to be near* or *present.* (1) Ac 17:17

παραυτίκα adv. (αὐτός) *on the spot; momentary* (adj. in NT). (1) 2 Cor 4:17

παραφέρω v. (φέρω) aor. παρήνεγκον. *to take* or *carry away, remove.* (4)

παραφίημι v. *to set aside, neglect.* (v.l.)

παραφρονέω v. (φρήν) *to be beside oneself, be irrational.* (1) 2 Cor 11:23

παραφρονία, ας, ἡ n. (φρήν) *madness, insanity.* (1) 2 Pt 2:16

παραχειμάζω v. (χιών) fut. παραχειμάσω; aor. παρεχείμασα; pf. παρακεχείμακα. *to spend the winter, winter.* (4)

παραχειμασία, ας, ἡ n. (χιών) *wintering.* (1) Ac 27:12

παραχρῆμα adv. (χράομαι) *at once, immediately.* (18)

πάρδαλις, εως, ἡ n. *leopard.* (1) Rev 13:2

παρέβην s. παραβαίνω (2 aor.).

παρεδρεύω v. (ἑδραῖος) *to apply oneself to, concern oneself with, serve.* (1) 1 Cor 9:13

παρειμένος s. παρίημι (pf. pass. ptc.).

πάρειμι v. (εἰμί) fut. παρέσομαι. *to be present* or *here, have come,* πρὸς τὸ παρόν *for the present; be at one's disposal, have.* (24)

παρεισάγω v. (ἄγω) fut. παρεισάξω. *to bring in, introduce.* (1) 2 Pt 2:1

παρείσακτος, ον adj. (ἄγω) *secretly brought in, smuggled* or *sneaked in.* (1) Gal 2:4

παρεισδύω v. (δύνω) aor. παρεισέδυσα. *to slip in stealthily, sneak in.* (1) Jd 4

παρεισενέγκας s. παρεισφέρω (aor. ptc.).

παρεισέρχομαι v. (ἔρχομαι) aor. παρεισῆλθον. *to slip in, come in.* (2)

παρεισήκειν s. παρίστημι (plpf.).

παρεισφέρω v. (φέρω) aor. παρεισήνεγκα. *to apply, bring to bear.* (1) 2 Pt 1:5

παρεκτός adv. (παρά, ἐκ) *besides, outside,* τῶν παρεκτός *things external* or *unmentioned; apart from, except for* (adv. prep. w. gen.). (3)

παρεμβάλλω v. (βάλλω) fut. παρεμβαλῶ. *to put around, surround, throw up.* (1) Lk 19:43

παρεμβολή, ῆς, ἡ n. (βάλλω) *(fortified) camp; barracks, headquarters; army, battle line.* (10)

παρένεγκε s. παραφέρω (2 aor. impv.).

παρενοχλέω v. (ὄχλος) *to cause difficulty, trouble, annoy.* (1) Ac 15:19

παρεπίδημος, ον adj. (δῆμος) *sojourning; stranger, sojourner, resident alien* (subst. in NT). (3)

παρέρχομαι v. (ἔρχομαι) fut. παρελεύσομαι; aor. παρῆλθον; pf. παρελήλυθα. *to go* or *pass by; pass, be over; pass away, disappear, lose force; transgress, neglect, disobey; go through; come to* or *by, come here.* (29)

πάρεσις, εως, ἡ n. (-ίημι) *passing over, letting go unpunished.* (1) Rom 3: 25

παρέχω v. (ἔχω) fut. παρέξω; aor. παρέσχον. *to give up, offer, present; grant, show; cause, make happen, bring about, give rise to;* mid. *show oneself to be something; grant (something).* (16)

παρηγορία, ας, ἡ n. (ἄγω) *comfort.* (1) Col 4:11

παρθενία, ας, ἡ n. (παρθένος) *virginity.* (1) Lk 2:36

παρθένος, ου, ἡ, ὁ n. (*) *virgin, chaste person* (female or male). (15)

Πάρθοι, ων, οἱ n. pla. *Parthians.* (1) Ac 2:9

παρίημι v. (-ίημι) aor. παρῆκα; pf. pass. παρεῖμαι. *to neglect; be weakened, listless, drooping* (pass.). (2)

παρίστημι and **παριστάνω** v. (ἵστημι) fut. παραστήσω; aor. παρέστησα, παρέστην; pf. παρέστηκα. trans. (pres., impf., fut., 1 aor. act.) *to place beside, put at someone's disposal, provide, yield, present, represent, make, render, bring before, prove, demonstrate; offer* (mid.); intr. (2 aor. act., pres, fut, aor. mid.) *approach, come to, appear before, come to the aid of, help, stand by;* intr. (pf., plpf.) *stand near* or *by, be present (with), stand before, be here, have come.* (41)

Παρμενᾶς, ᾶ, ὁ n. pers. *Parmenas.* (1) Ac 6:5

πάροδος, ου, ἡ n. (ὁδός) *passing (by).* (1) 1 Cor 16:7

παροικέω v. (οἶκος) aor. παρῴκησα. *to live nearby, dwell beside; be a stranger* (poss.), *migrate; inhabit, live in* (poss.). (2)

παροικία, ας, ἡ n. (οἶκος) *stay, sojourn, foreign country, strange land.* (2)

πάροικος, ον adj. (οἶκος) *strange; stranger, alien* (subst.). (4)

παροιμία, ας, ἡ n. *proverb, maxim; figure* (of speech), *veiled saying.* (5)

πάροινος, ον adj. (οἶνος) *addicted to wine, drunken.* (2)

παροίχομαι v. pf. pass. παρῴχημαι. *to be past.* (1) Ac 14:16

παρομοιάζω v. (ὅμοιος) *to be like.* (1) Mt 23:27

παρόμοιος, ον adj. (ὅμοιος) *like, similar.* (1) Mk 7:13

παρόν, τό s. πάρειμι (pres. ptc. neut.).

παροξύνω v. (ὀξύς) *to stimulate, irritate; become irritated* or *angry* (pass. in NT). (2)

παροξυσμός, οῦ, ὁ n. (ὀξύς) *stirring up, provoking, encouragement; sharp disagreement.* (2)

παροργίζω v. (ὀργή) fut. παροργιῶ. *to make angry.* (2)

παροργισμός, οῦ, ὁ n. (ὀργή) *angry mood, anger.* (1) Eph 4:26

παροτρύνω v. aor. παρώτρυνα. *to arouse, incite.* (1) Ac 13:50

παρουσία, ας, ἡ n. (εἰμί) *presence; coming, advent.* (24)

παροψίς, ίδος, ἡ n. (ὀψάριον) *dish, plate.* (1) Mt 23:25

παρρησία, ας, ἡ n. (πᾶς, ῥῆμα) *outspokenness, frankness, plainness,* παρρησίᾳ *plainly* or *openly,* μετὰ παρρησίας *plainly* or *confidently; openness to the public,* παρρησίᾳ *publicly,* ἐν παρρησίᾳ *make a public example of; courage, confidence, boldness, fearlessness,* ἐν παρρησίᾳ *fearlessly, joyousness.* (31)

παρρησιάζομαι v. (πᾶς, ῥῆμα) aor. ἐπαρρησιασάμην. *to speak freely, openly,* or *fearlessly; have courage, venture.* (9)

πᾶς, πᾶσα, πᾶν adj. (*) w. n. w. no art. *every, each, any; any and every, just* *any, any at all, anything; full, greatest, all; the whole; every kind of, all sorts of;* w. subst. w. art. *whoever, everything that, whatever, all; all* (as highest degree); *the whole, all (the);* w. pron. *all, everything;* attrib. *whole, all;* subst. *all* or *everyone* (masc. and fem.), *all things* or *everything* (neut.); *everyone without exception,* ἐν παντί *in every respect* or *in everything.* (1243)

πάσχα, τό n. Ara. *Passover; Passover lamb; Passover meal.* (29)

πάσχω v. (*) aor. ἔπαθον; pf. πέπονθα. *to experience; be badly off; suffer, endure, undergo.* (42)

Πάταρα, ων, τά n. pla. *Patara.* (1) Ac 21:1

πατάσσω v. fut. πατάξω; aor. ἐπάταξα. *to strike, hit, strike down, slay; strike* (fig.). (10)

πατέω v. (*) fut. πατήσω; aor. pass. ἐπατήθην. *to tread; tread on, trample; walk, move on foot* (intr.). (5)

πατήρ, πατρός, ὁ n. (*) *father* (lit. and fig.), οἱ πατέρες *parents; ancestor* (lit. and fig.), *forefather, progenitor, forebear; Father, Parent* (of God). (413)

Πάτμος, ου, ὁ n. pla. *Patmos.* (1) Rev 1:9

πατριά, ᾶς, ἡ n. (πατήρ) *family, clan, relationship; nation, people.* (3)

πατριάρχης, ου, ὁ n. (πατήρ, ἄρχω) *patriarch, father of a nation.* (4)

πατρικός, ή, όν adj. (πατήρ) *derived from* or *handed down by one's father, paternal.* (1) Gal 1:14

πατρίς, ίδος, ἡ n. (πατήρ) *fatherland, homeland; home town, one's own part of the country.* (8)

Πατροβᾶς, ᾶ, ὁ n. pers. *Patrobas.* (1) Rom 16:14

πατρολῴας, ου, ὁ n. (πατήρ, ἀλοάω) *one who murders one's father, a patricide.* (1) 1 Ti 1:9

πατροπαράδοτος, ον adj. (πατήρ, δίδωμι) *inherited, handed down from one's father* or *ancestors.* (1) 1 Pt 1:18

πατρῷος, α, ον adj. (πατήρ) *paternal,* *belonging to one's father, inherited from one's ancestors.* (3)

Παῦλος, ου, ὁ n. pers. *Paul.* (158)

παύω v. (*) fut. παύσω; aor. ἔπαυσα; pf. pass. πέπαυμαι. *to stop, cause to stop, quiet, relieve, hinder, keep from; stop (oneself), cease, be through with, have finished, be at an end* (mid.). (15)

Πάφος, ου, ἡ n. pla. *Paphos.* (2)

παχύνω v. aor. pass. ἐπαχύνθην. *to make gross* or *dull; become dull* (pass. in NT). (2)

πέδη, ης, ἡ n. (πεζεύω) *fetter, shackle.* (3)

πεδινός, ή, όν adj. (πεζεύω) *flat, level.* (1) Lk 6:17

πεζεύω v. (*) *to travel by land; travel on foot* (poss.). (1) Ac 20:13

πεζῇ adv. (πεζεύω) *by land.* (2)

πειθαρχέω v. (πείθω, ἄρχω) aor. ἐπειθάρχησα. *to obey, follow.* (4)

πειθός, ή, όν adj. (πείθω) *persuasive.* (1) 1 Cor 2:4

πειθώ, οῦς, ἡ n. *persuasiveness.* (v.l.)

πείθω v. (*) fut. πείσω; aor. ἔπεισα; pf. πέποιθα; pf. pass. πέπεισμαι; aor. pass. ἐπείσθην. *to convince, persuade, appeal to, cajole, mislead, win over, strive to please, conciliate, pacify, set at ease* or *rest, satisfy* (act.); *depend on, trust in, be convinced, be sure* or *certain* (2 pf. and plpf.); *be persuaded, believe, obey, follow, be persuaded by, take advice, follow* (pass. and mid.); *be convinced* or *certain* (pf. pass.). (52)

πεῖν s. πίνω (2 aor. inf.).

πεινάω v. (*) fut. πεινάσω; aor. ἐπείνασα. *to hunger, be hungry; hunger for.* (23)

πεῖρα, ας, ἡ n. (*) *attempt, trial, experiment; experience.* (2)

πειράζω v. (πεῖρα) aor. ἐπείρασα; pf. pass. πεπείρασμαι; aor. pass. ἐπειράσθην. *to try, attempt; make trial of, put to the test; test; tempt,* ὁ πειράζων *the tempter.* (38)

πειράομαι v. (πεῖρα) *to try, attempt, endeavor.* (1) Ac 26:21

πειρασμός, οῦ, ὁ n. (πεῖρα) *test, trial; temptation, enticement, tempting, being tempted*. (21)

πεισμονή, ῆς, ἡ n. (πείθω) *persuasion*. (1) Gal 5:8

πέλαγος, ους, τό n. *open sea, depths (of the sea); sea*. (2)

πελεκίζω v. pf. pass. πεπελέκισμαι. *to behead (with an ax)*. (1) Rev 20:4

πέμπτος, η, ον adj. (πέντε) *fifth*. (4)

πέμπω v. (*) fut. πέμψω; aor. ἔπεμψα; aor. pass. ἐπέμφθην. *to send, instruct, commission, appoint, eject, have transported; send (to)*. (79)

πένης, ητος adj. (πόνος) *poor, needy; poor person* (subst. in NT). (1) 2 Cor 9:9

πενθερά, ᾶς, ἡ n. (πενθερός) *mother-in-law*. (6)

πενθερός, οῦ, ὁ n. (*) *father-in-law*. (1) Jn 18:13

πενθέω v. (πένθος) fut. πενθήσω; aor. ἐπένθησα. *to be sad, grieve, mourn; mourn over* (trans.). (10)

πένθος, ους, τό n. (*) *grief, sadness, mourning, sorrow*. (5)

πενιχρός, ά, όν adj. (πόνος) *poor, needy*. (1) Lk 21:2

πεντάκις adv. (πέντε) *five times*. (1) 2 Cor 11:24

πεντακισχίλιοι, αι, α adj. (πέντε, χίλιοι) *five thousand*. (6)

πεντακόσιοι, αι, α adj. (πέντε) *five hundred*. (2)

πέντε adj. (*) *five*. (38)

πεντεκαιδέκατος, η, ον adj. (πέντε, καί, δέκα) *fifteenth*. (1) Lk 3:1

πεντήκοντα adj. (πέντε) *fifty*. (7)

πεντηκοστή, ῆς, ἡ n. (πέντε) *Pentecost*. (3)

πέποιθα s. πείθω (2 pf.).

πεποίθησις, εως, ἡ n. (πείθω) *trust, confidence*. (6)

πέπονθα s. πάσχω (2 pf.).

πέπραγμαι s. πράσσω (pf. pass.).

πέπρακα, πέπραμαι s. πιπράσκω (pf., pf. pass.).

πέπραχα s. πράσσω (2 pf.).

πέπτωκα s. πίπτω (pf.).

πέπωκα s. πίνω (pf.).

περαιτέρω adv. (πέραν) *further, beyond*. (1) Ac 19:39

πέραν adv. (*) *on the other side; (shore or land on the) other side* (subst.); *on the other side of, across*, πέραν τοῦ Ἰορδάνου *Perea* (adv. prep. w. gen.). (23)

πέρας, ατος, τό n. (πέραν) *end, limit, boundary; conclusion*. (4)

Πέργαμος, ου, ἡ and **Πέργαμον, ου, τό** n. pla. *Pergamus* or *Pergamum*. (2)

Πέργη, ης, ἡ n. pla. *Perga*. (3)

περί prep. (*) w. gen. *about, concerning, on account of, because of, for, with regard* or *reference to, in relation to, with respect to*, περὶ ἁμαρτίας *take away* or *atone for sin*, τὸ περὶ τῆς ἁμαρτίας *sin-offering*; w. acc. *around, about, near, with, with regard* or *respect to, for*. (333)

περιάγω v. (ἄγω) *to lead around, take about; go around* or *about, travel about on* (intr.). (6)

περιαιρέω v. (αἱρέω) aor. περιεῖλον. *to take away, remove, cast off* (of anchors); pass. *be removed; be abandoned*. (5)

περιάπτω v. (ἄπτω) aor. περιῆψα. *to kindle*. (1) Lk 22:55

περιαστράπτω v. (ἀστραπή) aor. περιήστραψα. *to shine around; shine* (intr.). (2)

περιβάλλω v. (βάλλω) fut. περιβαλῶ; aor. περιέβαλον; pf. pass. περιβέβλημαι. *to put on, clothe, dress*. (23)

περιβλέπω v. (βλέπω) aor. περιέβλεψα. *to look around* (mid. in NT). (7)

περιβόλαιον, ου, τό n. (βάλλω) *covering, wrap, cloak, robe*. (2)

περιδέω v. (δέω) pf. pass. περιδέδεμαι. *to bind* or *wrap around*. (1) Jn 11:44

περιέδραμον s. περιτρέχω (2 aor.).

περιεζωσμένος s. περιζώννυμι (pf. pass. ptc.).

περιέθηκα s. περιτίθημι (aor.).

περιελεῖν s. περιαιρέω (2 aor. inf.).

περιελθών s. περιέρχομαι (2 aor. ptc.).

περιελών s. περιαιρέω (2 aor. ptc.).

περιέπεσον s. περιπίπτω (2 aor.).

περιεργάζομαι v. (ἔργον) *to be a busybody* or *meddler.* (1) 2 Th 3:11

περίεργος, ον adj. (ἔργον) *meddlesome,* ὁ περίεργος *busybody; belonging to magic,* τὰ περίεργα *magic.* (2)

περιέρχομαι v. (ἔρχομαι) aor. περιῆλθον. *to go* or *wander about, be an itinerant.* (3)

περιέστην, περιεστώς s. περιΐστημι (2 aor., 2 pf. ptc.).

περιέτεμον, περιετμήθην s. περιτέμνω (2 aor., aor. pass.).

περιέχω v. (ἔχω) aor. περιέσχον. *to seize, come upon, befall; contain,* περιέχει ἐν γραφῇ *it stands* or *says in scripture* (intr.). (2)

περιζώννυμι v. (ζώννυμι) fut. περιζώσω; aor. περιέζωσα; pf. pass. περιέζωσμαι. *to gird about; gird oneself* (mid.). (6)

περίθεσις, εως, ἡ n. (τίθημι) *putting on, wearing.* (1) 1 Pt 3:3

περιΐστημι v. (ἵστημι) aor. περιέστην; pf. περιέστηκα. *to stand around; avoid, shun* (mid.). (4)

περικάθαρμα, ατος, τό n. (καθαρός) *dirt, refuse, off-scouring.* (1) 1 Cor 4:13

περικαλύπτω v. (καλύπτω) aor. περιεκάλυψα; pf. pass. περικεκάλυμμαι. *to cover, conceal.* (3)

περίκειμαι v. (κεῖμαι) *to be around, surround, be placed around; wear something, bear, be beset by.* (5)

περικεφαλαία, ας, ἡ n. (κεφαλή) *helmet.* (2)

περικρατής, ές adj. (κράτος) *having power, being in command* or *control.* (1) Ac 27:16

περικρύβω v. (κρύπτω) *to hide, conceal.* (1) Lk 1:24

περικυκλόω v. (κυκλόω) fut. περικυκλώσω. *to surround, encircle.* (1) Lk 19:43

περιλάμπω v. (λάμπω) aor. περιέλαμψα. *to shine around.* (2)

περιλείπομαι v. (λείπω) *to remain, be left behind.* (2)

περίλυπος, ον adj. (λύπη) *very sad, deeply grieved.* (5)

περιμένω v. (μένω) *to wait for.* (1) Ac 1:4

πέριξ adv. (περί) *around, in the vicinity.* (1) Ac 5:16

περιοικέω v. (οἶκος) *to be in the neighborhood of,* οἱ περιοικοῦντες αὐτούς *their neighbors.* (1) Lk 1:65

περίοικος, ον adj. (οἶκος) *living around; neighbor* (subst. in NT). (1) Lk 1:58

περιούσιος, ον adj. (εἰμί) *chosen, special.* (1) Tit 2:14

περιοχή, ῆς, ἡ n. (ἔχω) *content* or *wording (of a text); portion* or *section (of a text).* (1) Ac 8:32

περιπατέω v. (πατέω) fut. περιπατήσω; aor. περιεπάτησα. *to go (about), walk (around), appear; comport oneself, behave, live, conduct oneself, walk* (fig.). (95)

περιπείρω v. aor. περιέπειρα. *to pierce through, impale.* (1) 1 Ti 6:10

περιπίπτω v. (πίπτω) aor. περιέπεσον. *to strike; fall in with, fall into* or *among, become involved in.* (3)

περιποιέω v. (ποιέω) aor. περιεποίησα. *to save* or *preserve (for oneself); acquire, obtain, gain for oneself.* (3)

περιποίησις, εως, ἡ n. (ποιέω) *keeping safe, preserving, saving; gaining, obtaining; possessing, possession, property.* (5)

περιρήγνυμι v. (ῥήγνυμι) aor. περιέρρηξα. *to tear off.* (1) Ac 16:22

περισπάω v. (σπάω) *to be distracted, quite busy, overburdened* (pass. in NT). (1) Lk 10:40

περισσεία, ας, ἡ n. (περί) *surplus, abundance,* εἰς περισσείαν *greatly.* (4)

περίσσευμα, ατος, τό n. (περί)

abundance, fullness; what remains or
is left. (5)
περισσεύω v. (περί) aor. ἐπερίσσευσα;
aor. pass. ἐπερισσεύθην. to abound,
be more than enough, be left over,
be present in abundance, surpass, be
extremely rich or abundant, overflow,
grow, have an abundance, be rich, have
more, excel, have more than enough,
be outstanding or prominent; cause to
abound, grant richly (trans.). (39)
περισσός, ή, όν adj. (περί) extraordinary, remarkable; abundant, profuse,
going beyond what is necessary, su-
perfluous, unnecessary; neut. as adv.
in abundance; subst. advantage; whatever is more than. (6)
περισσότερος, α, ον adj. (περί) greater,
more, even more, excessive; more, even
more, even more clearly, much more
(neut. as adv.). (16)
περισσοτέρως adv. (περί) (even) more,
to a greater degree, far more or greater,
so much more; especially, all the more,
much more. (12)
περισσῶς adv. (περί) exceedingly, beyond measure, very; (even) more
(comp. sense). (4)
περιστερά, ᾶς, ἡ n. pigeon, dove. (10)
περιτέμνω v. (τομός) aor. περιέτεμον;
pf. pass. περιτέτμημαι; aor. pass.
περιετμήθην. to circumcise (lit. and
fig.). (17)
περιτίθημι v. (τίθημι) aor. περιέθηκα.
to put or place around, put or place on;
grant, bestow, show. (8)
περιτομή, ῆς, ἡ n. (τομός) circumcision, state of having been circumcised;
those who are circumcised, Jews (or
Judeans). (36)
περιτρέπω v. (τροπή) to turn. (1) Ac
26:24
περιτρέχω v. (τρέχω) aor. περιέδραμον.
to run about, go about in. (1) Mk 6:55
περιφέρω v. (φέρω) to carry about, carry
here and there. (3)
περιφρονέω v. (φρήν) to disregard, look
down on, despise. (1) Tit 2:15

περίχωρος, ον adj. (χωρέω) neigh-
boring; region around, neighborhood
(subst. in NT). (9)
περίψημα, ατος, τό n. (ψώχω) dirt, off-
scouring. (1) 1 Cor 4:13
περπερεύομαι v. to boast, brag. (1) 1
Cor 13:4
Περσίς, ίδος, ἡ n. pers. Persis. (1) Rom
16:12
πέρυσι adv. (πέραν) last year, a year
ago. (2)
πετεινόν, οῦ, τό n. (πέτομαι) bird. (14)
πέτομαι v. (*) to fly. (5)
πέτρα, ας, ἡ n. (*) rock, rocky grotto,
rocky ground; (piece of) rock, stone.
(15)
Πέτρος, ου, ὁ n. pers. Peter. (156)
πετρώδης, ες adj. (πέτρα, εἶδος) rocky,
stony; rocky ground (subst. in NT). (4)
πεφίμωμαι s. φιμόω (pf. pass.).
πήγανον, ου, τό n. rue (a garden herb).
(1) Lk 11:42
πηγή, ῆς, ἡ n. spring, fountain, flow, well.
(11)
πήγνυμι v. (*) aor. ἔπηξα. to put together,
build, set up. (1) Heb 8:2
πηδάλιον, ου, τό n. steering paddle,
rudder. (2)
πηλίκος, η, ον pron. (ἡλικία) correl.
how large; how great. (2)
πηλός, οῦ, ὁ n. clay; mud, mire. (6)
πήρα, ας, ἡ n. knapsack, traveler's bag,
beggar's bag (poss.). (6)
πηρόω v. to disable, maim, blind. (v.l.)
πῆχυς, εως, ὁ n. cubit (measure of
length, about 46 centimeters or 18
inches); hour or day (poss.). (4)
πιάζω v. (πιέζω) aor. ἐπίασα; aor. pass.
ἐπιάσθην. to grasp, take (hold of);
seize, arrest, take into custody, catch.
(12)
πίε, πιεῖν, πίεσαι s. πίνω (2 aor. impv.,
2 aor. inf., fut. mid. 2 sg.).
πιέζω v. (*) pf. pass. πεπίεσμαι. to press
down. (1) Lk 6:38
πιθανολογία, ας, ἡ n. (πείθω, λέγω)
persuasive speech, art of persuasion,
specious argument. (1) Col 2:4

πικραίνω v. (πικρός) fut. πικρανῶ; aor. pass. ἐπικράνθην. *to make bitter; be embittered* (pass.). (4)

πικρία, ας, ἡ n. (πικρός) *bitterness,* χολὴ πικρίας *bitter gall,* ῥίζα πικρίας *bitter root; animosity, anger, harshness.* (4)

πικρός, ά, όν adj. (*) *bitter; embittered, harsh.* (2)

πικρῶς adv. (πικρός) *bitterly.* (2)

Πιλᾶτος, ου, ὁ n. pers. *Pilate.* (55)

πίμπλημι v. (*) aor. ἔπλησα; aor. pass. ἐπλήσθην. *to fill, fulfill; be fulfilled, come to an end* (pass.). (24)

πίμπρημι v. (*) pass. in NT *to burn with fever; become distended, swell up.* (1) Ac 28:6

πινακίδιον, ου, τό n. (πίναξ) *little (wooden) tablet* (for writing). (1) Lk 1:63

πίναξ, ακος, ἡ n. (*) *platter, dish.* (5)

πίνω v. (*) fut. πίομαι; aor. ἔπιον; pf. πέπωκα. *to drink* (lit. and fig.). (73)

πιότης, τητος, ἡ n. *fatness, oily richness.* (1) Rom 11:17

πιπράσκω v. pf. πέπρακα; pf. pass. πέπραμαι; aor. pass. ἐπράθην. *to sell, sell* (as a slave). (9)

πίπτω v. (*) fut. πεσοῦμαι; aor. ἔπεσον, ἔπεσα; pf. πέπτωκα. *to fall, fall down, fall or throw oneself to the ground, fall* (dead), *fall to pieces, collapse, go down, fall* (in), *become invalid, come to an end, fail; be destroyed, fall* (morally), *be completely ruined, perish, disappear, pass from the scene.* (90)

Πισιδία, ας, ἡ n. pla. *Pisidia.* (1) Ac 14:24

Πισίδιος, α, ον adj. pla. *Pisidian.* (1) Ac 13:14

πιστεύω v. (πείθω) fut. πιστεύσω; aor. ἐπίστευσα; pf. πεπίστευκα; pf. pass. πεπίστευμαι; aor. pass. ἐπιστεύθην. *to believe, be convinced of, give credence* (to); *believe* (in), *trust, have confidence; entrust; be confident about;*

think or *consider (possible); believer* (ptc.). (241)

πιστικός, ή, όν adj. (πείθω) *genuine, unadulterated.* (2)

πίστις, εως, ἡ n. (πείθω) *faithfulness, reliability, fidelity, commitment, assurance, oath, proof, pledge, conviction; trust, confidence, faith; body of faith, belief*, or *teaching.* (243)

πιστός, ή, όν adj. (πείθω) *trustworthy, faithful, dependable, inspiring trust* or *faith, reliable; trusting, cherishing faith* or *trust, believing (in Christ), full of faith; (Christian) believer* (subst.). (67)

πιστόω v. (πείθω) aor. pass. ἐπιστώθην. *to feel confidence, be convinced* (pass. in NT). (1) 2 Ti 3:14

πλανάω v. (πλάνη) fut. πλανήσω; aor. ἐπλάνησα; pf. pass. πεπλάνημαι; aor. pass. ἐπλανήθην. *to mislead, deceive; go astray, be misled, wander about aimlessly, be deluded, wander away, be mistaken, be deceived, let oneself be misled* or *deceived* (pass.). (39)

πλάνη, ης, ἡ n. (*) *error, delusion, deceit, deception.* (10)

πλανήτης, ου, ὁ n. (πλάνη) *wanderer, roamer; wandering* (used as adj. in NT). (1) Jd 13

πλάνος, ον adj. (πλάνη) *leading astray, deceitful; deceiver, impostor* (subst.). (5)

πλάξ, πλακός, ἡ n. *tablet.* (3)

πλάσμα, ατος, τό n. (πλάσσω) *image, figure, what is molded.* (1) Rom 9:20

πλάσσω v. (*) aor. ἔπλασα; aor. pass. ἐπλάσθην. *to form, mold.* (2)

πλαστός, ή, όν adj. (πλάσσω) *fabricated, false.* (1) 2 Pt 2:3

πλατεῖα, ας, ἡ n. (πλατύς) *wide road, street.* (9)

πλάτος, ους, τό n. (πλατύς) *breadth, width.* (4)

πλατύνω v. (πλατύς) pf. pass. πεπλάτυμμαι; aor. pass. ἐπλατύνθην. *to make broad, enlarge, open wide.* (3)

πλατύς, εῖα, ύ adj. (*) *broad, wide*. (1) Mt 7:13

πλέγμα, ατος, τό n. (πλέκω) *braided hair*. (1) 1 Ti 2:9

πλείων, πλεῖστος s. πολύς (comp., superl.).

πλέκω v. (*) aor. ἔπλεξα. *to weave, plait*. (3)

πλέον s. πολύς (comp. neut.).

πλεονάζω v. (πληρόω) aor. ἐπλεόνασα. *to be* or *become more, be* or *become great, be present in abundance, grow, increase, multiply; have too much; cause to increase*. (9)

πλεονεκτέω v. (πληρόω, ἔχω) aor. ἐπλεονέκτησα; aor. pass. ἐπλεονεκτήθην. *to exploit, outwit, defraud, cheat, take advantage of*. (5)

πλεονέκτης, ου, ὁ n. (πληρόω, ἔχω) *greedy person*. (4)

πλεονεξία, ας, ἡ n. (πληρόω, ἔχω) *greediness, insatiableness, avarice, covetousness, something forced*. (10)

πλευρά, ᾶς, ἡ n. *side* (of the human body). (5)

πλέω v. (*) *to travel by sea, sail*, ὁ ἐπὶ τόπον πλέων *seafarer* or *sea traveler*. (6)

πληγή, ῆς, ἡ n. (πλήσσω) *blow, stroke; wound, bruise; plague, misfortune*. (22)

πλῆθος, ους, τό n. (πίμπλημι) *quantity, number; large number, multitude, host, bundle, crowd (of people), throng, meeting, assembly, people, populace, population, fellowship, community, congregation, church, group*. (31)

πληθύνω v. (πίμπλημι) fut. πληθυνῶ; aor. pass. ἐπληθύνθην. *to increase, multiply; be multiplied, grow, increase* (pass. and act. intr.). (12)

πλήκτης, ου, ὁ n. (πλήσσω) *pugnacious person, bully*. (2)

πλήμμυρα, ης, ἡ n. (πίμπλημι) *high water, flood*. (1) Lk 6:48

πλήν adv. (πληρόω) *but, only, nevertheless, in any case, on the other hand,* *except that* (conj.)*; except* (adv. prep. w. gen.). (31)

πλήρης, ες adj. (πληρόω) *filled, full, rich; complete, in full, fully ripened, covered with*. (16)

πληροφορέω v. (πληρόω, φέρω) aor. ἐπληροφόρησα; pf. pass. πεπληροφόρημαι; aor. pass. ἐπληροφορήθην. *to fill (completely), fulfill, accomplish; convince* or *assure fully*. (6)

πληροφορία, ας, ἡ n. (πληρόω, φέρω) *full assurance, certainty, conviction, fullness*. (4)

πληρόω v. (*) fut. πληρώσω; aor. ἐπλήρωσα; pf. pass. πεπλήρωμαι; aor. pass. ἐπληρώθην. *to fill (full); complete, bring to completion; fulfill, bring to fulfillment, perform, bring to full expression; finish;* pass. *be filled, become filled* or *full, be well supplied; pass; be made complete; be fulfilled; be accomplished, be finished; have the number made complete*. (86)

πλήρωμα, ατος, τό n. (πληρόω) *that which fills (up),* τὸ πλήρωμα αὐτῆς *everything that is in it, that which makes full* or *complete, supplement, complement, patch; that which is full; full number, sum total, full measure; fulfilling, fulfillment; fullness*. (17)

πλήσας, πλησθείς, πλησθῆναι s. πίμπλημι (aor. ptc., aor. pass. ptc., aor. pass. inf.).

πλησίον adv. (*) *near, close to* (adv. prep. w. gen.)*; neighbor, fellow human being* (subst.). (17)

πλησμονή, ῆς, ἡ n. (πίμπλημι) *satiety, satisfaction, gratification,* πρὸς πλησμονὴν τῆς σαρκός *self-indulgence*. (1) Col 2:23

πλήσσω v. (*) aor. pass. ἐπλήγην. *to strike*. (1) Rev 8:12

πλοιάριον, ου, τό n. (πλέω) *small ship, boat, skiff*. (5)

πλοῖον, ου, τό n. (πλέω) *ship; boat*. (68)

πλοῦς, πλοός, ὁ n. (πλέω) *voyage, navigation*. (3)

πλούσιος, α, ον adj. (πλοῦτος) *rich, wealthy; abound* or *rich (in); rich person* (subst.). (28)

πλουσίως adv. (πλοῦτος) *richly, abundantly.* (4)

πλουτέω v. (πλοῦτος) aor. ἐπλούτησα; pf. πεπλούτηκα. *to be rich, become rich; be generous.* (12)

πλουτίζω v. (πλοῦτος) aor. pass. ἐπλουτίσθην. *to make rich.* (3)

πλοῦτος, ου, ὁ, τό n. (*) *wealth; wealth* (fig.), *abundance.* (22)

πλύνω v. aor. ἔπλυνα. *to wash.* (3)

πνεῦμα, ατος, τό n. (πνέω) *blowing, breathing, wind; breath, (life-)spirit; spirit* (as inner life), *mind, very self, spiritual state, state of mind, disposition; spirit* (as type of being, often evil), *ghost; Spirit* (of God, often w. ἅγιον). (379)

πνευματικός, ή, όν adj. (πνέω) *caused by* or *filled with the (divine) spirit, pertaining* or *corresponding to the (divine) spirit, spiritual, given by the Spirit,* τὰ πνευματικά *spiritual things* or *matters,* ὁ πνευματικός *one who possesses the Spirit; pertaining to (evil) spirits.* (26)

πνευματικῶς adv. (πνέω) *in keeping* or *in a manner consistent with the Spirit, spiritual.* (2)

πνέω v. (*) aor. ἔπνευσα. *to blow.* (7)

πνίγω v. (*) aor. ἔπνιξα. *to strangle; choke; be choked, drown* (pass.). (3)

πνικτός, ή, όν adj. (πνίγω) *strangled, choked to death.* (3)

πνοή, ῆς, ἡ n. (πνέω) *wind, breath.* (2)

ποδήρης, ες adj. (πούς) *reaching to the feet; robe reaching to the feet* (subst. in NT). (1) Rev 1:13

πόθεν adv. (ὅς) interrog. *from what place, from where; from what source, brought about* or *given by whom, born of whom; how, why, in what way.* (29)

ποιέω v. (*) fut. ποιήσω; aor. ἐποίησα; pf. πεποίηκα; pf. pass. πεποίημαι. *to make, manufacture, produce, create, appoint; do, cause, bring, accomplish,*

prepare, perform, make, establish, provide, bring, wage (of war), *give* (of a meal), *celebrate, send out, produce, bear, yield, force, claim, pretend, send; keep, carry out, practice, commit, live, show, be guilty of, act, proceed; do to, do with, do for, treat, deal with; get, gain, assume, suppose, take as an example, spend* (of time), *stay; work, be active; make* or *do for oneself, make* or *do of oneself* (mid.). (568)

ποίημα, ατος, τό n. (ποιέω) *work, creation, thing created (by God).* (2)

ποίησις, εως, ἡ n. (ποιέω) *doing, working.* (1) Jas 1:25

ποιητής, οῦ, ὁ n. (ποιέω) *maker, poet; doer.* (6)

ποικίλος, η, ον adj. (*) *diversified, manifold, many* or *various kinds of; ambiguous, crafty, sly, deceitful.* (10)

ποιμαίνω v. (ποιμήν) fut. ποιμανῶ; aor. ἐποίμανα. *to herd, tend (sheep), (lead to) pasture; shepherd* (fig.), *tend, protect, care for, nurture, look after.* (11)

ποιμήν, ένος, ὁ n. (*) *shepherd, sheepherder; shepherd* (fig.), *pastor.* (18)

ποίμνη, ης, ἡ n. (ποιμήν) *flock* (lit. and fig.). (5)

ποίμνιον, ου, τό n. (ποιμήν) *flock* (fig. in NT). (5)

ποῖος, α, ον pron. interrog. *of what kind* or *sort; which, what.* (33)

πολεμέω v. (πόλεμος) fut. πολεμήσω; aor. ἐπολέμησα. *to wage* or *make war, fight; be hostile.* (7)

πόλεμος, ου, ὁ n. (*) *war, battle, fight; conflict, strife, quarrel.* (18)

πόλις, εως, ἡ n. (*) *city, town, capital* or *main city,* κατὰ τὴν πόλιν *anywhere in the city,* κατὰ πόλεις *from city to city,* κατὰ πόλιν *in every city; (heavenly) city, New Jerusalem; city* (as inhabitants). (162)

πολιτάρχης, ου, ὁ n. (πόλις, ἄρχω) *city official.* (2)

πολιτεία, ας, ἡ n. (πόλις) *citizenship; state, people, body politic.* (2)

πολίτευμα, ατος, τό n. (πόλις) *commonwealth, state.* (1) Phil 3:20

πολιτεύομαι v. (πόλις) pf. pass. πεπολίτευμαι. *to live, lead one's life.* (2)

πολίτης, ου, ὁ n. (πόλις) *citizen; fellowcitizen, compatriot.* (4)

πολλά s. πολύς (neut. pl.).

πολλάκις adv. (πολύς) *many times, often, frequently.* (18)

πολλαπλασίων, ον adj. (πολύς) *many times as much, manifold.* (1) Lk 18:30

πολυλογία, ας, ἡ n. (πολύς, λέγω) *much speaking, wordiness, long-windedness, many words.* (1) Mt 6:7

πολυμερῶς adv. (πολύς, μέρος) *in various parts,* πολυμερῶς καὶ πολυτρόπως *in various ways.* (1) Heb 1:1

πολυποίκιλος, ον adj. (πολύς, ποικίλος) *(very) many-sided.* (1) Eph 3:10

πολύς, πολλή, πολύ adj. (*) pos. *many, numerous, mighty,* οὐ πολλοί *a few* (pl.)*; large, great, extensive, plentiful, great deal of* (pl.)*; much, large, great, many, long* (sg.)*; strong, severe, hard, deep, profound, strict, complete, late* (sg.)*; πολλοί many, majority, most, crowd* (subst.)*; πολλά many things, much* (subst.)*; πολλά greatly, earnestly, strictly, loudly, often, freely, bitterly, hard, many, many times* (subst. as adv.)*; πολύ much, large sum of money,* ἐπὶ πολύ *(for) a long time,* πολύ *(or* πολλῷ*) μᾶλλον much more, to a greater degree* (subst.)*; πολύ greatly, very much, strongly, loudly* (subst. as adv.); comp. (πλείων, πλεῖον or πλέον) *many, greater numbers, many more, more than, greater* (pl.)*; more, longer* (sg.)*; πλείονες or πλείους majority, most, even greater numbers, many more, others, rest* (subst.)*; πλείονα various things* (subst.)*; πλεῖον or πλέον greater or larger sum, greater measure, greater, more* (subst.)*; πλεῖον or πλέον more, in greater measure,* *to a greater degree, more, any* or *even more, more than,* πολὺ πλέον *much more* or *much rather* (subst. as adv.); superl. (πλεῖστος, η, ον) *most* (pl.)*; very great* or *large, greatest part* (sg.)*;* τὸ πλεῖστον *at the most* (subst.). (416)

πολύσπλαγχνος, ον adj. (πολύς, σπλάγχνον) *sympathetic, compassionate, merciful.* (1) Jas 5:11

πολυτελής, ές adj. (πολύς, τέλος) *(very) expensive, costly.* (3)

πολύτιμος, ον adj. (πολύς, τιμή) *very precious, valuable.* (3)

πολυτρόπως adv. (πολύς, τροπή) *in many ways,* πολυμερῶς καὶ πολυτρόπως *in various ways.* (1) Heb 1:1

πόμα, ατος, τό n. (πίνω) *drink.* (2)

πονηρία, ας, ἡ n. (πόνος) *wickedness, baseness, maliciousness, sinfulness.* (7)

πονηρός, ά, όν adj. (πόνος) *wicked, evil, bad, base, worthless, vicious, degenerate, malicious, slanderous, guilty, vile; of poor quality, worthless; sick, painful, virulent, serious; wicked* or *evil-intentioned person, evildoer,* ὁ πονηρός *the evil one* (devil), τὸ πονηρόν *(that which is) evil, wicked thought, evil deed* (subst.). (78)

πόνος, ου, ὁ n. (*) *(hard) labor, toil; pain, distress, affliction, suffering.* (4)

Ποντικός, ή, όν adj. pla. *Pontian; a Pontian* (subst. in NT). (1) Ac 18:2

Πόντιος, ου, ὁ n. pers. *Pontius.* (3)

πόντος, ου, ὁ n. *(high* or *open) sea.* (v.l.)

Πόντος, ου, ὁ n. pla. *Pontus.* (2)

Πόπλιος, ου, ὁ n. pers. *Publius.* (2)

πορεία, ας, ἡ n. (πορεύομαι) *journey, trip; conduct, way.* (2)

πορεύομαι v. (*) fut. πορεύσομαι; pf. pass. πεπόρευμαι; aor. pass. ἐπορεύθην. *to go, proceed, travel, depart, appear, be on the way, pass by; live, walk, follow; die.* (153)

πορθέω v. aor. ἐπόρθησα. *to destroy, pillage, make havoc of, annihilate, try to destroy* or *annihilate.* (3)

πορισμός, οῦ, ὁ n. (πορεύομαι) *means of gain*. (2)

Πόρκιος, ου, ὁ n. pers. *Porcius*. (1) Ac 24:27

πορνεία, ας, ἡ n. (πόρνη) *prostitution, unchastity, fornication*, ἐκ πορνείας οὐ γεγένημαι *not to be an illegitimate child; fornication* (fig.), *immorality*. (25)

πορνεύω v. (πόρνη) aor. ἐπόρνευσα. *to engage in illicit sex, fornicate, whore; fornicate* (fig.), *practice idolatry*. (8)

πόρνη, ης, ἡ n. (*) *prostitute, whore; prostitute* (fig.). (12)

πόρνος, ου, ὁ n. (πόρνη) *fornicator, (sexually) immoral person*. (10)

πόρρω adv. (πρό) *far (away)*. (4)

πόρρωθεν adv. (πρό) *from* or *at a distance*. (2)

πορρώτερον s. πόρρω (comp.).

πορφύρα, ας, ἡ n. (*) *purple (cloth), purple garment*. (4)

πορφυρόπωλις, ιδος, ἡ n. (πορφύρα, πωλέω) *merchant dealing in purple cloth*. (1) Ac 16:14

πορφυροῦς, ᾶ, οῦν adj. (πορφύρα) *purple; purple garment* (subst.). (4)

ποσάκις adv. (ὅς) *how many times? how often?* (3)

πόσις, εως, ἡ n. (πίνω) *drinking; drink*. (3)

πόσος, η, ον adj. (ὅσος) *how great, how much*, πόσῳ μᾶλλον *how much more* (interrog. or excl.)*; how many, how much*, πόσα *how many things* (interrog.). (27)

ποταμός, οῦ, ὁ n. (πίνω) *river, stream, winter torrents*. (17)

ποταμοφόρητος, ον adj. (πίνω, φέρω) *swept away by a river* or *stream*. (1) Rev 12:15

ποταπός, ή, όν adj. (ποῦ, ἀπό) *of what sort* or *kind(?), how great, glorious*, or *wonderful*. (7)

πότε adv. (ποῦ) *when(?)* ἕως πότε *how long?* (19)

ποτέ part. (ποῦ) encl. *at some time or other, once, formerly*, ἤδη ποτέ *now at last*, οὐ... ποτέ *never; ever*. (29)

πότερον adv. (ποῦ, ἕτερος) *whether*. (1) Jn 7:17

ποτήριον, ου, τό n. (πίνω) *cup* (lit. and fig.). (31)

ποτίζω v. (πίνω) aor. ἐπότισα; pf. πεπότικα; aor. pass. ἐποτίσθην. *to give to drink, cause to drink, water*. (15)

Ποτίολοι, ων, οἱ n. pla. *Puteoli*. (1) Ac 28:13

πότος, ου, ὁ n. (πίνω) *drinking party, carousal*. (1) 1 Pt 4:3

ποῦ adv. (*) *where(?) at what place(?)*, οὐκ ἔχω ποῦ *have nowhere; whither(?), to what place(?)*. (48)

πού adv. (ποῦ) encl. *somewhere; about, approximately*, μή που *lest*. (4)

Πούδης, εντος, ὁ n. pers. *Pudens*. (1) 2 Ti 4:21

πούς, ποδός, ὁ n. (*) *foot* (lit. and fig.), *leg; foot* (as measure of length, about 30 centimeters or 12 inches). (93)

πρᾶγμα, ατος, τό n. (πράσσω) *deed, event, occurrence, matter; undertaking, occupation, task; thing, affair; dispute, lawsuit, legal process* (poss.). (11)

πραγματεία, ας, ἡ n. (πράσσω) *activity; undertakings, business, affairs* (pl. in NT). (1) 2 Ti 2:4

πραγματεύομαι v. (πράσσω) aor. ἐπραγματευσάμην. *to do business, trade*. (1) Lk 19:13

πραθείς, πραθῆναι s. πιπράσκω (aor. pass. ptc., aor. pass. inf.).

πραιτώριον, ου, τό n. Lat. *praetorium, imperial* or *palace guard*. (8)

πράκτωρ, ορος, ὁ n. (πράσσω) *bailiff, constable*. (2)

πρᾶξις, εως, ἡ n. (πράσσω) *acting, activity, function; act, action, deed, evil* or *disgraceful deed, magical practice*. (6)

πρασιά, ᾶς, ἡ n. (*) *group*, πρασιαὶ πρασιαί *group by group*. (2)

πράσσω v. (*) fut. πράξω; aor. ἔπραξα; pf. πέπραχα; pf. pass. πέπραγμαι. *to* *do, accomplish, commit, practice, busy oneself with,* πράσσω τὰ ἴδια *mind one's own affairs, observe, collect;* intr. *act, behave; be, be situated, get along.* (39)

πραϋπαθία, ας, ἡ n. (πραΰς, πάσχω) *gentleness.* (1) 1 Ti 6:11

πραΰς, πραεῖα, πραΰ adj. (*) *gentle, humble, considerate, meek.* (4)

πραΰτης, ητος, ἡ n. (πραΰς) *gentleness, humility, courtesy, considerateness, meekness.* (11)

πρέπω v. (*) *to be fitting; it is fitting* or *suitable* (impers. in NT). (7)

πρεσβεία, ας, ἡ n. (πρεσβύτης) *ambassador(s).* (2)

πρεσβεύω v. (πρεσβύτης) *to be an ambassador* or *representative, travel* or *work as an ambassador.* (2)

πρεσβυτέριον, ου, τό n. (πρεσβύτης) *council of elders.* (3)

πρεσβύτερος, α, ον adj. (πρεσβύτης) *older, old; older person, ancestor, ancient person, elder, presbyter* (subst.). (66)

πρεσβύτης, ου, ὁ n. (*) *old* or *elderly man.* (3)

πρεσβῦτις, ιδος, ἡ n. (πρεσβύτης) *old* or *elderly woman.* (1) Tit 2:3

πρηνής, ές adj. *forward, prostrate, head first, headlong.* (1) Ac 1:18

πρίζω v. (*) aor. pass. ἐπρίσθην. *to saw (in two).* (1) Heb 11:37

πρίν conj. (πρό) *before.* (13)

Πρίσκα, ης, ἡ n. pers. *Prisca* (same person as Πρίσκιλλα). (3)

Πρίσκιλλα, ης, ἡ n. pers. *Priscilla* (same person as Πρίσκα). (3)

πρό prep. (*) w. gen. *before* (of place), *in front of, at, ahead of; earlier than, before* (of time); *above.* (47)

προάγω v. (ἄγω) fut. προάξω; aor. προήγαγον. *to lead forward, lead* or *bring out, bring before; go before, lead the way, precede, walk ahead of, go too far, go* or *get ahead of* (intr.). (20)

προαιρέω v. (αἱρέω) pf. pass. προήρημαι. *to bring out; choose (for one-*

self), commit oneself to, prefer, undertake, determine, decide, make up one's mind (mid. in NT). (1) 2 Cor 9:7

προαιτιάομαι v. (αἰτία) aor. προητιασάμην. *to accuse beforehand, already charge.* (1) Rom 3:9

προακούω v. (ἀκούω) aor. προήκουσα. *to hear before.* (1) Col 1:5

προαμαρτάνω v. (ἁμαρτάνω) pf. προημάρτηκα. *to sin before.* (2)

προαύλιον, ου, τό n. (αὐλή) *forecourt, gateway.* (1) Mk 14:68

προβαίνω v. (-βαίνω) aor. προέβην; pf. προβέβηκα. *to go ahead, advance* (lit.); *advance* (fig.), προβέβηκα ἐν ταῖς ἡμέραις *be advanced in years.* (5)

προβάλλω v. (βάλλω) aor. προέβαλον. *to put forward; put out (leaves).* (2)

προβάς s. προβαίνω (2 aor. ptc.).

προβατικός, ή, όν adj. (-βαίνω) *pertaining to sheep,* ἡ προβατική *sheep gate.* (1) Jn 5:2

προβάτιον, ου, τό n. *lamb, sheep.* (v.l.)

πρόβατον, ου, τό n. (-βαίνω) *sheep* (lit. and fig.). (39)

προβεβηκώς s. προβαίνω (pf. ptc.).

προβιβάζω v. (-βαίνω) aor. pass. προεβιβάσθην. *to cause to come forward, push forward, coach.* (1) Mt 14:8

προβλέπω v. (βλέπω) aor. προέβλεψα. *to foresee; provide, select* (mid. in NT). (1) Heb 11:40

προγίνομαι v. (γίνομαι) pf. προγέγονα. *to happen* or *be done before,* τὰ προγεγονότα ἁμαρτήματα *the sins that were committed in former times.* (1) Rom 3:25

προγινώσκω v. (γινώσκω) aor. προέγνων; pf. pass. προέγνωσμαι. *to have foreknowledge, know before* or *in advance; choose beforehand, know from past time.* (5)

πρόγνωσις, εως, ἡ n. (γινώσκω) *predetermination,* κατὰ πρόγνωσιν θεοῦ *destined by God.* (2)

πρόγονος, ον adj. (γίνομαι) *born before; parents, forebears, ancestors* (pl. subst. in NT). (2)

προγράφω v. (γράφω) aor. προέγραψα; pf. pass. προγέγραμμαι; aor. pass. προεγράφην. *to write before* or *above, write in earlier times, mark out; show forth, portray publicly, proclaim* or *placard in public.* (4)

πρόδηλος, ον adj. (δῆλος) *clear, evident, known to all.* (3)

προδίδωμι v. (δίδωμι) aor. προέδωκα. *to give in advance.* (1) Rom 11:35

προδότης, ου, ὁ n. (δίδωμι) *traitor, betrayer.* (3)

πρόδρομος, ον adj. (τρέχω) *running before; forerunner* (subst. in NT). (1) Heb 6:20

προέγνων s. προγινώσκω (2 aor.).

προέδραμον s. προτρέχω (2 aor.).

προέδωκα s. προδιδωμι (aor.).

προεθέμην s. προτίθημι (2 aor. mid.).

προείρηκα s. προλέγω (pf.).

προέλαβον s. προλαμβάνω (2 aor.).

προελεύσομαι s. προέρχομαι (fut. mid.).

προελθών s. προέρχομαι (2 aor. ptc.).

προελπίζω v. (ἐλπίς) pf. προήλπικα. *to hope before, be the first to hope.* (1) Eph 1:12

προενάρχομαι v. (ἄρχω) aor. προενηρξάμην. *to begin (beforehand).* (2)

προεπαγγέλλω v. (ἄγγελος) aor. προεπηγγειλάμην; pf. pass. προεπήγγελμαι. *to promise beforehand* or *previously* (mid. and pass. in NT). (2)

προέρχομαι v. (ἔρχομαι) fut. προελεύσομαι; aor. προῆλθον. *to go forward, go before, proceed, go (along); go before; come* or *go before(hand), go on before* or *ahead, arrive before.* (9)

προετοιμάζω v. (ἕτοιμος) aor. προητοίμασα. *to prepare beforehand.* (2)

προευαγγελίζομαι v. (ἄγγελος) aor. προευηγγελισάμην. *to proclaim good news in advance.* (1) Gal 3:8

προέχω v. (ἔχω) *to excel; have an advantage, protect oneself* (if mid.); *be excelled, be disadvantaged* (if pass.). (1) Rom 3:9

προηγέομαι v. (ἄγω) *to consider better, esteem more highly.* (1) Rom 12:10

πρόθεσις, εως, ἡ n. (τίθημι) *setting forth, putting out, presentation,* οἱ ἄρτοι τῆς προθέσεως *bread of presentation; plan, purpose, resolve, will, way of thinking, design.* (12)

προθεσμία, ας, ἡ n. (τίθημι) *appointed day, fixed* or *limited time, set time.* (1) Gal 4:2

προθυμία, ας, ἡ n. (θυμός) *willingness, readiness, goodwill, zeal.* (5)

πρόθυμος, ον adj. (θυμός) *ready, willing, eager; eagerness, desire* (subst.). (3)

προθύμως adv. (θυμός) *willingly, eagerly, freely.* (1) 1 Pt 5:2

προϊδών s. προοράω (2 aor. ptc.).

πρόϊμος, ον adj. (πρό) *early; early rain* (subst. in NT). (1) Jas 5:7

προΐστημι v. (ἵστημι) aor. προέστησα; pf. προέστηκα. *to rule, direct, be at the head (of); show concern for, care for, give aid, busy oneself with, engage in.* (8)

προκαλέω v. (καλέω) *to provoke, challenge* (mid. in NT). (1) Gal 5:26

προκαταγγέλλω v. (ἄγγελος) aor. προκατήγγειλα. *to foretell.* (2)

προκαταρτίζω v. (ἄρτι) aor. προκατήρτισα. *to get ready, make arrangements for in advance.* (1) 2 Cor 9:5

προκατέχω v. *to gain possession of* or *occupy previously.* (v.l.)

πρόκειμαι v. (κεῖμαι) *to be exposed, be exhibited; lie before, be present; set before.* (5)

προκηρύσσω v. (κηρύσσω) aor. προεκήρυξα. *to proclaim beforehand.* (1) Ac 13:24

προκοπή, ῆς, ἡ n. (κόπτω) *progress, advancement, furtherance.* (3)

προκόπτω v. (κόπτω) fut. προκόψω; aor. προέκοψα. *to be advanced, be far gone; progress, advance, go on.* (6)

πρόκριμα, ατος, τό n. (κρίνω) *prejudgment, discrimination.* (1) 1 Ti 5:21
προκυρόω v. (κύριος) pf. pass. προκεκύρωμαι. *to validate in advance, ratify previously.* (1) Gal 3:17
προλαμβάνω v. (λαμβάνω) aor. προέλαβον; aor. pass. προελήμφθην. *to do before the usual time, anticipate, take* (of a meal); *detect, overtake, surprise.* (3)
προλέγω v. (λέγω) aor. προεῖπον, προεῖπα; pf. προείρηκα; pf. pass. προείρημαι. *to tell beforehand, proclaim in advance, foretell; say before* or *previously, say already, mention previously.* (15)
προμαρτύρομαι v. (μάρτυς) *to bear witness to beforehand, predict.* (1) 1 Pt 1:11
προμελετάω v. (μέλει) *to prepare, practice beforehand.* (1) Lk 21:14
προμεριμνάω v. (μεριμνάω) *to concern oneself* or *be anxious beforehand.* (1) Mk 13:11
προνοέω v. (νίπτω) *to take thought for, take into consideration, have regard for; care for, provide for.* (3)
πρόνοια, ας, ἡ n. (νίπτω) *forethought, foresight, providence, provision.* (2)
προοράω v. (ὁράω) aor. προεῖδον; pf. προεώρακα. *to foresee; see previously; see before one* (mid.). (4)
προορίζω v. (ὁρίζω) aor. προώρισα; aor. pass. προωρίσθην. *to predetermine.* (6)
προπάσχω v. (πάσχω) aor. προέπαθον. *to suffer previously.* (1) 1 Th 2:2
προπάτωρ, ορος, ὁ n. (πατήρ) *ancestor.* (1) Rom 4:1
προπέμπω v. (πέμπω) aor. προέπεμψα; aor. pass. προεπέμφθην. *to accompany, escort; send* or *help on one's way.* (9)
προπετής, ές adj. (πίπτω) *rash, reckless, thoughtless.* (2)
προπορεύομαι v. (πορεύομαι) fut. προπορεύσομαι. *to go on before.* (2)
πρός prep. (*) w. gen. *to the advantage of, advantageous for, in the interest of;* w. dat. *near, at, by, close to* (of place); w.

acc. *toward, towards, to, with, among; near, at, during, toward, for* (of time); *(aiming) at, (striving) toward, for, for the purpose of, on behalf of* (of goal); *against, with, for, to toward, before* (of relationship); *with reference* or *regard to, about,* τί πρὸς ἡμᾶς *what is that to us?* τί πρὸς σέ *how does it concern you? in accordance with, in comparison with, in order to, for the purpose of;* πρὸς φθόνον *jealously; by, at, near, with, among, to* (of person, place, or thing). (700)
προσάββατον, ου, τό n. (σάββατον) *day before the Sabbath, Friday.* (1) Mk 15:42
προσαγορεύω v. (ἄγω) aor. pass. προσηγορεύθην. *to call, name, designate.* (1) Heb 5:10
προσάγω v. (ἄγω) aor. προσήγαγον. *to bring (forward* or *to); come near, approach* (intr.). (4)
προσαγωγή, ῆς, ἡ n. (ἄγω) *access.* (3)
προσαιτέω v. (αἰτέω) *to beg.* (1) Jn 9:8
προσαίτης, ου, ὁ n. (αἰτέω) *beggar.* (2)
προσαναβαίνω v. (-βαίνω) aor. προσανέβην. *to go* or *move up.* (1) Lk 14: 10
προσαναλίσκω and **προσαναλόω** v. (ἄλωσις) aor. προσανέλωσα. *to spend (lavishly).* (1) Lk 8:43
προσαναπληρόω v. (πληρόω) aor. προσανεπλήρωσα. *to supply.* (2)
προσανατίθημι v. (τίθημι) aor. προσανέθηκα. mid. in NT *to add, contribute, submit* (poss.); *consult with.* (2)
προσανέχω v. *to rise up toward.* (v.l.)
προσαπειλέω v. (ἀπειλή) aor. προσαπείλησα. *to threaten further* or *in addition* (mid. in NT). (1) Ac 4:21
προσαχέω v. *to resound* (of the surf). (v.l.)
προσδαπανάω v. (δαπάνη) aor. προσεδαπάνησα. *to spend in addition.* (1) Lk 10:35
προσδέομαι v. (δέομαι) *to need.* (1) Ac 17:25

προσδέχομαι v. (δέχομαι) aor. προσεδεξάμην. *to take up, receive, welcome, receive in a friendly manner; wait for, await.* (14)

προσδοκάω v. (δοκέω) *to wait for, look for, expect.* (16)

προσδοκία, ας, ἡ n. (δοκέω) *expectation.* (2)

προσδραμών s. προστρέχω (2 aor. ptc.).

προσεάω v. (ἐάω) *to permit to go farther.* (1) Ac 27:7

προσεγγίζω v. *to approach, come near.* (v.l.)

προσεθέμην, προσέθηκα s. προστίθημι (2 aor. mid., aor.).

προσεκλίθην s. προσκλίνω (aor. pass.).

προσελαβόμην s. προσλαμβάνω (2 aor. mid.).

προσελήλυθα, πρόσελθε s. προσέρχομαι (2 pf., 2 aor. impv.).

προσενέγκαι, προσένεγκε, προσένεγκον, προσενεχθείς, προσενήνοχα s. προσφέρω (1 aor. inf., 2 aor. impv., 1 aor. impv., aor. pass. ptc., 2 pf.).

προσέπεσον s. προσπίπτω (2 aor.).

προσεργάζομαι v. (ἔργον) aor. προσηργασάμην. *to make more* (of earnings). (1) Lk 19:16

προσέρχομαι v. (ἔρχομαι) aor. προσῆλθον; pf. προσελήλυθα. *to come or go to, approach; turn to, occupy oneself with, devote oneself to.* (86)

προσευχή, ῆς, ἡ n. (εὔχομαι) *prayer, intercession; place of prayer.* (36)

προσεύχομαι v. (εὔχομαι) fut. προσεύξομαι; aor. προσηυξάμην. *to pray.* (85)

προσέχω v. (ἔχω) pf. προσέσχηκα. *to be concerned about, care for, take care, be careful, be on one's guard, beware of; pay attention to, give heed to, follow; occupy oneself with, devote or apply oneself to, officiate, be addicted to.* (24)

προσηλόω v. (ἧλος) aor. προσήλωσα. *to nail (securely).* (1) Col 2:14

προσήλυτος, ου, ὁ n. (ἔρχομαι) *convert, proselyte.* (4)

πρόσκαιρος, ον adj. (καιρός) *temporary, transitory, lasting only a little while.* (4)

προσκαλέω v. (καλέω) aor. προσεκάλεσα; pf. pass. προσκέκλημαι. mid. in NT *to summon, call on, call to oneself, invite, call (to); call in, summon, call* (in a legal or official sense). (29)

προσκαρτερέω v. (κράτος) fut. προσκαρτερήσω. *to attach oneself to, wait on, be faithful to, stand ready; busy oneself with, be busily engaged in, be devoted to, spend much time in; hold fast to, continue in, persevere in.* (10)

προσκαρτέρησις, εως, ἡ n. (κράτος) *perseverance, patience.* (1) Eph 6:18

προσκεφάλαιον, ου, τό n. (κεφαλή) *pillow, cushion.* (1) Mk 4:38

προσκληρόω v. (κλῆρος) aor. pass. προσεκληρώθην. *to allot; be attached to, join* (pass. in NT). (1) Ac 17:4

προσκλίνω v. (κλίνω) aor. pass. προσεκλίθην. *to attach oneself to, join* (pass. in NT). (1) Ac 5:36

πρόσκλισις, εως, ἡ n. (κλίνω) *inclination, partiality.* (1) 1 Ti 5:21

προσκολλάω v. (κολλάω) aor. pass. προσεκολλήθην. *to be faithfully devoted to, join* (pass. in NT). (2)

πρόσκομμα, ατος, τό n. (κόπτω) *stumbling, cause for offense, cause for making a misstep, offense, obstacle, hindrance.* (6)

προσκοπή, ῆς, ἡ n. (κόπτω) *occasion for taking offense* or *for making a misstep.* (1) 2 Cor 6:3

προσκόπτω v. (κόπτω) aor. προσέκοψα. *to strike against; beat against, stumble; take offense at, feel repugnance for, reject.* (8)

προσκυλίω v. (κυλίω) aor. προσεκύλισα. *to roll (up to).* (2)

προσκυνέω v. (*) fut. προσκυνήσω; aor. προσεκύνησα. *to worship, do obeisance to, prostrate oneself before, do reverence to, welcome respectfully, bow in worship.* (60)

προσκυνητής, οῦ, ὁ n. (προσκυνέω) *worshiper.* (1) Jn 4:23

προσλαλέω v. (λαλέω) aor. προσελάλησα. *to speak to* or *with, address.* (2)

προσλαμβάνω v. (λαμβάνω) aor. προσέλαβον. mid. in NT *to take (in); take aside; receive into one's home* or *circle of acquaintances; take along with oneself.* (12)

προσλέγω v. *to answer, reply.* (v.l.)

πρόσλημψις, εως, ἡ n. (λαμβάνω) *acceptance.* (1) Rom 11:15

προσμένω v. (μένω) aor. προσέμεινα. *to remain* or *stay with, remain true to, continue in; remain longer.* (7)

προσορμίζω v. aor. pass. προσωρμίσθην. *to come into harbor, come to anchor* (pass. in NT). (1) Mk 6:53

προσοφείλω v. (ὀφείλω) *to owe (besides), still owe.* (1) Phlm 19

προσοχθίζω v. aor. προσώχθισα. *to be angry, offended, provoked.* (2)

πρόσπεινος, ον adj. (πεινάω) *hungry.* (1) Ac 10:10

προσπήγνυμι v. (πήγνυμι) aor. προσέπηξα. *to fix* or *fasten to, nail to (a cross).* (1) Ac 2:23

προσπίπτω v. (πίπτω) aor. προσέπεσον, προσέπεσα. *to fall down before* or *at the feet of; fall* or *beat upon, strike against.* (8)

προσποιέω v. (ποιέω) aor. προσεποίησα. *to make* or *act as though, pretend* (mid. in NT). (1) Lk 24:28

προσπορεύομαι v. (πορεύομαι) *to come up to, approach.* (1) Mk 10:35

προσρήγνυμι and **προσρήσσω** v. (ῥήγνυμι) aor. προσέρηξα. *to burst upon.* (2)

προστάσσω v. (τάσσω) aor. προσέταξα; pf. pass. προστέταγμαι. *to command, order, give instructions, determine, prescribe,* προστεταγμένοι καιροί *fixed times.* (7)

προστάτις, ιδος, ἡ n. (ἵστημι) *patron, benefactor.* (1) Rom 16:2

προστίθημι v. (τίθημι) aor. προσέθηκα; aor. pass. προσετέθην. *to add (to), put to, increase, bring, gather, do again; provide, give, grant, do.* (18)

προστρέχω v. (τρέχω) aor. προσέδραμον. *to run up (to).* (3)

προσφάγιον, ου, τό n. (φάγος) *fish (to eat).* (1) Jn 21:5

πρόσφατος, ον adj. (φονεύω) *new, recent.* (1) Heb 10:20

προσφάτως adv. (φονεύω) *recently.* (1) Ac 18:2

προσφέρω v. (φέρω) aor. προσήνεγκα, προσήνεγκον; pf. προσενήνοχα; aor. pass. προσηνέχθην. *to bring (to), bring before, hold to; bring, offer, present; meet, deal with* (pass.). (47)

προσφιλής, ές adj. (φίλος) *pleasing, agreeable, lovely, amiable.* (1) Phil 4:8

προσφορά, ᾶς, ἡ n. (φέρω) *sacrificing, offering* (as an act)*; offering* (what is offered)*, sacrifice.* (9)

προσφωνέω v. (φωνή) aor. προσεφώνησα. *to call out, address; call to, summon.* (7)

πρόσχυσις, εως, ἡ n. (-χέω) *sprinkling, pouring, spreading.* (1) Heb 11:28

προσψαύω v. (ψώχω) *to touch.* (1) Lk 11:46

προσωπολημπτέω v. (ὁράω, λαμβάνω) *to show partiality.* (1) Jas 2:9

προσωπολήμπτης, ου, ὁ n. (ὁράω, λαμβάνω) *one who shows partiality.* (1) Ac 10:34

προσωπολημψία, ας, ἡ n. (ὁράω, λαμβάνω) *partiality.* (4)

πρόσωπον, ου, τό n. (ὁράω) *face, countenance, presence, personal appearance, relational circumstance,* θαυμάζω πρόσωπον *to flatter,* λαμβάνω πρόσωπον *to show partiality* or *favoritism,* ἀπὸ προσώπου *from the presence of,* εἰς πρόσωπον *before,* βλέπω εἰς πρόσωπον *to regard someone's opinion,* κατὰ πρόσωπον *face to face* or *in the presence of,* πρὸ προσώπου *before; person; surface; external things, appearance.* (76)

προτείνω v. (-τείνω) aor. προέτεινα. *to stretch* or *spread out.* (1) Ac 22:25

πρότερος, α, ον adj. (πρό) *earlier, former; earlier, formerly, in former times,* *beforehand, previously, before, once, first time* (neut. as adv.). (11)

προτίθημι v. (τίθημι) aor. προέθηκα. *to display* or *make available publicly; plan, propose, intend* (mid. in NT). (3)

προτρέπω v. (τροπή) aor. προέτρεψα. *to urge (on), encourage, impel, persuade* (mid. in NT). (1) Ac 18:27

προτρέχω v. (τρέχω) aor. προέδραμον. *to run (on) ahead.* (2)

προϋπάρχω v. (ἄρχω) *to exist before.* (2)

πρόφασις, εως, ἡ n. (φαίνω) *actual motive* or *reason, valid excuse; pretext, ostensible reason, excuse, false motive.* (6)

προφέρω v. (φέρω) *to yield.* (2)

προφητεία, ας, ἡ n. (φημί) *prophetic activity; gift of prophesying* or *prophecy; prophecy, prophetic saying.* (19)

προφητεύω v. (φημί) fut. προφητεύσω; aor. ἐπροφήτευσα. *to prophesy; tell, reveal; foretell.* (28)

προφήτης, ου, ὁ n. (φημί) *prophet; writing* or *book* (of a particular prophet), οἱ προφῆται *the prophets* (as a division of the Hebrew Scriptures). (144)

προφητικός, ή, όν adj. (φημί) *prophetic.* (2)

προφῆτις, ιδος, ἡ n. (φημί) *prophet.* (2)

προφθάνω v. (φθάνω) aor. προέφθασα. *to be ahead of, come before, anticipate,* προφθάνω... λέγων *speak first.* (1) Mt 17:25

προχειρίζομαι v. (χείρ) aor. προεχειρισάμην; pf. pass. προκέχειρσμαι. *to choose for oneself, select, appoint.* (3)

προχειροτονέω v. (χείρ, -τείνω) pf. pass. προκεχειροτόνημαι. *to choose* or *appoint beforehand.* (1) Ac 10:41

Πρόχορος, ου, ὁ n. pers. *Prochorus.* (1) Ac 6:5

πρύμνα, ης, ἡ n. *stern* (of a boat or ship). (3)

πρωΐ adv. (πρό) *early, early in the morning, morning,* εὐθὺς πρωῒ *as soon as morning came.* (12)

πρωΐα, ας, ἡ n. (πρό) *(early) morning.* (2)

πρωϊνός, ή, όν adj. (πρό) *early, belonging to the morning, morning.* (2)

πρῷρα, ης, ἡ n. (πρό) *bow, prow* (of a boat or ship). (2)

πρωτεύω v. (πρό) *to be first, have first place.* (1) Col 1:18

πρωτοκαθεδρία, ας, ἡ n. (πρό, ἑδραῖος) *seat of honor, best seat.* (4)

πρωτοκλισία, ας, ἡ n. (πρό, κλίνω) *place of honor.* (5)

πρῶτον s. πρῶτος (neut. sg. as adv.).

πρῶτος, η, ον adj. (πρό) *first, earliest, earlier, outer, anterior; first, foremost, most important, most prominent,* ἐν πρώτοις *as of first importance;* neut. sg. as adv. *first, in the first place, before, earlier, to begin with, before* (w. gen.), *the first time* (w. art.); *in the first place, above all, especially, first of all.* (155)

πρωτοστάτης, ου, ὁ n. (πρό, ἵστημι) *leader, ringleader.* (1) Ac 24:5

πρωτοτόκια, ων, τά n. (πρό, τίκτω) *birthright, right of primogeniture.* (1) Heb 12:16

πρωτότοκος, ον adj. (πρό, τίκτω) *first-born* (lit.); *firstborn* (fig. of Christ and God's people). (8)

πρώτως adv. (πρό) *for the first time.* (1) Ac 11:26

πταίω v. (*) aor. ἔπταισα. *to stumble, trip, make a mistake, go astray, sin; be ruined* or *lost.* (5)

πτέρνα, ης, ἡ n. *heel.* (1) Jn 13:18

πτερύγιον, ου, τό n. (πέτομαι) *end, edge, pinnacle, summit.* (2)

πτέρυξ, υγος, ἡ n. (πέτομαι) *wing.* (5)

πτηνός, ή, όν adj. (πέτομαι) *winged; bird* (subst. in NT). (1) 1 Cor 15:39

πτοέω v. (*) aor. pass. ἐπτοήθην. *to terrify; be terrified, be alarmed, frightened,* or *startled* (pass. in NT). (2)

πτόησις, εως, ἡ n. (πτοέω) *terrifying, intimidation* (poss.); *fear, terror* (prob.). (1) 1 Pt 3:6

Πτολεμαΐς, ΐδος, ἡ n. pla. *Ptolemais.* (1) Ac 21:7

πτύον, ου, τό n. (πτύω) *winnowing shovel*. (2)

πτύρω v. *to be terrified, frightened, intimidated* (pass. in NT). (1) Phil 1:28

πτύσμα, ατος, τό n. (πτύω) *saliva, spit*. (1) Jn 9:6

πτύσσω v. (*) aor. ἔπτυξα. *to fold up, roll up*. (1) Lk 4:20

πτύω v. (*) aor. ἔπτυσα. *to spit (out)*. (3)

πτῶμα, ατος, τό n. (πίπτω) *(dead) body, corpse*. (7)

πτῶσις, εως, ἡ n. (πίπτω) *fall, collapse*. (2)

πτωχεία, ας, ἡ n. (πτωχός) *poverty*, ἡ κατὰ βάθους πτωχεία *extreme poverty*. (3)

πτωχεύω v. (πτωχός) aor. ἐπτώχευσα. *to be* or *become poor*. (1) 2 Cor 8:9

πτωχός, ή, όν adj. (*) *dependent on others for support, poor* (lit.); *poor* (fig.); *miserable, shabby; poor person* (subst.). (34)

πυγμή, ῆς, ἡ n. (*) *fist*. (1) Mk 7:3

πυθέσθαι, πυθόμενος s. πυνθάνομαι (2 aor. mid. inf., 2 aor. mid. ptc.).

πύθων, ωνος, ὁ n. *spirit of divination* (from the Python). (1) Ac 16:16

πυκνός, ή, όν adj. (πυγμή) *frequent, numerous; often, frequently*, πυκνότερον *more often, more frequently, very often, quite frequently* (neut. as adv.). (3)

πυκτεύω v. (πυγμή) *to box* (with fists). (1) 1 Cor 9:26

πύλη, ης, ἡ n. (*) *gate, door*. (10)

πυλών, ῶνος, ὁ n. (πύλη) *gateway, gate, entrance; entrance* (as forecourt). (18)

πυνθάνομαι v. aor. ἐπυθόμην. *to inquire, ask; learn*. (12)

πῦρ, ός, τό n. (*) *fire* (lit. and fig.). (71)

πυρά, ᾶς, ἡ n. (πῦρ) *a fire* (as a pile of combustible or burning material). (2)

πύργος, ου, ὁ n. *tower; farm building*. (4)

πυρέσσω v. (πῦρ) *to suffer with a fever*. (2)

πυρετός, οῦ, ἡ n. (πῦρ) *fever*. (6)

πύρινος, η, ον adj. (πῦρ) *fiery* (as a color). (1) Rev 9:17

πυρόω v. (πῦρ) pf. pass. πεπύρωμαι; aor. pass. ἐπυρώθην. *to burn* (lit. and fig.), *be inflamed, burn with sexual desire; make red hot, cause to glow, heat thoroughly* (pass. in NT). (6)

πυρράζω v. (πῦρ) *to be (fiery) red* (of the sky). (2)

πυρρός, ά, όν adj. (πῦρ) *(fiery) red*. (2)

Πύρρος, ου, ὁ n. pers. *Pyrrhus*. (1) Ac 20:4

πύρωσις, εως, ἡ n. (πῦρ) *burning; burning* or *fiery ordeal*. (3)

πωλέω v. (*) aor. ἐπώλησα. *to sell*, οἱ πωλοῦντες *sellers* or *dealers; be offered for sale, be sold* (pass.). (22)

πῶλος, ου, ὁ n. *foal, colt; horse*. (12)

πώποτε adv. (-πω, ὅς) *ever, at any time*. (6)

πωρόω v. (*) aor. ἐπώρωσα; pf. pass. πεπώρωμαι; aor. pass. ἐπωρώθην. *to harden, make dull* or *blind, close the mind* (fig. in NT). (5)

πώρωσις, εως, ἡ n. (πωρόω) *dullness, insensibility, obstinacy, closed mind*. (3)

πῶς part. (ὅς) *in what way, how, what, in what sense, how is it (possible) that, how dare you, how can you say, what does he mean by saying, how could, how* or *that* (interrog.); *how!* (excl.). (103)

πώς part. (ὅς) encl. *somehow, in some way, perhaps* (as adv. w. εἰ); *lest, lest somehow, (lest) perhaps* (as conj. w. μή). (15)

P

'Ραάβ, ἡ n. pers. *Rahab*. (2)

ῥαββί (*) Heb. *master, sir, rabbi*. (15)

ῥαββουνι (ῥαββί) Ara. *my lord, my master*. (2)

ῥαβδίζω v. (ῥάβδος) aor. pass. ἐραβδίσθην. *to beat* (with a rod). (2)

ῥάβδος, ου, ἡ n. (*) *rod, staff, stick, scepter*. (12)

ῥαβδοῦχος, ου, ὁ n. (ῥάβδος, ἔχω) *constable, police officer*. (2)

'Ραγαύ, ὁ n. pers. *Reu*. (1) Lk 3:35

ῥαδιούργημα, ατος, τό n. (ἔργον) *crime, villainy*. (1) Ac 18:14

ῥαδιουργία, ας, ἡ n. (ἔργον) *wickedness, chicanery, villainy, deceit, fraud, unscrupulousness*. (1) Ac 13:10

ῥαίνω v. *to sprinkle*. (v.l.)

'Ραιφάν, ὁ n. pers. *Rephan*. (1) Ac 7:43

ῥακά Ara. *fool, numskull, empty-head*. (1) Mt 5:22

ῥάκος, ους, τό n. *piece of cloth, patch*. (2)

'Ραμά, ἡ n. pla. *Rama*. (1) Mt 2:18

ῥαντίζω v. (*) aor. ἐράντισα; pf. pass. ῥεράντισμαι. *to sprinkle; cleanse* or *purify (for) oneself* (mid.). (4)

ῥαντισμός, οῦ, ὁ n. (ῥαντίζω) *sprinkling*. (2)

ῥαπίζω v. (ῥάβδος) aor. ἐράπισα. *to slap*. (2)

ῥάπισμα, ατος, τό n. (ῥάβδος) *blow* (by an instrument)*; slap in the face*. (3)

ῥαφίς, ίδος, ἡ n. (*) *needle*. (2)

'Ραχάβ, ἡ n. pers. *Rahab*. (1) Mt 1:5

'Ραχήλ, ἡ n. pers. *Rachel*. (1) Mt 2:18

'Ρεβέκκα, ας, ἡ n. pers. *Rebecca*. (1) Rom 9:10

ῥέδη, ης, ἡ n. Lat. *carriage* (four-wheeled). (1) Rev 18:13

ῥέω v. (*) fut. ῥεύσω. *to flow*. (1) Jn 7:38

'Ρήγιον, ου, τό n. pla. *Rhegium*. (1) Ac 28:13

ῥῆγμα, ατος, τό n. (ῥήγνυμι) *wreck, ruin, collapse*. (1) Lk 6:49

ῥήγνυμι and ῥήσσω v. (*) fut. ῥήξω; aor. ἔρρηξα. *to tear (in pieces), break, burst; tear* or *break loose, break out, break forth; throw down*. (7)

ῥηθείς s. λέγω (aor. pass. ptc.).

ῥῆμα, ατος, τό n. (*) *word, saying, expression, prophecy* (sg. or pl.), *command(ment), order, direction, threat, proclamation* (pl.), *gospel, confession; thing, object, matter, event*. (68)

'Ρησά, ὁ n. pers. *Rhesa*. (1) Lk 3:27

ῥήτωρ, ορος, ὁ n. (ῥῆμα) *advocate, attorney*. (1) Ac 24:1

ῥητῶς adv. (ῥῆμα) *expressly, explicitly*. (1) 1 Ti 4:1

ῥίζα, ης, ἡ n. (*) *root; shoot, scion, descendant*. (17)

ῥιζόω v. (ῥίζα) pf. pass. ἐρρίζωμαι. *to be* or *become firmly rooted, be* or *become fixed* (pass. in NT). (2)

ῥιπή, ῆς, ἡ n. (ῥίπτω) *rapid movement, twinkling*. (1) 1 Cor 15:52

ῥιπίζω v. *to blow here and there, toss; be tossed about* (pass. in NT). (1) Jas 1:6

ῥίπτω and ῥιπτέω v. (*) aor. ἔρριψα; pf. pass. ἔρριμμαι. *to throw, take off* (of clothing), *throw down; put* or *lay down*. (8)

'Ροβοάμ, ὁ n. pers. *Rehoboam*. (2)

'Ρόδη, ης, ἡ n. pers. *Rhoda*. (1) Ac 12:13

'Ρόδος, ου, ἡ n. pla. *Rhodes*. (1) Ac 21:1

ῥοιζηδόν adv. *with a rushing noise, with a roar*. (1) 2 Pt 3:10

'Ρομφά, ὁ n. pers. *Rompha*. (v.l.)

ῥομφαία, ας, ἡ n. *sword* (lit. and fig.). (7)

ῥοπή, ῆς, ἡ n. *inclination, twinkling* (of an eye). (v.l.)

Ῥουβήν, ὁ n. pers. *Reuben.* (1) Rev 7:5

Ῥούθ, ἡ n. pers. *Ruth.* (1) Mt 1:5

Ῥοῦφος, ου, ὁ n. pers. *Rufus.* (2)

ῥύμη, ης, ἡ n. *narrow street, lane, alley.* (4)

ῥύομαι v. fut. ῥύσομαι; aor. ἐρρυσάμην; aor. pass. ἐρρύσθην. *to save, rescue, deliver, preserve, set free,* ὁ ῥυόμενος *the deliverer.* (17)

ῥυπαίνω v. (ῥύπος) aor. pass. ἐρρυπάνθην. *to defile, pollute; be defiled* or *polluted* (pass. in NT). (1) Rev 22:11

ῥυπαρία, ας, ἡ n. (ῥύπος) *moral uncleanness, vulgarity, sordid avarice, greediness.* (1) Jas 1:21

ῥυπαρός, ά, όν adj. (ῥύπος) *filthy, soiled; unclean, defiled.* (2)

ῥύπος, ου, ὁ n. (*) *dirt.* (1) 1 Pt 3:21

ῥύσις, εως, ἡ n. (ῥέω) *flow, flowing.* (3)

ῥυτίς, ίδος, ἡ n. *wrinkle.* (1) Eph 5:27

Ῥωμαϊκός, ή, όν adj. pla. *Roman, Latin.* (v.l.)

Ῥωμαῖος, α, ον adj. pla. *Roman; Roman person* or *citizen* (subst. in NT). (12)

Ῥωμαϊστί adv. pla. *in Latin.* (1) Jn 19:20

Ῥώμη, ης, ἡ n. pla. *Rome.* (8)

ῥώννυμι v. (*) pf. pass. ἔρρωμαι. *farewell, goodbye* (pf. pass. impv. in NT). (1) Ac 15:29

Σ

σαβαχθανι Ara. *you have forsaken me.* (2)

Σαβαώθ n. pers. *Sabaoth, of the armies* (lit.), κύριος Σαβαώθ *Lord of Hosts.* (2)

σαββατισμός, οῦ, ὁ n. (σάββατον) *sabbath rest, sabbath observance.* (1) Heb 4:9

σάββατον, ου, τό n. (*) Heb. sg. *Sabbath; week;* pl. *Sabbaths, Sabbath* (usu.); *week.* (68)

σαγήνη, ης, ἡ n. *seine, dragnet.* (1) Mt 13:47

Σαδδουκαῖος, ου, ὁ n. oth. *Sadducee; Sadducees* (pl. in NT). (14)

Σαδώκ, ὁ n. pers. *Zadok.* (2)

σαίνω v. pass. in NT *to be deceived* (poss.); *to be disturbed* (poss.). (1) 1 Th 3:3

σάκκος, ου, ὁ n. *sack, sackcloth.* (4)

Σαλά, ὁ n. pers. *Shelah.* (2)

Σαλαθιήλ, ὁ n. pers. *Shealtiel, Salathiel.* (3)

Σαλαμίς, ῖνος, ἡ n. pla. *Salamis.* (1) Ac 13:5

Σαλείμ, τό n. pla. *Salim.* (1) Jn 3:23

σαλεύω v. (ἄλλομαι) aor. ἐσάλευσα; pf. pass. σεσάλευμαι; aor. pass. ἐσαλεύθην. *to shake, cause to waver* or *totter, drive to and fro; disturb, shake* (fig.), *incite.* (15)

Σαλήμ, ἡ n. pla. *Salem.* (2)

Σαλμών, ὁ n. pers. *Salmon.* (2)

Σαλμώνη, ης, ἡ n. pla. *Salmone.* (1) Ac 27:7

σάλος, ου, ὁ n. (ἄλλομαι) *surge, waves* (of a rough sea). (1) Lk 21:25

σάλπιγξ, ιγγος, ἡ n. (σαλπίζω) *trumpet; trumpet-call, trumpet-sound.* (11)

σαλπίζω v. (*) fut. σαλπίσω; aor.

ἐσάλπισα. *to blow* or *sound a trumpet, trumpet, blow a trumpet* (fig.). (12)

σαλπιστής, οῦ, ὁ n. (σαλπίζω) *trumpeter.* (1) Rev 18:22

Σαλώμη, ης, ἡ n. pers. *Salome.* (2)

Σαμάρεια, ας, ἡ n. pla. *Samaria.* (11)

Σαμαρίτης, ου, ὁ n. pla. *a Samaritan.* (9)

Σαμαρῖτις, ιδος, ἡ n. pla. *a Samaritan woman.* (2)

Σαμοθράκη, ης, ἡ n. pla. *Samothrace.* (1) Ac 16:11

Σάμος, ου, ἡ n. pla. *Samos.* (1) Ac 20:15

Σαμουήλ, ὁ n. pers. *Samuel.* (3)

Σαμψών, ὁ n. pers. *Samson.* (1) Heb 11:32

σανδάλιον, ου, τό n. *sandal.* (2)

σανίς, ίδος, ἡ n. *board, plank.* (1) Ac 27:44

Σαούλ, ὁ n. pers. *Saul.* (9)

σαπρός, ά, όν adj. (σήπω) *bad, not good; evil, unwholesome.* (8)

Σάπφιρα, ης, ἡ n. pers. *Sapphira.* (1) Ac 5:1

σάπφιρος, ου, ἡ n. Heb. *sapphire.* (1) Rev 21:19

σαργάνη, ης, ἡ n. *(rope) basket.* (1) 2 Cor 11:33

Σάρδεις, εων, αἱ n. pla. *Sardis.* (3)

σάρδιον, ου, τό n. (*) *carnelian, sardius.* (2)

σαρδόνυξ, υχος, ὁ n. (σάρδιον) *sardonyx.* (1) Rev 21:20

Σάρεπτα, ων, τά n. pla. *Zarephath.* (1) Lk 4:26

σαρκικός, ή, όν adj. (σάρξ) *material, physical, human, fleshly; (merely) human, earthly, mediocre, worldly.* (7)

141

σάρκινος, η, ον adj. (σάρξ) *material, physical, human, fleshly; (merely) human*. (4)

σάρξ, σαρκός, ἡ n. (*) *flesh* (lit.), ἡ ἐν σαρκὶ περιτομή *physical circumcision; body, physical body, physical limitations, flesh* (opp. τὸ πνεῦμα), σάρξ (ἁμαρτίας) *sinful flesh; living being (with flesh), person*, αἵματος καὶ σαρκός (and reverse) *mortal nature; human* or *mortal nature, earthly descent, natural* or *physical descent*, μου τὴν σάρκα *my compatriots;* κατὰ (τὴν) σάρκα *according to human standards, from a human point of view, by outward standards;* ἐν σαρκί *in earthly things, as a human being*. (147)

σαρόω v. pf. pass. σεσάρωμαι. *to sweep*. (3)

Σάρρα, ας, ἡ n. pers. *Sarah*. (4)

Σαρών, ῶνος, ὁ n. pla. *Sharon*. (1) Ac 9:35

Σατανᾶς, ᾶ, ὁ n. pers. *Satan, the Enemy*. (36)

σάτον, ου, τό n. *seah* (Hebrew dry measure, about 13 liters or quarts). (2)

Σαῦλος, ου, ὁ n. pers. *Saul*. (15)

σβέννυμι v. (*) fut. σβέσω; aor. ἔσβεσα. *to extinguish, put out, quench, stifle, suppress; go out* (pass.). (6)

σέ s. σύ (acc.).

σεαυτοῦ, ῆς pron. (σύ, αὐτός) reflex. *(of) yourself*. (43)

σεβάζομαι v. (σέβω) aor. pass. ἐσεβάσθην. *to worship*. (1) Rom 1:25

σέβασμα, ατος, τό n. (σέβω) *devotional object*. (2)

σεβαστός, ή, όν adj. (σέβω) *imperial; (His Majesty) the Emperor* (subst.). (3)

σέβω v. (*) *to worship*, ὁ σεβόμενος (τὸν θεόν) *God-fearer, worshiper of God* (mid. in NT). (10)

σειρά, ᾶς, ἡ n. *cord, rope, chain*. (1) 2 Pt 2:4

σεισμός, οῦ, ὁ n. (σείω) *earthquake; storm* (on a body of water). (14)

σείω v. (*) fut. σείσω; aor. pass. ἐσείσθην. *to shake, agitate; be shaken, quake, be stirred, tremble* (pass.). (5)

Σεκοῦνδος, ου, ὁ n. pers. *Secundus*. (1) Ac 20:4

Σελεύκεια, ας, ἡ n. pla. *Seleucia*. (1) Ac 13:4

σελήνη, ης, ἡ n. (*) *moon*. (9)

σεληνιάζομαι v. (σελήνη) *to be moonstruck; be an epileptic* (fig. in NT). (2)

Σεμεΐν, ὁ n. pers. *Semein*. (1) Lk 3:26

σεμίδαλις, εως, ἡ n. Sem. *(best quality) wheat flour*. (1) Rev 18:13

σεμνός, ή, όν adj. (σέβω) *worthy of respect* or *honor, noble, dignified, serious, honorable, worthy, venerable, holy, above reproach*. (4)

σεμνότης, ητος, ἡ n. (σέβω) *dignity, seriousness, probity, holiness*. (3)

Σέργιος, ου, ὁ n. pers. *Sergius*. (1) Ac 13:7

Σερούχ, ὁ n. pers. *Serug*. (1) Lk 3:35

σέσηπα s. σήπω (2 pf.).

Σήθ, ἡ n. pers. *Seth*. (1) Lk 3:38

Σήμ, ὁ n. pers. *Shem*. (1) Lk 3:36

σημαίνω v. (σημεῖον) aor. ἐσήμανα. *to report, communicate; indicate, suggest, intimate*. (6)

σημεῖον, ου, τό n. (*) *sign, token, indication, (distinguishing) mark, mark of genuineness, signal; miracle, portent*. (77)

σημειόω v. (σημεῖον) *to mark, take note of* (mid. in NT). (1) 2 Th 3:14

σήμερον adv. (ἡμέρα) *today*, ἡ σήμερον ἡμέρα *today, this very day*, σήμερον ταύτῃ τῇ νυκτί *this very night, now;* ἡ σήμερον *today* (subst.). (41)

σήπω v. (*) pf. σέσηπα. *to decay, rot*. (1) Jas 5:2

σής, σητός, ὁ n. (*) *moth*. (3)

σητόβρωτος, ον adj. (σής, βιβρώσκω) *motheaten*. (1) Jas 5:2

σθενόω v. (*) fut. σθενώσω. *to strengthen, make strong*. (1) 1 Pt 5:10

σιαγών, όνος, ἡ n. *cheek*. (2)

σιγάω v. (σιγή) aor. ἐσίγησα; pf. pass. σεσίγημαι. *to say nothing, keep still, keep silent, hold one's tongue, stop* speaking, become silent; keep secret, conceal (trans.). (10)

σιγή, ῆς, ἡ n. (*) silence, quiet. (2)

σίδηρος, ου, ὁ n. (*) iron. (1) Rev 18:12

σιδηροῦς, ᾶ, οῦν adj. (σίδηρος) (made of) iron. (5)

Σιδών, ῶνος, ἡ n. pla. Sidon. (9)

Σιδώνιος, α, ον adj. pla. Sidonian; country around Sidon, region of Sidon, a Sidonian (subst.). (2)

σικάριος, ου, ὁ n. Lat. assassin, terrorist, dagger man. (1) Ac 21:38

σίκερα, τό n. Ara. beer. (1) Lk 1:15

Σιλᾶς, ᾶ, ὁ n. pers. Silas. (12)

Σιλουανός, οῦ, ὁ n. pers. Silvanus. (4)

Σιλωάμ, ὁ n. pla. Siloam. (3)

σιμικίνθιον, ου, τό n. Lat. apron. (1) Ac 19:12

Σίμων, ωνος, ὁ n. pers. Simon. (75)

Σινᾶ n. pla. Sinai. (4)

σίναπι, εως, τό n. mustard (plant). (5)

σινδών, όνος, ἡ n. linen cloth; shirt. (6)

σινιάζω v. aor. ἐσινίασα. to sift. (1) Lk 22:31

σιρικός, ή, όν adj. silken; silk cloth (subst. in NT). (1) Rev 18:12

σιρός, οῦ, ὁ n. pit, cave. (v.l.)

σιτευτός, ή, όν adj. (σῖτος) fattened. (3)

σιτίον, ου, τό n. (σῖτος) grain; food (pl. in NT). (1) Ac 7:12

σιτιστός, ή, όν adj. (σῖτος) fattened; fattened cattle (neut. pl. subst. in NT). (1) Mt 22:4

σιτομέτριον, ου, τό n. (σῖτος, μέτρον) food allowance, ration. (1) Lk 12:42

σῖτος, ου, ὁ n. (*) wheat, grain. (14)

Σιών, ἡ n. pla. (Mount) Zion; Jerusalem; people of God. (7)

σιωπάω v. fut. σιωπήσω; aor. ἐσιώπησα. to keep silent, say nothing, make no sound; be or become quiet, be silent or mute. (10)

σκανδαλίζω v. (σκάνδαλον) aor. ἐσκανδάλισα; aor. pass. ἐσκανδαλίσθην. to cause to sin; give offense to, anger, shock; pass. fall away, be led into sin, be repelled by; take offense. (29)

σκάνδαλον, ου, τό n. (*) trap, reason for falling; temptation (to sin), enticement; fault, stain, stumbling-block, that which offends. (15)

σκάπτω v. (*) fut. σκάψω; aor. ἔσκαψα. to dig, cultivate. (3)

σκάφη, ης, ἡ n. (σκάπτω) (small) boat, skiff. (3)

σκέλος, ους, τό n. leg. (3)

σκέπασμα, ατος, τό n. covering, clothing, house. (1) 1 Ti 6:8

Σκευᾶς, ᾶ, ὁ n. pers. Sceva. (1) Ac 19:14

σκευή, ῆς, ἡ n. (σκεῦος) equipment or gear (of a ship), tackle or rigging. (1) Ac 27:19

σκεῦος, ους, τό n. (*) thing, object, driving-anchor, τὰ σκεύη property, equipment; vessel, jar, dish; instrument, vessel (fig.), body, wife, penis (poss.). (23)

σκηνή, ῆς, ἡ n. (*) tent, hut, lodging, dwelling, Tabernacle or Tent of Testimony; dwelling (celestial). (20)

σκηνοπηγία, ας, ἡ n. (σκηνή, πήγνυμι) Feast of Tabernacles or Booths. (1) Jn 7:2

σκηνοποιός, οῦ, ὁ n. (σκηνή, ποιέω) tentmaker; maker of stage properties (poss.). (1) Ac 18:3

σκῆνος, ους, τό n. (σκηνή) tent, lodging (fig. in NT). (2)

σκηνόω v. (σκηνή) fut. σκηνώσω; aor. ἐσκήνωσα. to live, settle, take up residence. (5)

σκήνωμα, ατος, τό n. (σκηνή) habitation, dwelling, body. (3)

σκιά, ᾶς, ἡ n. (*) shade; shadow; shadow (as representation). (7)

σκιρτάω v. aor. ἐσκίρτησα. to leap, spring about. (3)

σκληροκαρδία, ας, ἡ n. (σκληρός, καρδία) hardness of heart, coldness, obstinacy, stubbornness. (3)

σκληρός, ά, όν adj. (*) hard, rough; harsh, unpleasant, strong; difficult; strict, cruel, merciless. (5)

σκληρότης, ητος, ἡ n. (σκληρός) hardness (of heart), stubbornness. (1) Rom 2:5

σκληροτράχηλος, ον adj. (σκληρός, τράχηλος) stiff-necked, stubborn. (1) Ac 7:51

σκληρύνω v. (σκληρός) aor. ἐσκλήρυνα; aor. pass. ἐσκληρύνθην. to harden; be or become hardened (pass.). (6)

σκολιός, ά, όν adj. crooked; crooked (fig.), unscrupulous, dishonest, harsh. (4)

σκόλοψ, οπος, ὁ n. thorn, splinter. (1) 2 Cor 12:7

σκοπέω v. (σκοπός) to look (out) for, notice, keep one's eyes on, consider. (6)

σκοπός, οῦ, ὁ n. (*) goal, mark. (1) Phil 3:14

σκορπίζω v. (*) aor. ἐσκόρπισα; aor. pass. ἐσκορπίσθην. to scatter, disperse, chase in all directions; scatter abroad, distribute. (5)

σκορπίος, ου, ὁ n. scorpion. (5)

σκοτεινός, ή, όν adj. (σκότος) dark. (3)

σκοτία, ας, ἡ n. (σκότος) darkness, gloom, dark, secret; darkness (fig.). (16)

σκοτίζω v. (σκότος) aor. pass. ἐσκοτίσθην. pass. in NT to be or become dark, be darkened; be or become inwardly darkened. (5)

σκότος, ους, τό n. (*) darkness, gloom; darkness (as hiddenness); darkness (mor.); bearer, victim, or instrument of darkness. (31)

σκοτόω v. (σκότος) pf. pass. ἐσκότωμαι; aor. pass. ἐσκοτώθην. pass. in NT be or become darkened; be or become darkened in mind. (3)

σκύβαλον, ου, τό n. refuse, garbage, crud. (1) Phil 3:8

Σκύθης, ου, ὁ n. pla. a Scythian. (1) Col 3:11

σκυθρωπός, ή, όν adj. (ὁράω) sad, gloomy, sullen, dark. (2)

σκύλλω v. (*) pf. pass. ἔσκυλμαι. to weary, harass; trouble, bother, annoy; trouble oneself (mid.); be dejected (pass.). (4)

σκῦλον, ου, τό n. (σκύλλω) booty, spoils (pl. in NT). (1) Lk 11:22

σκωληκόβρωτος, ον adj. (σκώληξ, βιβρώσκω) eaten by worms. (1) Ac 12:23

σκώληξ, ηκος, ὁ n. (*) worm. (1) Mk 9:48

σμαράγδινος, η, ον adj. (σμάραγδος) (of) emerald, made of emerald, emerald in color. (1) Rev 4:3

σμάραγδος, ου, ὁ n. (*) emerald. (1) Rev 21:19

σμῆγμα, ατος, τό n. ointment, salve. (v.l.)

σμύρνα, ης, ἡ n. (*) myrrh. (2)

Σμύρνα, ης, ἡ n. pla. Smyrna. (2)

σμυρνίζω v. (σμύρνα) pf. pass. ἐσμύρνισμαι. to treat or flavor with myrrh. (1) Mk 15:23

Σόδομα, ων, τά n. pla. Sodom. (9)

Σολομών, ῶνος, ὁ n. pers. Solomon. (12)

σορός, οῦ, ἡ n. coffin, bier. (1) Lk 7:14

σός, σή, σόν adj. (σύ) your, yours (sg.); your own people, what is yours (subst.). (27)

σουδάριον, ου, τό n. Lat. face-cloth, cloth. (4)

Σουσάννα, ης, ἡ n. pers. Susanna. (1) Lk 8:3

σοφία, ας, ἡ n. (σοφός) wisdom, cleverness; Wisdom (personif.). (51)

σοφίζω v. (σοφός) aor. ἐσόφισα; pf. pass. σεσόφισμαι. to make wise, teach, instruct; be craftily devised (pass.). (2)

σοφός, ή, όν adj. (*) clever, skillful, experienced; wise, learned. (20)

Σπανία, ας, ἡ n. pla. Spain. (2)

σπαράσσω v. (σπάω) aor. ἐσπάραξα. to shake to and fro, convulse. (3)

σπαργανόω v. aor. ἐσπαργάνωσα; pf. pass. ἐσπαργάνωμαι. to wrap up in cloths (of infants). (2)

σπαρείς s. σπείρω (2 aor. pass. ptc.).

σπαταλάω v. aor. ἐσπατάλησα. to live luxuriously or voluptuously. (2)

σπάω v. (*) aor. ἔσπασα. to draw (of a sword), pull out (mid. in NT). (2)

σπεῖρα, ης, ἡ n. *cohort* (tenth part of a legion, about 600 men). (7)

σπείρω v. (*) aor. ἔσπειρα; pf. pass. ἔσπαρμαι; aor. pass. ἐσπάρην. *to sow (seed)*, ὁ σπείρων *sower*. (52)

σπεκουλάτωρ, ορος, ὁ n. Lat. *courier, executioner*. (1) Mk 6:27

σπένδω v. (*) *to offer a drink-offering; be poured out as a drink-offering, be offered up* (pass. in NT). (2)

σπέρμα, ατος, τό n. (σπείρω) *seed* (of plants and of males); *posterity, descendants, children, survivors; nature, disposition, character*. (43)

σπερμολόγος, ον adj. (σπείρω, λέγω) *picking up seeds; scrapmonger, scavenger* (subst. in NT). (1) Ac 17:18

σπεύδω v. (*) aor. ἔσπευσα. *to hurry, make haste, hasten; hasten (something)*. (6)

σπήλαιον, ου, τό n. *cave, hideout*. (6)

σπιλάς, άδος, ἡ n. (σπίλος) *(hidden) reef; spot, stain* (poss.). (1) Jd 12

σπίλος, ου, ὁ n. (*) *spot, stain, blemish*. (2)

σπιλόω v. (σπίλος) pf. pass. ἐσπίλωμαι. *to stain, defile*. (2)

σπλαγχνίζομαι v. (σπλάγχνον) aor. pass. ἐσπλαγχνίσθην. *to have pity, feel sympathy*. (12)

σπλάγχνον, ου, τό n. (*) *inward parts, entrails, heart; love, affection, beloved* (pl. in NT). (11)

σπόγγος, ου, ὁ n. *sponge*. (3)

σποδός, οῦ, ἡ n. *ashes*. (3)

σπορά, ᾶς, ἡ n. (σπείρω) *seed; origin, sowing* (poss.). (1) 1 Pt 1:23

σπόριμος, ον adj. (σπείρω) *sown; standing grain, grain fields* (pl. subst. in NT). (3)

σπόρος, ου, ὁ n. (σπείρω) *seed, store of seed*. (6)

σπουδάζω v. (σπεύδω) fut. σπουδάσω; aor. ἐσπούδασα. *to hurry, hasten; be zealous* or *eager, take pains, make every effort, be conscientious*. (11)

σπουδαῖος, α, ον adj. (σπεύδω) *eager, zealous, earnest, diligent*, σπουδαιό-τερος *very earnest*, πολύ σπουδαιότερος *much more zealous*. (3)

σπουδαίως adv. (σπεύδω) *with haste*, σπουδαιοτέρως *with special urgency; diligently, earnestly, zealously, strongly*. (4)

σπουδή, ῆς, ἡ n. (σπεύδω) *haste, speed*, μετὰ σπουδῆς *in haste; eagerness, earnestness, diligence, willingness, zeal, good will, devotion, effort*. (12)

σπυρίς, ίδος, ἡ n. *basket, hamper*. (5)

στάδιον, ου, τό n. *stade* (Roman measure of distance, about 192 meters or 210 yards); *arena, stadium*, ἐν σταδίῳ τρέχω *run a race*. (7)

στάμνος, ου, ἡ n. (ἵστημι) *jar*. (1) Heb 9:4

στασιαστής, οῦ, ὁ n. (ἵστημι) *rebel, revolutionary*. (1) Mk 15:7

στάσις, εως, ἡ n. (ἵστημι) *existence, occurrence, standing, place, position; uprising, riot, revolt, rebellion; strife, discord, disunion, dispute, dissension*. (9)

στατήρ, ῆρος, ὁ n. (ἵστημι) *stater* (Greek silver coin, four drachmas). (1) Mt 17:27

σταυρός, οῦ, ὁ n. (σταυρόω) *cross* (lit. and fig.). (27)

σταυρόω v. (*) fut. σταυρώσω; aor. ἐσταύρωσα; pf. pass. ἐσταύρωμαι; aor. pass. ἐσταυρώθην. *to crucify* (lit. and fig.). (46)

σταφυλή, ῆς, ἡ n. *(bunch of) grapes*. (3)

στάχυς, υος, ὁ n. *head of grain* or *wheat*. (5)

Στάχυς, υος, ὁ n. pers. *Stachys*. (1) Rom 16:9

στέγη, ης, ἡ n. (στέγω) *roof*. (3)

στέγω v. (*) *to cover, pass over in silence; endure, bear, stand*. (4)

στεῖρα, ας, ἡ n. (στερεός) *barren woman; incapable of bearing children, barren, infertile* (adj.). (5)

στέλλω v. (*) mid. in NT *to keep away, stand aloof; avoid, try to avoid*. (2)

στέμμα, ατος, τό n. (στέφανος) *wreath* or *garland (of flowers)*. (1) Ac 14:13

στεναγμός, οῦ, ὁ n. (στενός) *sigh, groan, groaning.* (2)

στενάζω v. (στενός) aor. ἐστέναξα. *to sigh, groan; complain.* (6)

στενός, ή, όν adj. (*) *narrow.* (3)

στενοχωρέω v. (στενός, χωρέω) *to restrict;* pass. in NT *be confined, restricted; be distressed, crushed.* (3)

στενοχωρία, ας, ἡ n. (στενός, χωρέω) *distress, difficulty, anguish, trouble.* (4)

στερεός, ά, όν adj. (*) *firm, hard, solid, strong; firm* (fig.), *steadfast.* (4)

στερεόω v. (στερεός) aor. ἐστερέωσα; aor. pass. ἐστερεώθην. *to make strong* or *firm; be strengthened* (pass.). (3)

στερέωμα, ατος, τό n. (στερεός) *firmness, steadfastness.* (1) Col 2:5

Στεφανᾶς, ᾶ, ὁ n. pers. *Stephanas.* (3)

Στέφανος, ου, ὁ n. pers. *Stephen.* (7)

στέφανος, ου, ὁ n. (*) *wreath, crown; adornment, pride; prize, reward.* (18)

στεφανόω v. (στέφανος) aor. ἐστεφάνωσα; pf. pass. ἐστεφάνωμαι. *to wreathe, crown; honor, reward, crown* (fig.). (3)

στῆθος, ους, τό n. *chest, breast.* (5)

στήκω v. (ἵστημι) *to stand; stand firm, be steadfast.* (10)

στηριγμός, οῦ, ὁ n. (στηρίζω) *safe position, firm hold; steadfastness, firmness of commitment* (poss.). (1) 2 Pt 3:17

στηρίζω v. (*) fut. στηρίξω; aor. ἐστήριξα, ἐστήρισα; pf. pass. ἐστήριγμαι; aor. pass. ἐστηρίχθην. *to set up, establish, support, fix; confirm, strengthen,* τὸ πρόσωπον στηρίζω *set one's face* (denoting firmness of purpose). (13)

στιβάς, άδος, ἡ n. *leafy branch.* (1) Mk 11:8

στίγμα, ατος, τό n. (*) *mark, brand.* (1) Gal 6:17

στιγμή, ῆς, ἡ n. (στίγμα) *moment.* (1) Lk 4:5

στίλβω v. *to shine, be radiant.* (1) Mk 9:3

στοά, ᾶς, ἡ n. (ἵστημι) *portico, porch.* (4)

Στοϊκός, ή, όν adj. oth. *Stoic.* (1) Ac 17:18

στοιχεῖον, ου, τό n. (στοιχέω) *elements, fundamental principles; elemental spirits* (poss.). (7)

στοιχέω v. (*) fut. στοιχήσω. *to agree with, hold to, follow, confirm.* (5)

στολή, ῆς, ἡ n. (στέλλω) *(long, flowing) robe.* (9)

στόμα, ατος, τό n. (*) *mouth,* στόμα πρὸς στόμα λαλέω *to speak face to face, lips, jaws; utterance, eloquence; mouth* (of the earth)*; edge* (of a sword). (78)

στόμαχος, ου, ὁ n. (στόμα) *stomach.* (1) 1 Ti 5:23

στρατεία, ας, ἡ n. (στρατιά) *expedition, campaign, warfare, fight.* (2)

στράτευμα, ατος, τό n. (στρατιά) *army, troops.* (8)

στρατεύομαι v. (στρατιά) *to serve in the army, serve as a soldier; fight, wage battle.* (7)

στρατηγός, οῦ, ὁ n. (στρατιά, ἄγω) *chief magistrate, praetor; captain (of the temple).* (10)

στρατιά, ᾶς, ἡ n. (*) *army, host.* (2)

στρατιώτης, ου, ὁ n. (στρατιά) *soldier* (lit. and fig.). (26)

στρατολογέω v. (στρατιά, λέγω) aor. ἐστρατολόγησα. *to enlist (soldiers).* (1) 2 Ti 2:4

στρατοπεδάρχης and στρατοπέδαρχος, ου, ὁ n. *military commander, commandant of a camp.* (v.l.)

στρατόπεδον, ου, τό n. (στρατιά, πεζεύω) *army, legion.* (1) Lk 21:20

στρεβλόω v. (στρέφω) *to twist, distort.* (1) 2 Pt 3:16

στρέφω v. (*) aor. ἔστρεψα; aor. pass. ἐστράφην. *to turn, turn around, turn toward* or *to; bring back, return; change; turn (away); make a turn-about, turn around* (pass. as act.). (21)

στρηνιάω v. (στρῆνος) aor. ἐστρηνίασα. *to live in luxury, live sensually.* (2)

στρῆνος, ους, τό n. (*) *sensuality, luxury*. (1) Rev 18:3

στρουθίον, ου, τό n. *sparrow*. (4)

στρωννύω v. (*) aor. ἔστρωσα; pf. pass. ἔστρωμαι. *to spread, make* (a bed); *furnish* (a room). (6)

στυγητός, ή, όν adj. (*) *loathsome, despicable*. (1) Tit 3:3

στυγνάζω v. (στυγητός) aor. ἐστύγνασα. *to be shocked, appalled; be* or *become gloomy, dark*. (2)

στῦλος, ου, ὁ n. *pillar, column; pillar* (fig.), *support*. (4)

σύ, σού; ὑμεῖς, ὑμῶν pron. (*) encl. forms σου, σοι, σε *you* (sg.); *you* (pl.). (2907)

συγγένεια, ας, ἡ n. (γίνομαι) *relationship, kinship, relatives*. (3)

συγγενής, ές adj. (γίνομαι) *related;* subst. in NT *relative; compatriot, kin*. (11)

συγγενίς, ίδος, ἡ n. (γίνομαι) *kinswoman, relative*. (1) Lk 1:36

συγγνώμη, ης, ἡ n. (γινώσκω) *concession, indulgence, pardon*. (1) 1 Cor 7:6

συγκάθημαι v. (ἑδραῖος) *to sit with*. (2)

συγκαθίζω v. (καθίζω) aor. συνεκάθισα. *to cause to sit down with; sit down with* (intr.). (2)

συγκακοπαθέω v. (κακός, πάσχω) aor. συνεκακοπάθησα. *to suffer together with, suffer hardship with, join one in suffering*. (2)

συγκακουχέομαι v. (κακός, ἔχω) *to suffer* or *be mistreated with*. (1) Heb 11:25

συγκαλέω v. (καλέω) aor. συνεκάλεσα. *to call together, summon; call to one's side, summon* (mid.). (8)

συγκαλύπτω v. (καλύπτω) pf. pass. συγκεκάλυμμαι. *to conceal*. (1) Lk 12:2

συγκάμπτω v. (κάμπτω) aor. συνέκαμψα. *to (cause to) bend*. (1) Rom 11:10

συγκαταβαίνω v. (-βαίνω) aor. συγκατέβην. *to go down with*. (1) Ac 25:5

συγκατάθεσις, εως, ἡ n. (τίθημι) *agreement, union*. (1) 2 Cor 6:16

συγκατατίθημι v. (τίθημι) *to agree with, consent to* (mid. in NT). (1) Lk 23:51

συγκαταψηφίζομαι v. (ψύχω) aor. pass. συγκατεψηφίσθην. *to be chosen together with, be added* (pass. in NT). (1) Ac 1:26

συγκεράννυμι v. (κεράννυμι) aor. συνεκέρασα; pf. pass. συγκεκέρασμαι. *to compose, unite*. (2)

συγκινέω v. (κινέω) aor. συνεκίνησα. *to stir up, move, arouse* or *excite*. (1) Ac 6:12

συγκλείω v. (κλείω) aor. συνέκλεισα. *to close up together, hem in, enclose; confine, imprison, lock in*. (4)

συγκληρονόμος, ον adj. (κλῆρος, νόμος) *co-heir* (subst. in NT). (4)

συγκοινωνέω v. (κοινός) aor. συνεκοινώνησα. *to be connected with, participate in, take a sympathetic interest in*. (3)

συγκοινωνός, οῦ, ὁ n. (κοινός) *participant, partner, sharer*. (4)

συγκομίζω v. (κόσμος) aor. συνεκόμισα. *to bury*. (1) Ac 8:2

συγκρίνω v. (κρίνω) aor. συνέκρινα. *to combine; compare; explain, interpret*. (3)

συγκύπτω v. (κύπτω) *to be bent over, bent double*. (1) Lk 13:11

συγκυρία, ας, ἡ n. *coincidence, chance*. (1) Lk 10:31

συγχαίρω v. (χαίρω) aor. pass. συνεχάρην. *to rejoice with; congratulate*. (7)

συγχέω and συγχύννω v. (-χέω) pf. pass. συγκέχυμαι; aor. pass. συνεχύθην. *to confuse, confound, trouble, stir up; be amazed, surprised, excited, agitated* (pass.). (5)

συγχράομαι v. (χράομαι) *to have dealings with*. (1) Jn 4:9

σύγχυσις, εως, ἡ n. (-χέω) *confusion, tumult*. (1) Ac 19:29

συζάω v. (ζάω) fut. συζήσω. *to live with, live together*. (3)

συζεύγνυμι v. (ζυγός) aor. συνέζευξα. *to join together, pair.* (2)

συζητέω v. (ζητέω) *to discuss; dispute, debate, argue.* (10)

συζήτησις, εως, ἡ n. *dispute, discussion.* (v.l.)

συζητητής, οῦ, ὁ n. (ζητέω) *disputant, debater.* (1) 1 Cor 1:20

σύζυγος, ου, ὁ n. (ζυγός) *comrade.* (1) Phil 4:3

συζωοποιέω v. (ζάω, ποιέω) aor. συνεζωοποίησα. *to make alive together with.* (2)

συκάμινος, ου, ἡ n. *mulberry tree.* (1) Lk 17:6

συκῆ, ῆς, ἡ n. (σῦκον) *fig tree.* (16)

συκομορέα, ας, ἡ n. (σῦκον) *fig-mulberry tree, sycamore tree.* (1) Lk 19:4

σῦκον, ου, τό n. (*) *fig, ripe fig.* (4)

συκοφαντέω v. (σῦκον, φαίνω) aor. ἐσυκοφάντησα. *to harass, squeeze, shake down, blackmail; extort.* (2)

συλαγωγέω v. (συλάω, ἄγω) *to make captive of, rob.* (1) Col 2:8

συλάω v. (*) aor. ἐσύλησα. *to rob, sack, loot, raid.* (1) 2 Cor 11:8

συλλαλέω v. (λαλέω) aor. συνελάλησα. *to talk, discuss,* or *converse with.* (6)

συλλαμβάνω v. (λαμβάνω) fut. συλλήμψομαι; aor. συνέλαβον; pf. συνείληφα; aor. pass. συνελήμφθην. *to seize, grasp, apprehend, arrest; catch; become pregnant, conceive;* mid. *seize, arrest; help.* (16)

συλλέγω v. (λέγω) fut. συλλέξω; aor. συνέλεξα. *to collect, gather (in), pick.* (8)

συλλογίζομαι v. (λέγω) aor. συνελογισάμην. *to reason, discuss, debate.* (1) Lk 20:5

συλλυπέω v. (λύπη) *to grieve with; be (deeply) grieved with, feel sympathy* (pass. in NT). (1) Mk 3:5

συμβαίνω v. (-βαίνω) aor. συνέβην; pf. συμβέβηκα. *to happen, come about.* (8)

συμβάλλω v. (βάλλω) aor. συνέβαλον. *to converse, confer; consider, ponder; meet, fall in with; engage, fight someone; help, be of assistance* (mid.). (6)

συμβασιλεύω v. (βασιλεύς) fut. συμβασιλεύσω; aor. συνεβασίλευσα. *to rule (as king) with.* (2)

συμβιβάζω v. (-βαίνω) fut. συμβιβάσω; aor. συνεβίβασα; aor. pass. συνεβιβάσθην. *to unite, hold together, knit together; conclude; demonstrate, prove; instruct, teach, advise.* (7)

συμβουλεύω v. (βούλομαι) aor. συνεβούλευσα. *to advise; consult, plot* (mid.). (4)

συμβούλιον, ου, τό n. (βούλομαι) *plan, purpose,* συμβούλιον λαμβάνω *to form a plan, decide, consult, plot; council.* (8)

σύμβουλος, ου, ὁ n. (βούλομαι) *advisor, counselor.* (1) Rom 11:34

Συμεών, ὁ n. pers. *Symeon, Simeon.* (7)

συμμαθητής, οῦ, ὁ n. (μανθάνω) *fellow-pupil, fellow-disciple.* (1) Jn 11:16

συμμαρτυρέω v. (μάρτυς) *to confirm, support by testimony.* (3)

συμμερίζω v. (μέρος) *to share with* (mid. in NT). (1) 1 Cor 9:13

συμμέτοχος, ον adj. (ἔχω) *sharing with; sharing, sharer* (subst. in NT). (2)

συμμιμητής, οῦ, ὁ n. (μιμέομαι) *fellow-imitator, one who joins in following someone's example.* (1) Phil 3:17

συμμορφίζω v. (μορφή) *to take on the same form as, be conformed to* (pass. in NT). (1) Phil 3:10

σύμμορφος, ον adj. (μορφή) *similar in form* or *appearance.* (2)

συμπαθέω v. (πάσχω) aor. συνεπάθησα. *to sympathize with.* (2)

συμπαθής, ές adj. (πάσχω) *sympathetic, understanding.* (1) 1 Pt 3:8

συμπαραγίνομαι v. (γίνομαι) aor. συμπαρεγενόμην. *to come together.* (1) Lk 23:48

συμπαρακαλέω v. (καλέω) aor. pass. συμπαρεκλήθην. *to encourage together; receive encouragement* or *comfort together* (pass. in NT). (1) Rom 1:12

συμπαραλαμβάνω v. (λαμβάνω) aor. συμπαρέλαβον. *to take along with, take along as adjunct* (prob.). (4)

συμπάρειμι v. (εἰμί) *to be together, present with.* (1) Ac 25:24

συμπάσχω v. (πάσχω) *to suffer with, suffer the same thing as.* (2)

συμπέμπω v. (πέμπω) aor. συνέπεμψα. *to send with* or *at the same time.* (2)

συμπεριλαμβάνω v. (λαμβάνω) aor. συμπεριέλαβον. *to embrace.* (1) Ac 20:10

συμπίνω v. (πίνω) aor. συνέπιον. *to drink with.* (1) Ac 10:41

συμπίπτω v. (πίπτω) aor. συνέπεσον. *to fall in, collapse.* (1) Lk 6:49

συμπληρόω v. (πληρόω) *to be swamped; fulfill, approach, come* (pass. in NT). (3)

συμπνίγω v. (πνίγω) aor. συνέπνιξα. *to choke; crowd around, press upon, crush.* (5)

συμπολίτης, ου, ὁ n. (πόλις) *fellow-citizen, compatriot.* (1) Eph 2:19

συμπορεύομαι v. (πορεύομαι) *to go (along) with; come together, flock.* (4)

συμπόσιον, ου, τό n. (πίνω) *group* (eating together), *party,* συμπόσια συμπόσια *in parties* or *groups.* (2)

συμπρεσβύτερος, ου, ὁ n. (πρεσβύτης) *fellow-elder, fellow-minister.* (1) 1 Pt 5:1

συμφέρω v. (φέρω) aor. συνήνεγκα. *to bring together; it is good, something is useful* or *helpful, it is better* (impers.); *profitable, what is good,* τὸ συμφέρον *profit, advantage* (ptc.). (15)

σύμφημι v. (φημί) *to concur, agree with.* (1) Rom 7:16

σύμφορος, ον adj. (φέρω) *beneficial; benefit, advantage* (subst. in NT). (2)

συμφυλέτης, ου, ὁ n. (φύω) *compatriot, member of the same people group.* (1) 1 Th 2:14

σύμφυτος, ον adj. (φύω) *identified with.* (1) Rom 6:5

συμφύω v. (φύω) aor. pass. συνεφύην. *to grow up with* (pass. in NT). (1) Lk 8:7

συμφωνέω v. (φωνή) fut. συμφωνήσω; aor. συνεφώνησα; aor. pass. συνεφωνήθην. *to fit (in) with, match (with), agree with; be of one mind, agree.* (6)

συμφώνησις, εως, ἡ n. (φωνή) *agreement.* (1) 2 Cor 6:15

συμφωνία, ας, ἡ n. (φωνή) *music; band, orchestra* (poss.); *bagpipe* (poss.). (1) Lk 15:25

σύμφωνος, ον adj. (φωνή) *agreeing; agreement* (subst. in NT). (1) 1 Cor 7:5

συμψηφίζω v. (ψῶχω) aor. συνεψήφισα. *to count up, compute.* (1) Ac 19:19

σύμψυχος, ον adj. (ψύχω) *harmonious.* (1) Phil 2:2

σύν prep. (*) w. dat. *with, beside, at the same time with, just as,* εἰμὶ σύν *to be with, accompany, follow, be a companion* or *disciple of, be among someone's attendants; to the aid of; at the same time as, (together) with, besides, in addition to.* (128)

συνάγω v. (ἄγω) fut. συνάξω; aor. συνήγαγον; pf. pass. συνῆγμαι; aor. pass. συνήχθην. *to gather (in); gather up, gather together, bring* or *call together; invite* or *receive as a guest; advance, move* (intr.); *be gathered* or *brought together, gather, come together* (pass.). (59)

συναγωγή, ῆς, ἡ n. (ἄγω) *synagogue; congregaton of a synagogue; meeting (for worship), gathering.* (56)

συναγωνίζομαι v. (ἀγών) aor. συνηγωνισάμην. *to fight* or *contend along with, help, assist.* (1) Rom 15:30

συναθλέω v. (ἀθλέω) aor. συνήθλησα. *to contend* or *struggle along with, fight at one's side.* (2)

συναθροίζω v. (θροέω) aor. συνήθροισα; pf. pass. συνήθροισμαι. *to gather, bring together; be gathered, meet* (pass.). (2)

συναίρω v. (αἴρω) aor. συνῆρα. *to settle,* συναίρω λόγον *settle accounts.* (3)

συναιχμάλωτος, ου, ὁ n. (ἅλωσις) *fellow-prisoner.* (3)

συνακολουθέω v. (ἀκολουθέω) aor. συνηκολούθησα. *to follow, follow (as a disciple).* (3)

συναλίζω v. (ἅλας) *to eat with* (poss.)*; bring together, assemble* (poss.)*; be with, stay with* (poss. alt. spelling of συναυλίζομαι *spend the night with*). (1) Ac 1:4

συναλλάσσω v. (ἄλλος) *to reconcile.* (1) Ac 7:26

συναναβαίνω v. (-βαίνω) aor. συνανέβην. *to come* or *go up with.* (2)

συνανάκειμαι v. (κεῖμαι) *to eat with,* οἱ συνανακείμενοι *fellow guests* or *banqueters.* (7)

συναναμίγνυμι v. (μίγνυμι) *to mix up together; mingle* or *associate with* (pass. in NT). (3)

συναναπαύομαι v. (παύω) aor. συνανεπαυσάμην. *to rest with.* (1) Rom 15: 32

συναντάω v. (σύν, ἀντί) fut. συναντήσω; aor. συνήντησα. *to meet; happen.* (6)

συναντιλαμβάνομαι v. (λαμβάνω) aor. συναντελαβόμην. *to help.* (2)

συναπάγω v. (ἄγω) aor. pass. συναπήχθην. *to lead away with;* pass. in NT *be led* or *carried away by; accommodate.* (3)

συναποθνῄσκω v. (θνήσκω) aor. συναπέθανον. *to die with.* (3)

συναπόλλυμι v. (ὄλεθρος) aor. συναπώλεσα. *to destroy with; be destroyed* or *perish with* (mid. in NT). (1) Heb 11:31

συναποστέλλω v. (στέλλω) aor. συναπέστειλα. *to send with.* (1) 2 Cor 12:18

συναρμολογέω v. (ἁρμόζω, λέγω) *to join* or *fit together; be joined* or *fit together* (pass. in NT). (2)

συναρπάζω v. (ἁρπάζω) aor. συνήρπασα; pf. συνήρπακα; aor. pass. συνηρπάσθην. *to seize; be caught, torn away* (pass.). (4)

συναυξάνω v. (αὐξάνω) *to grow together* (pass. in NT). (1) Mt 13:30

συνβ- s. συμβ-.

συνγ- s. συγγ-.

σύνδεσμος, ου, ὁ n. (δέω) *fastener, ligament; (uniting) bond; fetter; bundle.* (4)

συνδέω v. (δέω) pf. pass. συνδέδεμαι. *to bind (with); be bound with, be put in chains with,* συνδεδεμένοι *fellow-prisoners* (pass. in NT). (1) Heb 13:3

συνδοξάζω v. (δοκέω) aor. pass. συνεδοξάσθην. *to be glorified with, share in someone's glory* (pass. in NT). (1) Rom 8:17

σύνδουλος, ου, ὁ n. (δοῦλος) *fellow-slave; slave.* (10)

συνδρομή, ῆς, ἡ n. (τρέχω) *running* or *rushing together.* (1) Ac 21:30

συνεγείρω v. (ἐγείρω) aor. συνήγειρα; aor. pass. συνηγέρθην. *to raise with.* (3)

συνέδριον, ου, τό n. (ἑδραῖος) *council, Sanhedrin; council meeting; meeting room.* (22)

συνείδησις, εως, ἡ n. (εἶδος) *conscience, consciousness.* (30)

συνεῖδον s. συνοράω (2 aor.).

συνειδυῖα s. σύνοιδα (2 pf. ptc. fem.).

συνείληφα s. συλλαμβάνω (2 pf.).

σύνειμι v. (εἰμί) *to be with, join.* (2)

σύνειμι v. (-εἶμι) *to come together, gather.* (1) Lk 8:4

συνεισέρχομαι v. (ἔρχομαι) aor. συνεισῆλθον. *to enter* or *go in(to) with.* (2)

συνέκδημος, ου, ὁ n. (δῆμος) *traveling companion.* (2)

συνεκλεκτός, ή, όν adj. (λέγω) *also chosen; one also chosen* (fem. subst. in NT). (1) 1 Pt 5:13

συνεπιμαρτυρέω v. (μάρτυς) *to testify at the same time.* (1) Heb 2:4

συνεπιτίθημι v. (τίθημι) aor. συνεπέθηκα. *to join in an attack* (mid. in NT). (1) Ac 24:9

συνέπομαι v. *to accompany.* (1) Ac 20:4

συνεργέω v. (ἔργον) *to work together with, assist, help.* (5)

συνεργός, όν adj. (ἔργον) *helping; helper, fellow-worker, co-worker* (subst. in NT). (13)

συνέρχομαι v. (ἔρχομαι) aor. συνῆλθον; pf. συνελήλυθα. *to assemble, gather, come together with, meet; travel together with, come with; have sexual relations.* (30)

συνεσθίω v. (ἐσθίω) aor. συνέφαγον. *to eat with.* (5)

σύνεσις, εως, ἡ n. (-ἵημι) *intelligence, acuteness, shrewdness; insight, understanding.* (7)

συνεστώς s. συνίστημι (2 pf. ptc.).

συνετός, ή, όν adj. (-ἵημι) *intelligent, wise, sagacious, with good sense.* (4)

συνευδοκέω v. (δοκέω) *to agree with, approve of, consent to, sympathize with.* (6)

συνευωχέομαι v. (ἔχω) *to feast together.* (2)

συνέφαγον s. συνεσθίω (2 aor.).

συνεφίστημι v. (ἵστημι) aor. συνεπέστην. *to join in an attack.* (1) Ac 16: 22

συνέχω v. (ἔχω) fut. συνέξω; aor. συνέσχον. *to stop, shut; press hard, crowd; guard; seize, attack, distress, torment, overcome; be occupied with, absorbed in* (pass.); *urge on, impel; direct, control* (poss.). (12)

συνζ- s. συζ-.

συνήδομαι v. (ἡδονή) *to delight in, (joyfully) agree with.* (1) Rom 7:22

συνήθεια, ας, ἡ n. (ἔθος) *being or becoming accustomed, custom, habit, usage.* (3)

συνῆκα s. συνίημι (aor.).

συνῆλθον s. συνέρχομαι (2 aor.).

συνηλικιώτης, ου, ὁ n. (ἡλικία) *contemporary person.* (1) Gal 1:14

συνηρπάκειν s. συναρπάζω (plpf.).

συνῆσαν s. σύνειμι (impf. 3 pl.).

συνήσω, συνῆτε s. συνίημι (fut., 2 aor. subj. 2 pl.).

συνήχθην s. συνάγω (aor. pass.).

συνθάπτω v. (θάπτω) aor. pass. συνετάφην. *to bury (together) with; be buried with* (pass. in NT). (2)

συνθλάω v. aor. pass. συνεθλάσθην. *to crush, dash to pieces; be broken to pieces* (pass. in NT). (2)

συνθλίβω v. (θλίβω) *to press together, press upon.* (2)

συνθρύπτω v. (τρυφή) *to break (in pieces).* (1) Ac 21:13

συνιδών s. συνοράω (2 aor. ptc.).

συνίημι and συνίω v. (-ἵημι) fut. συνήσω; aor. συνῆκα. *to understand, comprehend, gain an insight.* (26)

συνίστημι and συνιστάνω v. (ἵστημι) aor. συνέστησα; pf. συνέστηκα. trans. (act., mid., pass.) *present, introduce* or *recommend, commend; demonstrate, show, bring out;* intr. (pres. mid. and pf. act.) *stand with* or *by; continue, endure, exist, hold together.* (16)

συνίων s. συνίημι (pres. ptc.).

συνιών s. σύνειμι (pres. ptc.).

συνιῶσιν s. συνίημι (pres. subj. 3 pl.).

συνκ- s. συγκ-.

συνλ- s. συλλ-.

συνμ- s. συμμ-.

συνοδεύω v. (ὁδός) *to travel together with.* (1) Ac 9:7

συνοδία, ας, ἡ n. (ὁδός) *caravan.* (1) Lk 2:44

σύνοιδα v. (οἶδα) pf. σύνοιδα. pf. used as pres. *to be privy to; know, be conscious of.* (2)

συνοικέω v. (οἶκος) *to live with.* (1) 1 Pt 3:7

συνοικοδομέω v. (οἶκος, δῶμα) *to build together; be built up together* (pass. in NT). (1) Eph 2:22

συνομιλέω v. (ὅμοιος, -εἴλω) *to talk* or *converse with.* (1) Ac 10:27

συνομορέω v. (ὅμοιος, ὁρίζω) *to border on, be next door to.* (1) Ac 18:7

συνοράω v. (ὁράω) aor. συνεῖδον. *to become aware of, perceive; comprehend, realize.* (2)

συνοχή, ῆς, ἡ n. (ἔχω) *distress, dismay, anguish.* (2)

συνπ- s. συμπ-.

συνρ- s. συρρ-.

συνσ- s. συσσ-.

συνσπ- s. συσπ-.

συνστ- s. συστ-.

συντάσσω v. (τάσσω) aor. συνέταξα. *to order, direct, prescribe.* (3)

συνταφείς s. συνθάπτω (2 aor. pass. ptc.).

συντέλεια, ας, ἡ n. (τέλος) *completion, close, end.* (6)

συντελέω v. (τέλος) fut. συντελέσω; aor. συνετέλεσα; aor. pass. συνετελέσθην. *to bring to an end, complete, finish, close; carry out, fulfill, accomplish, establish; come to an end, be over, fulfill, accomplish.* (6)

συντέμνω v. (τομός) *to cut short, shorten, limit.* (1) Rom 9:28

συντηρέω v. (τηρέω) *to protect, defend, save, preserve; hold, treasure up.* (3)

συντίθημι v. (τίθημι) aor. συνέθηκα; pf. pass. συντέθειμαι. *to put with*; mid. in NT *agree; decide.* (3)

συντόμως adv. (τομός) *promptly, readily; briefly, concisely.* (2)

συντρέχω v. (τρέχω) aor. συνέδραμον. *to run together; go with, dash with.* (3)

συντρίβω v. (τρίβος) fut. συντρίψω; aor. συνέτριψα; pf. pass. συντέτριμμαι; aor. pass. συνετρίβην. *to shatter, smash, crush; mistreat* or *beat severely; annihilate; be bent, be broken* (pass.). (7)

σύντριμμα, ατος, τό n. (τρίβος) *destruction, ruin.* (1) Rom 3:16

σύντροφος, ον adj. (τρέφω) *raised with; foster-brother, companion, intimate friend* (subst. in NT). (1) Ac 13:1

συντυγχάνω v. (τυγχάνω) aor. συνέτυχον. *to meet, join.* (1) Lk 8:19

Συντύχη, ης, ἡ n. pers. *Syntyche.* (1) Phil 4:2

συνυποκρίνομαι v. (κρίνω) aor. pass. συνυπεκρίθην. *to join in pretense* or *hypocrisy.* (1) Gal 2:13

συνυπουργέω v. (ἔργον) *to join in helping, co-operate with.* (1) 2 Cor 1:11

συνφ- s. συμφ-.

συνχ- s. συγκ-.

συνψ- s. συμψ-.

συνωδίνω v. (ὠδίν) *to suffer agony together.* (1) Rom 8:22

συνωμοσία, ας, ἡ n. (ὀμνύω) *conspiracy, plot.* (1) Ac 23:13

Συράκουσαι, ῶν, αἱ n. pla. *Syracuse.* (1) Ac 28:12

Συρία, ας, ἡ n. pla. *Syria.* (8)

Σύρος, ου, ὁ n. pla. *a Syrian.* (1) Lk 4:27

Συροφοινίκισσα, ης, ἡ n. pla. *a Syrophoenician woman.* (1) Mk 7:26

Σύρτις, εως, ἡ n. pla. *the Syrtis.* (1) Ac 27:17

σύρω v. (*) *to drag, pull, draw, drag away, sweep away.* (5)

συσπαράσσω v. (σπάω) aor. συνεσπάραξα. *to pull about, convulse.* (2)

σύσσημον, ου, τό n. (σημεῖον) *signal, sign.* (1) Mk 14:44

σύσσωμος, ον adj. (σῶμα) *belonging to the same body.* (1) Eph 3:6

συστατικός, ή, όν adj. (ἴστημι) *introducing, commendatory,* συστατικὴ ἐπιστολή *letter of recommendation.* (1) 2 Cor 3:1

συσταυρόω v. (σταυρόω) pf. pass. συνεσταύρωμαι; aor. pass. συνεσταυρώθην. *to crucify with; be crucified with, be jointly crucified* (pass. in NT). (5)

συστέλλω v. (στέλλω) aor. συνέστειλα; pf. pass. συνέσταλμαι. *to limit, shorten; cover, wrap up; pack, fold up, snatch up* (poss.); *take away, remove* (poss.). (2)

συστενάζω v. (στενός) *to lament, groan (together).* (1) Rom 8:22

συστοιχέω v. (στοιχέω) *to correspond (to).* (1) Gal 4:25

συστρατιώτης, ου, ὁ n. (στρατιά) *fellow-soldier, comrade in arms* (fig. in NT). (2)

συστρέφω v. (στρέφω) aor. συνέστρεψα. *to gather up, bring together; be gathered, gather, come together.* (2)

συστροφή, ῆς, ἡ n. (στρέφω) *disorderly* or *seditious gathering, commotion; plot, conspiracy.* (2)

συσχηματίζω v. (ἔχω) *to form after; be formed like, be conformed to, be guided by* (pass. in NT). (2)

Συχάρ, ἡ n. pla. *Sychar.* (1) Jn 4:5

Συχέμ, ἡ n. pla. *Shechem.* (2)

σφαγή, ῆς, ἡ n. (σφάζω) *slaughter,* πρόβατα σφαγῆς *sheep to be slaughtered.* (3)

σφάγιον, ου, τό n. (σφάζω) *victim* (sacrificial), *offering.* (1) Ac 7:42

σφάζω v. (*) fut. σφάξω; aor. ἔσφαξα; pf. pass. ἔσφαγμαι; aor. pass. ἐσφάγην. *to slaughter, butcher, murder,* ἐσφαγμένη εἰς θάνατον *mortally wounded.* (10)

σφόδρα adv. (*) *extremely, greatly, very* (*much*). (11)

σφοδρῶς adv. (σφόδρα) *very much, greatly, violently.* (1) Ac 27:18

σφραγίζω v. (σφραγίς) aor. ἐσφράγισα; pf. pass. ἐσφράγισμαι; aor. pass. ἐσφραγίσθην. *to seal; seal up; mark* (with a seal); *attest, certify, acknowledge; seal* (for delivery). (15)

σφραγίς, ῖδος, ἡ n. (*) *signet; seal; mark, inscription; attestation, confirmation, certification.* (16)

σφυδρόν, οῦ, τό n. *ankle.* (1) Ac 3:7

σχεδόν adv. (ἔχω) *nearly, almost.* (3)

σχῆμα, ατος, τό n. (ἔχω) *outward appearance, form, shape; way of life, present form.* (2)

σχίζω v. (*) fut. σχίσω; aor. ἔσχισα; aor. pass. ἐσχίσθην. *to split, divide, separate, tear* (*apart*), *tear off;* pass. *be divided, be split, be torn; become divided* or *disunited.* (11)

σχίσμα, ατος, τό n. (σχίζω) *tear, crack; division, dissension, schism.* (8)

σχοινίον, ου, τό n. *rope, cord.* (2)

σχολάζω v. (σχολή) aor. ἐσχόλασα. *to busy oneself with, devote oneself to, give one's time to; be unoccupied, stand empty.* (2)

σχολή, ῆς, ἡ n. (*) *lecture hall.* (1) Ac 19:9

σῴζω v. (*) fut. σώσω; aor. ἔσωσα; pf. σέσωκα; pf. pass. σέσωσμαι, σέσωμαι; aor. pass. ἐσώθην. *to save, keep from harm, preserve, rescue, save* (*from death*), *bring out safely, save* or *free* (*from disease*); *save* or *preserve* (*from eternal death*), *bring salvation, bring to salvation;* pass. *be restored to health, get well; be saved, attain salvation, save oneself,* οἱ σῳζόμενοι *those who are to be* or *are being saved.* (106)

σῶμα, ατος, τό n. (*) *body, dead body, corpse, living body,* εἰμὶ ἐν σώματι *subject to mortal ills,* διὰ τοῦ σώματος *during the time of one's mortal life; slaves* (pl.); *body* (of a plant or seed); *reality, thing itself; body* (fig. of the Christian community). (142)

σωματικός, ή, όν adj. (σῶμα) *bodily, corporeal; body-related.* (2)

σωματικῶς adv. (σῶμα) *bodily, corporeally, in reality.* (1) Col 2:9

Σώπατρος, ου, ὁ n. pers. *Sopater.* (1) Ac 20:4

σωρεύω v. (*) fut. σωρεύσω; pf. pass. σεσώρευμαι. *to heap* or *pile up; load up with, overwhelm.* (2)

Σωσθένης, ους, ὁ n. pers. *Sosthenes.* (2)

Σωσίπατρος, ου, ὁ n. pers. *Sosipater.* (1) Rom 16:21

σωτήρ, ῆρος, ὁ n. (σῴζω) *Savior, deliverer, preserver.* (24)

σωτηρία, ας, ἡ n. (σῴζω) *deliverance, preservation; salvation.* (46)

σωτήριος, ον adj. (σῴζω) *saving, delivering, preserving, bringing salvation; means of deliverance, deliverance, salvation* (neut. subst.). (5)

σωφρονέω v. (φρήν) aor. ἐσωφρόνησα. *to be of sound mind; be reasonable, sensible, serious.* (6)

σωφρονίζω v. (φρήν) *to encourage, advise, urge.* (1) Tit 2:4

σωφρονισμός, οῦ, ὁ n. (φρήν) *moderation, self-discipline, prudence; advice, improvement* (poss.). (1) 2 Ti 1:7

σωφρόνως adv. (φρήν) *soberly, moderately, showing self-control.* (1) Tit 2:12

σωφροσύνη, ης, ἡ n. (φρήν) *reasonableness, rationality; good judgment, moderation, self-control, decency, chastity.* (3)

σώφρων, ον adj. (φρήν) *prudent, thoughtful, self-controlled, chaste, decent, modest.* (4)

ταβέρναι, ῶν, αἱ s. Τρεῖς Ταβέρναι

Ταβιθά, ἡ n. pers. *Tabitha*. (2)

τάγμα, ατος, τό n. (τάσσω) *class, group.* (1) 1 Cor 15:23

τακτός, ή, όν adj. (τάσσω) *fixed, appointed.* (1) Ac 12:21

ταλαιπωρέω v. (ταλαίπωρος) aor. ἐταλαιπώρησα. *to endure sorrow* or *distress, feel miserable, lament.* (1) Jas 4:9

ταλαιπωρία, ας, ἡ n. (ταλαίπωρος) *wretchedness, distress, trouble, misery.* (2)

ταλαίπωρος, ον adj. (*) *miserable, wretched, distressed.* (2)

ταλαντιαῖος, α, ον adj. (τάλαντον) *weighing a talent* (of the weight of a hailstone). (1) Rev 16:21

τάλαντον, ου, τό n. (*) *talent* (Greek monetary unit, 6,000 drachmas). (14)

ταλιθα Ara. *girl, little girl.* (1) Mk 5:41

ταμεῖον, ου, τό n. (τομός) *storeroom; inner room.* (4)

τάξις, εως, ἡ n. (τάσσω) *fixed succession* or *order; order, proper procedure*, κατὰ τάξιν *in order, in an orderly manner; arrangement, nature, manner, condition, outward aspect*, κατὰ τὴν τάξιν Μελχισέδεκ *just like Melchizedek.* (9)

ταπεινός, ή, όν adj. (*) *lowly, undistinguished, of no account, downcast; pliant, subservient, abject; humble.* (8)

ταπεινοφροσύνη, ης, ἡ n. (ταπεινός, φρήν) *humility, modesty.* (7)

ταπεινόφρων, ον adj. (ταπεινός, φρήν) *humble.* (1) 1 Pt 3:8

ταπεινόω v. (ταπεινός) fut. ταπεινώσω; aor. ἐταπείνωσα; aor. pass. ἐταπεινώθην. *to lower, level; humble, humiliate, abuse, degrade; make humble; constrain, mortify*, οἶδα ταπεινοῦσθαι *I know how to do with little.* (14)

ταπείνωσις, εως, ἡ n. (ταπεινός) *humiliation, downfall; lowliness, humility, humble station*, τὸ σῶμα τῆς ταπεινώσεως *the humble body.* (4)

ταράσσω v. (*) aor. ἐτάραξα; pf. pass. τετάραγμαι; aor. pass. ἐταράχθην. *to shake together, stir up, move; disturb, unsettle, throw into confusion, trouble, agitate*; pass. *be moved, stirred; be troubled, frightened, terrified, intimidated.* (17)

ταραχή, ῆς, ἡ n. *stirring up; disturbance, tumult, rebellion.* (v.l.)

τάραχος, ου, ὁ n. (ταράσσω) *consternation; disturbance, commotion.* (2)

Ταρσεύς, έως, ὁ n. pla. *person from Tarsus, a Tarsian.* (2)

Ταρσός, οῦ, ἡ n. pla. *Tarsus.* (3)

ταρταρόω v. aor. ἐταρτάρωσα. *to hold captive in Tartarus* (the Netherworld). (1) 2 Pt 2:4

τάσσω v. (*) aor. ἔταξα; pf. pass. τέταγμαι. *to arrange, put in place, put over* or *in charge of, devote to; order, fix, determine, appoint; belong to* (pass.)*; set* (mid. as act.). (8)

ταῦρος, ου, ὁ n. *bull, ox.* (4)

ταφή ῆς, ἡ n. (θάπτω) *burial-place, burial ground.* (1) Mt 27:7

τάφος, ου, ὁ n. (θάπτω) *grave, tomb; tomb* (fig.). (7)

τάχα adv. (ταχύς) *perhaps, possibly, probably.* (2)

ταχέως adv. (ταχύς) pos. *quickly, at once, without delay, too quickly, too easily, hastily; soon*; comp. (τάχιον) *more quickly, faster, quickly, soon,* τέξομαι

without delay; superl. (τάχιστα) ὡς
τάχιστα *as soon as possible.* (15)

ταχινός, ή, όν adj. (ταχύς) *coming soon,
imminent, swift.* (2)

τάχιον, τάχιστα s. ταχέως (comp., superl.).

τάχος, ους, τό n. (ταχύς) *speed, quickness, swiftness, haste,* ἐν τάχει *quickly,
at once, without delay;* ἐν τάχει *soon,
in a short time, shortly.* (8)

ταχύς, εῖα, ύ adj. (*) *quick, swift,
speedy;* neut. sg. as adv. *without delay,
quickly, at once; in a short time, soon
(afterward).* (13)

τέ part. (*) encl., postpos. *and likewise,
and so, so; and,* τὲ... τέ *as... so, not
only... but also,* τὲ καί *and; even.*
(215)

τέθεικα, τέθειμαι, τεθῆναι s. τίθημι
(pf., pf. pass., aor. pass. inf.).

τεθλιμμένος s. θλίβω (pf. pass. ptc.).

τεθνάναι, τέθνηκα s. θνῄσκω (pf. inf.,
pf.).

τέθραμμαι s. τρέφω (pf. pass.).

τεθῶ s. τίθημι (aor. pass. subj.).

τεῖχος, ους, τό n. (*) *wall.* (9)

τεκεῖν s. τίκτω (2 aor. inf.).

τεκμήριον, ου, τό n. *proof.* (1) Ac 1:3

τεκνίον, ου, τό n. (τίκτω) *(little) child*
(voc. pl. in NT). (8)

τεκνογονέω v. (τίκτω, γίνομαι) *to bear
children.* (1) 1 Ti 5:14

τεκνογονία, ας, ἡ n. (τίκτω, γίνομαι)
bearing of children. (1) 1 Ti 2:15

τέκνον, ου, τό n. (τίκτω) *child, son;
child* (as a term of endearment)*; child*
(as one who has the characteristics
of another); pl. *descendants, posterity;
children* (as inhabitants of a city)*; children* (as people with specific characteristics). (99)

τεκνοτροφέω v. (τίκτω, τρέφω) aor.
ἐτεκνοτρόφησα. *to bring up children.*
(1) 1 Ti 5:10

τέκτων, ονος, ὁ n. (τίκτω) *builder, carpenter.* (2)

τέλειος, α, ον adj. (τέλος) *perfect; full-
grown, mature, adult, grown-up; initi-*

ated; perfect (in mor. sense), *fully developed;* subst. *what is perfect; adult.*
(19)

τελειότης, ητος, ἡ n. (τέλος) *perfection, completeness, maturity.* (2)

τελειόω v. (τέλος) aor. ἐτελείωσα; pf.
τετελείωκα; pf. pass. τετελείωμαι;
aor. pass. ἐτελειώθην. *to complete,
bring to an end, finish, accomplish,
spend all; bring to its goal* or *accomplishment, make perfect; consecrate,
initiate;* pass. *receive final fulfillment,
reach one's goal; be fulfilled, become
perfect, be perfected; be consecrated,
become an initiate.* (23)

τελείως adv. (τέλος) *fully, perfectly,
completely, altogether.* (1) 1 Pt 1:13

τελείωσις, εως, ἡ n. (τέλος) *perfection;
fulfillment.* (2)

τελειωτής, οῦ, ὁ n. (τέλος) *perfecter.*
(1) Heb 12:2

τελεσφορέω v. (τέλος, φέρω) *to bear
fruit to maturity.* (1) Lk 8:14

τελευτάω v. (τέλος) aor. ἐτελεύτησα;
pf. τετελεύτηκα. *to die,* θανάτῳ
τελευτάτω *let someone surely die.*
(11)

τελευτή, ῆς, ἡ n. (τέλος) *end, death.* (1)
Mt 2:15

τελέω v. (τέλος) aor. ἐτέλεσα; pf.
τετέλεκα; pf. pass. τετέλεσμαι; aor.
pass. ἐτελέσθην. *to bring to an
end, finish, complete; carry out, accomplish, perform, fulfill, keep; pay.*
(28)

τέλος, ους, τό n. (*) *end, termination,
cessation; close, conclusion, end* (as
cosmic act), (τὸ) τέλος *finally,* ἄχρι
(or ἕως, μέχρι) τέλους *to the end,*
εἰς τέλος *in the end, finally, forever,
decisively, fully; goal, outcome, aim,
destiny; rest, remainder; (indirect) tax,
toll-tax, customs duties.* (40)

τελώνης, ου, ὁ n. (τέλος, ὠνέομαι) *tax-
collector, revenue officer.* (21)

τελώνιον, ου, τό n. (τέλος, ὠνέομαι)
revenue or *tax office.* (3)

τέξομαι s. τίκτω (fut. mid.).

τέρας, ατος, τό n. *prodigy, portent, omen, wonder* (pl. w. σημεῖα in NT). (16)

Τέρτιος, ου, ὁ n. pers. *Tertius.* (1) Rom 16:22

Τέρτυλλος, ου, ὁ n. pers. *Tertullus.* (2)

τέσσαρες, α adj. (*) *four.* (41)

τεσσαρεσκαιδέκατος, η, ον adj. (τέσσαρες, καί, δέκα) *fourteenth.* (2)

τεσσεράκοντα adj. (τέσσαρες) *forty.* (22)

τεσσερακονταετής, ές adj. (τέσσαρες, ἔτος) *forty years.* (2)

τεταρταῖος, α, ον adj. (τέσσαρες) *happening on the fourth day,* τεταρταῖός ἐστιν *he has been (dead) four days.* (1) Jn 11:39

τέταρτος, η, ον adj. (τέσσαρες) *fourth; fourth part, quarter* (neut. subst.). (10)

τετρααρχέω v. (τέσσαρες, ἄρχω) *to be tetrarch.* (3)

τετραάρχης, ου, ὁ n. (τέσσαρες, ἄρχω) *tetrarch.* (4)

τετράγωνος, ον adj. (τέσσαρες, γωνία) *(four-)square, shaped like a cube* (poss.). (1) Rev 21:16

τετράδιον, ου, τό n. (τέσσαρες) *detachment* or *squad of four soldiers.* (1) Ac 12:4

τετρακισχίλιοι, αι, α adj. (τέσσαρες, χίλιοι) *four thousand.* (5)

τετρακόσιοι, αι, α adj. (τέσσαρες) *four hundred.* (4)

τετράμηνος, ον adj. (τέσσαρες, μήν) *lasting four months; period of four months, third of a year* (subst. in NT). (1) Jn 4:35

τετραπλοῦς, ῆ, οῦν adj. (τέσσαρες) *four times (as much), fourfold.* (1) Lk 19:8

τετράπους, ουν adj. (τέσσαρες, πούς) *four-footed; four-footed animal, quadruped* (subst. in NT). (3)

τέτυχα s. τυγχάνω (2 pf.).

τεφρόω v. (τύφω) aor. ἐτέφρωσα. *to cover with* or *reduce to ashes.* (1) 2 Pt 2:6

τέχνη, ης, ἡ n. (τίκτω) *skill, trade.* (3)

τεχνίτης, ου, ὁ n. (τίκτω) *craftsperson, artisan, designer, architect.* (4)

τήκω v. *to melt; melt* (intr.), *dissolve* (pass. in NT). (1) 2 Pt 3:12

τηλαυγῶς adv. (αὐγή) *(very) plainly* or *clearly.* (1) Mk 8:25

τηλικοῦτος, αὕτη, οῦτο pron. (ἡλικία, οὗτος) demonstr. correl. *so great, so large; so important* or *mighty.* (4)

τηρέω v. (*) fut. τηρήσω; aor. ἐτήρησα; pf. τετήρηκα; pf. pass. τετήρημαι; aor. pass. ἐτηρήθην. *to keep watch over, guard* οἱ τηροῦντες *the guards; keep, hold, reserve, preserve, support* (poss.), *keep from harm; keep, observe, fulfill, pay attention to, take to heart.* (70)

τήρησις, εως, ἡ n. (τηρέω) *prison; keeping, observance.* (3)

Τιβεριάς, άδος, ἡ n. pla. *Tiberias.* (3)

Τιβέριος, ου, ὁ n. pers. *Tiberius.* (1) Lk 3:1

τίθημι v. (*) fut. θήσω; aor. ἔθηκα; pf. τέθεικα; pf. pass. τέθειμαι; aor. pass. ἐτέθην. *to lay (away), put (away), set up, place, explain, take off, give up, remove, lay down, show deference to, bend* (of knees), *place before, serve, have* or *keep (in mind), effect, arrange for, provide* or *set up (an example); put aside, store up, deposit; appoint, assign; make, consign;* mid. *have (in mind), effect, arrange for, put (in custody); appoint to* or *for; fix, establish, set, arrange; make, consign* (w. double acc.). (100)

τίκτω v. (*) fut. τέξομαι; aor. ἔτεκον; aor. pass. ἐτέχθην. *to give birth (to), bear; bring forth, produce.* (18)

τίλλω v. *to pluck, pick.* (3)

Τιμαῖος, ου, ὁ n. pers. *Timaeus.* (1) Mk 10:46

τιμάω v. (τιμή) fut. τιμήσω; aor. ἐτίμησα; pf. pass. τετίμημαι. *to estimate, value, set a price on; honor, revere.* (21)

τιμή, ῆς, ἡ n. (*) *(selling) price, value, money; honor, reverence, respect,* *showing of honor* or *respect, respectability, place of honor; honorarium, compensation; privilege.* (41)

τίμιος, α, ον adj. (τιμή) *costly, precious, of great worth* or *value, held in honor; held in high regard, respected.* (13)

τιμιότης, ητος, ἡ n. (τιμή) *richness, prosperity, abundance.* (1) Rev 18:19

Τιμόθεος, ου, ὁ n. pers. *Timothy.* (24)

Τίμων, ωνος, ὁ n. pers. *Timon.* (1) Ac 6:5

τιμωρέω v. (τιμή, αἴρω) aor. pass. ἐτιμωρήθην. *to punish, have someone punished.* (2)

τιμωρία, ας, ἡ n. (τιμή, αἴρω) *punishment.* (1) Heb 10:29

τίνω v. (*) fut. τίσω. *to pay, undergo a penalty.* (1) 2 Th 1:9

τίς, τί pron. (*) interrog. *who? which (one)? what? what sort of person* or *thing? which (of two)?* διὰ τί *why? for what reason?* εἰς τί *why? for what purpose?* ἐν τίνι *with what? through whom?* πρὸς τί *why?* τί γάρ *what does it matter?* τί ὅτι *what has happened that? why?* τίς τί *what each; what (sort of)* (adj.)*; why?* τί καί *why indeed?* (adv.)*; how!* (excl.). (556)

τὶς, τὶ pron. (*) encl., indef. *someone, anyone, somebody, a certain person,* ἐάν (or εἴ) τις *whoever, something, anything,* εἶναί τι *be* or *amount to something; some, any, a certain* (adj.)*; person of importance, somebody.* (525)

Τίτιος, ου, ὁ n. pers. *Titius.* (1) Ac 18:7

τίτλος, ου, ὁ n. Lat. *inscription, notice.* (2)

Τίτος, ου, ὁ n. pers. *Titus.* (13)

τοιγαροῦν part. (-τοί, γάρ, οὖν) somet. postpos., infer. *then, therefore, for that very reason.* (2)

τοίνυν part. (-τοί, νῦν) somet. postpos., infer. *hence, so, well (then), indeed.* (3)

τοιόσδε, άδε, όνδε adj. (ὁ) *such as this, of this kind.* (1) 2 Pt 1:17

τοιοῦτος, αύτη, οῦτον adj. (ὁ, οὗτος) *of such a kind, such as this, like such,*

such, like this; such a person or *thing* (subst.). (57)

τοίχος, ου, ὁ n. (τεῖχος) *wall.* (1) Ac 23:3

τόκος, ου, ὁ n. (τίκτω) *interest* (on money loaned). (2)

τολμάω v. (*) fut. τολμήσω; aor. ἐτόλμησα. *to dare, bring oneself, have the courage, be brave enough, venture, presume, be courageous, show boldness.* (16)

τολμηρότερον adv. (τολμάω) *rather boldly.* (1) Rom 15:15

τολμηροτέρως adv. *rather boldly.* (v.l.)

τολμητής, οῦ, ὁ n. (τολμάω) *bold, audacious person.* (1) 2 Pt 2:10

τομός, ή, όν adj. (*) *cutting, sharp,* τομώτερος *sharper.* (1) Heb 4:12

τόξον, ου, τό n. *bow* (of an archer). (1) Rev 6:2

τοπάζιον, ου, τό n. *topaz.* (1) Rev 21:20

τόπος, ου, ὁ n. (*) *place, space, building, location, (definite) place, (particular) spot, scene, place* (to live), *room, place* (as customary location), *place* (of destiny); *place* (in a book), *passage; position, office; possibility, opportunity, chance; regions, districts,* κατὰ τόπους *in various regions* (pl.). (94)

τοσοῦτος, αύτη, οῦτον adj. (οὗτος) correl. *so many* (pl.); *so much, so great, so long; so great* or *strong, to such extent, as strong; so much and no more; so much, as much.* (20)

τότε adv. (ὅς, τέ) *at that time, then* (past or fut.), ἀπὸ τότε *from that time on; then, thereupon, thereafter.* (160)

τοὐναντίον adv. (ἐν, ἀντί) *on the other hand* (= τὸ ἐναντίον). (3)

τοὔνομα n. (ὄνομα) *named, by name* (= τὸ ὄνομα). (1) Mt 27:57

τοῦτ' = τοῦτο before ἐστί (v).

τοῦτο s. οὗτος (neut.).

τράγος, ου, ὁ n. (τρώγω) *he-goat.* (4)

τράπεζα, ης, ἡ n. (τέσσαρες, πεζεύω) *table, bank; meal, food.* (15)

τραπεζίτης, ου, ὁ n. (τέσσαρες,

πεζεύω) *money changer, banker.* (1) Mt 25:27

τραῦμα, ατος, τό n. (*) *wound.* (1) Lk 10:34

τραυματίζω v. (τραῦμα) aor. ἐτραυμάτισα; pf. pass. τετραυμάτισμαι. *to wound.* (2)

τραχηλίζω v. (τράχηλος) pf. pass. τετραχήλισμαι. *to lay bare; be laid bare* (pass. in NT). (1) Heb 4:13

τράχηλος, ου, ὁ n. (*) *neck, throat,* ἐπιπίπτω ἐπὶ τὸν τράχηλόν τινος *to embrace someone.* (7)

τραχύς, εῖα, ύ adj. *rough, uneven.* (2)

Τραχωνῖτις, ιδος, ἡ n. pla. *Trachonitis.* (1) Lk 3:1

τρεῖς, τρία adj. (*) *three.* (68)

Τρεῖς Ταβέρναι n. pla. *Three Taverns.* (1) Ac 28:15

τρέμω v. (*) *to tremble, quiver; tremble (at), be in awe (of), be afraid.* (3)

τρέφω v. (*) aor. ἔθρεψα; pf. pass. τέθραμμαι. *to feed, nourish, nurse, support; rear, bring up, train.* (9)

τρέχω v. (*) aor. ἔδραμον. *to run, rush, advance; exert oneself, strive to advance, make progress; progress, speed on.* (20)

τρῆμα, ατος, τό n. *opening, hole, eye* (of a needle). (1) Lk 18:25

τριάκοντα adj. (τρεῖς) *thirty.* (11)

τριακόσιοι, αι, α adj. (τρεῖς) *three hundred.* (2)

τρίβολος, ου, ὁ n. (τρεῖς, βάλλω) *thistle.* (2)

τρίβος, ου, ἡ n. (*) *path.* (3)

τριετία, ας, ἡ n. (τρεῖς, ἔτος) *(period of) three years.* (1) Ac 20:31

τρίζω v. *to gnash, grind* (of teeth). (1) Mk 9:18

τρίμηνος, ον adj. (τρεῖς, μήν) *of three months; (period of) three months* (subst. in NT). (1) Heb 11:23

τρίς adv. (τρεῖς) *three times,* ἐπὶ τρίς *a third time* (prob.). (12)

τρίστεγον, ου, τό n. (τρεῖς, στέγω) *third story* (of a building). (1) Ac 20:9

τρισχίλιοι, αι, α adj. (τρεῖς, χίλιοι) *three thousand.* (1) Ac 2:41

τρίτος, η, ον adj. (τρεῖς) *third; third time, for the third time, in the third place* (neut. as adv.); *third part, a third, one-third* (neut. subst.). (56)

τρίχινος, η, ον adj. (θρίξ) *made of hair.* (1) Rev 6:12

τρόμος, ου, ὁ n. (τρέμω) *trembling, quivering.* (5)

τροπή, ῆς, ἡ n. (*) *turn, turning, change.* (1) Jas 1:17

τρόπος, ου, ὁ n. (τροπή) *manner, way, kind, guise,* κατὰ πάντα τρόπον *in every way* or *respect,* κατὰ μηδένα τρόπον *by no means,* καθ᾽ ὃν τρόπον *in the same way as,* ὃν τρόπον *(just) as; ways, customs, kind of life.* (13)

τροποφορέω v. (τροπή, φέρω) aor. ἐτροποφόρησα. *to bear* or *put up with someone's manner* or *mood.* (1) Ac 13:18

τροφή, ῆς, ἡ n. (τρέφω) *nourishment, food.* (16)

Τρόφιμος, ου, ὁ n. pers. *Trophimus.* (3)

τροφός, οῦ, ἡ n. (τρέφω) *nurse, mother* (poss.). (1) 1 Th 2:7

τροφοφορέω v. *to care for.* (v.l.)

τροχιά, ᾶς, ἡ n. (τρέχω) *wheel-track, course, way, path.* (1) Heb 12:13

τροχός, οῦ, ὁ n. (τρέχω) *wheel, course* (poss.). (1) Jas 3:6

τρύβλιον, ου, τό n. *bowl, dish.* (2)

τρυγάω v. aor. ἐτρύγησα. *to harvest (grapes), gather.* (3)

τρυγών, όνος, ἡ n. *small pigeon, turtledove.* (1) Lk 2:24

τρυμαλιά, ᾶς, ἡ n. (*) *hole, eye* (of a needle). (1) Mk 10:25

τρύπημα, ατος, τό n. (τρυμαλιά) *hole, eye* (of a needle). (1) Mt 19:24

Τρύφαινα, ης, ἡ n. pers. *Tryphaena.* (1) Rom 16:12

τρυφάω v. (τρυφή) aor. ἐτρύφησα. *to live for pleasure, revel, carouse.* (1) Jas 5:5

τρυφή, ῆς, ἡ n. (*) *indulgence, reveling; luxury, splendor.* (2)

Τρυφῶσα, ης, ἡ n. pers. *Tryphosa*. (1) Rom 16:12

Τρῳάς, άδος, ἡ n. pla. *Troas*. (6)

Τρωγύλλιον, ου, τό n. pla. *Trogyllium*. (v.l.)

τρώγω v. (*) *to eat* (audibly). (6)

τυγχάνω v. (*) aor. ἔτυχον; pf. τέτυχα. *to meet, attain, gain, find, experience; happen, turn out*, εἰ τύχοι *if it should turn out that way, perhaps*, τυχόν *if possible, perhaps*, δυνάμεις οὐ τὰς τυχούσας *extraordinary miracles*. (12)

τυμπανίζω v. (τύπος) aor. pass. ἐτυμπανίσθην. *to torment, torture; be tortured* (pass. in NT). (1) Heb 11:35

τυπικῶς adv. (τύπος) *as an example* or *warning*. (1) 1 Cor 10:11

τύπος, ου, ὁ n. (*) *mark, trace; image, statue; form, figure, pattern, form (of expression)*, ἔχουσαν τὸν τύπον τοῦτον *somewhat as follows, after this manner, to this effect; text, content; type, model, design, example*. (15)

τύπτω v. (τύπος) *to strike, beat, wound, assault*. (13)

Τύραννος, ου, ὁ n. pers. *Tyrannus*. (1) Ac 19:9

τυρβάζω v. *to trouble oneself, be troubled, be agitated* (pass.). (v.l.)

Τύριος, ου, ὁ n. pla. *a Tyrian*. (1) Ac 12:20

Τύρος, ου, ἡ n. pla. *Tyre*. (11)

τυφλός, ή, όν adj. (*) *blind; blind* (fig.), *incapable of comprehending; subst. blind person* (lit. and fig.). (50)

τυφλόω v. (τυφλός) aor. ἐτύφλωσα; pf. τετύφλωκα. *to blind* (fig. in NT). (3)

τυφόω v. (τύφω) pf. pass. τετύφωμαι; aor. pass. ἐτυφώθην. *to delude;* pass. in NT *be puffed up, conceited; be blinded, become foolish* (poss.)*; be mentally ill* (poss.). (3)

τύφω v. (*) *to give off smoke; smoke, smolder, glimmer* (pass. in NT). (1) Mt 12:20

τυφωνικός, ή, όν adj. *like a whirlwind*, ἄνεμος τυφωνικός *typhoon, hurricane*. (1) Ac 27:14

τυχεῖν, τύχοι s. τυγκάνω (2 aor. inf., 2 aor. opt. 3 sg.).

Τυχικός, οῦ, ὁ n. pers. *Tychicus*. (5)

τυχόν s. τυγχάνω (2 aor. ptc. neut.).

ὑακίνθινος, η, ον adj. (ὑάκινθος)
hyacinth-colored. (1) Rev 9:17

ὑάκινθος, ου, ὁ n. (*) jacinth, hyacinth.
(1) Rev 21:20

ὑάλινος, η, ον adj. (ὕαλος) of glass,
transparent as glass. (3)

ὕαλος, ου, ἡ n. (*) crystal, glass. (2)

ὑβρίζω v. (ὕβρις) aor. ὕβρισα; aor. pass.
ὑβρίσθην. to mistreat, scoff at, insult.
(5)

ὕβρις, εως, ἡ n. (*) shame, insult, mistreatment; hardship, disaster, damage.
(3)

ὑβριστής, οῦ, ὁ n. (ὕβρις) violent or
insolent person. (2)

ὑγιαίνω v. (ὑγιής) to be healthy; be
correct. (12)

ὑγιής, ές adj. (*) healthy, well; correct,
sound. (11)

ὑγρός, ά, όν adj. (ὕδωρ) moist, pliant,
green (of wood). (1) Lk 23:31

ὑδρία, ας, ἡ n. (ὕδωρ) water jar. (3)

ὑδροποτέω v. (ὕδωρ, πίνω) to drink
(only) water. (1) 1 Ti 5:23

ὑδρωπικός, ή, όν adj. (ὕδωρ) suffering
from dropsy or edema. (1) Lk 14:2

ὕδωρ, ατος, τό n. (*) water (lit. and fig.).
(76)

ὑετός, οῦ, ὁ n. (ὕδωρ) rain. (5)

υἱοθεσία, ας, ἡ n. (υἱός, τίθημι) adop-
tion. (5)

υἱός, οῦ, ὁ n. (*) son, (male) offspring,
descendant, foal; son (ext. sense), follower, pupil, οἱ υἱοὶ τῶν ἀνθρώπων
humans, one who shares a special relationship with (w. gen.), Son (in various
designations of Jesus). (377)

ὕλη, ης, ἡ n. (*) forest; wood, pile of
wood, wood used for building (poss.).
(1) Jas 3:5

ὑμεῖς s. σύ (pl.).

Ὑμέναιος, ου, ὁ n. pers. Hymenaeus.
(2)

ὑμέτερος, α, ον adj. (σύ) belonging to
or incumbent upon you (pl.), your (pl.),
τῷ ὑμετέρῳ ἐλέει by the mercy shown
to you, νὴ τὴν ὑμετέραν καύχησιν ἣν
ἔχω by the pride that I have in you,
τὸ ὑμέτερον ὑστέρημα that which is
lacking in you. (11)

ὑμνέω v. (ὕμνος) fut. ὑμνήσω; aor.
ὕμνησα. to sing in praise to or of, sing
a song of praise to; sing a hymn (intr.).
(4)

ὕμνος, ου, ὁ n. (*) hymn or song of
praise. (2)

ὑπ' = ὑπό before smooth breathing.

ὑπάγω v. (ἄγω) to go away, go home; go,
take one's departure; die. (79)

ὑπακοή, ῆς, ἡ n. (ἀκούω) obedience.
(15)

ὑπακούω v. (ἀκούω) aor. ὑπήκουσα. to
obey, follow, be subject to; open or
answer (the door). (21)

ὕπανδρος, ον adj. (ἀνήρ) married (of a
woman). (1) Rom 7:2

ὑπαντάω v. (ὑπό, ἀντί) aor. ὑπήντησα.
to meet; encounter, oppose. (10)

ὑπάντησις, εως, ἡ n. (ὑπό, ἀντί) coming to meet, εἰς ὑπάντησιν to meet
(someone). (3)

ὕπαρξις, εως, ἡ n. (ἄρχω) property,
possession. (2)

ὑπάρχω v. (ἄρχω) to be (= εἰμί);
exist, be present, be at one's disposal,
τὰ ὑπάρχοντα property, possessions,
means. (60)

ὑπέβαλον s. ὑποβάλλω (2 aor.).

ὑπέδειξα s. ὑποδείκνυμι (aor.).

ὑπέθηκα s. ὑποτίθημι (aor.).

ὑπείκω v. (εἴκω) *to yield, give way, submit.* (1) Heb 13:17

ὑπέλαβον s. ὑπολαμβάνω (2 aor.).

ὑπελείφθην s. ὑπολείπω (aor. pass.).

ὑπέμεινα s. ὑπομένω (aor.).

ὑπεμνήσθην s. ὑπομιμνήσκω (aor. pass.).

ὑπεναντίος, α, ον adj. (ὑπό, ἐν, ἀντί) *opposed, contrary, hostile; opponent, adversary* (subst.). (2)

ὑπενεγκεῖν s. ὑποφέρω (aor. inf.).

ὑπέπλευσα s. ὑποπλέω (aor.).

ὑπέρ prep. (*) w. gen. *for, in behalf of, for the sake of someone* or *something, in place of, instead of, in the name of,* εἰμὶ ὑπέρ τινος *to be for someone* or *on someone's side,* ὑπὲρ (τῶν) ἁμαρτιῶν *in order to atone for* or *remove (the) sins; because of, for the sake of, for; about, concerning, with reference to;* w. acc. *over and above, beyond, more than, more exalted than;* adv. *even more.* (150)

ὑπεραίρω v. (αἴρω) *to rise up, exalt oneself, be elated,* (mid. and pass. in NT). (3)

ὑπέρακμος, ον adj. (ἄκρον) *past one's prime, past marriageable age, past the bloom of youth* (of a woman); *at one's sexual peak* (of a woman), *with strong passions* (of a man). (1) 1 Cor 7:36

ὑπεράνω adv. (ὑπέρ, ἀνά) adv. prep. w. gen. in NT *(high) above.* (3)

ὑπεραστίζω v. *to protect.* (v.l.)

ὑπεραυξάνω v. (αὐξάνω) *to grow wonderfully, increase abundantly.* (1) 2 Th 1:3

ὑπερβαίνω v. (-βαίνω) *to trespass, sin.* (1) 1 Th 4:6

ὑπερβαλλόντως adv. (βάλλω) *surpassingly, to a much greater degree.* (1) 2 Cor 11:23

ὑπερβάλλω v. (βάλλω) *to go beyond, surpass, outdo,* ὑπερβάλλων *surpassing, extraordinary, outstanding.* (5)

ὑπερβολή, ῆς, ἡ n. (βάλλω) *excess, extraordinary quality* or *character,* καθ᾽ ὑπερβολήν *to an extraordinary degree, beyond measure, utterly,* καθ᾽ ὑπερβολὴν εἰς ὑπερβολήν *beyond all measure and proportion.* (8)

ὑπερεῖδον s. ὑπεροράω (2 aor.).

ὑπερέκεινα adv. (ἐκεῖ) adv. prep. w. gen. in NT *beyond.* (1) 2 Cor 10:16

ὑπερεκπερισσοῦ adv. (ὑπέρ, ἐκ, περί) *quite beyond all measure, as earnestly as possible; infinitely more than* (adv. prep. w. gen.). (3)

ὑπερεκτείνω v. (-τείνω) *to stretch out beyond, overextend.* (1) 2 Cor 10:14

ὑπερεκχύννω v. (-χέω) *to pour out over; overflow* (pass. in NT). (1) Lk 6:38

ὑπερεντυγχάνω v. (τυγχάνω) *to plead, intercede.* (1) Rom 8:26

ὑπερέχω v. (ἔχω) *to have power over, be in authority (over), be highly placed,* ἐξουσίαι ὑπερέχουσαι *governing authorities; be better than, surpass, excel,* τὸ ὑπερέχον *surpassing greatness.* (5)

ὑπερηφανία, ας, ἡ n. (φαίνω) *arrogance, haughtiness, pride.* (1) Mk 7:22

ὑπερήφανος, ον adj. (φαίνω) *arrogant, haughty, proud.* (5)

ὑπερλίαν adv. (λίαν) *exceedingly; special,* οἱ ὑπερλίαν ἀπόστολοι *super-apostles* (adj. in NT). (2)

ὑπερνικάω v. (νίκη) *to prevail completely, win a most glorious victory.* (1) Rom 8:37

ὑπέρογκος, ον adj. (ὄγκος) *haughty, pompous, bombastic.* (2)

ὑπεροράω v. (ὁράω) aor. ὑπερεῖδον. *to overlook, disregard.* (1) Ac 17:30

ὑπεροχή, ῆς, ἡ n. (ἔχω) *superiority, preeminence,* καθ᾽ ὑπεροχὴν λόγου ἢ σοφίας *as a superior person in speech or wisdom; authority.* (2)

ὑπερπερισσεύω v. (ὑπέρ, περί) aor. ὑπερεπερίσσευσα. *to be in great excess, present in abundance; overflow* (pass.). (2)

ὑπερπερισσῶς adv. (ὑπέρ, περί) *beyond all measure.* (1) Mk 7:37

ὑπερπλεονάζω v. (πληρόω) aor. ὑπερεπλεόνασα. *to abound, run over, overflow.* (1) 1 Ti 1:14

ὑπερυψόω v. (ὕψος) aor. ὑπερύψωσα. *to raise, exalt, raise to the loftiest height.* (1) Phil 2:9

ὑπερφρονέω v. (φρήν) *to think too highly of oneself, be haughty.* (1) Rom 12:3

ὑπερῷον, ου, τό n. (ὑπέρ) *upper story, room upstairs.* (4)

ὑπέχω v. (ἔχω) *to undergo punishment.* (1) Jd 7

ὑπήκοος, ον adj. (ἀκούω) *obedient.* (3)

ὑπήνεγκα s. ὑποφέρω (aor.).

ὑπηρετέω v. (ὑπηρέτης) aor. ὑπηρέτησα. *to serve, be helpful.* (3)

ὑπηρέτης, ου, ὁ n. (*) *helper, assistant, minister.* (20)

ὕπνος, ου, ὁ n. (*) *sleep* (lit. and fig.). (6)

ὑπό prep. (*) w. gen. *by, at the hands of*; w. acc. *under, below, at; under (the control or power of), under obligation; about.* (220)

ὑποβάλλω v. (βάλλω) aor. ὑπέβαλον. *to instigate (secretly), suborn.* (1) Ac 6:11

ὑπογραμμός, οῦ, ὁ n. (γράφω) *example.* (1) 1 Pt 2:21

ὑπόδειγμα, ατος, τό n. (δείκνυμι) *example, model, pattern; outline, sketch, symbol.* (6)

ὑποδείκνυμι v. (δείκνυμι) fut. ὑποδείξω; aor. ὑπέδειξα. *to show, give direction, prove, set forth.* (6)

ὑποδέχομαι v. (δέχομαι) aor. ὑπεδεξάμην; pf. pass. ὑποδέδεγμαι. *to receive, welcome, entertain as a guest.* (4)

ὑποδέω v. (δέω) aor. ὑπέδησα; pf. pass. ὑποδέδεμαι. *to tie or bind beneath, put on shoes* (mid. in NT). (3)

ὑπόδημα, ατος, τό n. (δέω) *sandal, footwear.* (10)

ὑπόδικος, ον adj. (δίκη) *answerable, accountable.* (1) Rom 3:19

ὑποδραμών s. ὑποτρέχω (2 aor. ptc.).

ὑποζύγιον, ου, τό n. (ζυγός) *donkey.* (2)

ὑποζώννυμι v. (ζώννυμι) *to undergird, brace* (of a ship). (1) Ac 27:17

ὑποκάτω adv. (ὑπό, κατά) adv. prep. w. gen. in NT *under, below, down at.* (11)

ὑποκρίνομαι v. (κρίνω) *to pretend.* (1) Lk 20:20

ὑπόκρισις, εως, ἡ n. (κρίνω) *playacting, pretense, outward show, dissembling, hypocrisy.* (6)

ὑποκριτής, οῦ, ὁ n. (κρίνω) *actor, pretender, dissembler, hypocrite.* (17)

ὑπολαμβάνω v. (λαμβάνω) aor. ὑπέλαβον. *to take up; receive as a guest, support; reply; assume, think, believe, be of the opinion (that), suppose.* (5)

ὑπόλειμμα, ατος, τό n. (λείπω) *remnant.* (1) Rom 9:27

ὑπολείπω v. (λείπω) aor. pass. ὑπελείφθην. *to leave remaining; be left remaining* (pass. in NT). (1) Rom 11:3

ὑπολήνιον, ου, τό n. (ληνός) *wine trough, vat.* (1) Mk 12:1

ὑπολιμπάνω v. (λείπω) *to leave (behind).* (1) 1 Pt 2:21

ὑπομένω v. (μένω) fut. ὑπομενῶ; aor. ὑπέμεινα; pf. ὑπομεμένηκα. *to remain or stay (behind); stand one's ground, hold out, endure.* (17)

ὑπομιμνήσκω v. (μιμνήσκομαι) fut. ὑπομνήσω; aor. ὑπέμνησα; aor. pass. ὑπεμνήσθην. *to remind, call to mind, bring up; remember, think of* (pass.). (7)

ὑπόμνησις, εως, ἡ n. (μιμνήσκομαι) *reminding*, ἐν ὑπομνήσει *by a reminder; remembrance.* (3)

ὑπομονή, ῆς, ἡ n. (μένω) *patience, (steadfast) endurance, fortitude, steadfastness, perseverance; expectation.* (32)

ὑπονοέω v. (νίπτω) *to suspect, suppose.* (3)

ὑπόνοια, ας, ἡ n. (νίπτω) *suspicion, conjecture.* (1) 1 Ti 6:4

ὑποπλέω v. (πλέω) aor. ὑπέπλευσα. *to sail under the lee or shelter of.* (2)

ὑποπνέω v. (πνέω) aor. ὑπέπνευσα. *to blow gently.* (1) Ac 27:13

ὑποπόδιον, ου, τό n. (πούς) *footstool.* (7)

ὑπόστασις, εως, ἡ n. (ἵστημι) *substantial nature, essence, actual being, realization; plan, project, undertaking, endeavor, obligation; situation,*

condition, frame of mind; title deed.
(5)
ὑποστέλλω v. (στέλλω) aor. ὑπέστειλα.
to draw back, withdraw; shrink back,
shrink from, avoid, be timid about, keep
silent about (mid.). (4)
ὑποστολή, ῆς, ἡ n. (στέλλω) hesitancy,
timidity. (1) Heb 10:39
ὑποστρέφω v. (στρέφω) fut. ὑποστρέψω;
aor. ὑπέστρεψα. to turn back, return,
ὑποστρέφω ἐκ turn away. (35)
ὑποστρωννύω v. (στρωννύω) to spread
out underneath. (1) Lk 19:36
ὑποταγή, ῆς, ἡ n. (τάσσω) subjection, subordination, submission, ἐν
ὑποταγῇ under control. (4)
ὑποτάσσω v. (τάσσω) aor. ὑπέταξα; pf.
pass. ὑποτέταγμαι; aor. pass. ὑπετά-
γην. to subject, subordinate, bring to
subjection; become subject, subject
oneself, be subjected or subordinated,
obey (pass.). (38)
ὑποτίθημι v. (τίθημι) aor. ὑπέθηκα. to
lay down, risk; make known, teach
(mid.). (2)
ὑποτρέχω v. (τρέχω) aor. ὑπέδραμον. to
run or sail under the lee or shelter of.
(1) Ac 27:16
ὑποτύπωσις, εως, ἡ n. (τύπος) proto-
type, standard, outline (poss.). (2)
ὑποφέρω v. (φέρω) aor. ὑπήνεγκα. to
submit to, endure. (3)
ὑποχωρέω v. (χωρέω) aor. ὑπεχώρησα.
to go off, go away, retire, steal away.
(2)
ὑπωπιάζω v. (ὁράω) to give a black eye,
strike in the face; wear down, brow-
beat, slander; punish, treat roughly,
torment. (2)
ὗς, ὑός, ἡ n. sow. (1) 2 Pt 2:22

ὑσσός, οῦ, ὁ n. javelin. (v.l.)
ὕσσωπος, ου, ὁ, ἡ n. Heb. hyssop. (2)
ὑστερέω v. (ὕστερος) aor. ὑστέρησα;
pf. ὑστέρηκα; aor. pass. ὑστερήθην.
to miss, fail to reach, be excluded; fail,
give out, lack; be needy; be less than,
be inferior to; lack, fall short; pass.
be needy; lack, be lacking, go without,
come short. (16)
ὑστέρημα, ατος, τό n. (ὕστερος) need,
want, deficiency, absence; lack, short-
coming. (9)
ὑστέρησις, εως, ἡ n. (ὕστερος) need,
lack, poverty, καθ᾽ ὑστέρησιν because
of need or want. (2)
ὕστερος, α, ον adj. (*) last, future
(poss.); neut. sg. as adv. in the second
place, latter, then, thereafter; finally,
ὕστερον πάντων last of all. (12)
ὑφ᾽ = ὑπό before rough breathing.
ὑφαίνω v. to weave. (v.l.)
ὑφαντός, ή, όν adj. woven. (1) Jn 19:23
ὑψηλός, ή, όν adj. (ὕψος) tall, high,
ὑψηλότερος greater heights; exalted,
proud, haughty; subst. ἐν ὑψηλοῖς on
high, in heaven; what is considered exalted, something that is (too) high. (11)
ὑψηλοφρονέω v. (ὕψος, φρήν) to be
proud, haughty. (1) 1 Ti 6:17
ὕψιστος, η, ον adj. (ὕψος) highest; subst. τὰ ὕψιστα the highest
heights (= heaven), highest heaven; ὁ
ὕψιστος the Most High (of God). (13)
ὕψος, ους, τό n. (*) height, heaven; high
position. (6)
ὑψόω v. (ὕψος) fut. ὑψώσω; aor. ὕψωσα;
aor. pass. ὑψώθην. to lift up, raise high;
exalt, make great, consider better. (20)
ὕψωμα, ατος, τό n. (ὕψος) world above;
arrogance, pride, proud obstacle. (2)

φαγεῖν, φάγομαι s. ἐσθίω (2 aor. inf., fut. mid.).

φάγος, ου, ὁ n. (*) *glutton.* (2)

φαιλόνης, ου, ὁ n. Lat. *cloak.* (1) 2 Ti 4:13

φαίνω v. (*) fut. φανῶ; aor. ἔφανα; aor. pass. ἐφάνην. *to shine, give light, be bright;* pass. *shine, flash; appear, be* or *become visible, be revealed, be seen, make one's appearance, show oneself; be recognized, be apparent, be revealed; appear as something, appear to be something; have the appearance, seem.* (31)

Φάλεκ, ὁ n. pers. *Peleg.* (1) Lk 3:35

φανερός, ά, όν adj. (φαίνω) *visible, clear, plainly to be seen, open, plain, evident, known; (in) the open, public notice,* εἰς φανερὸν ἐλθεῖν *to come to light,* ὁ ἐν τῷ φανερῷ Ἰουδαῖος *the Jew* (or *Judean*) *who is one outwardly* (subst.). (18)

φανερόω v. (φαίνω) fut. φανερώσω; aor. ἐφανέρωσα; pf. pass. πεφανέρωμαι; aor. pass. ἐφανερώθην. *to reveal, expose publicly; disclose, show, make known, teach, make plain;* pass. *show* or *reveal oneself, be revealed, appear, become visible; become public knowledge, be disclosed, become known, be made known, be shown.* (49)

φανερῶς adv. (φαίνω) *openly, publicly; clearly, distinctly.* (3)

φανέρωσις, εως, ἡ n. (φαίνω) *disclosure, announcement, open proclamation.* (2)

φανός, οῦ, ὁ n. (φαίνω) *lamp, lantern.* (1) Jn 18:3

Φανουήλ, ὁ n. pers. *Phanuel.* (1) Lk 2:36

φαντάζω v. (φαίνω) *to make visible; appear, become visible to;* φανταζόμενον *sight, spectacle* (pass. in NT). (1) Heb 12:21

φαντασία, ας, ἡ n. (φαίνω) *pomp, pageantry.* (1) Ac 25:23

φάντασμα, ατος, τό n. (φαίνω) *apparition, ghost.* (2)

φανῶ s. φαίνω (fut.).

φάραγξ, αγγος, ἡ n. *ravine, valley.* (1) Lk 3:5

Φαραώ, ὁ n. pers. *Pharaoh.* (5)

Φάρες, ὁ n. pers. *Perez.* (3)

Φαρισαῖος, ου, ὁ n. oth. *Pharisee.* (98)

φαρμακεία, ας, ἡ n. (φάρμακον) *sorcery, magic.* (2)

φάρμακον, ου, τό n. (*) *magic potion, charm.* (1) Rev 9:21

φάρμακος, ου, ὁ n. (φάρμακον) *sorcerer, magician.* (2)

φάσις, εως, ἡ n. (φαίνω) *report, announcement, news.* (1) Ac 21:31

φάσκω v. (φαίνω) *to say, assert, claim.* (3)

φάτνη, ης, ἡ n. *manger, crib, stable* (poss.), *feeding place* (poss.). (4)

φαῦλος, η, ον adj. *base, bad; ordinary.* (6)

φέγγος, ους, τό n. *light, radiance.* (2)

φείδομαι v. (*) fut. φείσομαι; aor. ἐφεισάμην. *to spare; refrain.* (10)

φειδομένως adv. (φείδομαι) *sparingly.* (2)

φέρω v. (*) fut. οἴσω; aor. ἤνεγκα; aor. pass. ἠνέχθην. *to carry, bear, bring with one, bring* or *take along, bear* or *grant a favor; bring (on), bring (to), fetch, lead; be moved, be driven, let oneself be moved, rush* (pass.); *put, place, reach out; sustain, bear up; lead* *(to); utter, make; establish; bear patiently, endure, put up with; bear* (of plants), *produce.* (66)

φεύγω v. (*) fut. φεύξομαι; aor. ἔφυγον. *to flee; escape; flee from, avoid, shun; vanish, disappear.* (29)

Φῆλιξ, ικος, ὁ n. pers. *Felix.* (9)

φήμη, ης, ἡ n. (φημί) *report, news.* (2)

φημί v. (*) encl. forms φημι, φησι(ν) *to say, affirm,* φησίν *it is said, it says; mean.* (66)

Φῆστος, ου, ὁ n. pers. *Festus.* (13)

φθάνω v. (*) aor. ἔφθασα. *to come before, precede; arrive, reach,* w. ἐπι *come upon, overtake; attain.* (7)

φθαρτός, ή, όν adj. (φθείρω) *perishable, mortal.* (6)

φθέγγομαι v. (*) aor. ἐφθεγξάμην. *to speak, utter, proclaim.* (3)

φθείρω v. (*) aor. ἔφθειρα; aor. pass. ἐφθάρην. *to ruin (financially), spoil; ruin, corrupt; destroy; be led astray* (pass.). (9)

φθινοπωρινός, ή, όν adj. (φθείρω, ὀπώρα) *belonging to late autumn.* (1) Jd 12

φθόγγος, ου, ὁ n. (φθέγγομαι) *tone, voice.* (2)

φθονέω v. (φθόνος) *to envy, be jealous.* (1) Gal 5:26

φθόνος, ου, ὁ n. (*) *envy, jealousy.* (9)

φθορά, ᾶς, ἡ n. (φθείρω) *dissolution, deterioration, corruption, state of being perishable, that which is perishable, decay; depravity; destruction.* (9)

φιάλη, ης, ἡ n. *bowl.* (12)

φιλάγαθος, ον adj. (φίλος, ἀγαθός) *loving what is good.* (1) Tit 1:8

Φιλαδέλφεια, ας, ἡ n. pla. *Philadelphia.* (2)

φιλαδελφία, ας, ἡ n. (φίλος, ἀδελφός) *love of brother or sister.* (6)

φιλάδελφος, ον adj. (φίλος, ἀδελφός) *having brotherly love, having mutual affection.* (1) 1 Pt 3:8

φίλανδρος, ον adj. (φίλος, ἀνήρ) *having affection or love for a husband.* (1) Tit 2:4

φιλανθρωπία, ας, ἡ n. (φίλος, ἄνθρωπος) *(loving) kindness.* (2)

φιλανθρώπως adv. (φίλος, ἄνθρωπος) *benevolently, kindly.* (1) Ac 27:3

φιλαργυρία, ας, ἡ n. (φίλος, ἄργυρος) *love of money, miserliness, avarice.* (1) 1 Ti 6:10

φιλάργυρος, ον adj. (φίλος, ἄργυρος) *fond of money, avaricious.* (2)

φίλαυτος, ον adj. (φίλος, αὐτός) *loving oneself, selfish.* (1) 2 Ti 3:2

φιλέω v. (φίλος) aor. ἐφίλησα; pf. πεφίληκα. *to have affection for, like, consider someone a friend, love, like* or *love to do; kiss.* (25)

φίλη, ης, ἡ s. φίλος (fem. subst.).

φιλήδονος, ον adj. (φίλος, ἡδονή) *loving pleasure.* (1) 2 Ti 3:4

φίλημα, ατος, τό n. (φίλος) *kiss.* (7)

Φιλήμων, ονος, ὁ n. pers. *Philemon.* (1) Phlm 1

Φίλητος, ου, ὁ n. pers. *Philetus.* (1) 2 Ti 2:17

φιλία, ας, ἡ n. (φίλος) *friendship, love.* (1) Jas 4:4

Φιλιππήσιος, ου, ὁ n. pla. *a Philippian.* (1) Phil 4:15

Φίλιπποι, ων, οἱ n. pla. *Philippi.* (4)

Φίλιππος, ου, ὁ n. pers. *Philip.* (36)

φιλόθεος, ον adj. (φίλος, θεός) *devout.* (1) 2 Ti 3:4

Φιλόλογος, ου, ὁ n. pers. *Philologus.* (1) Rom 16:15

φιλονεικία, ας, ἡ n. (φίλος) *dispute, argument.* (1) Lk 22:24

φιλόνεικος, ον adj. (φίλος) *quarrelsome, contentious.* (1) 1 Cor 11:16

φιλοξενία, ας, ἡ n. (φίλος, ξένος) *hospitality.* (2)

φιλόξενος, ον adj. (φίλος, ξένος) *hospitable.* (3)

φιλοπρωτεύω v. (φίλος, πρό) *to wish to be first, like to be leader.* (1) 3 Jn 9

φίλος, η, ον adj. (*) *beloved, dear, loving, kindly disposed, devoted;* subst. *friend* (masc. and fem.). (29)

φιλοσοφία, ας, ἡ n. (φίλος, σοφός) *philosophy.* (1) Col 2:8

φιλόσοφος, ου, ὁ n. (φίλος, σοφός)
philosopher. (1) Ac 17:18
φιλόστοργος, ον adj. (φίλος, -στέργω)
loving dearly, devoted. (1) Rom 12:10
φιλότεκνος, ον adj. (φίλος, τίκτω) loving one's children. (1) Tit 2:4
φιλοτιμέομαι v. (φίλος, τιμή) to have
as one's ambition, consider it an honor,
aspire. (3)
φιλοφρόνως adv. (φίλος, φρήν) in a
friendly manner, hospitably. (1) Ac
28:7
φιμόω v. fut. φιμώσω; aor. ἐφίμωσα; pf.
pass. πεφίμωμαι; aor. pass. ἐφιμώθην.
to muzzle; silence, put to silence; be
silenced or silent (pass.). (7)
Φλέγων, οντος, ὁ n. pers. Phlegon. (1)
Rom 16:14
φλογίζω v. (φλόξ) to set on fire. (2)
φλόξ, φλογός, ἡ n. (*) flame, ἐν πυρὶ
φλογός in flaming fire. (7)
φλυαρέω v. (φλύαρος) to talk nonsense
(about), disparage, chatter maliciously
about. (1) 3 Jn 10
φλύαρος, ον adj. (*) gossipy. (1) 1 Ti
5:13
φοβερός, ά, όν adj. (φόβος) causing fear,
fearful, terrible, frightful. (3)
φοβέω v. (φόβος) aor. pass. ἐφοβήθην.
pass. in NT be afraid, be or become
frightened (aor.), φοβέομαι ἀπό be
afraid of, fear; (have) reverence, respect. (95)
φόβητρον, ου, τό n. (φόβος) terrible
sight or event, horror, dreadful portent.
(1) Lk 21:11
φόβος, ου, ὁ n. (*) intimidation, something terrible or awe-inspiring, a terror, that which causes fear; fear, alarm,
fright, apprehension, feeling of anxiety,
slavish fear, reverence, respect. (47)
Φοίβη, ης, ἡ n. pers. Phoebe. (1) Rom
16:1
Φοινίκη, ης, ἡ n. pla. Phoenicia. (3)
φοῖνιξ and φοίνιξ, ικος, ὁ n. date-palm,
palm tree; palm-branch. (2)
Φοῖνιξ, ικος, ὁ n. pla. Phoenix. (1) Ac
27:12

φονεύς, έως, ὁ n. (φονεύω) murderer.
(7)
φονεύω v. (*) fut. φονεύσω; aor. ἐφό-
νευσα. to (commit) murder, kill.
(12)
φόνος, ου, ὁ n. (φονεύω) murder, killing.
(9)
φορέω v. (φέρω) fut. φορέσω; aor.
ἐφόρεσα. to bear constantly, wear;
bear. (6)
Φόρον, ου, τό s. Ἀππίου Φόρον.
φόρος, ου, ὁ n. (φέρω) tribute, tax. (5)
φορτίζω v. (φέρω) pf. pass. πεφόρτισμαι.
to load, burden, cause to carry; be bur-
dened (pass.). (2)
φορτίον, ου, τό n. (φέρω) load, cargo;
burden. (6)
Φορτουνᾶτος, ου, ὁ n. pers. Fortunatus.
(1) 1 Cor 16:17
φραγέλλιον, ου, τό n. (*) Lat. whip,
lash. (1) Jn 2:15
φραγελλόω v. (φραγέλλιον) Lat. aor.
ἐφραγέλλωσα. to flog, scourge. (2)
φραγμός, οῦ, ὁ n. (φράσσω) fence,
hedge; partition. (4)
φράζω v. aor. ἔφρασα. to explain, interpret. (1) Mt 15:15
φράσσω v. (*) aor. ἔφραξα; aor. pass.
ἐφράγην. to shut, close, stop, silence;
block, bar. (3)
φρέαρ, ατος, τό n. well; pit, shaft. (7)
φρεναπατάω v. (φρήν, ἀπάτη) to deceive. (1) Gal 6:3
φρεναπάτης, ου, ὁ n. (φρήν, ἀπάτη) deceiver, misleader. (1) Tit 1:10
φρήν, φρενός, ἡ n. (*) thinking, understanding (pl. in NT). (2)
φρίσσω v. to shudder. (1) Jas 2:19
φρονέω v. (φρήν) fut. φρονήσω. to think,
form or hold an opinion, judge, feel,
regard, cherish thoughts, ὑπέρ τινος
φρονέω be concerned about someone,
ὑψηλὰ φρονέω be proud; set one's
mind on, be intent on, φρονέω τά τινος
take someone's side; be minded or disposed, τοῦτο φρονεῖτε ἐν ὑμῖν let the
same kind of thinking dominate you.
(26)

φρόνημα, ατος, τό n. (φρήν) *way of thinking, mind(-set), aim, aspiration, striving*. (4)

φρόνησις, εως, ἡ n. (φρήν) *way of thinking, (frame of) mind; understanding, insight, intelligence*. (2)

φρόνιμος, ον adj. (φρήν) *sensible, thoughtful, prudent, wise*, φρονιμώτερος *shrewder*. (14)

φρονίμως adv. (φρήν) *prudently, shrewdly*. (1) Lk 16:8

φροντίζω v. (φρήν) *to think of, be intent on, be careful* or *concerned about, pay attention to*. (1) Tit 3:8

φρουρέω v. (ὁράω) fut. φρουρήσω. *to guard; detain, confine, hold in custody; protect, keep*. (4)

φρυάσσω v. aor. ἐφρύαξα. *to be arrogant, haughty, insolent*. (1) Ac 4:25

φρύγανον, ου, τό n. *pieces of dry wood* or *brushwood* (pl. in NT). (1) Ac 28:3

Φρυγία, ας, ἡ n. pla. *Phrygia*. (3)

Φύγελος, ου, ὁ n. pers. *Phygelus*. (1) 2 Ti 1:15

φυγή, ῆς, ἡ n. (φεύγω) *flight*. (1) Mt 24:20

φυλακή, ῆς, ἡ n. (φυλάσσω) *guarding, watch*, φυλάσσω φυλακάς *keep watch, do guard duty; guard, sentinel; prison* (lit. and fig.), *haunt; watch* (period of the night). (47)

φυλακίζω v. (φυλάσσω) *take into custody, imprison*. (1) Ac 22:19

φυλακτήριον, ου, τό n. (φυλάσσω) *prayer-band, prayer-case*. (1) Mt 23:5

φύλαξ, ακος, ὁ n. (φυλάσσω) *guard, sentinel*. (3)

φυλάσσω v. (*) fut. φυλάξω; aor. ἐφύλαξα. *to watch, guard*, φυλάσσω φυλακάς *keep watch; protect, preserve, entrust; observe, follow*; mid. *look out for, avoid; keep, observe, follow*. (31)

φυλή, ῆς, ἡ n. (φύω) *tribe; nation, people*. (31)

φύλλον, ου, τό n. *leaf; foliage* (pl. in NT). (6)

φύραμα, ατος, τό n. *mixture* or *batch of dough; lump* (of soft clay). (5)

φυσικός, ή, όν adj. (φύω) *natural, in accordance with nature*, φυσικά *creatures of instinct*. (3)

φυσικῶς adv. (φύω) *naturally, by instinct*. (1) Jd 10

φυσιόω v. (φύω) pf. pass. πεφυσίωμαι; aor. pass. ἐφυσιώθην. *to puff up, make proud; become puffed up* or *conceited, put on airs, be inflated* (pass.). (7)

φύσις, εως, ἡ n. (φύω) *nature, natural endowment* or *condition*, κατὰ φύσιν *natural, by nature*, παρὰ φύσιν *contrary to nature; natural characteristic* or *disposition*, ἡ φύσις ἡ ἀνθρωπίνη *human nature, humankind*, φύσει *spontaneously; nature* (as established order)*; natural being, creature, species*. (14)

φυσίωσις, εως, ἡ n. (φύω) *swelled-headedness, pride, conceit*. (1) 2 Cor 12:20

φυτεία, ας, ἡ n. (φύω) *plant*. (1) Mt 15:13

φυτεύω v. (φύω) aor. ἐφύτευσα; pf. pass. πεφύτευμαι; aor. pass. ἐφυτεύθην. *to plant*. (11)

φύω v. (*) aor. pass. ἐφύην. *to grow (up), come up*. (3)

φωλεός, οῦ, ὁ n. *den, lair, hole*. (2)

φωνέω v. (φωνή) fut. φωνήσω; aor. ἐφώνησα; aor. pass. ἐφωνήθην. *to crow* (of roosters), *call* or *cry out, speak loudly, say with emphasis; address as; summon, call; invite*. (43)

φωνή, ῆς, ἡ n. (*) *sound, tone, noise, blast; voice, call, cry, outcry, (loud* or *solemn) declaration, utterance; language*. (139)

φῶς, φωτός, τό n. (φαίνω) *light* (lit. and fig.), ἐν τῷ φωτί *in the open, publicly; torch, lamp, lantern, fire*. (73)

φωστήρ, ῆρος, ὁ n. (φαίνω) *star; splendor, radiance*. (2)

φωσφόρος, ον adj. (φαίνω, φέρω) *bearing light; morning star* (subst. in NT). (1) 2 Pt 1:19

φωτεινός, ή, όν adj. (φαίνω) *shining, bright, radiant, illuminated, full of light.* (5)

φωτίζω v. (φαίνω) fut. φωτίσω; aor. ἐφώτισα; pf. pass. πεφώτισμαι; aor. pass. ἐφωτίσθην. *to shine;* trans. *give light to, light (up), illuminate; enlighten, shed light upon, bring to light.* (11)

φωτισμός, οῦ, ὁ n. (φαίνω) *enlightenment, light, bringing to light, revealing.* (2)

X

χαίρω v. (*) fut. χαρήσομαι; aor. pass. ἐχάρην. *to rejoice, be glad, be delighted; with joy, gladly* (ptc.)*; welcome, good day, hail (to you), I am glad to see you, hello, good morning, farewell, good-bye,* χαίρειν *greetings* (impv.). (74)

χάλαζα, ης, ἡ n. *hail.* (4)

χαλάω v. (*) fut. χαλάσω; aor. ἐχάλασα; aor. pass. ἐχαλάσθην. *to let down, lower.* (7)

Χαλδαῖος, ου, ὁ n. pla. *a Chaldean.* (1) Ac 7:4

χαλεπός, ή, όν adj. *hard, difficult, hard to deal with, violent, dangerous.* (2)

χαλιναγωγέω v. (χαλάω, ἄγω) aor. ἐχαλιναγώγησα. *to bridle, hold in check.* (2)

χαλινός, οῦ, ὁ n. (χαλάω) *bit, bridle.* (2)

χαλκεύς, έως, ὁ n. (χαλκός) *(black) smith, metalworker.* (1) 2 Ti 4:14

χαλκηδών, όνος, ὁ n. (χαλκός) *chalcedony.* (1) Rev 21:19

χαλκίον, ου, τό n. (χαλκός) *bronze vessel, kettle.* (1) Mk 7:4

χαλκολίβανον, ου, τό and **χαλκολίβανος, ου, ὁ** n. (χαλκός) *fine brass* or *bronze.* (2)

χαλκός, οῦ, ὁ n. (*) *brass, bronze; gong, copper coin, small change, money.* (5)

χαλκοῦς, ῆ, οῦν adj. (χαλκός) *made of copper, brass,* or *bronze.* (1) Rev 9:20

χαμαί adv. *to* or *on the ground.* (2)

Χανάαν, ἡ n. pla. *Canaan.* (2)

Χαναναῖος, α, ον adj. pla. *Canaanite.* (1) Mt 15:22

χαρά, ᾶς, ἡ n. (χαίρω) *joy, state of joyfulness,* χαρᾶς εἰμί *to be pleasant; joy* (caused by a person or thing). (59)

χάραγμα, ατος, τό n. (*) *mark, stamp; thing formed, image.* (8)

χαρακτήρ, ῆρος, ὁ n. (χάραγμα) *reproduction, (exact) representation.* (1) Heb 1:3

χάραξ, ακος, ὁ n. (χάραγμα) *palisade, entrenchment, siege-work.* (1) Lk 19:43

χαρήσομαι s. χαίρω (fut. mid.).

χαρίζομαι v. (χαίρω) fut. χαρίσομαι; aor. ἐχαρισάμην; pf. pass. κεχάρισμαι; aor. pass. ἐχαρίσθην. *to give graciously, grant, give; cancel; forgive, pardon.* (23)

χάριν adv. (χαίρω) adv. prep. w. gen. in NT, usu. after n. *for the sake of, on behalf of, on account of,* τούτου χάριν *for this purpose,* χάριν τίνος *why,* οὗ χάριν *for this reason.* (9)

χάρις, ιτος, ἡ n. (χαίρω) *graciousness, attractiveness, charm, winsomeness,* οἱ λόγοι τῆς χάριτος *the gracious words; favor, grace, gracious care* or *help, goodwill, that which brings favor, (divine) favor,* κατὰ χάριν *as a favor,* ποία ὑμῖν χάρις ἐστίν *what credit is that to you; (sign of) favor, gracious deed* or *gift, benefaction, proof of goodwill, gracious deed* or *work,* ὑπὸ χάριν *under God's gracious will; favor* (as the product of generosity)*; thanks, gratitude, thankfulness, thankful spirit,* χάριν ἔχω *be grateful* or *thankful to.* (155)

χάρισμα, ατος, τό n. (χαίρω) *gift, favor bestowed.* (17)

χαριτόω v. (χαίρω) aor. ἐχαρίτωσα; pf. pass. κεχαρίτωμαι. *to bestow favor on, favor highly, bless.* (2)

Χαρράν, ἡ n. pla. *Haran.* (2)

χάρτης, ου, ὁ n. (χάραγμα) *papyrus, (sheet of) paper*. (1) 2 Jn 12

χάσμα, ατος, τό n. *chasm*. (1) Lk 16:26

χεῖλος, ους, τό n. *lip; shore, bank*. (7)

χειμάζω v. (χειμών) *to toss in a storm; be tossed in a storm* (pass. in NT). (1) Ac 27:18

χειμάρρους, ου, ὁ n. (χειμών, ῥέω) *winter torrent, ravine, wadi*. (1) Jn 18:1

χειμών, ῶνος, ὁ n. (*) *bad* or *stormy weather, storm; winter,* χειμῶνος *in winter*. (6)

χείρ, χειρός, ἡ n. (*) *hand, handwriting, arm, finger; hand (of), activity, power, help*. (177)

χειραγωγέω v. (χείρ, ἄγω) *to take* or *lead by the hand*. (2)

χειραγωγός, οῦ, ὁ n. (χείρ, ἄγω) *leader*. (1) Ac 13:11

χειρόγραφον, ου, τό n. (χείρ, γράφω) *account, record of debts*. (1) Col 2:14

χειροποίητος, ον adj. (χείρ, ποιέω) *made* or *brought about by human hands*. (6)

χειροτονέω v. (χείρ, -τείνω) aor. ἐχειροτόνησα; aor. pass. ἐχειροτονήθην. *to choose; appoint, install*. (2)

χείρων, ον adj. *worse, more severe*. (11)

Χερούβ, τό n. oth. *winged creature, cherub*. (1) Heb 9:5

χήρα, ας, ἡ n. *widow*. (26)

χιλίαρχος, ου, ὁ n. (χίλιοι, ἄρχω) *military tribune, high-ranking officer*. (21)

χιλιάς, αδος, ἡ n. (χίλιοι) *(group of) a thousand*. (23)

χίλιοι, αι, α adj. (*) *thousand*. (11)

Χίος, ου, ἡ n. pla. *Chios*. (1) Ac 20:15

χιτών, ῶνος, ὁ n. *tunic, shirt; clothes* (pl.). (11)

χιών, όνος, ἡ n. (*) *snow*. (2)

χλαμύς, ύδος, ἡ n. *cloak* (military), *mantle*. (2)

χλευάζω v. (*) *to mock, sneer, scoff*. (1) Ac 17:32

χλιαρός, ά, όν adj. *lukewarm*. (1) Rev 3:16

Χλόη, ης, ἡ n. pers. *Chloe*. (1) 1 Cor 1:11

χλωρός, ά, όν adj. *yellowish green,*

(light) green; pale, greenish gray; plant (neut. subst.). (4)

χοϊκός, ή, όν adj. (-χέω) *made of earth* or *dust, earthly*. (4)

χοῖνιξ, ικος, ἡ n. *choenix* (dry measure, about one liter or quart). (2)

χοῖρος, ου, ὁ n. *swine, pig*. (12)

χολάω v. (χολή) *to be angry*. (1) Jn 7:23

χολή, ῆς, ἡ n. (*) *something bitter, gall; gall* (fig.), χολὴ πικρίας *gall of bitterness, bitter gall*. (2)

Χοραζίν, ἡ n. pla. *Chorazin*. (2)

χορηγέω v. (χορός, ἄγω) fut. χορηγήσω; *to provide, supply (in abundance)*. (2)

χορός, οῦ, ὁ n. (*) *(choral) dance, dancing*. (1) Lk 15:25

χορτάζω v. (χόρτος) aor. ἐχόρτασα; aor. pass. ἐχορτάσθην. *to feed, fill;* pass. *gorge oneself; be satisfied*. (16)

χόρτασμα, ατος, τό n. (χόρτος) *food*. (1) Ac 7:11

χόρτος, ου, ὁ n. (*) *grass, hay*. (15)

Χουζᾶς, ᾶ, ὁ n. pers. *Chuza*. (1) Lk 8:3

χοῦς, χοός, ὁ n. (-χέω) *soil, dust*. (2)

χράομαι v. (*) aor. ἐχρησάμην; pf. pass. κέχρημαι. *to make use of, employ, use,* μᾶλλον χράομαι *make the most of, be all the more useful; act, proceed; treat*. (11)

χρεία, ας, ἡ n. (χράομαι) *need, what should be; lack, want, difficulty; necessary thing; office, duty, service*. (49)

χρεοφειλέτης, ου, ὁ n. (χράομαι, ὀφείλω) *debtor*. (2)

χρή v. (χράομαι) *it is necessary, it ought* (impers.). (1) Jas 3:10

χρῄζω v. (χράομαι) *to need, have need of*. (5)

χρῆμα, ατος, τό n. (χράομαι) *money;* usu. pl. *property, wealth, means; money*. (6)

χρηματίζω v. (χράομαι) fut. χρηματίσω; aor. ἐχρημάτισα; pf. pass. κεχρημάτισμαι; aor. pass. ἐχρηματίσθην. *to make known a divine injunction* or *warning; be called* or *named, be identified as; receive a warning, be directed, be revealed* or *prophesied* (pass.). (9)

χρηματισμός, οῦ, ὁ n. (χράομαι) *divine statement* or *answer*. (1) Rom 11:4

χρῆσαι s. χράομαι (aor. mid. inf.).

χρήσιμος, η, ον adj. (χράομαι) *useful, beneficial, advantageous*. (1) 2 Ti 2:14

χρῆσις, εως, ἡ n. (χράομαι) *relations, function* (of sexual intercourse). (2)

χρῆσον s. κίχρημι (aor. impv.).

χρηστεύομαι v. (χράομαι) *to be kind, loving, merciful*. (1) 1 Cor 13:4

χρηστολογία, ας, ἡ n. (χράομαι, λέγω) *smooth talk, plausible speech*. (1) Rom 16:18

χρηστός, ή, όν adj. (χράομαι) *easy; fine; reputable, kind, loving, benevolent; kindness* (neut. subst.). (7)

χρηστότης, ητος, ἡ n. (χράομαι) *uprightness, what is good; goodness, kindness, generosity*. (10)

χρῖσμα, ατος, τό n. (χρίω) *anointing*. (3)

Χριστιανός, οῦ, ὁ n. oth. *a Christian*. (3)

Χριστός, οῦ, ὁ n. pers. *Christ, Anointed One, Messiah; Christ* (as a name ascribed to Jesus). (529)

χρίω v. (*) aor. ἔχρισα. *to anoint* (fig. in NT). (5)

χρονίζω v. (χρόνος) fut. χρονίσω. *to stay (for a long time); take time, linger, fail to come* or *stay away for a long time, delay, take a long time*. (5)

χρόνος, ου, ὁ n. (*) *time, period of time*, πλείων χρόνος *a longer time*, ἱκανὸς χρόνος *a long time*, ὁ πᾶς χρόνος *the whole time*, χρόνον τινά *for a while*, χρόνοις αἰωνίοις *long ages ago*, πρὸ χρόνων αἰωνίων *before time began; occasion; respite, delay*. (54)

χρονοτριβέω v. (χρόνος, τρίβος) aor. ἐχρονοτρίβησα. *to spend time, lose time*. (1) Ac 20:16

χρυσίον, ου, τό n. (χρυσός) *gold; gold ornaments, jewelry; coined gold, money*. (12)

χρυσοδακτύλιος, ον adj. (χρυσός,

δείκνυμι) *with a gold ring on one's finger*. (1) Jas 2:2

χρυσόλιθος, ου, ὁ n. (χρυσός, λίθος) *chrysolite, yellow topaz*. (1) Rev 21:20

χρυσόπρασος, ου, ὁ n. (χρυσός, πρασιά) *chrysoprase*. (1) Rev 21:20

χρυσός, οῦ, ὁ n. (*) *gold; gold thing* (of an image), *coined gold, money*. (10)

χρυσοῦς, ῆ, οῦν adj. (χρυσός) *golden, made of* or *adorned with gold*. (18)

χρυσόω v. (χρυσός) pf. pass. κεχρύσωμαι. *to adorn with gold, gild*. (2)

χρώς, χρωτός, ὁ n. *skin, surface of the body*. (1) Ac 19:12

χωλός, ή, όν adj. *lame, crippled, deprived of one foot; lame person, what is lame, lame leg* (subst.). (14)

χώρα, ας, ἡ n. (χωρέω) *land* (in contrast to sea); *district, region; country* (in contrast to city); *field, cultivated land; place, land*. (28)

χωρέω v. (*) aor. ἐχώρησα. *to go, go out* or *away; reach, come; be in motion, go forward, make progress* or *headway; hold, contain, make room, grasp, accept, comprehend, understand*. (10)

χωρίζω v. (χωρίς) fut. χωρίσω; aor. ἐχώρισα; pf. pass. κεχώρισμαι; aor. pass. ἐχωρίσθην. *to divide, separate; separate oneself, be separated, be taken away, go away* (pass.). (13)

χωρίον, ου τό n. (χωρέω) *place, piece of land, field*. (10)

χωρίς adv. (*) adv. prep. w. gen. in NT, after n. *separately, apart, by itself; without, apart from, independent(ly), separated from, far from, besides, in addition to, except (for), outside (of), without making use of, without having obtained, without committing, without possessing, without relation to, without regard to*. (41)

χῶρος, ου, ὁ n. Lat. *northwest*. (1) Ac 27:12

ψάλλω v. (*) fut. ψαλω.; *to sing, sing praise, make melody*. (5)

ψαλμός, οῦ, ὁ n. (ψάλλω) *song of praise, psalm*. (7)

ψευδάδελφος, ου, ὁ n. (ψεύδομαι, ἀδελφός) *false brother, false member*. (2)

ψευδαπόστολος, ου, ὁ n. (ψεύδομαι, στέλλω) *false, spurious*, or *bogus apostle*. (1) 2 Cor 11:13

ψευδής, ές adj. (ψεύδομαι) *false, lying; liar* (subst.). (3)

ψευδοδιδάσκαλος, ου, ὁ n. (ψεύδομαι, διδάσκω) *false* or *bogus teacher, quack teacher*. (1) 2 Pt 2:1

ψευδολόγος, ον adj. (ψεύδομαι, λέγω) *speaking falsely, lying; liars* (pl. subst. in NT). (1) 1 Ti 4:2

ψεύδομαι v. (*) aor. ἐψευσάμην. *to lie*, ψεύδομαι εἰς or κατά *tell lies against; tell lies to, impose*. (12)

ψευδομαρτυρέω v. (ψεύδομαι, μάρτυς) fut. ψευδομαρτυρήσω; aor. ἐψευδομαρτύρησα. *to bear false witness, give false testimony*. (5)

ψευδομαρτυρία, ας, ἡ n. (ψεύδομαι, μάρτυς) *false witness*. (2)

ψευδόμαρτυς, υρος, ὁ n. (ψεύδομαι, μάρτυς) *one who gives false testimony, a false witness*. (2)

ψευδοπροφήτης, ου, ὁ n. (ψεύδομαι, φημί) *false* or *bogus prophet*. (11)

ψεῦδος, ους, τό n. (ψεύδομαι) *lie, falsehood, lying*. (10)

ψευδόχριστος, ου, ὁ n. (ψεύδομαι, χρίω) *false Christ, bogus Messiah*. (2)

ψευδώνυμος, ον adj. (ψεύδομαι, ὄνομα) *falsely bearing a name, falsely called*. (1) 1 Ti 6:20

ψεῦσμα, ατος, τό n. (ψεύδομαι) *lying,*

untruthfulness, undependability. (1) Rom 3:7

ψεύστης, ου, ὁ n. (ψεύδομαι) *liar*. (10)

ψηλαφάω v. (ψώχω) aor. ἐψηλάφησα. *to touch, handle; feel around for, grope for*. (4)

ψηφίζω v. (ψώχω) aor. ἐψήφισα. *to count (up), calculate, reckon; interpret, figure out*. (2)

ψῆφος, ου, ἡ n. (ψώχω) *voting-pebble, vote; amulet, stone*. (3)

ψιθυρισμός, οῦ, ὁ n. (*) *(secret) gossip, tale-bearing*. (1) 2 Cor 12:20

ψιθυριστής, οῦ, ὁ n. (ψιθυρισμός) *rumormonger, gossiper*. (1) Rom 1:29

ψίξ, χός, ἡ n. *bit, crumb* (of bread). (v.l.)

ψιχίον, ου, τό n. *very little bit, crumb*. (2)

ψυγήσομαι s. ψύχω (2 fut. pass.).

ψυχή, ῆς, ἡ n. (ψύχω) *(breath of) life, life-principle, soul, earthly life, life, that which possesses life; soul* (as inner life), ἐκ ψυχῆς *from the heart, gladly*, μιᾷ ψυχῇ *with one mind; person*, πᾶσα ψυχή *everyone*. (103)

ψυχικός, ή, όν adj. (ψύχω) *natural, unspiritual, worldly, physical; subst. the physical* (neut.)*; worldly person* (masc.). (6)

ψῦχος, ους, τό n. (ψύχω) *cold*. (3)

ψυχρός, ά, όν adj. (ψύχω) *cold, cool; cold water* (neut. subst.). (4)

ψύχω v. (*) aor. pass. ἐψύγην. *to make cool* or *cold; go out, be extinguished* (pass. in NT). (1) Mt 24:12

ψωμίζω v. (ψώχω) aor. ἐψώμισα. *to feed; give away, dole out*. (2)

ψωμίον, ου, τό n. (ψώχω) *(small) piece* or *bit of bread*. (4)

ψώχω v. (*) *to rub* (of grain). (1) Lk 6:1

Ω *omega* (last letter of the Greek alphabet), τὸ ῏Ω *the omega*. (3)

ὦ interj. *O . . . ! O; O, Oh, How . . . !* (17)

ὧδε adv. (ὁ) *here, to this place, hither, in this place,* ἕως ὧδε *this far; in this case, at this point, on this occasion, under these circumstances.* (61)

ᾠδή, ῆς, ἡ n. (*) *song* (of praise to God). (7)

ὠδίν, ῖνος, ἡ n. (*) *birth-pain(s), great pain, (endtime) woes.* (4)

ὠδίνω v. (ὠδίν) *to have birth-pains, be in labor* (lit. and fig.), *suffer greatly.* (3)

ὦμος, ου, ὁ n. *shoulder.* (2)

ὠνέομαι v. (*) aor. ὠνησάμην. *to buy.* (1) Ac 7:16

ᾠόν, οῦ, τό n. *egg.* (1) Lk 11:12

ὥρα, ας, ἡ n. (*) *time of day* (undefined), ὥρα πολλή *late hour; hour* (twelfth part of the daytime), *short period of time, while, moment,* αὐτῇ τῇ ὥρᾳ *at that very time, at once, instantly; time,* ἀπὸ τῆς ὥρας ἐκείνης *from that time on, at once.* (106)

ὡραῖος, α, ον adj. (ὥρα) *happening or coming at the right time, timely; beautiful, fair, lovely, pleasant.* (4)

ὠρύομαι v. *to roar* (of lions). (1) 1 Pt 5:8

ὡς part. (*) *as, like, in such a way as, how,* ἕκαστος ὡς *each one as* (comp. part.); *as,* οὕτως . . . ὡς *so . . . as,* ὡς καί *as . . . so, similar to* (comp. conj.); *as, as one who* (w. ptc.), *as though, alleged to be* (part. introducing the character of something); *so that* (conj.); *that,* the fact that (conj.); *about, approximately, nearly* (w. numbers); *how!* (excl.); *when, after* (w. aor.), *while, when, as long as* (w. pres. or impf.), ὡς ἄν *when, as soon as,* ὡς τάχιστα *as quickly as possible* (temp. conj.); *with a view to, in order to, in order that* (part. of purpose); *as if, as it were, so to speak.* (504)

ὡσαννά Ara. *hosanna.* (6)

ὡσαύτως adv. (ὡς, αὐτός) *(in) the same (way), similarly, likewise.* (17)

ὡσεί part. (ὡς, εἰ) *as, like; about.* (21)

῾Ωσηέ, ὁ n. pers. *Hosea.* (1) Rom 9:25

ὡσί s. οὖς (dat. pl.).

ὥσπερ part. (ὡς, -πέρ) *as, just as, like.* (36)

ὡσπερεί part. (ὡς, -πέρ, εἰ) *like, as though, as it were.* (1) 1 Cor 15:8

ὥστε part. (ὡς, τέ) *for this reason, therefore, so; so that, of such a kind that, for the purpose of, with a view to, in order that.* (83)

ὠτάριον, ου, τό n. (οὖς) *ear.* (2)

ὠτίον, ου, τό n. (οὖς) *ear.* (3)

ὠφέλεια, ας, ἡ n. (ὠφελέω) *use, gain, advantage, point.* (2)

ὠφελέω v. (*) fut. ὠφελήσω; aor. ὠφέλησα; aor. pass. ὠφελήθην. *to help, aid, benefit, be of use (to), be of value; accomplish; receive help, be benefited* (pass.). (15)

ὠφέλιμος, ον adj. (ὠφελέω) *useful, beneficial, advantageous.* (4)

ὤφθην s. ὁράω (aor. pass.).